China
Yunnan Province

THE BRADT TRAVEL GUIDE

The Bradt Story

The first Bradt travel guide was written by Hilary and George Bradt in 1974 on a river barge floating down a tributary of the Amazon in Bolivia. From their base in Boston, Massachusetts, they went on to write and publish four other backpacking guides to the Americas and one to Africa.

In the 1980s Hilary continued to develop the Bradt list in England, and also established herself as a travel writer and tour leader. The company's publishing emphasis evolved towards broader-based guides to new destinations – usually the first to be published on those countries – complemented by hiking, rail and wildlife guides.

Since winning *The Sunday Times* Small Publisher of the Year Award in 1997, we have continued to fill the demand for detailed, well-written guides to unusual destinations, while maintaining the company's original ethos of low-impact travel.

Travel guides are by their nature continuously evolving. If you experience anything which you would like to share with us, or if you have any amendments to make to this guide, please write; all your letters are read and passed on to the author. Most importantly, do remember to travel with an open mind and to respect the customs of your hosts – it will add immeasurably to your enjoyment.

Happy travelling!

Hilary Bradt

Hilary Bradt

19 High Street, Chalfont St Peter, Bucks SL9 9QE, England
Tel: 01753 893444 Fax: 01753 892333
Email: info@bradt-travelguides.com
Web: www.bradt-travelguides.com

China
Yunnan Province
THE BRADT TRAVEL GUIDE

Stephen Mansfield
**with contributions by
David Reynolds**

Bradt Travel Guides, UK
The Globe Pequot Press Inc, USA

First published in 2001 by Bradt Travel Guides,
19 High Street, Chalfont St Peter, Bucks SL9 9QE, England
Published in the USA by The Globe Pequot Press Inc, 246 Goose Lane,
PO Box 480, Guilford, Connecticut 06437-0480

British Library Cataloguing in Publication Data
A catalogue record for this book is available from the British Library
ISBN 1 84162 002 5

Library of Congress Cataloging-in-Publication Data is available

Photographs Stephen Mansfield
Illustrations Carole Vincer
Maps Alan Whitaker

Typeset from the author's disc by Wakewing, High Wycombe
Printed and bound in Italy by Legoprint, Trento

China
Yunnan Province

THE BRADT TRAVEL GUIDE

Stephen Mansfield
with contributions by
David Reynolds

Bradt Travel Guides, UK
The Globe Pequot Press Inc, USA

First published in 2001 by Bradt Travel Guides,
19 High Street, Chalfont St Peter, Bucks SL9 9QE, England
Published in the USA by The Globe Pequot Press Inc, 246 Goose Lane,
PO Box 480, Guilford, Connecticut 06437-0480

British Library Cataloguing in Publication Data
A catalogue record for this book is available from the British Library
ISBN 1 84162 002 5

Library of Congress Cataloging-in-Publication Data is available

Photographs Stephen Mansfield
Illustrations Carole Vincer
Maps Alan Whitaker

Typeset from the author's disc by Wakewing, High Wycombe
Printed and bound in Italy by Legoprint, Trento

Authors/Acknowledgements

AUTHORS

Stephen Mansfield is a British-born writer and photographer who has been based in Japan since the mid-1980s. His work has appeared in over 80 magazines and newspapers worldwide. He has also contributed photos for several books on Southeast Asia. He is the author and photographer of *Culture Shock! Laos*, *Cultures of the World Laos*, and another Bradt title, *Guide to Philippines*. He is author and co-photographer of *Birmanie: Le Temps Suspendu*, with Michel Huteau, and *Japan: Island of the Floating World*. He has travelled extensively throughout Asia and the Middle East and has lived at various times in London, Barcelona and Cairo. As one of the foremost travel writers on Laos he has published many articles on the people and culture of Indochina, as well as a coffee-table book entitled *Laos A Portrait*. New titles include a guide to Tokyo and *Lao Hill Tribes: Traditions and Patterns of Existence*. He now divides his time between projects in Asia and his home near Tokyo.

David Reynolds works for Silk Steps, a British tour operator that specialises in China and the Far East. Following a prolonged spell of travelling and working around the world with careers too numerous to mention, he settled in Hong Kong and Japan for several years. During this time he worked for a publisher of titles on Asian countries and began a love affair with the region that has yet to end. Now living in Bristol, UK, he continues to visit China and the Far East several times a year.

ACKNOWLEDGEMENTS

Very many thanks to David Reynolds (Silk Steps) and Neil Taylor (Regent Holidays) for checking the text and their helpful contributions. Thanks also to the following: Jim Goodman for his internet information on hill tribes; Xuan Ke, ethnomusicologist extraordinaire who supplied extra info on background to Naxi music; Zhou Yu for additional information and guide tips into minority areas; Peter Viuf Johansen for computer help in Dali; Audrey Swift for filling in the gaps on border area health challenges and problems; He Liyi for insights into Bai culture; Sarah at the Forest Café for out-of-the-way Jinghong; Dao Yuam Chun for further information on the Dai people and their culture and Helen Wang for the background on Dali and just about anything else.

A Thousand Flowers to Yuki

Contents

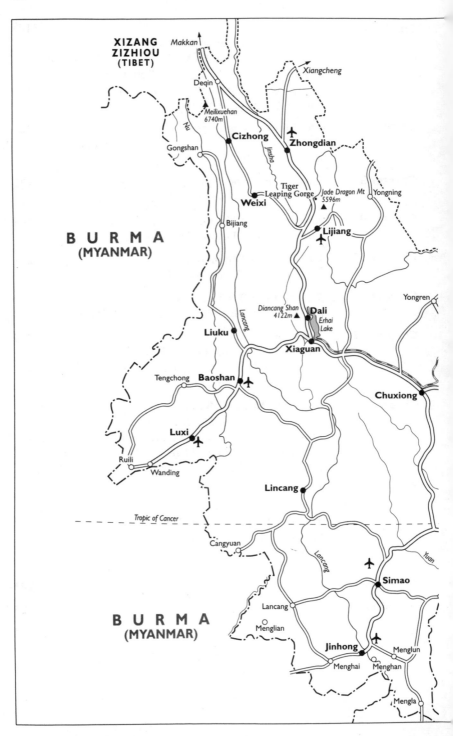

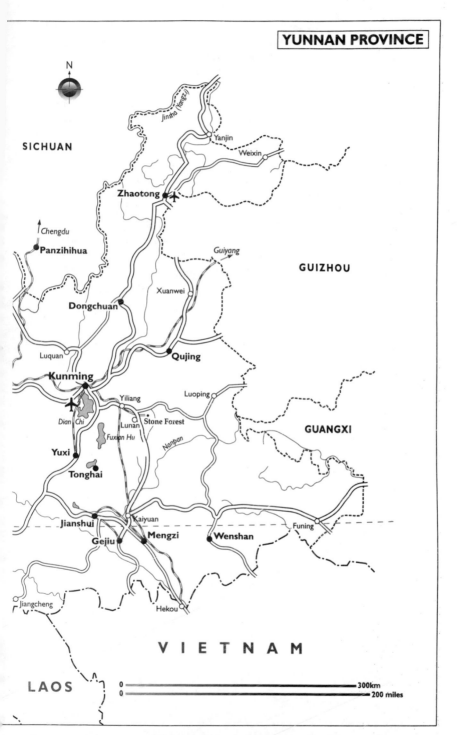

LIST OF MAPS

Introduction

Yunnan is China's most geographically and ethnically diverse province. With the exception of deserts and coastlines, Yunnan is in many ways a perfect microcosm of China, or what China should be, its staggeringly varied landscapes and richly varied ecology rarely seen in greater China today.

Yunnan's matchless landscapes have been the subject of Chinese poets for centuries. One ancient line reads:

Sunrise in the East
Cangshan's nineteen peaks in the West
Snow to the North
Endless hills and clouds to the South.

There are few regions in Asia that can provide so much visual stimulation within one defined area: Tibetan highland on its northwestern borders, central mountains, hills, plains, and plateaus; volcanic areas rich in hot springs. Legendary waters like the Yangzi, Mekong and Pearl rivers pass through its valleys and gorges, semi-tropical jungle and rain forest creep over its southern and southwestern borders with Laos, Burma and Vietnam. Although industries have been relocated here, Yunnan has not yet been turned into the environmental eyesore that characterises much of post-Mao China and all its ill-conceived attempts at progress.

Nowhere in China is the flora and fauna more diverse than here. Over half of China's animal and plant species inhabit Yunnan, lending it great appeal to naturalists and hikers. Yunnan is the basin into which the culture of the Han Chinese from the east, Tibetan influences from the northwest, and the rich cultures of Southeast Asia have been poured and blended. Over a third of all the country's ethnic minorities live here. The most intriguing and 'exotic' of them are some of the least affected in many ways by China's pervasive social policies. Historically and ethnographically, Yunnan is the gene-pool from which the Tai peoples who now inhabit Laos, Thailand, parts of Burma and Vietnam and further afield, originally sprang before migrating south.

Travellers are drawn to Yunnan for a number of reasons. The province is regarded as one of the most relaxed, stress- and bureaucracy-free places in China, a place to stimulate but also recuperate the battered traveller. Yunnan is an all-seasons destination, a place where you can find good weather somewhere in the province for most of the year. For active, exploration-minded travellers, Yunnan offers a full itinerary. Highlights include the provincial capital of Kunming, renowned for its food and laid-back atmosphere; a petrified forest at nearby Shilin; Xishuangbanna, home of the stunning Dai people; and the drug town of Ruili near the Burmese border, with its Buddhist pagodas, ethnic minorities and shady deals. Tiger Leaping Gorge, one of the deepest ravines in the world, is a challenging trek, but there are countless others, most of them unexplored. The ancient town of Lijiang, now a UNESCO World Heritage Site, and its nearby monasteries on the road to Tibet, the lakeside town of Dali with its Bai-style architecture, and the province's many festivals are other persuasive reasons to spend time in Yunnan.

Yunnan often seems like a separate geographical and cultural land mass from the rest of China. Traditionally, its historical isolation from the mainstream helped to save it from Chinese domination. Unfortunately, nothing lasts forever. Tour operators in Beijing have already begun calling the province 'Shangri-la', a prophetic epithet certain to shorten the life of this unique corner of China.

Part One

General Information

'Ahead of us now lay the very much wayward world of the non-Chinese, the world of those who have been incorporated into the Chinese Empire, but who live irredeemably and steadfastly beyond it.'

The River At The Centre Of The World, Simon Winchester

Hornbill

Background Information

'Of all the Chinese the Yun-nanese are the least social sticklers; perhaps because they live so far on China's farthest outskirt, perhaps because of all Chinese their blood is the most mixed.'

In A Yunnan Courtyard, Louise Jordan Miln

GEOGRAPHY AND CLIMATE

The province covers a total area of 394,000km^2, and shares its borders with Laos, Vietnam and Burma in the south and west. Northwestern Yunnan is less than 100km from the borders of Arunachal Pradesh in India.

Yunnan's geographical diversity is incredible, featuring towering, permanently snow-covered peaks, limestone, marble and karst mountains, volcanoes, tropical jungles and some of the world's deepest gorges. Many of its bizarre formations, like the Stone Forest at Shilin, are the result of carbonate rock erosions that have eaten into layers and strata of the Yunnan–Guizhou Plateau on which the province sits. Yunnan's distinctive landscape has been, and continues to be, formed by the slow collision of the Asian and Indian continents. Extensions of the Himalayas penetrate western Yunnan in the form of the long Hengduan Mountain Range. Lijiang's Jade Dragon Snow Mountain and Deqin's Mount Kagebo are the most visible extensions of the Qinghai–Tibet Plateau which sinks into the province, fusing with the Yunnan–Guizhou Plateau and creating at the same time some of the most spectacular ravines in northern Yunnan, Tiger Leaping Gorge being the finest example.

The erosion and fracturing of its crust has resulted in the region's instability, a fact that was demonstrated with devastating effects in the 1995 earthquake that hit the Lijiang regions. Tengchong in southwest Yunnan is a major volcanic area, replete with hot springs and geysers.

There are few land masses in the world that can lay claim to having so many famous rivers gathered together in temporary proximity as there are in Yunnan. As if China's great river, the Yangzi, wasn't enough, the Mekong and Salween also pass through the province, rushing headlong down from Tibet. Southeast Yunnan is also the source of the Pearl River. Lake Dian near Kunming, and Dali's Erhai Lake are well-known tourist destinations, but there is a whole lake district region running for over 150km south from the capital, halfway to the border with Vietnam.

The Tropic of Cancer slices across southern Yunnan. Moisture arrives to this region from the Indian Ocean, resulting in heavy monsoon rains. High or cool winds are a rarity in this sub-tropical region, the Himalayas acting as a wind barrier, deflecting any chill blasts from the north. Yunnan has no single climate, more like a series of micro-climates, mostly dependent upon elevation. Altitudes vary immensely, from the 6,740m peak of Mount Kagebo to the confluence of the Honghe and Nanxi rivers in Hekou County which lie at a mere 76m. Yunnan's average altitude is 2,000m. Trying to accommodate this range, the climate is defined rather bewilderingly as a sub-tropical highland monsoon type. It's actually not a bad description, giving some idea of what to expect at almost any time of the year, taking in humid, temperate and frigid zones.

Temperatures and weather conditions in central Yunnan are generally mild. Kunming is often described as the 'City of Eternal Spring' because of its temperate, even, climate accompanied by lots of rain. Southern and southwestern parts of the province, those contiguous with neighbouring Southeast Asian countries, have tropical rainforest climates, and a quasi-monsoon season that lasts from about May to the end of October. The northwest and east can be bitterly cold even in the summer months. Snowfall is common during the winter and areas like Lugu Lake and Deqin are virtually inaccessible at these times. Almost anywhere north of Kunming in fact, is vulnerable to freezing from November to February. The summer months from May to August are generally mild, but characterised by high rainfall. Areas like Xishuangbanna are warm throughout the year.

NATURAL HISTORY AND ECOLOGY

Yunnan's spectrum of flora and fauna reflects the varied micro-climates and graduated elevations that support and provide habitats for a phenomenal range of species. By the same token that has condemned much of its architectural heritage, Yunnan's environment has suffered much as a result of intensive farming and the rapid overdevelopment of its industries and urban centres.

Many forests were cleared during Mao's time and replaced with rubber plantations which quickly depleted the soil. Although Yunnan is China's fourth largest timber supplier, little more than 20% of Yunnan is now covered in forest. Slash-and-burn methods have destroyed vast stretches of primary forest in the south. In places like Xishuangbanna and Simao, barely 20% of the original forest still stands. To be fair to the government, it is doing what it can. After disastrous floods in the middle reaches of the river took a huge toll in human lives and property in both 1998 and the following year, laws to severely restrict deforestation in the Upper Yangzi regions of Yunnan were strictly implemented.

Having signed the Convention on the International Trade in Endangered Species, worked with the WWF in its Xishuangbanna nature reserve project, and become a fully accredited member of UNESCO's Man and Biosphere Programme, the Chinese government has earned some respect from the international community. A few environmental groups have also sprung up across China, though it is unclear just how outspoken or proactive they are allowed to be when it comes to projects perceived as being economically profitable.

Yunnan's rich flora has been exploited for centuries by locals and minorities who have been able to find a natural orchard and pharmacopoeia in its mountain ranges, forests and jungles. Walnuts, oil-palm, wild fungi, betel nuts, camphor, lacquer, chillies, longan, pomelo, angelica, devil-wood, countless kinds of medicinal plants and sundry other natural products grow wild in the province. Xishuangbanna is especially rich in flora, with over 5,000 species of plants growing here alone. Over half the plant species in the whole of China, are found in Yunnan. A quarter of the country's medicinal plants and herbs grow here, hundreds of varieties of trees and over 2,000 species of ornamental plants and rare flowers. Ornamental plants which are native to Yunnan include primrose, camellia, lily, *Gentiana scabra*, orchid, rhododendron and magnolia. 650 different kinds of azalea grow in Yunnan alone.

Traditionally the Chinese have viewed wild animals as a resource to be exploited rather than preserved for posterity. China's market oriented economy has only fuelled that way of thinking. Business people have tried to cash in on the curiosity of the emerging middle classes by opening animal parks. Although there is nothing particularly sinister about that, the conditions the animals are kept in are often cruel, insanitary and humiliating.

China has no laws against cruelty to animals. It's not uncommon in China to come across displays of horse fighting or parks that feature such crowd pleasures as hunting ranges where patrons can use bows and arrows to stalk tethered rabbits. At one zoo, which was actually criticised by the local media, customers prepared to pay enough could witness the gory spectacle of a live calf being torn apart by a tiger.

Ironically, the same rise in incomes that has fuelled the creation of freak animal shows has generated a new breed of urban pet-owners who would rather pamper their dogs or cats than eat or bate them. The Communists, who banned dog ownership after labelling it bourgeois, would be surprised at the recent proliferation of pet stores and veterinary clinics in places like Kunming. Although dogs are still more commonly found on the menu than the leash, China has a long history of dog ownership. Wealthy families and members of the imperial court during the Qin dynasty (221–207BC) kept dogs, cats, rabbits and birds as pets, and a detailed record of raising and treating canines, called the *Classic on Dogs*, dating from the Han dynasty (207BC–AD220) has been found.

Tourists are often offended at the sight of dogs being skinned in front of them, animals gasping their last in open markets. Call them relative values or double standards, but most visitors prefer a sanitary slaughtering to the raw live shows at Chinese markets and restaurants. That old joke about the Chinese eating everything with four legs except tables and chairs translates into a grim humour in many restaurants, where not only cats and dogs appear on the menu, but also turtles, salamanders, pangolin, bear and monkey brain. Health food in Yunnan, as elsewhere in China, is more likely to mean snake blood, extracted bear bile, ground tiger's paw, and shreds of rhino horn than carrot juice and tofu. Considered antidotes to fatigue and a short life, these products, now in increasingly short supply, are highly esteemed.

Having said that, there are many officially protected animals in Yunnan. Among the 379 vertebrates listed as worthy of state protection are golden-haired monkeys, gibbons, wild elephants, snow leopards, loris, hornbills, white-tailed red pheasants, tragopan, crested ibis, and red-crowned cranes.

The government has established several nature reserves in Yunnan. Bitahai in Zhongdian is an important reserve as migrating birds and waterfowl come here. Napahai Reserve, also in Zhongdian, though considerably smaller, is another precious allotment of space for birds and keen ornithologists. Baima Reserve in Deqin covers a huge area (1,800km² in all), representing a complete ecosystem. The Xishuangbanna Nature Reserve is even bigger at 2,420km². You are unlikely to see much in the way of fauna here or elsewhere in the province as the increasingly embattled wildlife is withdrawing into the remaining fastnesses of Yunnan or vanishing altogether. Over 400 different types of birds are said to live in the greenery of the reserve, though. The prospect for Yunnan's plant life looks good, with half of China's protected plant species represented in this luxuriant and green reserve. Some of Yunnan's geological marvels, like the terraces at Baishui and the Stone Forest at Shilin, have also been designated as protected areas.

Many of these reserves, unfortunately, are being targeted for tourist resort development, a rather self-defeating process involving the construction of hotels, souvenir stalls, restaurants, attraction parks and new highways that no one seems able or willing to halt.

HISTORY AND POLITICS

Yunnanese history, like the tributaries of its great rivers the Yangzi, Mekong and Salween, has for long periods, run an independent, self-determined course, but inevitably returned to the massive land mass and cultural centrality of China. Strongly influenced by relations with its neighbours, landlocked Yunnan, larger than either Britain or Sweden, was able to go its own way, squatting high up on its citadel-like plateau, but its integration into greater China was only a question of time.

Yunnan's origins reach far back in time. For several decades Peking Man, discovered in 1921, remained the oldest evidence of human life in China. Later discoveries of vital, missing pieces in Yunnan's own anthropological puzzle have significantly changed the view of Chinese pre-history. In 1965 geologists surveying the route for the construction of the Kunming-Chengdu railway came across a large collection of fossils. Locals explained that they ground down these 'dragon bones' for medical uses. When the team examined rock galleries in the nearby village of Yuanmou, they found substantial quantities of mammal fossils. Even more significant, the men found two human teeth, 1.5–2.5 million years old, establishing the remains of this Homo erectus yuanmouensis (Yuanmou Man) as the ancestor of Peking Man. Further discoveries in 1973 established Yuanmou Man, a lake-side inhabiting contemporary of primitive horses and elephants, familiar with the use of fire, as China's oldest hominid to date. The last major find in 1988, of fossil skulls at Hudieliangzi, a village near Yuanmou, provided another important piece of evidence proving that the complete evolutionary process, from hominid to Man, occurred in China. The discovery that Yunnan may have been the first inhabited area of China has forced a revision in the view or perception of the region as a remote, late-developer in the long and venerable history of China.

Another adjustment to the view of Yunnan as a savage, uncivilized outland beyond the influence of Chinese culture, an opinion endorsed in annals chronicling the first millennium of recorded Chinese history, was made in 1955 with the discovery of a highly refined Bronze Age culture centred around the shores of Lake Dian, a few kilometers south of Kunming. Among the objects found within 48 intact tombs dating back to 1200BC were a number of bronze treasury vessels whose lid-figurines vividly portray the daily life and rituals of the small agricultural kingdom of Dian – a head-hunting, slave-owning society that could also produce accomplished artists.

Other distinct societies and ethic groups may also have existed at this time. The Bai and Yi minority nationalities, for example, claim to have migrated to Yunnan as long as 3,000–4,000 years ago. The Han historian Sima Qian, makes the first mention of Yunnan in an account of the first Chinese invasion of Dian in 339BC. During the Warring States Period (453–221BC) China, concerned for the first time with security on its western frontier, had also begun to consider the possibility of a trade passage across southern China, through Burma to India and beyond. Accordingly, the Chu general Zhuang Qiao, was dispatched to Dian to suppress the 'southern barbarians.' After a ten-year campaign, his return blocked by the armies of rival states, the general decided to stay. Appointing himself sovereign ruler of the Kingdom of Dian, the new state, ruled by descendants of Zhuang Qiao, kept its independence in total isolation from the affairs of China until 109BC.

During the early years of the Qin dynasty an important road link between Sichuan and Qujing in the northeast of Yunnan was completed and the first of Yunnan's prefectures set up. With the advent of the more dynamic Han dynasty (207BC–AD220), a second invasion of Yunnan was launched, this time with the approval of the king of Dian who hoped that as allies, the Chinese would help him conquer neighbouring tribes. Although the Chinese troops were not able to penetrate Yunnan's awesome western mountains, an imperial seal was issued by the Emperor Wu Di establishing Dian as a tributary state of the Han empire. The Han established a prefecture in Baoshan in AD69, thereby affirming their dominance over the important transcontinental stretch of the Southern Silk Route, as it had become, to Burma and India.

The Han interfered very little in the goings-on of all but eastern Yunnan. Dian continued to be ruled by tribal chiefs who paid nominal tribute to the emperor. With the dissolution of the Han the kingdom of Dian fractured and weakened, falling into the hands of tribes from the south. The Three Kingdoms Period (AD220–280) saw the creation of a loosely formed kingdom after a rebellion headed by Yunnan's intellectuals and elite was put down. Parts of northwestern Sichuan were integrated into this new state whose continued existence through the Western Jin Period (AD265–316) brought the region under closer Chinese control.

Six princes ruled southwest Yunnan during the early years of the eighth century. One of them, on a mission to north China, is said to have been asked where he came from, replying that it was a land south of Sichuan's rainy belt. According to the story which is widely disputed, the emperor, hearing this description named the prince's home Yunnan, meaning the 'land south of the clouds.' During a banquet ostensibly to welcome and consolidate the different states, the most ruthless and politically ambitious of the princes had the hall set on fire with the other five consorts inside. Seizing their lands, and creating the unified state of Nanzhao, the kingdom expanded over the next two centuries into parts of Burma and Vietnam. Sometimes allied with the Chinese against Tibet, it also threatened and defeated the mighty Tang army, took control of large areas of southwest Yunnan and oversaw trade passing along the lucrative Southern Silk Route.

Nanzhao's successor, the Kingdom of Dali, a strong and independent state based in Dali on the shores of Erhai Lake, remained a power to reckon with until 1253 when it was ransacked by the armies of Kublai Khan, the Mongol grandson of Genghis Khan. The general's invasion of southwest Yunnan was part of a larger strategy to subdue the Song dynasty by firstly occupying

ZHENG HE: THE AMBITIOUS EUNUCH

When the Ming army stormed into Yunnanfu in 1368, Ma Ho's family, decendents of a Mongol governor of Yunnan, bravely but unwisely put up resistance to China's new rulers. Trapped by the overwhelming forces of the Ming, Ma Ho and several of his other 10-year old friends were rounded up, castrated and then pressed into the army as orderlies.

Rising through the ranks of the military, Ma Ho showed exceptional skills in war and diplomacy. Promoted to officer and then court eunuch in Nanning the capital, the emperor renamed him Zheng He. In 1405, the ambitious He was appointed as admiral of a fleet of 62 ships carrying over 27,000 men whose mission was to explore sea routes and establish commercial centres for the trading of spices, pottery, and raw materials. In He's seven extraordinary voyages he laid anchor in ports as remote as Arabia, the Indian Ocean, Persia and parts of Africa. The objects he traded in during these voyages can still be found in parts of the world as far apart as Sri Lanka and Java.

Interestingly, the maritime dominance China enjoyed at the time as a result of Zheng He's voyages of discovery were not to lead, as they would in the case of European powers like the Portuguese and British, to the establishment of trading ports that would be used as the beachheads of colonialism, but to the immigration of large numbers of Chinese, eager to make their fortunes overseas.

Yunnan and then pressing his advantage north and west. With the collapse of the Kingdom of Dali, most of the population dispersed to southern and western Yunnan. Among the mercenaries, soldiers of fortune and recruited bandits the Mongols took along with them on their Yunnan campaign were a tough breed of Muslims from Central Asia and Persia who were used to repopulate evacuated areas of the province. When Yunnan eventually fell to the armies of the resurgent Ming dynasty in 1368, an ethnic cleansing of the area took place resulting in the genocide or expulsion of thousands of foreigners. Only a small number of Muslims were permitted to remain. A few even rose to positions of power and eminence. Zheng He, a eunuch appointed as the new Ming emperor's admiral, became a great explorer opening up trade routes to the Middle East and elsewhere. Although Yunnan continued to resist the presence of Ming armies, the viceroys of the new order were able to express Ming influence in a series of infrastructure projects that included the construction of Chinese temples, a city wall around Yunnanfu, as Kunming was then known, and a comprehensive canal system.

Yunnan continued to be ruled as a distant colony rather than a province of China until 1658 when Manchu troops drove the last Ming emperor into Burma. Because of their distance and isolation from the administrative centre, the Chinese garrisons in Yunnan remained a largely symbolic presence, subordinate to local chieftains, warlords and aboriginal groups. Quick to rebel against the northern government, the province also served at this time as a kind of gulag for dissidents, bureaucrats and criminals who had fallen out of favour with the emperor. Although a relatively small group, the exiled intellectuals and progressives who were banished to Yunnan brought with them the sophisticated customs, language and advanced architectural styles of north China.

In the 18th century Yunnan was used to launch a series of successful attacks on neighbouring Burma. Tribute in the form of jade and rubies henceforth passed by elephant along the Burma Road from Mandalay to Yunnanfu, where it was transferred onto mules and pack horses for the journey to Beijing.

During the declining years of the Qing dynasty, Yunnan turned towards Burma and Indochina to read its political future, as it did toward the Chinese. At the same time as Burma fell under the influence of the British, the French were advancing into Tonkin, the first step in their eventual colonisation of Vietnam, Cambodia and Laos. The two empires, keen to establish land routes across southwestern Yunnan, also coveted Yunnan's rich mineral wealth, particularly its copper and tin mines.

A dispute between Chinese and Hui (Muslim) miners in 1855 escalated into a fully-fledged rebellion against Chinese rule. The Hui ransacked Yunnanfu, razing many of its Buddhist monasteries and temples as well as torching public buildings and private houses before withdrawing to Dali where they set up their own independent state. The European powers were quick to take advantage of the ensuing chaos. In a proxy conflict that was to be replicated a century later by the superpowers in Indochina, France supplied arms and money to the emperor from their bases in present day Vietnam, while the British dispatched weapons to the Muslims from Burma. The Muslims were eventually subdued with great ferocity in 1873. Whole communities of Muslims and those ethnic minorities who had supported them, including women and children, were massacred. An outbreak of plague killed off many of the survivors. The Muslim stronghold of Dali and other Hui settlements were virtually depopulated. The British and French were able to extract generous concessions from the exhausted Qing dynasty: the British to open trade, and the French to construct a narrow-gauge railway line connecting Yunnan with Hanoi.

In the late 19th and early 20th centuries, a handful of Western explorers, surveyors and botanists had begun penetrating Yunnan's difficult terrain. The French historian and traveller, J P G Pauthier introduced the region of Lijiang and its magnificent snow range, the Yulongxueshan, or Jade Dragon Snow Mountain, to readers with his *L'Universe Chine* and Francis Garnier, on an expedition to open a trade route up the Mekong from Vietnam to China, explored the waters of the Lancanijiang (Mekong River) in Deqin Prefecture. The British botanist Horace began collecting herbs in the Lijiang region in 1888, and was followed in the 1920s by the famous Dr Joseph Rock (see *Dr Rock: Botanist-Explorer*, page 162–3) and others like Frank Kingdon-Ward who scoured the reaches of Yunnan's Upper Mekong in search of exotic plants.

In 1911, after the final collapse of the Qing dynasty, China became a republic and Yunnan fell once again into the hands of contending local warlords and feuding clans. With the Japanese invasion of eastern China in 1937 the Nationalist government withdrew to Chongqing, in Sichuan. Yunnan became an important strategic centre for transferring food, arms and other important supplies by road from Burma, overland from eastern Tibet by caravan, and by air from India to Allied war bases in West China. Airstrips in Lijiang and Kunming became important American bases. It was from here that General Sitwell's ground forces and General Chenault's Flying Tiger pilots operated.

Civil war, the semi-feudal rule of warlords and drug barons and the barbaric example of the Japanese convinced the ethnically mixed Yunnanese that their future would be best served by full integration with China. Accordingly, when Chairman Mao's Red Army crossed into Yunnan in 1949 the majority of the peasants in Yunnan welcomed the liberation. Although certain tribal groups were obliged to abolish practices regarded as undesirable by the new government – land reforms among the Bai, Dai and Naxi, the termination of slavery among the Cool Mountain Yi and Jingpo, and head-hunting by the Wa – the minorities fared well under the new administration until the advent of the Cultural Revolution. Any form of ethnicity was condemned as 'little nation chauvinism', minority traditions as 'superstitious' and 'backward'. The Deng Xiaoping regime did much to rectify the damage caused by over-zealous Red Guards, and the minorities, many empowered with their own autonomous prefectures and counties, were once again allowed, encouraged in fact, to practice their indigenous traditions and customs. Although remote areas of Yunnan lag far behind the rest of China, since the province decided to throw in its lot with China it has enjoyed a higher level of prosperity than at any time in its recorded history.

THE ECONOMY

Mao's economic experiments, involving hundreds of millions of people, inflicted enormous physical and psychological suffering. During the famine of 1959–61, during which grain production figures were grossly inflated, peasants were left hungry and an estimated 20–30 million people died. The miseries in rural areas like Yunnan were compounded by bizarre and idiotic edicts issuing from Beijing. A peculiar movement launched in 1958, for example, required all families and individuals to smash their cooking stoves. The explanation, given over the radio at the time, announced that: 'Too much precious time is wasted on cooking our daily meals. True happy communism means not only working together but also eating together from a big pot, like workers and students in the cities.' The movement to melt stoves, pots and other domestic utensils seems to have conveniently coincided with a government drive to increase steel production. In Yunnan, action groups were formed to search houses for the incriminating stoves.

China's first economic break came with the death of the rigidly ideological Mao, and the emergence of the pragmatic Deng Xiaoping at the helm of the party. Deng's reforms, characterised by his 'Four Modernisations', (of industry, agriculture, science and technology and defenses), led the way to steady economic growth and a very real rise in the standard of living of the ordinary person. Hailing from Sichuan, the province north of Yunnan, Deng's agricultural reforms during the late 1970s allowed farmers to sell their produce on the free market. Productivity rose almost immediately.

Attempts to modernise the economy have meant grappling with some painful historical legacies. The irrational policies of central planning, and the Marxist fixation with expanding industrial capacity left China with a great number of unprofitable state-owned enterprises that were motivated more by political ideology than sound economic incentives. Although the government finally recognises the importance of the nonstate sector, the Communist Party, fearing that if it completely abandons its old policies it will face extinction, has not deviated much in principle from the old Marxist-Leninist ideal of government control of the means of production.

Despite respectably high economic growth, unemployment has risen sharply. Many of China's large state-owned commercial banks are technically insolvent, with huge non-performing loans. Corruption in the economic sector is rampant. The country, however, largely managed to escape the Asian financial crises which struck in the 1990s but whose effects are still felt at the beginning of this century. China has carefully taken warning of the effects of crony capitalism and pegged exchange rates. Its own strict capital controls have so far shielded it from the worst effects of the financial meltdown.

At least China is facing up to, rather than ignoring, its economic problems. Resolute steps have been taken, for example, to make the economy more

PARKING LOTS IN THE JUNGLE

From the Thai side of the Mekong, a convoy of unlicensed Japanese cars, mostly Hondas destined for the Chinese border, are being loaded on to a ferry that will take them across the river to Ban Houei Xai on the Lao side. Although nobody seems particularly troubled by the shady legalities surrounding these highly visible commodities – the very act of smuggling in broad daylight, as it were – tensions are high on this stretch of the border. As if to prove the point, a scowling Thai, already exasperated at how much he has had to pay to police and other officials to get this far, screams at a Lao stevedore who is parking an oil-streaked motorbike a little too close to his investment.

An even more improbable sight awaits those who find themselves on the Lao side of the border, a few miles from the Chinese settlement of Boten where giant car parks appear to have been shaved out of the jungle. Here, the cars, on the last leg of their journey across the border into the hands of awaiting dealers in Yunnan, are carefully washed, waxed and polished before being delivered. Most stand out in the blistering sun; others are parked under wattle and pandanus-roofed constructions that look more like the consecrated halls of tribal shamans than car ports.

Where there are roads there are, by definition, exponentially higher levels of traffic, or, in this case, trafficking. New roads and older upgraded routes will make the trade even more lucrative and inflict a lot less wear and tear on the cars and drivers who deliver them. There are two main routes for conveying vehicles up to the Yunnan border. The first involves

market-friendly and to boost domestic spending. Buying shares on the stock market has been declared a patriotic duty. China's investment environment is also on an upswing with much of the red tape and obfuscation that made foreign investors nervous now being swept away. An increase in foreign investment has also meant the introduction of valuable technology and expertise. China's likely membership of the World Trade Organisation will help to bring it into the global fold.

Per capita income in Yunnan still lags behind China's frantically prosperous east coast urban economies despite some major infrastructure developments in the region like the Kunming-Nanning railway, new expressways, and Kunming's superb expanded airport facilities.

Yunnan has good reason to be optimistic though. Tourism is increasingly important for the province with earnings rising steadily with each successive year. The resource-rich province is well aware of its strategic position on the overland trade route between mainland Southeast Asia and China's large industrial and commercial cities, and is looking forward to exploiting it. A series of highways already under construction in Laos will permit trucks and private vehicles to drive from Singapore all the way to Beijing through Yunnan's land corridors.

driving the cars up through Thailand to the Ban Houei Xai crossing, and then scrambling them along a deplorably rutted road to Luang Nam Tha in the far north of Laos, where they will stay for a few days in their temporary holding spaces cut from the undergrowth, before making their way over the border. The other, arguably more arduous route, involves getting the cars over the Mittraphab, or 'Friendship' Bridge, which connects Thailand and Laos to warehouses in the capital Vientiane, from where drivers, working in pairs, must negotiate pot-holed, bandit-infested mountain roads before reaching the same destination. The dangers here are palpably real, with several Lao as well as foreigners having been killed or wounded along this route in the last few years. But if the risks are high, so too are the profits.

Second-hand BMWs and other upmarket German sedans are shipped from Gulf states like Bahrain, where used cars are extremely cheap due to their fast turnover, for as little as $1,500 per vehicle. New Japanese cars, officially exported to Thailand, are transshipped to Bangkok from the United States. Dealers expect to incur almost as much in so-called 'handling charges' as the shipping costs in order to get these hot items through Thailand. Once the cars reach the Yunnan border four or five days later, import duties and other more arbitrarily negotiable fees, are slapped on. Border delays caused, as the local authorities would have it, by inexplicable and random crackdowns, are usually understood to mean that the border police are trying to inflate the fees. Even so, the profit on a single car once it is safely in Yunnan can still be as much as $6,000.

The obstacles preventing engineers, surveyors, and road gangs from building great inter-continental trunk roads have, until recently, not been the region's deserts, marble mountains, or petrified forests of karst, but the more obdurate realities of geo-politics. Conversely, when the political climate has proved to be more amenable, frontiers more flexible, the asphalt has flowed unchecked. Southeast Asia is one region where the current entente cordiale among nations formerly wracked by conflict, is helping, quite literally, to pave the way for road projects that seem to have been gathering dust for decades.

All Asian roads invariably lead, as they did in Marco Polo's day, to China, the Middle Kingdom. Increased productivity and a necessity to import more raw materials from abroad have created the need for a major land bridge connecting China to Southeast Asia. In the view of some critics and military analysts, the implications of China's imminent overreach into Southeast Asia via new roads, may not be entirely benign. Local residents in the north of Laos, where influences from over the border are most apparent, are especially fearful of Chinese expansion. One elderly resident living in the market town of Muong Sing, still recalls the Moroccan and Singalese troops who were garrisoned there during the colonial period when it was France's remotest outpost in the country. 'The forces the French tried to contain,' he regaled me, 'are pouring in over the border now. The Chinese are hungry for our resources. They think they can trade them for their cheap clothes, toys and thermos flasks.'

Not only vectors for cross-border trade, land bridges between China and Southeast Asia are likely to have a dramatic impact on the lifestyles and cultural values found along these transforming conduits. How these changes are likely to affect, not only the volume of traffic passing through the new land corridors, but also the communities in their catchment areas, remains to be seen.

THE PEOPLE

Gloriously underpopulated, with less than 40 million souls of various nationalities, Yunnan is a fascinating crossroads or compression point for the mingling of people of Chinese, Tibetan, Thai, Burmese and other origins and ethnic affiliations. In Yunnan, the drab homogeneity that characterises many other parts of China splinters into a rich multiplicity of ethnic groups.

When minorities were classified for the first time in the 1950s, over 250 groups were found to exist in Yunnan. Twenty-four of these have received official recognition. How do you define a people who are of China, but not precisely Chinese? The answer is to treat them as fully accredited Chinese citizens but to call them Minority Nationalities. So far the terminology, with a few exceptions, has worked fairly well. China is one place which has never pretended to be fully homogeneous. The Han Chinese may be numerically dominant, accounting for 94% of the population, but 55 distinctly different nationalities, China's ethnic minorities, occupy over 60% of the country's land mass, a great deal of which is in potentially vital economic and strategic border areas.

Xishuangbanna has the highest concentration of ethnic tribes in the whole of China. Many minorities have kin on the other sides of the borders. The Yao are known in Laos as the Mien, the Miao as the Hmong, while the Jingpo are called the Kachin in Burma. This rich diversity presents a formidable ethnographic map. Yunnan's importance in terms of Southeast Asian population flows cannot be underestimated, the region being the gene-pool for the so-called Tai races. The Tai probably originated in southern China's Kwangsi region. Sixth-century Chinese records speak of Tai peoples inhabiting an area south of the Yangzi river. The real dispersal of tribes had probably begun as early as the 1st century AD, as a result of expansion by the Han Chinese into the Red River delta region of Vietnam. Proto-Tai people, under increasing pressure from the expansionist Han Chinese, moved from Kwangsi, southwest into Yunnan and to the Sip Song Chau Tai region of present day northwestern Vietnam. The Tai were sufficiently unified by the 8th and 9th centuries to establish their own kingdom in Nanzhao in the west and northwest of Yunnan province. The Tai appear in Chinese records from this period as the 'barbarians beyond the Yangtze.'

Under increasing pressure and persecution from the land-hungry Han Chinese, tribes began moving towards the southwest in large numbers. By the

YUNNAN'S MINORITY NATIONALITIES

The following is a list of Yunnan's officially recognised 24 ethnic minorities: their name, language group, population, and the regions in which large numbers of the groups live. The Kuchong are a small minority of only 3,000 members living along the border with Vietnam and in some remote parts of the north. At present they are not recognised by the state as a separate minority.

Name	Language group	Population	Habited region
Yi	Tibeto-Burman	4,054,000	Dali, Xishuangbanna, Wenshan, Qujing, Zhaotong, Dongchuan, Kunming
Bai	Sino Tibetan	1,339,000	Dali, Lijiang, Nujiang, Kunming
Hani	Tibeto-Burman	1,248,000	Simao, Lincang, Xishuangbanna, Yuxi, Honghe, Baoshan, Dehong, Chuxiong, Lijiang
Dai	Tai-Kedai	1,014,000	Lincang, Simao, Yuxi, Xishuangbanna, Honghe
Zhuang	Tai-Kedai	1,003,000	Wenshan, Qujing
Miao	Miao-Yao	896,000	Zhaotong, Qujing, Kunming, Chuxiong, Honghe, Wenshan
Lisu	Tibeto-Burman	557,000	Deqin, Nujiang, Baoshan, Dehong, Lijiang
Hui	Sinitic	522,000	Zhaotong, Dongchuan, Qujing, Honghe, Yuxi, Kunming, Dali, Baoshan, Dehong
Lahu	Tibeto-Burman	408,000	Lincang, Simao, Xishuangbanna
Wa	Mon-Khmer	347,000	Lincang, Simao
Naxi	Tibeto-Burman	265,000	Lijiang, Deqin, Dali
Yao	Miao-Yao	173,000	Wenshan, Honghe, Xishuangbanna
Jingpo	Tibeto-Burman	118,000	Dehong, Nujiang
Tibetan	Tibeto-Burman	111,000	Deqin, Lijiang
Bulang	Mon-Khmer	81,000	Xishuangbanna, Lincang, Simao
Buyi	Tai-Kedai	34,000	Qujing
Pumi	Tibeto-Burman	29,000	Lijiang, Nujiang
Achang	Tibeto-Burman	27,000	Dehong, Baoshan
Nu	Tibeto-Burman	26,000	Nujiang, Deqin
Jinuo	Tibeto-Burman	17,000	Xishuangbanna
De'ang	Mon-Khmer	15,000	Dehong, Lincang
Mongolian	Mongol	13,000	Yuxi
Shui	Tai-Kedai	7,700	Kunming, Qujing
Dulong	Tibeto-Burman	5,600	Nujiang

middle of the 13th century the level of migration increased dramatically as invading Mongol armies under Kublai Khan swept into Nanzhao, capturing its capital, Ta-li, in 1253.

The Cultural Revolution and disastrous Great Leap Forward were grim times for Yunnan's minorities. Attempts to dismantle the so-called 'four olds', meaning old culture, ideas, customs and habits, were often brutal. Village shamans and priests, regarded as conveyors of superstition, were rounded up and either interned or sent to work in communes, headmen were quickly dispatched to re-education camps, and old burial customs were replaced with cremation. Although Yunnan's minorities are now referred to as 'equal brothers' with the Chinese, Han chauvinism still exists.

Yunnan's rich and bewildering trove of ethnic minorities includes names like the Buyi, Jingpo, Pumi and Dulong, groups few of us have ever heard of. Their highly distinct cultures and ethnic diversity, and the fact that relatively little has been written about them, make these groups some of the most intriguing minorities left in Asia, and their habitat, at least until now, one of the least exposed to tourism. Strikingly individualistic, with their own styles of dress, customs, beliefs, and rituals, many of the ethnic minorities of Yunnan live a life apart. Others have bent to pressures imposed by an increasing number of Han Chinese and allowed themselves to be thoroughly Sinonised.

The dismantling of ethno-geographical divisions and the integration of the minorities into mainstream Chinese life is clearly a mixed blessing. 'Ethno tourism' is increasing every year, inspired, ironically, by the very thing which is likely to hasten the demise of their environment – the survival of authentic living cultures. The gradual disappearance of Yunnan's forests as a dietary, medical and cultural resource, not to mention the protective canopy it affords to the more socially introspective hill tribes, is an issue of great concern.

There is something of a minority revival afoot in the southwest of China. Local festivals and customs are receiving more state endorsement and support, preferential choice is given to the children of minorities in education such as university places, and minority families are exempt from China's one-child policy. In every aspect of life the cultural quality of the minorities is improving.

Some, however, fear that these micro-cultures are being increasingly packaged for the delectation of the tourist market, that ethnic groups are the victims of a campaign that portrays them as 'happy, innocent children of nature' as one brochure puts it. The economic development of the minorities, the last to have benefited from China's recent prosperity, however desirable, is certain to erode and modify their cultures.

RELIGION

Despite attempts by the communists to reduce its influence, Buddhism is enjoying a considerable revival in today's China. All religions have to be registered under Chinese law, and there is a good deal of state control, but freedom to worship, though frowned upon by the atheist party, is guaranteed under the law. A softening in the government's policies towards Buddhism has spurred the restoration, redecorating and reoccupancy by monks and lamas, of temples, monasteries and other religious sites. Alms-giving and other forms of donation to the Buddhist clergy which were illegal, are now acceptable practices, and attendance figures at religious festivals, ceremonies and other rites have increased as China reconnects with its cultural past. The state's support for the restoration of Tibetan monasteries and lamaseries in the northeast, and its enthusiastic endorsement for the revival of religious and ethnic festivals, is largely linked to tourism, particularly foreign tourism.

Chinese Buddhists follow the widely practised Mahayana, or 'Greater Vehicle' doctrine of Mahayana Buddhism, also common in places like Japan and Korea. The essence of Buddhism is expressed in the Four Noble Truths which conclude, putting it simply, that all life is suffering and that the cause is desire. Only the extinction of our cravings by detaching ourselves from material and physical desires, can break the cycle of suffering and inch us closer to Nirvana, a word that can be broadly translated at 'extinction of the self'. In this highly causative world we are responsible for our actions in both our present and former lives. We are accountable for the evil actions or wrongdoings that accumulate doing our lifetimes and must atone for them by suffering in future lives. Suffering in this life as a result of past incarnations is unavoidable, but acts of merit in the present cycle can improve our lot in the next.

The most direct way to achieve this is by following the Buddha's Eight Fold Path. These are listed as right understanding, right speech, right conduct, right purpose, right vocation, right thinking, right effort and right meditation. A person's chances of improving his or her karma and enjoying a higher form of existence in the next life can also be improved by following some basic moral tenets, which include prohibitions on killing any living thing, stealing, incontinence, falsehood and the consumption of alcohol. The very opposite in many ways of Chinese style communism, tolerance and a remarkable acceptance of man's fallibility characterise Buddhism. Neither authoritarian nor prescriptive, nor excluding in its attitude towards its followers or other religions, Buddhism simply offers a way forward for those who wish to follow it.

Gaining merit for the afterlife is less important to Chinese Buddhists than improving the quality of this one. In the same way that animists hold rites to ensure a good harvest, Buddhism in modern China has, through suitable offerings and the honouring of certain saints, deities and other religious figures, been co-opted as a means of achieving materialistic or life-improving ends. This pragmatic approach to religion, propitiating the divine as a means to an end, is apparent in the number of people at Buddhist or Taoist temples praying for success in business, entrance to a good university, recovery from illness, or any number of favours and requests.

In normal everyday life there are a number of ways in which to achieve one's desires. These include offering food and alms to monks, supporting local temples with monetary gifts, and offerings of fruit, flowers, gold leaf and incense. Becoming a monk for a period of time or dedicating a son into the monkhood, something that is still practised to a limited extent among certain groups in Yunnan like the Dai in Xishuangbanna, are other ways of currying favour with the powers that be. One popular belief among the people of southern Yunnan is that a family whose son has entered the monkhood, even for only a very short period of time, will be spared the torments of hell.

Taoism is China's only truly indigenous religion. The founder of Taoism, Lao-tzu, is believed to have been born in 604BC. His *Tao Te Ching*, much read among New Agers in the West, is an extremely short tract, and there is some doubt that the master really intended his ideas to form the basis of a religion with temples, festivals, rites and all the other trappings of institutionalised beliefs. Dao, the Way of the Universe, is the core of Taoism. Nature is the engine that drives all life, and certain practices, including physical and spiritual exercises, meditation, and formerly alchemy, must be followed in order to align yourself with the Dao and maintain balance and harmony. The concept of Yin and Yang, the feminine-masculine duality is well known. In your travels through Yunnan you are sure to come across several Taoist temples and shrines and even, if you are lucky, a Taoist festival.

Despite its temples of learning and the offerings made at them, Confucianism is more of a philosophy or moral code than a religion. Confucius, who lived at more or less the same time as Lao-tzu, wished to change the organisation of Chinese society through its administrative and educational systems. His seminal writings, *The Analects*, were widely applied after his death with the support of the thinker and writer Mencius, who helped to promote the master's principles through his own work, *The Book of Mencius*. The influence of Confucianism on Chinese society, seeping into every walk of life, cannot be overstated. Its rigid authoritarianism, its stress on allegiance to rulers, strong patriarchal family values, ancestor worship, and emphasis on obedience have been endlessly exploited by unscrupulous rulers. Yunnan's most famous Confucian temple is the marvellous Temple of Learning in Jianshui.

Yunnan has a sizeable Muslim community, mostly descended from Arab traders and soldiers of fortune who found lucrative work in the area after Kublai Khan's Mongol armies subdued the region in the 13th century. Most cities and many towns have a mosque. Muslim quarters are often easy to recognise from their concentration of restaurants, often white-tiled affairs, with strips of wind-dried beef, a conspicuous absence of pork, bags full of raisins and spices, and a green crescent emblem above the door. Most of the Muslim population was wiped out in the terrible reprisals that followed the Muslim Rebellion of 1855–73.

An ancient and pervasive animism in which spirits exercise great power and influence over the destinies of men, predates Buddhism by many centuries and exerts a hold over many of the remoter hill tribe communities. The communists regarded all such practices as superstition, witchcraft and black magic. The jungles, forests and remoter highlands of Yunnan are inhabited by a host of different spirits. Many of Yunnan's ethnic minorities follow their own idiosyncratic forms of spirit worship, which often have an admixture of Buddhism, Taoism and ancestor worship. The paramount deities are the gods of the soil, and complex rituals connected to the cultivation of rice and other crops are conducted. This belief system is common on the other side of

Yunnan's southern borders, particularly among strongly Sinicised groups like the Hmong and Yao in Laos and Vietnam where a combination of animism, ancestor worship and elements of primitive Taoism, is presided over by local sorcerers and shamans.

The wearing of protective tattoos was quite common among many tribes until recently, especially in remote villages. Amulets are worn for the same purpose. Astrologers and other kinds of diviners are often consulted. In urban areas it is quite common to come across spirit mediums whose ability to make contact with the spirit world and occasionally relay messages from the dead and departed, is in increasing demand.

Catholic and Protestant missionaries did well in the southwest during the period of Western incursion into China in the 19th century. Methodist missionaries gained many converts among hill tribes like the Miao. There has been a small rekindling of Christianity in Yunnan, although the number of converts remains low and the influence of Christianity on the social order slight. The Protestant Church is required to be affiliated with, and answerable to, the state controlled Three-Self Patriotic Movement, the Catholic Church with the Catholic Patriotic Association. Tensions exist between the Catholic church and the state because the church refuses to disavow the Pope as its spiritual leader. Much to China's chagrin the Vatican maintains diplomatic relations with Taiwan instead.

Only atheists are allowed to become members of the Communist Party. The restriction has meant a very low membership figure among the minorities, most of whom profess to some form of religion.

LANGUAGE

Chinese is an uncommonly difficult language to learn. This is understood by the Chinese themselves who, generally speaking, will not expect you to know their language to any degree of fluency. A few words and phrases are useful though, not just to help explain yourself, but to break the ice (see *Appendix 1* on page 281 for useful words and phrases). China's official language, the one everyone will learn at school, is called Mandarin in the West, but known in China as Putonghua. It is also known as Hanyu, the 'language of the Han.'

Despite its apparent complexity, Chinese grammar, following the basic 'subject-verb-object' pattern of European languages, and having a much simplified system of grammar with no tricky articles, tenses and singular-plural distinctions, is easy enough to master. The stumbling block for most foreigners is the tonal system, the scores of sounds, homonyms, rising, falling and neutral tones that are difficult but essential to differentiate if you wish to express yourself clearly and meaningfully.

Learning the characters is time-consuming and requires enormous concentration on the part of foreigners. There are over 50,000 registered ideograms in Chinese, though may of these are anachronisms now and only found in classical literature. Educated Chinese are said to be familiar in their daily lives with seven or eight thousand characters. Half that number would allow you to read a newspaper with a fair level of proficiency.

Although proficiency in foreign languages is limited mostly to the young, well-educated and urban, the importance of English in the economic development of China has now been finally recognised. An increasing number of Chinese study abroad and are returning with different language skills. Many cities have an English Corner which takes place one day a week, usually on a Sunday. You may also be approached sometimes by people eager to practise their English, although this seems to be less common in Yunnan than other places.

Although there are many forms of Chinese, including Cantonese, Shanghainese, and Fujianese – as well as culturally and geographically determined tongues like Tibetan, and countless dialects of which Yunnan has more than its fair share – Mandarin Chinese is the overarching language that makes it possible for most, though by no means all, Chinese to communicate with each other.

Among Yunnan's minority nationalities there are four main language groups: the Tibeto-Burman, Mon-Khmer, Miao-Yao and Tai-Zhuang. A large number of dialects are also spoken. Though taught in schools, Chinese is largely understood as a second language. Chinese characters are mostly used as a written medium, although some minorities have retained their original scripts.

Practical Information

'If you wish to travel quickly in China, never be in a hurry ... Emulate, too, that leading trait in the Chinese character, and never understand anything which you do not wish to understand.'

An Australian in China, G E Morrison, 1895

Morrison was an obnoxious enough traveller, a wealthy white man among peasant farmers and Yunnanese coolies, always ready to thrash a native for insolence but with all the time in the world to be discourteous. He did however, get a few things right. For the long-haul traveller, China at times can seem more ordeal than pleasure. Surly manners, infested hotels and bland food are only half the story. Finding yourself in a border town having your visa checked by a self-important and over-zealous official is enough to put most people off travelling to China's remoter, potentially more interesting, regions. When in doubt or if you think a verdict might go against you, plead ignorance.

WHEN TO VISIT

Yunnan is generally acknowledged to have China's best overall climate. Its varied weather means that there is always somewhere else to go if you encounter bad weather. Generally speaking, most travellers agree that spring, from March to May, and the autumn months from September to November, are the best overall times of the year.

Spring and autumn are usually dry, with plenty of sunny days and Kodachrome-perfect skies. Yunnan's sobriquet, 'The Kingdom of Flowers and Plants', justifies the tourist hype during the spring months when the countryside bursts into flower. Autumn in the north is particularly lovely for the changing colours of its leaves. Spring can be very hot and humid in the south and southwest, however. If you like steamy weather, then head for Xishuangbanna or Dehong.

Late May to September is the rainy season. This can seriously upset your travel plans, so you may have to be flexible. Roads are often blocked or partially washed away in places like Dehong and Deqin in the far northwest. If you find yourself trapped by the rain, check out the weather forecast and move on. Likewise, higher altitudes can be freezing during the autumn and winter months, roads frozen over or blocked by snow. Public holidays and the

Chinese New Year are notoriously congested times to travel. It may also be difficult to obtain air tickets at these times or to book accommodation.

Timing your visit to coincide with a festival will add interest to your itinerary. Many of Yunnan's best festivals take place during the spring and autumn months. China is eight hours ahead of GMT, 16 ahead of US Pacific Standard Time, 13 ahead of US Eastern Standard and two hours behind Australian Eastern Standard Time.

HIGHLIGHTS

The following is a personal list but one which, hopefully, includes places of historical and cultural importance, and also destinations that reflect an interest in a number of fields from temple architecture, hot springs, botany, and trekking to pure travel and serendipity.

Kunming For its vibrant streets, up-to-the-minute shopping, excellent food and nearby Lake Dian.

Dali A wonderful old town full of character. The centre of the Bai minority culture, Dali sits on a fertile plain between the marble screen of the Cangshan Mountain Range and the blue surface of Erhai Lake. Some of the best travellers' cafés, and most relaxing hotels and guesthouses in Yunnan are found here.

Lijiang The old town, now a UNESCO World Heritage Site, looks and feels the way Chinese towns used to be. Old wooden and stone buildings, cobbled backstreets, gurgling streams and willow trees. Lijiang, the centre of the Naxi people and their virile culture, has bags of atmosphere and plenty to see.

Tiger Leaping Gorge One of the world's deepest gorges, with sheer cliffs, thundering waterfalls, dramatic views of the Upper Yangzi River, the gorge is not for the faint-hearted. One of China's great natural sights.

Mounts Deqin and Kagebo Peaks that soar to well over 6,000m, a Tibetan region of glaciers, rare plants and herbs, major river basins and spectacular views of terraced valleys, distant monasteries and prayer flags, Deqin is Yunnan's most remote region.

Tengchong A traditional town at the epicentre of a highly active volcanic region, Tengchong, and its nearby volcanoes, geysers and hot springs evoke an otherworldly landscape.

Ruili At the remote western edge of the empire, Ruili obeys no laws except its own. A wild and woolly frontier town, by day Ruili is a great street trading emporium on the old Southern Silk Route: by night rowdy, flashy and ostentatious, a neon crystal in the jungle.

Ganlanba The homeland of the Dai people and many other minority nationalities. The villages, ancient temples and pagodas of sub-tropical

Ganlanba (the 'Olive Plain'), are easily explored by bicycle. The plain sits in the middle of Xishuangbanna, a prefecture which provides the conditions for over half of China's plant species to grow. This most southern region of Yunnan with its Rousseauesque jungles, rain forests, tropical orchards and rubber plantations, seems to be both geographically and spiritually more a part of Southeast Asia than China.

Jianshui A town of well-preserved traditional homes, ancient bridges and fascinating backstreets, Jianshui, with its incredible Confucius Temple, is on the brink of becoming a major tourist sight.

Kunming to Hekou by rail A must for train buffs, this old French line extends all the way from Kunming to the Vietnamese capital of Hanoi. The narrow-gauge line chugs through eye-catching countryside, temperate to sub-tropical, stopping at small colonial style stations whose yellow and ochre stucco walls seem timeless.

RED TAPE
Visa and entry requirements
All foreign visitors require a visa to enter China. **Tourist visas** are valid for one month after the date of entry and have to be used within three months of the date they were issued. Extensions can be applied for once you are in China. Double-entry visas are also available if you intend to visit a neighbouring country and then return to China. Both single- and double-entry visas can be applied for with a standard Chinese visa form. You will need one entirely blank page in your passport for the tourist visa, which is classified as an L category. Multiple-entry six-month visas are harder to obtain and are usually granted only to businesspeople or those who have been to China before. Visas are obtainable worldwide from Chinese embassies and consulates or through accredited or specialist tour operators. Hong Kong is one of the easiest and fastest places to obtain a Chinese visa. Here you have the option of a 30-day, 60-day, 90-day or six-month single-entry visa, or a multiple-entry visa. Prices vary according to the validity and the speed of service you require. Try CTS (China Travel Service) at 1st floor, Alpha House, 27–33 Nathan Road, Kowloon; tel: 852 2721 4481; fax: 852 2721 6251 or Shoestring Travel on the 4th Floor of the same building; tel: 852 2723 2306.

When applying for a visa you will be required to submit an application form, one passport-size photograph, and your passport which must be valid for a minimum of six months after your entry into China. Fees are usually required to be paid in cash. It usually takes between three and four working days to have a normal tourist visa issued. **Business visas** are usually valid for three months. Officially (though rarely enforced) you should have a return ticket out of the country and, when applying for the visa, list your itinerary in detail. However, you should avoid mentioning Tibet or Xinjiang on your application, as listing these politically sensitive areas can affect your chances of obtaining a visa. Similarly China is quite hostile towards journalists, writers and others with media-related occupations, so you would be well advised to avoid mentioning such details even if your purpose in visiting China is purely for sightseeing. Clerics can also face difficulty in obtaining visas and if you have a letter of invitation from an official body or organisation in China this would be helpful to include with your application. If you are travelling on a tour, then seek advice from your tour operator about the visa application process. Visa costs are levied more or less according to how much your own embassy is charging Chinese visitors for theirs. This seems a fair enough practice. Thank god they don't do the same with airport taxes!

Visa extensions are issued, or denied, by the Foreign Affairs section of the Public Security Bureau (PSB) – the local police station. This means that you don't have to go back to Kunming to apply. Any large town should have a PSB office able to issue an extension. First extensions are usually no problem, but second ones are rarer. It often depends on the place, people and tourist season. Some offices kindly waive the fee, others charge as much as Y110 for an extension.

Don't forget to take some backup ID just in case you lose your passport. If you overstay your visa the fines can be quite high.

Chinese embassies and consulates overseas

Australia 15 Coronation Drive, Yarralumla, ACT 2600; tel: 02 6273 4780
Canada 515 St Patrick, Ottawa, Ontario KIN 5H3; tel: 13 789 3509
France 11 Avenue George V, Paris; tel: 01 47 23 36 77
Germany Kurfislrstenallee 125-300, Bonn 2; tel: 0228 361 095
Italy Via Della Camilluccia 613, Rome 00135; tel: 06 3630 8534
Japan 3-4-33 Moto-Azabu, Minato-ku, Tokyo 106; tel: 03 3403 3380
New Zealand 104A Korokoro Rd, Petone, Wellington; tel: 04 587 0407
Singapore 11-01/03 Tanglin Shopping Centre, 19 Tanglin Rd; tel: 734 3361
Thailand 57 Ratchadaphisek Rd, Dindaeng, Bangkok 10210; tel: 02 245 7032
UK 49 Portland Place, London W1D 1QD; tel: 020 7636 8845. Visa Section 31 Portland Place, London W1D 1QD; tel: 020 7631 1430. 24-hr visa information (premium rate call) 0891-880808
USA 2300 Connecticut Ave NW, Washington, DC 20008; tel: 202 328 2500

Consulates
UK
Manchester Denison House, Denison Rd, Victoria Park, Manchester M14 5RX; tel: 0161 224 7443
Edinburgh 43 Station Rd, Edinburgh EH12; tel: 0131 334 8501

USA
Chicago 100 West Erie St, Chicago, IL 60610; tel: 312 803 0095; fax: 312 803 0122
Houston 3417 Montrose Bd, Houston, TX 77066; tel: 713 524 4311; fax: 713 524 7656
Los Angeles 443 Shatto Place, Los Angeles, CA 90020; tel: 213 380 2506; fax: 213 380 1961

New York 520 12th Av, New York, NY 10036; tel: 212 330 7409; fax: 212 502 0245
San Francisco 1450 Laguna St, San Francisco, CA 94115; tel: 415 563 4857; fax: 415 563 0494

Kunming
Thailand Next to the Kunming Hotel; tel: 871 313 8888
Burma (Myanmar) 3rd Floor, Building Three, Camellia Hotel; tel: 871 317 6609
Laos 2nd Floor, Building Three, Camellia Hotel; tel: 871 317 6623

Please note that there is no Vietnamese consulate in Kunming so you should obtain a Vietnamese visa prior to arrival.

Foreign embassies in China (Beijing)
Australia 21 Donzhi-menwai Dajie; tel: 010 6532 2331
Canada 19 Dongzhi-menwai Dajie; tel: 010 6532 3536
France 3 Sanlitun Dong 3 Jie; tel: 010 6532 1331
Germany 5 Dongzhi-menwai Dajie; tel: 010 6532 2161
Ireland 3 Ritan Dong Lu; tel: 010 6532 2691
Japan 7 Ritan Lu; tel: 010 6532 2361
New Zealand 1 Ritan Dong 2 Jie; tel: 010 6532 2731
Singapore 1 Xiushui Beijie; tel: 010 6532 3962
Thailand 40 Guanghua Lu; tel: 010 6532 1903
UK 11 Guanghua Lu; tel: 010 6532 1961
USA 3 Xiushui Beijie; tel: 010 6532 3831

Some of the embassies in Beijing do not have jurisdiction for Yunnan, but the following consulates cover Yunnan and should be contacted in the event of an emergency:

US Consulate in Chengdu 4 Lingshiguan Lu, Chengdu; tel: 0378 558 3992; fax: 0378 558 3520
British Consulate in Guangzhou 2nd Floor Guangdong International Hotel, 339 Huanshi Dong Lu, Guangzhou; tel: 020 8335 1354; fax: 020 8333 6485

GETTING THERE AND AWAY
By air
There are various international gateways which have direct connections to Kunming, most of which are located in southern Asia. Many travellers include a trip to Yunnan as part of an overall visit to China; visiting Beijing, Guilin, Shanghai or Guangzhou and then flying directly into the province from one of these airports. Kunming has an extensive network of international flights, with direct connections to Hong Kong, Bangkok, Singapore, Kuala Lumpur, Rangoon, Vientiane, Osaka and Macau. Thai Airways has daily Bangkok–Kunming flights. These have become one of the most popular gateways to Yunnan for travellers from the USA and UK, as there are cheap through fares available with this route. Hong Kong also remains a favoured route, with daily direct flights on Dragonair and China Southern Airlines.

China's national carrier is referred to as CAAC (Civil Aviation Administration of China), but is generally known on its international routes as Air China. Yunnan and the southwest are mainly served by three local carriers: Yunnan Airlines, China Southern Airlines and China Southwest Airlines. Chinese aviation in general has been much criticised in the past, but services have improved tremendously in recent years as demand and profitability have increased, and you will find Yunnan served by a well-maintained, newish fleet of Boeing 733s and 737s.

If you have any concerns about air services in China you should check which type of aircraft you will be flying in before booking. Many Western governments will have a listing of airlines and aircraft in China approved for their safety record. Check the British Foreign Office website at www.fco.gov.uk for examples. The safety record of Chinese carriers has greatly improved in recent years and whilst it doesn't do any harm to be cautious, bear in mind that the fatality record of road travel in China is far, far worse!

Air China offices overseas
Australia Suite 2, 5thF, 454 Collins St, Melbourne, Victoria 3000; tel: 9642 1555
Canada Suite 1005, 655 Bay St, Toronto MSG 2K4; tel: 5818833
France 10 Bd Malesherbes, Paris 75008; tel: 01 42 66 58
Germany Duesseldorfer Str 4, D-60329, Frankfurt-am-Mian; tel: 233038
Japan Air China Building, 2-5-2, Toranomon, Minato-ku, Tokyo 105; tel: 03 52510711
Singapore 01-53 Anson Centre, 51 Anson Rd, Singapore 0207; tel: 225 2177
Thailand CP Tower 2/F, 313 Silom Rd, Bangrak, Bangkok 10500; tel: 662 631 0728
UK 41 Grosvenor Gdns, London SWIW OBP; tel: 020 7630 0919
USA 49th St, New York, NY 10017; tel: 212 371 9898

Tickets and stopovers
Long-haul travellers on round-the-world or open tickets can try to factor Bangkok into their schedule and then fly into Kunming directly on one of the daily Thai Air flights or one of the popular routes that goes via Chiang Mai. The Thai through fares from Bangkok remain one of the best deals for people originating from Europe, Australia or the US, though many prefer to fly via Beijing or Hong Kong, from where there are connections to more or less anywhere in China.

Travel agencies overseas specialising in China can usually easily book you onward tickets to Yunnan, although they will be more expensive. On the other hand, you may be able to get a same-day connection, obviating, and at the same time saving you the cost, of an overnight stay while you sort out your bookings. Domestic and international tickets bought in either Hong Kong or Macau (newly returned to China) are among the cheapest deals available.

Tour specialists
UK
Asian Journeys 6 Willows Gate, Stratton Audley, Oxon OX27 9AU; tel: 01869 276 200; fax: 01869 276 214; email: mail@asianjourneys.com; web: www.asianjourneys.com

China Direct 109 Ferguson Close, London E14 3SJ; tel: 020 7538 2840; fax: 020 75366 9088; email: info@chinadirect-travel.co.uk; web: www.chinadirect-travel.co.uk

China Travel Service (CTS) 7 Upper St Martin's Lane, London WC2H 9DL; tel: 020 7836 9911; fax: 020 7836 3121; email: cts@ctsuk.com

Exodus Expeditions 9 Weir Rd, London SW12 0LT; tel: 0181 675 5550

Explore Worldwide 1 Frederick St, Aldershot, Hants GUII ILQ; tel: 01252 319448

Imaginative Traveller 14 Barley Mow Passage, Chiswick, London W4 4PH; tel: 0181 742 8612

Magic of the Orient 2 Kingsland Court, Three Bridges Rd, Crawley, W Sussex RH10 1HL; tel: 01293 537700; fax: 01293 537888; web: www.magicoftheorient.com

Master Travel FREEPOST (SE 7045), London SE24 9BR; tel: 020 8678 5320; fax: 020 8674 2712; email: tours@mastertravel.co.uk; web: www.mastertravel.co.uk

Regent Holidays 15 John St, Bristol BS1 2HR; tel: 0117 921 1711; fax: 0117 925 4866; email: regent@regent-holidays.co.uk; web: www.regent-holidays.co.uk

Silk Steps 83 Quakers Rd, Downend, Bristol BS16 6NH; tel: 0117 940 2800; fax: 0117 940 6900; email: info@silksteps.co.uk; web: www.silksteps.co.uk

Steppes East The Travel House, 51 Castle St, Cirencester GL7 1QD; tel: 01285 651010; fax: 01285 885888; email: sales@steppeseast.co.uk; web: www.steppeseast.co.uk

USA

Asian Pacific Adventures 826 South Sierra Bonita Av, Los Angeles, CA 90036-4704; tel: 800 825 1680

Earth River Expeditions 180 Towpath Rd, Accord, NY 12404; tel: 914 626 4423

Earth Science Expeditions 202 North Av, No 102, Grand Junction, CO 81501; tel: 970 242 108

Australia

Intrepid Travel 11–12 Spring St, Fitzroy, Victoria, Australia; tel: 613 9473 2626; fax: 613 9419 4426; email: info@intrepidtravel.com.au; web: www.intrepidtravel.com

Peregrine Adventures 285 Lonsdale St, Melbourne, Victoria; tel/fax: 03 9662 2700.

Direct flights to Kunming from southeast Asia

The following countries and airlines fly direct to Kunming from Southeast Asian destinations. With the opening up of the province, the number of flights and routes is likely to increase.

From Thailand Daily Bangkok–Kunming flights by Yunnan Airlines and Thai Airways. Three of the Thai Airways weekly flights go via Chiang Mai.

From Singapore Both Yunnan Airlines and Silk Air, a Singapore Airlines subsidiary, have twice-weekly flights between Singapore and Kunming. Kuala Lumpur Yunnan airlines has recently launched a direct service once a week from Kuala Lumpur to Kunming.

From Laos Both Lao Aviation and China Southern operate once a week flights between Vientiane and Kunming.

From Burma Air China and Myanmar Airways have one weekly flight each from Rangoon (Yangon) to Kunming.

From Kuala Lumpur Yunnan Airlines has recently launched a direct service once a week from Kuala Lumpur to Kunming.

Flights to Beijing/Hong Kong
From the UK

Both British Airways and Air China have direct non-stop flights from London Heathrow to Beijing, that currently operate three times a week. The competition between these two airlines has kept fares down and with low season prices of £360, they represent very good value for money. It is worth bearing in mind that Air China also offers discounts on their domestic fares when booked in conjunction with an international ticket. A London–Beijing–Kunming return ticket costs £575 with Air China. There are also plans underway by Air China to increase their number of flights from London to Beijing to five a week. British Airways also offers good-value open-jaw tickets flying into Beijing and out of Hong Kong (or vice versa) for as little as £450 in low season.

Cathay Pacific, Virgin Atlantic and British Airways all operate daily direct flights from London to Hong Kong. Virgin also has a direct service to Shanghai twice a week. Fares to Hong Kong start from £440 with Virgin or British Airways in the low season and £390 for Shanghai.

There are also a number of international airlines who all have indirect flights from the UK to Beijing and Hong Kong, with fares from as little as £340 for an indirect return from London to Beijing. Thai Airways has a daily service that goes via Bangkok to Kunming with fares from £600.

Aeroflot 70 Piccadilly London W1; tel: 020 7355 2233
Air China 41 Grosvenor Gdns , London SW1W; tel: 020 7630 0919
Alitalia 4 Portman Sq, London; tel: 020 7602 7111
British Airways Various locations throughout Britain; tel: 020 7828 4895
Cathay Pacific 7 Appletree Yd, Duke of York St, London SW1; tel: 020 7747 8888
Emirates Airlines 95 Cromwell Rd, London; tel: 020 7808 0808
Finnair 144 Clifford St, London W; tel: 020 7408 1222
Gulf Air 10 Albemarle St, London W1 tel: 020 7408 1717
KLM Terminal 4, Heathrow Airport; tel: 0870 507 4074
Lufthansa 7-8 Conduit St, London W1; tel: 0345 737747
Pakistan International Airlines 44 Dover St, London; tel: 020 7499 5500
Singapore Airlines 143–147 Regent St, London W1; tel: 020 7747 0007
Swissair Swiss Centre, 1 Swiss Ct, London; tel: 020 7434 7300
Thai International 41 Albemarle St, London W1; tel: 020 7499 9113
Turkish Airlines 125 Pall Mall, London SW1; tel: 020 7760 9300
Virgin Atlantic 14–16 Oxford St, London W1; tel: 01293 747747

From the USA

Most direct flights to China operate from the west coast, with the exception of Northwest Airlines. There are twice-weekly direct flights with

Northwest Airlines from Detroit to Beijing, China Eastern has four flights a week from Los Angeles to Beijing and Air China also has a number of direct flights to Beijing and Shanghai from Los Angeles and San Francisco. Fares start from as little as $700 with China Eastern or Air China in the low season. There are a number of airlines serving Hong Kong; Cathay Pacific has daily flights from Los Angeles, United has daily direct flights from both San Francisco and Los Angeles and Air China, Thai International and Singapore Airlines all have direct services from San Francisco and Los Angeles.

There are also a number of airlines with indirect services which connect on to Beijing or Hong Kong. Thai Airways is probably the most convenient and economical way to reach Kunming via Bangkok.

Air China tel: 212 371 9899
Asiana Airlines tel: 1 800 227 4262
Cathay Pacific tel: 1 800 233 2742
China Airlines tel: 917 368 2000-10-28
China Eastern Airlines tel: 0206 343 5582
EVA Airlines tel: 1 800 695 1188
Japan Airlines tel: 1 800 525 3663
Korean Airlines tel: 1 800 438 5000
Northwest Airlines tel: 1 800 438 5000
Singapore Airlines tel: 1 800 742 3333
Thai International tel: 1 800 426 5204
United Airlines tel: 1 800 538 2929

From Australia and New Zealand

Coming from Australia and New Zealand, the nearest point of entry to China is Hong Kong, which is served by a number of carriers with direct flights. Air China, British Airways, Cathay Pacific, Ansett Australia and Qantas all have direct flights from Australia's east coast. Air New Zealand is the only direct flight from Auckland to Hong Kong. The cheapest fares to Hong Kong are with Royal Brunei Airlines who have indirect flights for as little as A$850 from Brisbane, Darwin and Perth.

Air China tel: 03 9642 1555
Air New Zealand tel: 1 800 737 000 (New Zealand)
Ansett Australia tel: 1800 131 414
British Airways Melbourne tel: 039 603 1133; Sydney tel: 02 8904 8800; Auckland tel: 09 356 8690
Cathay Pacific Australia tel: 1800 131 747; New Zealand tel: 09 379 0861
Garuda Melbourne tel: 03 9654 2522; Sydney tel: 1300 365 331; Auckland tel: 09 366 1855
Malaysian Airlines Sydney tel: 1 800 269 9988; Auckland tel: 09 366 1855
Qantas Australia tel: 131 313; New Zealand tel: 09 357 8900
Royal Brunei Brisbane tel: 07 3221 7757
Singapore Airlines Australia tel: 1 800 131 011; New Zealand tel: 09 303 2129

From Canada
Canadian Airlines have a direct service from Vancouver to Beijing several times a week. Air Canada, Canadian and Cathay Pacific all have direct daily services to Hong Kong from Vancouver with connecting services from Toronto and Montreal.

Air Canada tel: 1 800 555 1212
Canadian tel: 1 800 426 7000
Cathay Pacific tel: 1 800 233 2742

Routes via Beijing and Hong Kong
There are several daily flights from both Beijing and Hong Kong to Kunming. These remain popular routes for foreign travellers to Yunnan. China Southern, China Southwest and Dragonair are the carriers. Dragonair out of Hong Kong offers the cheapest tickets to Kunming at present. A cheaper route, though a longer one, is to book a Guangzhou to Kunming flight in Hong Kong. You will then have to make your way to Guangzhou by train. You might save yourself Y400–500 doing this.

Recommended discount ticket agencies/carriers
Australia
Flight Centre 157 Ann St, Brisbane, Queensland 4000; tel: 133133; web: www.flightcentre.com.au. Over 200 branches.
STA Travel 855 George St, Ultimo, Sydney, NSW 2007; tel: 02 9212 1255; web: www.sta-travel-group.com. Branches in all major Australian cities.

Canada
Avia Tel: 514 284 5040. A Montreal-based agency.
Mars Tours Tel: 416 536 5458. Based in Toronto.
Travel Cuts 187 College St, Toronto MST 1P7; trel: 416 979 2406; web: www.travelcuts.com. Student travel agency. All major cities.

Japan
No 1 Travel Tel: 03 3200 8871. One of the largest discount agencies. Offices in most major cities.

Malaysia
China Southern has flights to Beijing, Guangzhou and Hong Kong.
Malaysia Airlines flies from Kuala Lumpur to Beijing and Guangzhou.

New Zealand
Flight Centre 3A National Bank Tower, 2015–225 Queen St, Auckland; tel: 0800 FLIGHTS.
Garuda Airlines operates the cheapest flights at present to Hong Kong and Beijing.

Philippines
Manila–Beijing flights are twice-weekly on **China Southern**. There is also a Guangzhou–Manila weekly flight.

South Korea

Regular **Air China**, **Korean Air** and **Asiana Air** flights from Seoul to major Chinese cities like Beijing, Shanghai and Hong Kong.

Joy Travel Service 10th Floor, 24-2 Mukyo-dong, Chung-gu, Seoul; tel: 776 9871
Korean International Student Exchange Society (KISES) Room 505, YMCA Building, Chongno 2-ga, Seoul; tel: 733 9494
Top Travel Room 506, YMCA Building, Chongno 2-ga, Seoul; tel: 739 5231

UK

Bridge the World 47 Chalk Farm Rd, London NW1 8AJ; tel: 020 7911 0900; fax: 020 7813 3350; email: sales@bridgetheworld.co.uk
Campus Travel 52 Grosvenor Gdns, London SW1W 0UA; tel: 0207 730 8111. Several branches.
China Travel Service (CTS) 7 Upper St Martin's Lane, London WC2H 9DL; tel: 0207 836 9911; email: cts@ctsuk.com
China Travel Service and Information Centre (CTSIC) 124 Euston Rd, London NWI 2AL
Council Travel 28a Poland St, London W1F 8QP; tel: 0207 437 7767
Fly Now Cheetham Hill Rd, Manchester M8 5EJ; tel: 0161 721 4000; fax: 0161 7214202
Holiday Planners 111 Bell St, Marylebone Rd, London NW1 6TL; tel: 020 7724 2255; fax: 020 7724 8282
Jade Travel 5 Newport Place, London WC2H 7QU; tel: 020 7734 7726; fax: 020 7734 2149
STA Travel 86 Old Brompton Rd, London SW7 3LQ; tel: 020 7361 6262; email: enquiries@statravel.co.uk. Several branches.
Trailfinders Travel Centre 42–50 Earls Court Rd, London W8 6TF; tel: 020 7938 3366; web: www.trailfinders.com. Several branches.
Travel Bug 597 Cheetham Hill Rd, Manchester M8 5EU; tel: 0161 721 4000
Union Travel 93 Piccadilly, London W1J 7NQ; tel: 020 7493 4343

USA

Air Brokers International 150 Post St, San Francisco; tel: 1 800 883 3273
Council Travel Tel: 800 226 8624; web: www.ciee.org. Big student travel group. All major cities.
Gateway Travel Tel: 214 960 2000. Based in Dallas. Branches in most major cities.
High Adventure Travel Inc 442 Post St, San Francisco; tel: 1 800 4288735; web: www. airtreks.com
Overseas Tours Tel: 415 692 4892; web: www.overseastours.com. Based in Millbrae, California.
STA Travel 10 Downing St, New York; tel: 1 800 777 0112 (freephone)

Departure taxes

When leaving China by air the departure tax is Y90. Domestic flights charge something called an 'airport construction fee', costing Y50. The procedure is the same and both must be paid for in *yuan*.

Land routes

A few long-haul travellers make it to Yunnan overland from Europe and other Asian destinations. The easiest routes into Yunnan by land are from the southeast Asian countries of Laos and Vietnam which both border the south of the province. Coming from Laos you will cross into the border checkpoint close to Mengla in Xishuangbanna. (See *Chapter 13* for more information.) If you intend to enter from Vietnam then the narrow-gauge train which links Hanoi with Kunming is an interesting and scenic option, entering Yunnan at Hekou. (See below for more detail). Arriving from Burma is always difficult as the border at Ruili is more often than not closed to foreigners The other options for arriving overland into Yunnan would involve considerable journeys if you are thinking of coming from Europe via the Trans-Siberian express (one week) and then connecting with one of the train routes from Beijing to Kunming. Coming over the Himalayas via Nepal and Tibet is a mammoth journey which is beset with both physical and bureaucratic difficulties. Independent travel is frowned upon by the Chinese authorities in Tibet and it is now very difficult to reach Tibet from Nepal as anything other than part of an organised group. People have travelled this route into Yunnan before but the journey on the Lhasa–Sichuan Highway is extremely arduous and should deter all but the most determined and hardy travellers.

By train

China has a vast passenger rail network that serves most of its main cities, though routes from one region to another can sometimes be quite convoluted and time-consuming. It remains nonetheless an excellent and economical way to see the country and meet her peoples.

Several possible routes into Yunnan can be attempted by train, but all involve fairly long journeys. Hong Kong to Kunming is possible by first of all boarding the Kowloon Light Railway, for the three-hour journey to Guangzhou main railway station; alternatively there is now a high-speed express service which can do the journey in one hour twenty minutes but is naturally more expensive. When you reach Guangzhou you can transfer to a Nanning-bound train. There is now a high-speed electrified line between Kunming and Nanning which has reduced this section of the journey to 16 hours; expect the entire journey to take about two days. There are also daily trains from Guiyang to Kunming (12 hours), if you are coming from Guizhou province.

If coming through China from Beijing the most interesting route is to travel from Beijing to Xian, to Chengdu to Kunming, a journey that can be accomplished with three overnight legs – not necessarily consecutively. There are frequent trains along this route between some of China's most interesting and ancient cities. Another faster possibility would be to go from Beijing to Zhengzhou (high-speed line), to Changsha to Guiyang, to Kunming which can be done in 48 exhausting hours. Tickets can be purchased through the various CITS branches in each stop or arranged in advance as part of a travel package by a specialist tour operator abroad. See the descriptions on pages 51–2 for more details of types of ticket/seat available.

The Vietnamese capital of Hanoi is linked with Kunming by the old colonial, narrow-gauge line. Built in 1910 with a total length of 762km, this antiquated but fascinating line stops on the Vietnamese side at Lao Cai and then crosses to Hekou in Yunnan. The journey time is around 27 hours on the international train. This route is highly rated by rail journey enthusiasts for its beautiful mountain scenery as the train rolls along the Red River Valley in Vietnam and into the uplands of southern Yunnan. International trains arrive and depart on the Yunnan side from Kunming's north railway station twice a week on Mondays and Fridays. The journey takes 29 hours in total. A soft sleeper ticket costs Y680 one way and can be booked through Kunming CITS or a China specialist tour operator abroad. There are also local trains running daily to Hekou, some 16 hours from Kunming, but the carriages are basic and leave something to be desired. Trains depart daily at 09.30 from Kunming to Hekou with a connecting service on the Vietnamese side and at 14.45 from Hekou to Kunming. Once you reach Hekou you have to walk over the Red River bridge to Lao Cai where you can board another train for Hanoi. The border crossing is open from 07.30 to 17.00 daily and can involve some fairly elaborate checks and searches.

If you are entering Vietnam from Kunming you will need to have your point of entry (Hekou) and means of conveyance stated on your Vietnamese visa. As there is no Vietnamese consulate in Kunming this precludes any spontaneous decisions to use this route once you are there. Your visa and plans need to be fixed in advance of arriving in Kunming, either from the Vietnamese embassy in Beijing or your home country. There are no such problems entering China from Vietnam though, and this train journey comes highly recommended.

By bus

For the true travel masochist there is always the option of reaching Yunnan on one of the sleeper bus routes through southern China from Hong Kong. The fastest route would be to take a bus from Hong Kong's China–Hong Kong city bus station in Kowloon to Guangzhou. From Guangzou's long-distance bus station there are frequent regular and sleeper buses to Nanning and from there onwards to Kunming. Expect this journey to take around two or three days. You would be better advised to use the train for these longer journeys, though, and save bus travel for journeys within Yunnan province. Similarly, most big cities in China will have sleeper buses which will connect through to Yunnan and the southwest, but are of questionable value when compared to the advantages of the train.

You can enter Yunnan quite easily these days from Laos via the border crossing at Boten in Luang Nam Tha province. Buses ferry people up to the Chinese border from Luang Nam Tha town and Udomxai. Travellers entering Laos usually go from Jinghong in Xishuangbanna, overnight in Mengla, and then press on early the next morning to the border.

HEALTH AND TRAVEL ISSUES

Travellers to Yunnan should exercise some caution as Xishuangbanna contains one of China's few malarial risk areas. Overall, however, a visit to Yunnan does not present any serious health risks. Traffic accidents and stomach upsets rank as the most common dangers and annoyances in a province that sends the majority of its visitors away with a clean bill of health and a vow to return. Yunnan's geographical variety, its staggering number of climatic zones, means, however, that the potential range of medical problems varies from frostbite and altitude sickness to heatstroke and fungal infections.

Chinese doctors are well educated and trained and practise an interesting mixture of Western and Chinese medicine. Note that there is no supply of Rh-negative blood in China. Stocks of drugs can run low in remote areas, so if you require a regular medication it is best to bring enough with you to last the trip. The same applies to carrying enough contact-lens solution, tampons and other regularly administered necessities. Watch out for dehydration, a common complaint. This is easily combated with plenty of bottled liquids or mineral water. Even without diarrhoea you should try to drink three litres of water a day. Electrolyte rehydration powder is useful in the event that you do succumb to this.

Water, raw vegetables and fruit which cannot be peeled, should be avoided wherever possible. Minor stomach upsets are common but rarely amount to anything and should certainly not stop travellers from enjoying Yunnanese cooking. The general rule is to eat at restaurants which appear to be clean and well patronised. Many Chinese dishes are stir-fried which should kill off most of the bacteria. Make sure that chopsticks are sealed in plastic and new. Otherwise take your own. Milk is not always pasteurised and is best avoided.

Yunnan has a relatively low incidence of illness, and its health care standards, by and large, are reasonably good. Visitors can go to public hospitals, or to community and rural health centres for medical consultation and treatment. Even quite small towns usually have fairly decently stocked pharmacies. A little care and prevention will help to minimise the potential number of health problems you could incur in Yunnan.

Unfair as it is, foreigners often receive preferential treatment in hospitals, and may find themselves being ushered to the head of long queues of waiting patients.

Before the trip

It is important to consult a doctor at least two months in advance of your trip to find out about the timing of vaccinations. It may also be necessary to try out prophylactic malaria tablets before departure to see if they suit you. A check-up at the dentist, a couple of months before the trip, is a good idea. Dental facilities in the provinces are not, on average, as good as medical ones.

There are no legal requirements for vaccinations for Yunnan except for yellow fever vaccine which is only required if you are arriving from an infected area (eg: South America or Sub Saharan Africa). Nevertheless it is wise to be up to date with tetanus, diphtheria, polio (all ten yearly), typhoid and hepatitis A. Hepatitis A vaccine (eg: Havrix Monodose, Avaxim) is now considered to be the best way to protect against the disease and may even be taken close to the time of travel although it is preferable to have it at least two weeks in advance. The blood product gamma globulin has fallen out of favour and is now seldom used. The newer typhoid vaccines are about 85% effective and cause fewer side effects than the older ones.

If you intend to be in Yunnan for some time, or have plans to get off the beaten track, further vaccinations against hepatitis B, rabies, TB, and Japanese encephalitis (April to October) may be required. Allow at least eight weeks for these vaccinations to be completed.

Medical insurance

Try to find a good all-round insurance policy that provides cover for theft, illness and serious accidents. There are a number of different high to low risk policies on offer, so check carefully with your local travel agent. It is a good idea to carry a paper listing any medical problems that you have, blood type, emergency contact numbers and details of any prescriptions or special medication that you use regularly.

Medical kits

A light medical kit is a must. Contents should be stored in an easily sealed bag that can be taken on planes as hand luggage. A basic kit could include plasters, an antibiotic powder and salve for treating cuts and scratches, painkillers, a stopping agent for diarrhoea, such as Imodium, antiseptic cream, a small set of hypodermics, a thermometer and tweezers, Q-tips to prevent ear infections, aspirins, Pepto-Bismol for general stomach problems, malaria pills if you are going into jungle or rainforest areas in the monsoon season, a calamine lotion to alleviate irritation from stings, rashes and bites, antiseptic and sun block creams, a rehydration mixture such as Electrolyte, water purification tablets, an insect repellent, sunscreen lotion. A bottle of Tiger Balm is useful for muscle aches and pains and can provide relief from insect bites. Mosquito coils and nets are useful in sub-tropical areas.

General travel health care

Most problems can be avoided with a little planning and attention to your health on the trip. You should be in reasonably good shape before you depart, but if you are taking medication, make sure that you have a sufficient supply and take your prescription or bottle labels with you in case you need a top up. Be sure to take an extra pair of glasses or contact lenses with you as this will save a lot of hassle and expense. Contact lens solution is available in cities and large towns throughout Yunnan, but may be almost impossible to find off-the-beaten-track.

Allow yourself a couple of easy days to adjust to a tropical climate and throw off any jet lag you might experience. Any small cuts or grazes incurred on the road should be addressed immediately as they can become septic within a very short time, especially in the humid southern regions of Yunnan. Cuts and grazes should be cleaned immediately and covered with a clean dry dressing.

Tap water is said to be treated but it is best to be cautious and avoid drinking it directly as the quality will vary greatly from one region to another. Use purification tablets or keep a supply of easily-available mineral water handy. Ice cubes and salads washed in suspect water are the usual causes of stomach upsets. Tea and coffee should be safe as the water is boiled.

Watch your diet in general and be aware of unpasteurised daily foods (especially milk), unwashed fruit, and inadequately cooked, or lukewarm dishes. Fruit that can be peeled, plenty of grains and roughage, eggs, nuts, and beans will help to ensure some regular protein intake. Iron and vitamin pills can help. Drink more than you think you need to rehydrate your body in high temperatures. Extra doses of salt on food are better than taking salt tablets.

It is not advisable to walk barefoot or in open thongs in obviously garbage-strewn urban areas. Don't swim in slow flowing rivers, lakes or ponds as eye and ear infections are easily picked up. This is also a good way of contracting parasitic infections like bilharzia. Personal hygiene is important. Try to take at least one shower a day, wash hands before meals, brush teeth with purified or mineral water, not straight from the tap, cover yourself sufficiently when there are droves of insects around, stay out of direct sunlight for long periods and avoid extremes of temperature whenever possible.

Travel clinics
UK
British Airways Travel Clinic and Immunisation Service 156 Regent St, London W1, tel: 020 7439 9584. This place also sells travellers' supplies and has a branch of Stanford's travel book and map shop. There are now BA clinics all around Britain and three in South Africa. To find your nearest one, phone 01276 685040.

MASTA (Medical Advisory Service for Travellers Abroad) Keppel St, London WC1 7HT; tel: 09068 224100. This is a premium-line number, charged at 50p per minute.

Nomad Travel Pharmacy and Vaccination Centre 3–4 Wellington Terrace, Turnpike Lane, London N8 0PX; tel: 020 8889 7014; recorded information service (premium rate call): 09068 633 414; web: www.nomadtravel.co.uk. There is also a branch on Queen's Rd, Bristol; tel: 0117 922 6567.

Thames Medical 157 Waterloo Rd, London SE1 8US; tel: 020 7902 9000. Competitively priced, one-stop travel health service. All profits go to their affiliated company InterHealth which provides health care for overseas workers on Christian projects.

Trailfinders Immunisation Centre 194 Kensington High St, London W8 7RG; tel: 020 7938 3999. Also 254–284 Sauchiehall St, Glasgow G2 3EH; tel: 0141 353 0066. NHS travel website, www.fitfortravel.scot.nhs.uk, provides country-by-country advice on immunisation and malaria, plus details of recent developments, and a list of relevant health organisations.

USA

Centers for Disease Control 1600 Clifton Road, Atlanta, GA 30333; tel: 877 FYI TRIP; 800 311 3435; web: www.cdc.gov/travel. This organisation is the central source of travel information in the USA. Each summer they publish the invaluable Health Information for International Travel which is available from the Division of Quarantine at the above address.

Connaught Laboratories PO Box 187, Swiftwater, PA 18370; tel: 800 822 2463. They will send a free list of specialist tropical-medicine physicians in your state.

IAMAT (International Association for Medical Assistance to Travelers) 736 Center St, Lewiston, NY 14092. A non-profit organisation which provides lists of English-speaking doctors abroad.

Australia

TMVC tel: 1300 65 88 44; website: www.tmvc.com.au. TMVC has 20 clinics in Australia, New Zealand and Thailand, including:

Brisbane Dr Deborah Mills, Qantas Domestic Building, 6th floor, 247 Adelaide St, Brisbane, QLD 4000; tel: 7 3221 9066; fax: 7 3321 7076

Melbourne Dr Sonny Lau, 393 Little Bourke St, 2nd floor, Melbourne, VIC 3000; tel: 3 9602 5788; fax: 3 9670 8394

Sydney Dr Mandy Hu, Dymocks Building, 7th floor, 428 George St, Sydney, NSW 2000; tel: 2 221 7133; fax: 2 221 8401

South Africa

There are four British Airways travel clinics in South Africa: *Johannesburg*, tel: (011) 807 3132; *Cape Town*, tel: (021) 419 3172; *Knysna*, tel: (044) 382 6366; *East London*, tel: (0431) 43 2359.

Travel and healthcare books

The Traveller's Handbook, Melissa Shales, a WEXAS Publication
Where There is No Doctor, David Werner, Hersperian Foundation
The Traveller's Health, Richard Dawood, OUP
The Tropical Traveller, John Hatt, Pan Books
Staying Healthy in Asia, Africa & Latin America, Moon Publications
The Traveller's Health Guide, Dr Antony Turner, Roger Lascales

Health problems

Flying in

The most important thing about your time in the air, although you may only realise it afterwards, is the effect of the experience on your body. Cabin air is under slightly reduced pressure and relatively dry, space is restricted and the body is noticeably more sensitive to the adverse effects of alcohol, caffeine and certain kinds of food. Apart from some simple neck, shoulder, arm, lower back and feet stretching exercises, there is not that much you can do at 30,000 feet but wait for terra firma. There are, however, a few precautions that you can take prior to and after you arrive at your hotel which will, in most cases, eliminate or partially alleviate any unpleasant effects of flying and also help you relax during the flight. Drink plenty of water and fruit juices both before, during and after the flight to combat dehydration. The application of a good quality moisturiser before you depart will keep the exposed parts of your skin in the right condition during the flight. Try to avoid drinking alcohol altogether and cut down on the amount of tea and coffee you drink both during and immediately before the flight. It is also helpful to avoid eating fatty foods. Prepare comfortable, loose-fitting clothes, preferably made from natural fibres that will allow your skin to breathe. Try to take a relaxing soak in the tub or a hot shower after you get to your hotel room, providing of course, that it has a bath and hot water. This will help to restore your normal circulation and prepare you for your holiday.

Jet lag

Jet lag is caused when travellers pass through three or more time zones, setting their body's internal clocks on a confusing course that can result in sensations of nausea, fatigue, disorientation, loss of appetite and irregular sleeping patterns. According to the experts, the effects of jet lag can be reduced by exercising immediately after a flight, eating sensibly during it, forgoing smoking, laying off the booze, and taking at least one day easy after arrival. There may be a way to avoid this kill-joy regime and catch a few winks of sleep at the same time. The new wonder drug melatonin may just be the answer to getting your biological clock in step with other time zones. A synthetic version of this apparently harmless hormone is now being marketed as a pill, one of which is popped as soon as you board your plane. Subsequent doses are taken before bedtime for the next two days in the new time zone, a course that its manufacturers claim will reset the body's internal clock. The drug is already available in Singapore, Hong Kong and other parts of Asia. If melatonin fails, you can always pick up a copy of Charles Ehret's helpful book, *Overcoming Jet Lag*.

Respiratory infections

China is plagued by various strains of flu with more multiplying each year. Massive crowding, notoriously smoggy air, and the proximity of many people to chickens, ducks and pigs means quick infection and rapid spread of viruses. Underpopulated and less industrialised Yunnan, because of its chilly highland and alpine areas, is less of a breeding ground for respiratory infections like flu and the common cold, but care should be taken. Bring along whatever cold remedies work for you back home.

Altitude sickness

Yunnan is well above sea level and, with mountains soaring to over 6,000m, altitude sickness is fairly common. Reduced air pressure causes the blood to malfunction in its absorption of oxygen. Some people acclimatise quicker than others, of course, and for many people a gradual ascent will be no problem. It normally takes the body two to three days initially to adjust to higher altitudes, so if you are visiting towns such as Zhongdian and Deqin which are above

3,000m then you should try to take a bus in from Lijiang rather than flying straight from Kunming.

If you do fly into Zhongdian then it is important that you rest for a day or two and do not attempt anything strenuous, while your body adjusts to the high altitude. If you are trekking, try to sleep at a lower altitude than the height you climbed to during the day. Avoid alcohol, nicotine and drugs. Acute mountain sickness (AMS) usually results from too rapid an ascent to high altitudes. Mild symptoms of AMS, such as headaches, sleeplessness and loss of appetite are quite common for the first few days above 3,000m. Other symptoms of AMS include fatigue, nausea, disorientation, shortness of breath and aches and pains in muscles. AMS has to be taken seriously as it can quickly develop into more fatal forms of illness such as HACE (high altitude cerebral oedema) and HAPE (high altitude pulmonary oedema). Its effects can also be delayed and you may suffer ill effects some days or even weeks after you think you have adjusted to the altitude. If you are suffering from AMS then the only effective solution is to descend to a lower altitude immediately – 500m will do. In most cases the benefits will be almost instant. Drinking plenty of water and taking paracetamol or aspirin will also help alleviate ill effects.

Hepatitis

You may have given up eating sushi in Bangkok restaurants, or slurping cockles on the quay at Shanghai, because you were worried about picking up hepatitis A, but there are other ways to catch this disease which might, along with malaria, justifiably be called the 'travellers' curse'. You can get it through contaminated food or drink, by using unhygienic eating utensils, or by being in places where sanitation and hygiene leave much to be desired; situations in short, which many independent travellers frequently find themselves in. The symptoms are fairly easy to recognise. Sufferers experience headaches, fever, tiredness, stomach pains, diarrhoea and vomiting, the emission of orange-tinged urine; all or a combination of some of them making you feel like you are coming down with food poisoning. The skin and whites of the eyes will usually turn yellow. Absolute rest and a simple, balanced diet is the best cure, with absolutely no alcohol! Vaccine prevention is better (see page 35).

Hepatitis B is contracted mainly through sexual contact, the mingling of body fluids or through the blood. Infected syringes can also be transmitters. It is a more serious illness altogether than hepatitis A as people who have this disease can remain carriers throughout their life. The symptoms and treatment are almost identical to A. A vaccine to Hepatitis B does exist and is worth taking for trips of two months or longer if you are working in hospitals or with children: both situations can increase the likelihood of acquiring the disease. Avoid things like having your ears pierced, acupuncture or tattooing if you feel the conditions are not completely sanitary.

Malaria

Malaria exists in variable degrees in China. If you intend exploring the borderlands of places like Xishuangbanna which are contiguous with

Southeast Asian countries such as Laos, Vietnam and Burma then it is wise to take antimalarial tablets. Shaking fits, headaches, fever, sweating and chills are the normal symptoms of malaria, which is spread by mosquito bites. It can, in severe cases, be fatal, although this is fairly rare if treatment is sought quickly. Unfortunately the malaria in this area is resistant to the common prophylactic agents, and currently mefloquine (Lariam) is the most effective. This drug has to be prescribed by a doctor as it is not suitable for everybody. It should be tried at least two weeks in advance to see if there are any serious side effects. Alternatively, the antibiotic doxycycline can be used, but this must also be prescribed by a doctor. It has the advantage that it need only be started the day before arriving in Yunnan.

All prophylactics should be taken at night with or just after food, washed down with plenty of fluids and continued for four weeks after leaving the area. For those who are unable to take either of these drugs or who may be a long way from medical help, carrying a treatment for malaria (eg: quinine and another drug) is a sensible precaution. Advice should be sort from a doctor experienced in travel medicine to obtain the latest information.

Mosquitoes are at their most active at dusk and throughout the evening and night. Prevention, as they say, is always better than cure. Mosquito bites can largely be avoided by using liberal amounts of insect repellent (containing DEET such as the Autan or Jungle Formula brands), carrying a mosquito net for rural areas, burning mosquito coils in your room and wearing long-sleeved shirts or blouses and trousers. A burning candle can help to repel mosquitoes. Perfume, eau de toilette, and dark colours are said to attract mosquitoes. Large numbers of mosquitoes mass for the rainy season which hits the south of Yunnan from late May to September.

If you are not planning to visit Xishuangbanna or other tropical areas of southern Yunnan then there is no need to consider malarial prophylactics as mosquitoes are generally absent at altitudes of 1,700m and above, which would include Kunming and all areas north from there.

Dengue fever
This mosquito-borne disease resembles malaria but there is no prophylactic available to deal with it. The mosquitoes which carry this virus bite during the day time, so it worth applying repellent if you see them around. Symptoms include strong headaches, rashes and excruciating joint and muscle pains and high fever. Dengue fever only lasts for a week or so and is not usually fatal. Complete rest and paracetamol are the usual treatment. Plenty of fluids also help. Some patients are given an intravenous drip to keep them from dehydrating.

Cholera
Fortunately, this disease is quite rare in Yunnan. When there are cases they are generally well publicised in the media, so that travellers will usually know when to avoid an infected area. Vomiting, watery stools, bad diarrhoea and cramp in the muscles and joints, and feeling completely enervated are some of

the obvious symptoms of cholera. Vaccinations against the disease are not particularly effective. Seek medical help as soon as you can and try to treat yourself for dehydration which can be severe in the case of cholera.

Diarrhoea

The Chinese call this problem 'spicy stomach'. More of an irritation and inconvenience in most cases than an illness, dehydration can be a problem, especially for children, so it is necessary to replace fluids with plenty of unappealing beverages like weak tea and diluted soft drinks. Rehydration tablets may be necessary if the body is not replenishing its fluids quickly enough. These should be supplemented with a simple diet such as watery rice. Imodium and Lomotil can help to alleviate the unpleasantness of diarrhoea but not cure it. They are only advisable if you have to travel.

More serious bouts of diarrhoea (dysentery) involving blood, slime and/or a fever require medical treatment. If you are not close to facilities then using an antibiotic such as ciprofloxacin (500mg twice daily for three days) may help. Diarrhoea which is greasy and is accompanied by tummy cramps and 'eggy' burps needs tinidazole (2g in one dose repeated a week later if symptoms persist). However, self-treatment can be dangerous and an expert opinion is always preferable.

Amoebic dysentery is more serious, and if not properly addressed can cause long-term problems. Like standard diarrhoea, dysentery is caused by contaminated food or water, and can be exacerbated by a sudden change to a tropical climate from a temperate or high altitude one.

Heat and sun problems

Sunburn, fatigue and heat stroke can also take place even when there is plenty of cloud cover. Calamine lotion is handy to alleviate mild sunburn, but as a precaution against more severe exposure, a good zinc-based sun cream is vital. A broad-brimmed hat, long sleeves if you can stand them in the heat, a lip salve to prevent chapping, or a barrier cream of some kind for the nose, will protect you from the harmful effects of the sun. Usually these are not much more than an intense rawness of the skin which can be excruciatingly uncomfortable.

Other affects include chills, headache, vomiting and nausea. Heat exhaustion is generally caused by dehydration and salt deficiency. This can cause exhaustion, dizziness, muscle cramps and headaches. Salt and fluid replacement and a quiet readjustment spell are the best cures. Heat stroke is the most extreme form of illness in this category and can be fatal. People who suffer an attack of heat stroke will need to be hospitalised without delay. Heat stroke is caused by a dangerous rise in body temperature caused by over long exposure to direct sunlight or high temperatures. Like sunburn and heat exhaustion, sun stroke can be avoided with a little common sense. If you suffer from heat stroke the immediate measures include having your clothes removed, lying down covered in a wet cloth, and being fanned. Copious amounts of fluids will help.

Prickly heat is quite common in all the tropical countries. Prickly heat is caused when perspiration forms under skin whose pores have not sufficiently adjusted to the new rate of sweat. As the name suggests, these itchy rashes on the skin can be very irritating. Taking regular cool showers, not spending too much time in the humidity, and applying talcum powder can bring relief.

Rabies
This extremely dangerous viral infection is caused by a bite or contact with saliva into an open wound from an infected warm-blooded mammal, usually, but not always, a dog. Regardless of whether you have had pre-exposure doses of rabies vaccine before being attacked, it is imperative to act quickly. The bitten area should be scrubbed for about five minutes in clean water using soap and an iodine or spirit solution. Then go as quickly as possible for medical help to receive tretament. Travellers who have already had at least two doses of rabies vaccine will need less treatment to complete the course and will avoid having to find a source of the very expensive rabies Immunoglobulin (RIG) which costs about US$800. Remember that it is never too late to seek help as the incubation period of the disease can be very long. Nevertheless try to get help as soon as you can.

Japanese encephalitis
This potentially fatal mosquito- borne viral disease is prevalent in Yunnan from April to October. It exists in rural areas where pigs are found close to paddy fields during the rainy season. An unlicensed vaccine is available in the UK (it is licensed elsewhere in the world eg: USA and Japan) and is advised for travellers who are not allergic to bee or wasp stings and who intend to spend four weeks or more in rural areas of this province during the rainy months. Three doses of vaccine should be taken about six weeks or more in advance of travel. For those who have no time or who are unable to take the vaccine, rest assured that this disease is rare in the Western traveller, and simple precautions to avoid night-biting mosquitoes will reduce the risk even further.

Fungal problems
Anti-fungal creams and powders such as Tinaderm generally work wonders in combating problems like ringworm, athlete's foot and other infections that thrive between toes, fingers, and in the groin areas and other body crevices. Loose fitting cotton garments help to reduce body dampness. Communal showers, unwashed towels and bathing areas where the floor is inadequately scrubbed and obviously damp, are classic spots to pick up fungal infections. Plenty of exposure to air and sunlight, along with regular rinses in medicated soap, can help to clear up infected areas.

Worm and parasitic infestations
If treated, parasitic invasion of skin or alimentary tracks, is not a serious problem. It is, however, fairly common in southern Yunnan. Humid, tropical climates are the perfect incubation conditions for the various kinds of worms

that can cause harm. The eggs of thread-worms hatch in the intestines, and problems relating to infestation can occur if not treated promptly. Round-worms are even known to enter the blood stream. In most cases you will be able to diagnose your own condition as their presence is visible in faeces. Infestations of this kind can usually be cleared fairly easily by taking Mebendazole. Avoid being a host to hook-worms which enter the body through the sole of the feet, by not walking around barefoot, except in the most pristine environments.

Stings, cuts and bites
If you are allergic to stings you should bring an antihistamine with you. Most stings are painful but not serious. Calamine lotion will help to bring the swelling down and provide some relief. Otherwise, you could try an ice-pack. Antihistamine creams, calamine lotion and analgesics will help to relieve the pain.

Cuts and scratches should be treated quickly in hot, tropical climates as infection can be rapid. Cuts can be cleaned with mercurochrome or an antiseptic solution. You should be careful not to scratch bites, which can easily become infected in tropical conditions.

There are several species of snake in Yunnan, although only a few are deadly. If you are unlucky enough to be bitten, wrap the affected limb with a cloth and proceed straight away to the nearest hospital. If you have the offending reptile with you, it can help with identification and the choice of the right serum or antivenin.

Other irritations
If you are staying at the lower end of budget travel accommodation, look out for bedbugs and lice. They are usually found in linen which has not been sufficiently cleaned. Tell-tale spots and flecks of blood on the sheets and walls near to the bed are giveaway signs. Lice are worse as they like to settle in the scalp, clothing and pubic hair. Lice can be caught from other people but easily treated with plenty of soap and shampoo and regular dousings in water slightly hotter than you are normally used to. Leeches are not generally a problem unless you are planning to do any trekking in damp rainforest areas. Don't attempt to pull off the leeches though. They should be burnt off with a lighter or dousing of salt. Ticks can be persuaded to withdraw with an application of oil, vaseline or alcohol solution to the affected area.

Respiratory problems
Some people suffer from respiratory problems in China's urban areas because of the high population density, lax pollution controls (though these are improving) and high incidence of smokers, with all the related illnesses. Smoking is almost impossible to escape in China and an estimated 150 billion cigarettes, a third of the world's total, are smoked here. Buses are probably the worst places to be confined with smokers; at least on trains there are no-smoking carriages, though there are still plenty of offenders.

Also, new strains of flu viruses often develop in China and you should be careful to rest if you feel yourself coming down with flu.

Sexually transmitted diseases

Gonorrhoea and syphilis are the most common sexually transmitted diseases (STDs) found in Yunnan. Antibiotics are used to treat these conditions, but syphilis continues throughout one's life, often leading to serious complications later on. The only real prevention is total sexual abstinence. There is absolutely no effective cure at this time for either herpes or HIV/AIDS cases. The number of these cases is increasing dramatically in Yunnan, most of them originating from the Ruili area where intravenous drug use and casual or paid sex are rampant. Condoms are the most effective deterrent but make sure that they are not one of the more inferior brands that exist. Price will usually give you a good idea of quality, although this is not a completely foolproof yardstick. The spread of AIDS by infected needles is a much more risky business since prevention from contamination is sometimes out of the hands of the patient. One possibility if you do need an injection is to buy a supply of new syringes from a pharmacy and get the doctor to use them. The cost of screening blood for transfusions is prohibitively high and China does not have a good record in this field. This is sure to have an adverse effect on the number of AIDS carriers, as infection is easily spread through contaminated blood. A relatively low consciousness about STDs in general in Yunnan seems likely to result in a steady increase in the number of people affected with these diseases.

SAFETY

Criminal matters are dealt with almost exclusively by the police or PSB who act as apprehenders, judge and jury, all rolled into one. Punishment is uniformly harsh with a whole range of offences from official corruption and drug-dealing to rape, receiving the death sentence. Offenders receive a well-publicised, sometimes publicly staged, bullet in the back of head. In the good old Confucian tradition of shared responsibility or culpability for one's offspring, the family are billed for the cost of the bullet.

Foreigners rarely have much to do with the police who take a rather tolerant view of visitors. Unless there are Chinese involved in a dispute, they will seldom intervene. Whether it is fair or not, crimes committed against foreigners are generally dealt with far more harshly than if the victim were Chinese.

Given the above, it comes as a surprise to learn that crime is actually on the rise in China generally, although the incidence of crime in Yunnan cannot be compared with China's big cities or its booming east coast. Although Western-style freedoms have been largely blamed for the sudden rise in crime rates, there is no question that massive unemployment and China's new creed of materialism are also responsible. Corrupt officials and juveniles are the main offenders.

Drugs, particularly opium and its derivatives, are synonymous with colonialism. British traders introduced the drug to the Chinese in 1773, causing enormous suffering and addiction which continued unabated until the communists took over. The bosses who run the Golden Triangle and their official friends in high places like Rangoon, have made considerable inroads into southwset Yunnan. Prostitution, though severely punished, is staging a strong comeback. Having said that, Yunnan is still a far safer place to travel than many other parts of Asia.

Theft is the most common problem and travellers, perceived to be rich and merely passing through, are occasionally targeted. There are always a few pickpockets around the crowded bus and train stations. Hard-seat carriages of trains can be a little risky, especially at night. Some travellers use a padlock and chain to attach their luggage to the overhead rack. Hotel rooms are generally quite safe, but if in doubt leave small valuables like passport, jewellery or cash, in the safe. Dormitories are definitely more likely to be a problem. Many people have complained of fellow travellers stealing. A money belt, carefully concealed under a T-shirt or loose over-blouse is the best way of carrying money. Try to divide cash into two or three different internal pockets as well. If you are unlucky enough to have something stolen, you will have to make out a detailed loss report at the Foreign Affairs Branch of the PSB. You will need this if you make an insurance claim.

Violent crimes are not common, although you should be vigilant at night. A fairly common scene, however, is to see a large group of people standing around watching two or three people engaged in what appears to be a violent altercation. Usually these arguments are restricted to slanging matches, the ocassional shove or accusative poke. They rarely get out of control. The same cannot be said for the language.

Women travellers

Women are unlikely to experience much sexual harassment in Yunnan. Most women give a glowing report of the behaviour of men here which is generally rather polite and deferential. This contrasts strongly with some other parts of Asia. The police generally pursue crimes against foreigners with more zest than normal, and the penalties are often more severe. This definitely gives women an extra level of protection. Some Western women travelling with male partners from home complain of being ignored by Chinese men who have the tendency, if given the option, of addressing their questions to men rather than women.

It should not be taken for granted though, that everyone will follow a chivalrous code of conduct in regard to women travellers. Care should still be taken in country locations when visiting remote villages, monasteries and other sights. Women who dress in skimpy skirts and see-through blouses on the east coast are occasionally taken for Russian prostitutes. This is unlikely to happen in most of Yunnan where few people will have heard of foreign women working in the red-light field. However, offence can be given by under-dressing in rural areas where they are not accustomed to the personal freedoms and fashion statements made by foreigners. Minority areas are particularly sensitive on this issue.

WHAT TO TAKE

Lightweight and mobile is the rule when travelling through regions like Yunnan where you are likely to acquire and discard things as the journey dictates. A decent, non-frame backpack is the most practical container for all the following suggested items, though a medium-sized, nylon bag will often do, particularly if you are carrying a fairly heavy or lumpy camera bag on one of your shoulders. Suitcases, unless you are on a very well-defined itinerary or arranged tour, can be a frustration when trying to fit your luggage on to a bus or train.

Sleeping bags are only recommended if you intend to stay overnight in exceedingly remote places or high altitude locations, if you think you might be stranded somewhere between connections, or if you intend to trek into some of the more inaccessible hill tribe areas in the south or southwest.

Strong shoes or boots for the rugged terrain, and sturdy sandals for the tropical climes, are vital. Layered clothing which can be stripped down or added to as the temperatures change, sometimes within one day, is useful. A light jacket with detachable arms and a sweater are handy items. Think light, tropical cotton clothing for the south where the humidity levels are often high. High-factor sunblock cream, a hat, and a good pair of sunglasses are essential as the light can be intense especially in the mountains. Lip salve and skin cream are useful as the dry, high plateau air will cause cracked skin and chapped lips.

A universal plug adapter may be handy if you are taking along an electric shaver or laptop computer. Universal sink plugs are also useful as these are often mysteriously absent from baths. A torch, a Swiss army-style, all-purpose knife, personal chopsticks for hygiene, and a money belt are all handy items. A small plastic alarm clock is essential. Tampons, condoms, shaving cream, toilet paper, contact lens solution and other specific items are all available in the cities, but if these are important it is wise to have a reserve stock for more off-the-beaten-track locations of which there are many in Yunnan. Earplugs to deal with the more deafening evenings of karaoke on the floor below or occupants in the room next door, are a godsend. Depending on the season and location, mosquito repellent and coils are advisable. A well-planned medical kit is essential. (See page 35.)

With a few exceptions such as Dali, you won't find much in the way of Western literature (translations of the classics are available but you might not feel like reading Francis Bacon or Thackeray in Yunnan), so bring along a good book or two. A good map is strongly recommended.

MAPS

Although the Chinese were amongst the first peoples to produce detailed maps of their towns and cities, the continued development of this most ancient skill was halted by the paranoia of the communist era. Maps are now no longer considered espionage tools by the Chinese authorities and are widely available, though mostly in Chinese. These are available from street vendors, kiosks, hotel shops and book shops. Maps are available for every city and town in Yunnan. Unfortunately, though, the quality tends to be poor and it is rare to find an English-labelled map that is an improvement on what you can find in a guidebook. It is currently impossible to find detailed relief or hiking maps.

The more visited cities will have maps in English available at the more expensive hotels, CITS offices, the ticket offices at tourist sights, and from the Xinhua chain of bookshops. You may also find some surprisingly good, handmade maps in the traveller cafés in cities like Dali and Lijiang. These are often more up-to-date than the official ones, though the scales may be misleading.

It's a good idea to get hold of a map or two before leaving for Yunnan. Nelle's Southern China is the most widely available map that covers the province in detail, but it does not cover the northern tip of Yunnan around Deqin; also some of the southern border areas with Laos have been cut short. The National Tourist Administration's tourist map is also recommended if you can get hold of it. NTA maps are produced in China by their tourist board and are occasionally available overseas. For very high-resolution maps detailing the precise contours of the terrain, the Operational Navigation Charts, a formerly classified series, are superb, especially for cyclists and trekkers. They are published by the Defence Mapping Agency at the Aerospace Centre, St Louis Air Force Station, Missouri 63118, USA.

The following shops and organisations should have good cartographic materials on Yunnan.

UK
John Smith and Sons 57–61 Vincent St, Glasgow G2 5TB; tel: 0141 221 7472
National Map Centre 22–24 Caxton St, London SW1; tel: 020 7222-2466
Stanfords 12–14 Long Acre, London WC2; tel: 020 7836 1321. Also at 29 Corn St, Bristol; tel: 0117 929 9966
The Travel Bookshop 13-15 Blenheim Crescent, London W11; tel: 020 7229 5260

USA and Canada
Traveller's Bookstore 22 W 52nd St, New York, NY 10019; tel: 212 664 0995
The Complete Traveller Bookstore 199 Madison Av, New York, NY 10016; tel: 212 685 9007
Phileas Foggs Books & Maps #87 Stanford Shopping Centre, Palo Alto, CA 94304; tel: 1-800/233
Forsyth Travel Library 9154 W 57th St, Shawnee Mission, KS 66201; tel: 1 800 367 7984
Open Air Books & Maps 25 Toronto St, Toronto, ON M5R 2CI; tel: 416 363 0719
World Wide Books & Maps 736 Granville St, Vancouver, BC V6Z 1E4; tel: 604 687 3320

Australia
Bowyangs 372 Little Bourke St, Melbourne; tel: 03 9670 4383
Travel Bookshop Shop 3, 175 Liverpool St, Sydney; tel: 02 9261 8200

China Maps, an online service, has simple political and geographical maps, plus some road routes: www.info.usaid.gov/hum_response/ofda/reliefweb/mapc/asi_chn/index.html

MONEY MATTERS

Generally speaking Yunnan is great value for the traveller. Although room costs in Kunming are over the odds, they are vastly different to the east coast of China where you can expect to pay similar rates to those found at the bottom end hotels in Shanghai and Hong Kong. Shared dorms in Yunnan can average US$3–5, while a double with air-con and a bathroom can usually be found for US$10–30. There is a lot of price variation between regions. Kunming's higher rates are unrepresentative of the province as a whole.

Food is cheap throughout China. A bowl of noodles will cost less than half a dollar, slightly less than a bottle of locally produced beer. If you are on a tight budget it is possible to exist on US$12–20 a day, excluding travel expenses. If you are staying in mid-range accommodation and sharing a room you can expect to spend about US$30–40 a day for all your expenses (excluding flights). Transport costs depend on the style and level of comfort you wish to travel at. Buses are good value. A six-hour bus ride will cost around US$4. Hard seats on trains are the cheapest but these can be tough going on the longer routes like the Kunming to Hekou run. There are several options for more comfortable bus and train journeys (see page 50–4, *Getting around Yunnan*).

Price tiering, by which foreigners end up paying twice the local rate for everything, has been gradually phased out, mostly because of the considerable flak and bad publicity that the government received. Although the official policy of price rigging for foreigners was stopped a few years ago its after-effects may still be felt. Once people have become accustomed to charging foreigners more for services and goods it can be a hard habit to break, so you should always be wary of paying over the odds. (Of course this is by no means a uniquely Chinese problem!) You may also end up paying more to enter a park or museum than a local.

Tipping is not common in Yunnan. Though it may increase your chances of getting better service or jumping the queue, it is not recommended as the travellers who follow you will be the negative beneficiaries of this practice. Only in large upmarket hotels has the practice of tipping become customary, introduced with foreign management and guests. Here you should look to add about 10% to your bill but only if you have been very satisfied with the service. **Bargaining** is common in many situations, whether in the market, shop, unmetered taxi or even hotel. Bargaining is an accepted practice and, as you can expect to be overcharged on many occasions anyway, it is a legitimate means of redressing the balance. The practice should not be taken to extremes though. Aggressive foreigners who regard it as their right to purchase objects at humiliatingly low costs are not very highly regarded by the Chinese. Try not to lose your perspective on prices, particularly with shopping; if you are reasonably happy with the price then why try to beat the price down further. Your absolute bargain can end up being someone else's loss.

Mercifully, the cumbersome old system of FECs, or Foreign Exchange Certificates, is now obsolete and travellers can deal in real money just like the Chinese. **Chinese currency** is called the *renminbi* (RMB), which means the 'People's Money'. *Yuan*, also known in its spoken form as *kuai*, are its currency units. Although you might occasionally see the odd one-yuan coin floating around in your change, most of the units appear in note form. The Chinese were the first people to use paper money, in fact. The denominations of *yuan* are Y100, Y50, Y10, Y5 and Y1. *Yuan* are divided into units of ten called *mao*, also known as *jiao*, and one-hundred sub-divisions of *fen*, which you will probably never have the chance to use in practice. The most common use for *fen* and *jiao* is for entrance to public toilets, so it's handy to keep some for this if nothing else.

The safest way to carry money in Yunnan is in **travellers' cheques** which can be issued through banks and travel agencies. The exchange rate for cheques is fixed in China and comes out slightly better than for cash transactions. The snag is that, generally speaking, they can only be cashed in at large Bank of China branches and the more upmarket tourist hotels of which there are very few in country areas. American Express and Thomas Cook are probably the best type to carry. It can also be useful having some different kinds of foreign currency handy. US dollars are the most widely accepted currency and many small shops and services will accept dollars if you are caught out with no Chinese currency. As a rule though you should avoid paying in dollars unless you have to, as it generally works out more expensive with the conversion rates you will be given by traders. **Credit cards** are useful, with Visa, Mastercard and American Express the easiest to draw on. Most Chinese banks in main cities will be able to issue cash advances on Visa cards within an hour. Wiring money through the Bank of China is definitely a last resort as it can take weeks to materialise.

There are increasing numbers of cash-dispensing machines now appearing in Kunming and tourist hot spots, like Lijiang, where you can use your credit card to withdraw cash, but don't rely on these for anything more than an emergency supply as they are frequently out of action.

A black market in foreign exchange exists in Yunnan but, given the marginal benefits, the risk of being cheated and the illegality of the act, it is hardly worth the trouble. More counterfeit money seems to end up in black market circles than in normal circulation.

The *yuan* is a non-convertible currency and cannot be bought abroad before you begin your trip. Similarly you do not want to end up carrying any of your Chinese currency out of the country at the end of your stay. Keep any exchange receipts as you will be required to produce these if you want to change any money back again.

Exchange rates at the time of writing are as follows: US$1 = Y8.3; £1 = Y12.4; Aus $ = Y4.6; Can $ = Y5.5.

Banking hours vary from branch to branch, but as a general rule banks open from 09.00 to 12.00, and 14.00 to 17.00, Monday to Friday, and from 09.00 to 12.30 on Saturdays. Most banks do not open for foreign exchange transactions on Saturdays. Banks close for the three official days of the Chinese New Year, and for the national holiday at the beginning of October, for which many businesses can be closed for a week; reduced hours often apply for the following ten or eleven days.

GETTING AROUND YUNNAN
By air

The number of airports and flight schedules has increased quite rapidly in Yunnan recently. Kunming and its superb newly redesigned and extended airport are at the hub of the province's air routes. Yunnan is served by several air companies including Air China, Yunnan Airlines, China Northwest, China Southwest, China Eastern and other carriers like Shanghai Airlines.

You need to produce your passport when buying a ticket at a CAAC office or agency like CITS (China International Travel Service). All tickets have to be paid for in local currency. It is not possible to pay by credit card at the present time, but you might check this out to see if any changes have been made. If you buy from an agent or across the counter from one of the larger hotels in Yunnan, expect to pay a surcharge.

Air travel is relatively inexpensive on domestic routes in Yunnan and can save you a lot of time if you are travelling between destinations such as Lijiang or Zhongdian, in the northwest of the province, and Jinhong in the southeast. Many travellers take the bus one way, choosing a route where there are good connections, eg: between places such as Kunming and Dali, and then fly back to avoid having to do the same route again, thus maximizing time but still seeing some of the countryside.

As mentioned earlier the safety record of China's airlines has improved considerably over the past few years and, as long as you are travelling on one of the bigger airline's Boeing 733 or 737 flights, there is no need to be concerned. Delays, however, remain a common feature of domestic flights and you should always plan any connecting flights with this in mind. With the

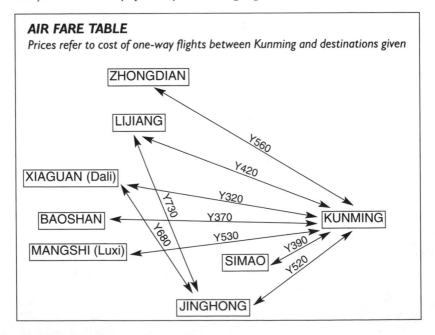

AIR FARE TABLE
Prices refer to cost of one-way flights between Kunming and destinations given

upsurge in domestic tourism it is also becoming more difficult to find seats on the popular routes such as Kunming–Lijiang and Jinhong–Lijiang during peak travel months and festival times. The periods around the Chinese New Year, April, September and October are especially busy and flights should be booked well in advance to avoid disappointment. If you are planning your visit to coincide with a major festival you should contact a tour operator which specialises in China for help with booking domestic flights and accommodation.

By bus

Buses are the real kings of the road in Yunnan. They provide the easiest, cheapest and most interesting way of getting around the province and seeing the countryside close-up. Road conditions can vary greatly through the province, from bone jarring, pot-holed unmetalled roads to the new smooth asphalt highways that have appeared in recent years. It must be said that journey times and conditions have improved dramatically on the more popular tourist routes such as Kunming–Dali–Lijiang–Zhongdian and travelling times have been halved.

On the down side, buses often break down, are subject to unscheduled stops and, on long-distance routes, can be wearing. Almost everyone, except women passengers, seem to be chain-smokers. Confirmed smokers say the marathon sleeper bus routes are an excellent way of giving up the habit. Accidents occur often, particularly on high mountain roads and on bends. Although government-run buses are said to be fractionally safer, there isn't much you can do about this. Most Chinese people will try to sit at the front as there is more leg space. These are obviously the most risky places to sit in the event of an accident. The safest seats are probably two-thirds of the way back along the bus. Try to get an aisle seat if you are in for a long ride. You may also want to bring along a pair of ear-plugs as most buses are fitted out with bulky cassette stereo speakers. A number of super-luxury, non-smoking buses have been introduced in the last couple of years. These new express buses are by far the quickest and most comfortable option and can whisk you from Kunming to Dali in five hours, to Lijiang in eight hours and to Zhongdian in eleven hours.

Sleeper buses are extremely popular, reasonably cheap, and run to places as far away from Kunming as Jinghong, Ruili and Deqin. There are usually two bunks with decent, though sometimes unwashed duvets and pillows. Luggage is stored underneath the bottom bunk but, because of the incidence of theft on sleepers, it is best to keep valuables close at hand, especially when you sleep. If you are booking a sleeper ticket, try to enquire what make of vehicle the bus is and avoid the old Eastern-European-made models, which have a bad record of breaking down en route. Unless you are on a very tight budget it is worth paying the extra money to use a more reliable form of transport.

Privately owned mini- and micro-buses cover many of the shorter and medium-length routes. There isn't usually quite so much room but they are faster than government-run vehicles. It may be difficult to fit large rucksacks onto these type of vehicles. If you intend using buses in general it is better to travel fairly lightly as the overhead racks are shallow and you may not wish to entrust your belongings to the roof.

When buying a ticket you will have to find the right window as each destination is designated by a different one. It is better, if you have time, to buy the ticket on the day before. Bus stations are often large affairs and can seem initially confusing. Cities like Xiaguan, and even large towns like Zhongdian, often have two bus stations.

By train

Trains are another option, though a more limited one than buses, for getting around certain parts of the province and beyond. While train services in Yunnan have perhaps not improved at the same rate as air transport, there have been some gains, such as the completion of the Kunming–Xiaguan line and the new plush express train between Kunming and the Stone Forest. A newly electrified line between Kunming and Nanning has also made travel out of the province to southern China a lot easier.

Most trains have quite a good selection of basic foods and drinks. In addition to a dining car, trolleys of noodles, boxed lunches, snacks, beer and soft drinks get pushed around the carriages from time to time. There are usually plenty of things you can stock up on at the train station before leaving.

The following is a breakdown of the different kinds of seats available on Chinese trains. If you board a train without a reserved seat and don't like what seems to be on offer, you can always try and seek out the conductor and ask to be upgraded to a better seat. If one is available they will happily oblige.

Types of seat

The cheapest type of seat available is called a **hard seat**. The description is a little unfair as the seats are slightly padded and not bad for the first couple of hours. These upright seats provide little longterm comfort though. Generally speaking on the trains, like the buses, you get what you pay for. There are no allotted seat numbers with hard seats if you buy them on the same day, meaning that you usually have to push and shove to get a space at all. Considering that passengers might be on the train for 13 or 14 hours at a stretch or more, the competition can get fierce. Passengers are in the habit of spitting on the floor, smoking endlessly and heaping garbage down onto the nether parts of the carriage or out of the window, making you feel part of a moving environmental disaster zone. This, however, is what the majority of Chinese, yet to benefit from the economic reforms that have made some of them rich overnight, have to put up with.

Hard sleepers are considerably more comfortable and the compartments are limited to a certain number of passengers. Bunk beds are arranged in three tiers, the middle generally being the best option if you can get it. The blankets, sheets and pillows provided are usually pretty clean as well. The bright lights and loud music are switched off at night which does not happen in the hard seat section.

Previous page A typical street scene in Old Lijiang

Above A butterfly alights on the blooms of a tropical plant in Xishuangbanna.

Below A fan palm seen in a tropical garden in Xishuangbanna

Below right An ancient tree trunk in a forest in the semi-tropical region of Simao

Soft seats are the next step up in comfort. Not many trains, unfortunately, have soft seat compartments. If you are lucky enough to find one that does, you should have a pleasant trip. The price is similar to hard sleeper. Smoking is not allowed in this section and the compartments rarely get crowded out.

Soft sleeper is the ultimate luxury. There are only four bunks in each of the closed compartments, and the non-smoking carriages are fitted out with nice touches like flowers, clean toilets and air-conditioning. The cost works out about twice that of a hard sleeper. If you can afford it, treat yourself at least once on the trip. A few years ago it was extremely easy to book soft sleepers as very few Chinese people could afford them. Times have changed and you may occasionally be disappointed to find everything booked up. Reserving in advance is the best approach.

Tickets and bookings

There is usually no problem in buying a hard seat on the same day or even slightly before the train departs as there are proportionally more of these available. Tickets for soft seats and the two types of sleeper tend to get snapped up more quickly. If you have problems buying these over the counter you can always resort to a travel agency like CITS or some private operator. Naturally, you will have to pay a bit over the odds but it might be worth it.

Self-reliancy

If you want to tour Yunnan by car you will have to hire a driver through a travel agency like CITS or one of the more savvy travellers' hotels or guesthouses. If you are planning a long itinerary with a car and driver and would like to attempt some of the driving yourself it may be possible to obtain a temporary Chinese driver's licence if your tour operator is open to the idea. These generally need to be applied for by the agent in China at least two months in advance of your arrival. The same applies to motorbikes which is even more of a shame as they would be the perfect way of getting out into the countryside and exploring some of Yunnan's backwaters.

What you can do however, is rent a bicycle. There don't appear to be any restrictions in this field. Despite the hills and the risk on main roads of thundering trucks, Yunnan is good biking country. This is one of the best ways to get off-the-beaten-track and escape the traffic. Bike hire is not that well developed yet in Yunnan but it is definitely getting there. Most towns have hire shops and hotels and guesthouses have now twigged that there is a market as well. Lijiang, Dali and Jinghong are particularly good.

Many travellers bring their own bikes into Yunnan, which is essential if you are attempting long distances or off-roading, as the quality of the locally available bikes is pretty poor. Most rental bikes will be Chinese brands such as Flying Pigeon – fine for pedalling around town but not for extended trips. Mountain bikes are still a rarity and, even where available, are not up to the same standard as those found in the West. If you are interested in arranging a cycling tour through Yunnan then you should contact one of the locally based operators such as Hai-Wei trails (www.haiweitrails.com) who should be able to offer advice and arrange a travel package to suit you.

You can hire bikes by the hour, day, or even longer if you are planning a few days away. Rates vary but generally fall into the Y12–25 a day category. You may be asked to pay a deposit which could be as much as Y200. You will almost certainly be asked to leave behind some form of identification. Check that the bike you have chosen suits you by taking it for a quick spin. Get the shop, café or guesthouse people to adjust the saddle if necessary and test all the separate parts like the chain, brakes and gears if it has them. You will be expected to replace them or fork out the equivalent or more if these are broken, even if it is just a case of wear and tear. Get the tyres pumped up beforehand as well.

TOURIST INFORMATION

The idea of tourist promotion through the dispensing of free maps, brochures and other information has not really taken root in Yunnan. **Traveller's cafés** are always a good, some would say the best, source of information. They usually have a guest book with dated comments by fellow travellers. Information is often posted on the bulletin board or walls as well.

The state-endorsed **CITS** (China International Travel Service) functions like a travel agent suggesting tours and itineraries as well as acting as a source for tickets to cultural events and performances and providing, at a suitable markup, bus, train and plane seats. CITS have offices in almost every town and city in China that attracts foreign tourists. Any maps you are likely to find on their shelves you will probably have to pay for. The service at these offices is generally friendly and you may be able to spend a companionable hour or so chatting with a member of staff keen to practice his or her English in some of the remoter branches. A few years ago, after it had dawned on them that the solo traveller market was a potentially lucrative one, CITS introduced **Family and Independent Traveller** (FIT) departments to some of their larger Yunnan branches. This might be worth checking out as it has promise.

You may also come across a similar organisation to CITS in the form of the much smaller **CTS** (China Travel Service). CTS was originally established to serve Hong Kong, Macau and Taiwanese Chinese visitors to China but now it has broadened its scope and provides services to other visitors as well. CTS is well represented by offices throughout China and generally provides an efficient service. The Hong Kong offices of CTS are an excellent place to obtain visas quickly and to organise accommodation, flights and tours.

CYTS (China Youth Travel Service) is another organisation you may come across which has expanded its scope beyond its original remit of youth-oriented travel and is again represented by various offices across China. In some towns such as Dali and Lijiang you will also come across small private tour operations and cafés which can help you book tickets and arrange tours and local transport. Although they sometimes have a limited scope, these small ventures are often the best places to unearth information on local attractions and book tickets. If nothing else, they understand the importance of good service to their survival.

The China National Tourist office is a government body that promotes China as a destination and stocks information pamphlets and basic maps on the most popular destinations. You can usually pick up some leaflets and maps on Kunming, Lijiang, Dali and Xishuangbanna at the office and the staff will also be happy to recommend Chinese tour operators in your home country. Overseas offices of the China National Tourist office are listed below:

Australia 19F, 44 Market St, Sydney, NSW 2000; tel: 12 9299 4057
France 116 Avenue des Champs-Elysees, 75008, Paris; tel: 1 44218282
Germany IIkenhanstra. 6, D-60433 Frankfurt am Main; tel: 169 520135
Japan 6F Hamamatsu Chu Building, 1-27-13, Hamamatsu-cho, Minato-ku, Tokyo; tel 81/03 3433 1461
Singapore 1 Shenton Way, No 17-05, Ribina House, Singapore 0106; tel: 65 221 8681
UK 4 Glentworth St, London NW1; tel: 020 7935 9787
USA 350 Fifth Ave, Suite 6413, Empire State Building, New York, NY 10018; tel: 212 760 1710

The **Hong Kong** branch is on the 12th Floor, Tower A, New Mandarin Plaza, 14 Science Museum Rd, Tsimshatsui East.

On-line information

Email and internet are in their early, somewhat restricted stages in Yunnan. The easiest way to access your email is by signing up for one of the free account services like Hotmail (www.hotmail.com) or Rocketmail (www.rocketmail.com) and then use one of the growing number of internet cafés that are springing up in Yunnan. The best places at the moment are Dali, Lijiang, Jinghong and Kunming.

There isn't a great deal of specific information on Yunnan available on the net and recommendations are likely to be out of date very quickly. At the time of writing, some of the sites on China which may have material on Yunnan are listed below.

Dark Wing www.darkwing.uoregon.edu. China maps: general, city, historical, miscellaneous, provincial.
Internet Travel Guide China www-students.inisg.ch/~pgeiser/china/china
China Today www.chinatour.com
China News Digest www.cnd.org
China National Tourist Association www.cnta.com and www.Kunming-China.com
Current website listings on China from www.aweto.com/china/

POST AND TELECOMMUNICATIONS

In recent years China has put a lot of money and expertise into developing a very modern and, generally speaking, efficient communications system.

Postal services

Postal services are fast and reliable and the rates reasonable. Standard letters cost Y2.2–6.7 depending on the weight, postcards Y5. Express Mail Services (EMS) operate to most countries. Main post offices in Yunnan open every day of the week, usually 08.00–18.00. Smaller branches may close over the weekend or for lunch. If you wish to send parcels abroad it is best to go to the post office, buy the right box there and let them help you assemble it. China's parcel service is generally very good. Expect to pay something like Y50 for a 1kg parcel by surface mail to Europe, Y80 for air delivery. Most of the major hotels also handle post and parcels.

There are only a few reliable poste restante offices in Yunnan. Most of these are located in places where there is a high concentration of overseas visitors, notably Dali and Lijiang. You will have to pay a couple of *yuan* to collect your mail.

Telephones and telecommunications

It is getting increasingly easy to make both local and long-distance domestic and international calls from Yunnan. Local calls, by the way, are free from your hotel. International calls on the other hand are quite expensive. The minimum charge is for three minutes. Expect to pay about Y30 a minute to place a call to Europe, Y27 for the US or Australia. The most efficient place to make an international call is from a telecommunication office. These are usually located next door to or adjoining a main post office and are open 24 hours. The system is straightforward. You hand over a deposit of Y200, are allotted a booth, and then dial your number. When you have finished you will be handed back the difference. You will be not be charged if no connection is made, but will have to pay the whole amount if you are put through to a answering machine. Local and long-distance domestic calls can be made from a public booth, smarter, privately run booths, and from hotel lobbies.

Telephone cards may be useful, although currently you can only use them within the province. Cards are sold in units of Y20, Y50 and Y100. Faxes can be sent from the telecommunication offices or business centres found in some of the more upmarket hotels. It is expensive to send a fax as there is a three minute minimum which will be levied even if you only dispatch one page. Some hotels have now even started to charge customers for receiving faxes.

Dialling data

The following are some useful telephone numbers and codes:

China country code (086)
International access code (00)
International access code from outside China (86)

Ambulance	20	International enquiries	115
Fire services	119	Local directory enquiries	114
Police	110	Long-distance enquiries	113

Some Yunnan area codes

Baoshan	0875	Jinghong	0691	Tengchong	0875
Dali	0872	Kunming	871	Tonghai	0877
Dehong	0692	Lijiang	0888	Yuxi	0877
Gejiu	0873	Luxi	0873	Zhongdian	0887
Jiangchuan	0877	Qujing	0874		
Jianshui	0873	Ruili	0692		

WHERE TO STAY

Travellers familiar with other Asian accommodation – the beauty, elegance and character of a Thai resort hotel, Balinese cottage or Japanese inn – may be disappointed by what is on offer in Yunnan where anonymous, purpose-built blocks with drab interiors and worn-out furniture are common. Quality however, has been improving rapidly, and there are even guesthouses now in places like Lijiang, Dali, Jianshui and Jinghong which are creatively exploiting local and ethnic architecture and design to create more pleasant environments for guests. The old system of automatically overcharging foreigners has now been phased out.

Apart from guesthouses, there are several kinds of accommodation options in Yunnan. Upmarket hotels call themselves *da jiudian*, or *da jiulou*, which translates as something like 'big hotel and wine shop'. The word *binguan* is also used to indicate a smart, quality establishment. *Zhaodaisuo* (rock-bottom boarding house) and the humble, dirt-cheap *luguan* rarely accept foreigners, but you might end up in one if you are in a remote rural area. Wherever you stay you can be sure of finding a pair of plastic slippers or flip-flops, and a thermos of hot water with a few bags of tea leaves. Many hotel rooms, even the cheaper ones, also have TVs.

Room rates in Yunnan and across the southwest are far cheaper than in most other parts of China. The cheapest, though not usually the nicest or quietest rooms, are found near or around bus and railway stations. There are few single rooms, though they do exist. As a solo traveller you will often end up paying for a room that has two or three beds. Generally speaking, in dorm set-ups you pay per person, whereas in doubles you pay for the room. Travelling with a companion will halve your costs. Rooms in twins or dormitories can be under US$2. Generally speaking, dorm beds, or single beds in rooms containing three or fours beds, will cost US$1.5–4. A clean, spacious, mid-range hotel with TV, air-conditioning, attached bathroom and 24-hour hot water will cost US$15–35.

Two- and three-star hotel rooms in China all seem to have been designed and furnished from exactly the same blueprint and apart from levels of cleanliness they tend to be pretty much identical to one another. There are some hotels and guesthouses with individual character that are worth seeking out but otherwise you can expect a monotonous conformity to your accommodation in this category of hotels. It is worth checking the rooms first though to ensure that the lighting and plumbing is working as it should be. Staff usually speak only a very limited amount of English but in most cases do try hard to help.

Top-notch four- and five-star hotels, of which there are a surprising number being built now, will often have excellent facilities including satellite TV, telephone, air-con, permanent hot water and a free newspaper. They may also have a limousine service, and business centre with fax facilities. At US$50–130 they are affordable for many foreigners, but few independent travellers use them unless they need to treat themselves or recuperate.

On checking in, foreigners are required to fill out a simple ID form which will then be forwarded to the local PSB. Although Yunnan feels considerably less like it than other places, China is essentially a police state. Check-out time is generally noon the next day, but if you have a flight or connection later, you can pay for half a day and stay until 6pm. After six you are charged at the full rate for a complete day. It is a good idea to have a look at a room before you sign anything. This is perfectly normal procedure in Yunnan. You will probably have to pay in advance, although more places are operating on a trust-the-guest basis these days. In some older mid-range hotels you will be issued with a plastic card with your room number on it. You take this to the receptionist who should be permanently in situ on your floor, hand it to her, and she will open your room for you. It can be an inconvenient system if you need to return to your room several times a day, but it guarantees some added security for your belongings. In most places now the usual system of being issued with your own key from reception applies, though you may sometimes be asked for a key deposit.

WHERE TO EAT
Food in Yunnan is generally tasty, varied, plentiful and cheap. Travellers who have come from other parts of China will delight not only in the variety of minority cuisines on offer but also the many Western favourites served in the travellers' cafés. What more could you ask for? The Chinese adore food and you should benefit from this. Only in the very remote areas are choices limited.

A year-round supply of fresh vegetables, plus various seasonal offerings, enrich the selection on Yunnan menus. Yunnan, with its highland meadows and plateaux, is one of the few places in China where dairy products like goat's cheese, yoghurt and milk are available.

Cantonese and occasionally Beijing-style dishes are found at the more upmarket restaurants and in hotels. Peking duck, sweet and sour dishes and dim sum are common. Most independent travellers will opt for family-run restaurants, humble brick or wooden shacks where they cook over a wood or charcoal fire, using a wok to produce mostly stir-fry dishes. Canteen-style restaurants, street stalls and vendors who set up shop in or around bus and train stations offer a wide range of filling snacks such as charcoal-grilled skewers of meat, vegetable and meat-stuffed pancakes, grilled corn-on-the-cob, kebabs, baked yams and steamed dumplings. Within the bus depots there are often sheltered, open-sided canteens dishing out simple, extremely cheap noodles, rice dishes, and bowls of soup and broth.

If you are eating at these more basic restaurants then you will often find that there is no menu available. The usual method with the cheaper eateries is that you will be invited into the kitchen or cooking-range area and asked to point out what you want which will then be prepared for you. You can get an idea from what other people are eating. It never does any harm to have a look at the cooking area anyway so that you can ascertain the level of hygiene. Any eatery where you can see the food being prepared and freshly cooked in front of you is usually a safe bet. Avoid buffets where the food has already been cooked and left standing, as these are the most likely places to pick up food poisoning.

Pork and chicken are China's main meats and Chinese cooking tends to leave the bone in the chopped meat. You are expected to chew the meat from the bone and then leave the bone at the side of your plate. Cafés that cater to foreigners more often than not serve the meat de-boned. It is possible to order boneless pieces (*ding*) or slices (*pian*). For vegetarians Yunnan can be a problem. You might be able to select your own vegetable, rice or noodle hashes direct from the kitchen but most soups and broths use animal stock. The same applies to fried food which is prepared in animal fats and oils. The best places to find strict, honest-to-goodness vegetarian dishes are in nearby Buddhist temples and monasteries. There are three basic types of vegetarian food available in such places. Plain vegetable dishes will be served at the more basic restaurants attached to such religious centres. So-called 'Buddhist' cooking involves simple rice and noodle veggy dishes which avoid supposedly stimulating ingredients like garlic, ginger and onion. Imitation meat dishes are interesting. They copy the shapes and presentational forms of meat dishes like spare ribs and pork medallions, but are purely vegetarian. Tofu is another good standby.

Certain dishes, such as hotpots, are widely available wherever you go. The Mongols introduced the hotpot (*huoguo*), in which several ingredients are cooked together in a broth at the dining table. Chicken casseroles are often cooked up in a broth that has medicinal herbs in it. Eel, freshwater fish, preserved duck eggs (*pidan*), horsebeans (*candou*) and a host of mushrooms and edible fungi are popular and widely available throughout Yunnan.

Different regions are known for their local specialties. In Kunming the most famous preparation is Across-the-Bridge-Noodles (*guoqiaomixian*), a self-serve dish where the customer places slices of raw chicken, ham and other meats and raw vegetables into a boiling hot broth covered in a thin layer of oil to keep everything warm. *Huotui*, Yunnan's slightly sweet, cured ham is delicious.

Elsewhere, local dishes include roast duck in Yiliang, stir-fried dishes with tangerine peel and glutinous rice cakes in Miao areas, bean curd in Shiping, chicken steamed in an earthen pot (*qiguoji*) in Jianshui, three-year-cured ham at Lugu Lake, fried goat cheese (*rubing*) in Lunan, fish casserole (*shaguoyu*) in Dali, deep fried bee larvae in Yuanyang, and fish or chicken baked with lemon grass in Xishuangbanna.

Dai food, as found in Xishuangbanna and the counties that border it, is more exotic, influenced by the cuisines and climates of Southeast Asia. It

TEAHOUSE CULTURE

In spite of its excellent coffee, Yunnan's tea is *the* drink for visitors. You could devote a whole trip to tea appreciation. The choice, ranging from chrysanthemum and hay tea, Tibetan and green teas, eucalyptus, ginger and liquorice, to various herb brews is staggering. Taken in one of the courtyard teahouses of Kunming, Dali and Lijiang, tea drinking in Yunnan can be what it was always meant to be in China – a rare and refined pleasure.

Yunnan is one of China's most important tea producing regions. Its best known leaf is *pu'er*, known in Hong Kong and Taiwan as *bolei*. The weather in the district of Menghai in Xishuangbanna is ideal for cultivating *pu'er*. The tea produced on the plantation slopes here is superb in taste, fragrance and texture. Tea which is mix-cropped with camphor trees is said to be the finest. Tibet, where tea is drunk not only for pleasure but hydration, has always been a major market for its teas. Tea merchants would arrange for great caravans of mules to transport the precious consignments from Xiaguan near Dali. To prevent damage the tea was steam-pressed into two and four-kilo bricks called *jincha*.

Teas are to be enjoyed for their taste and appeal, but also for their restorative and curative features. Teahouses and cafés in Yunnan often advertise the health benefits of their brews. Lijiang Snow Tea, for example, is said to have ploredive effects that moisten the throat, alleviating soreness and coughs, dispelling heat and relieving fever. The leaves are grown on the lower slopes of Jade Dragon Snow Mountain. The taste, bitter and acerbic, a woody, dry root flavour, is an acquired one. Another leaf, Yunnan's Flower Tea, a light and fragrant concoction, claims to have anti-inflammatory, sedative, analgesic merits, reducing lipids in serum and promoting liver function. It also claims to ease haemorrhoids. A quality tea called *tuocha*, drunk as a slimmer's brew, offering to reduce cholesterol, is popular in parts of Europe, especially France where it is known as 'beauty tea'. A slightly sweet black tea, it is sold in a shape that resembles Yunnan's steamed corn bread loaves.

In Dali connoisseurs of tea can try the 'Bai Nationalities Three Courses' tea set, consisting of bitter, sweet and after-flavour teas. The custom started at wedding ceremonies and festivals and then began to be served during musical performances. A typical set begins with bitter tea made with Mao Jin Spring Tea; the second course with slices of local cheese and black tea with honey and walnuts; the third, a 'return tea taste' course, consisting of a dry, fragrant tea mixed with prickly ash. Like wine tasting, this is not to be hurried. A three courses tea set can take about an hour to prepare and consume.

makes a nice change to find dishes on the menu that make liberal use of coconut milk, glutinous rice, banana leaves, lemon grass, hollowed and stuffed tubes of bamboo, and river moss. The fertile sub-tropical south is perfect for the cultivation of such fruits as mango, papaya, pomelos, rambutans and lychee.

Naxi cuisine in the north is based on corn, wheat, barley and beans with the addition of rice. *Baba*, deep-fried wheat flatbreads, are sold plain or stuffed with meat and vegetables. Naxi bean jelly is a popular dessert. Snacks in the mountain areas include walnuts, sunflower seeds, baked potatoes, buckwheat bread and, in the northwest, barley flour (*tsampa*) and yak cheese. Muslim Hui restaurants offer wind-dried beef, mutton and goat dishes. Their spicy beef noodles are particularly tasty.

Western dishes are also widely available in Yunnan in the various travellers' cafés and hotels. Kunming has a scattering of the fast-food outlets that have now appeared like a rash across the rest of China. Cafés in Dali and Lijiang serve up some good renditions of Western favourites from travellers' recipes that have been shared over the years, and it is possible to eat a good variety of food very cheaply in these towns. Kunming has Italian, French and Japanese restaurants as well as others that offer everything from Mexican cuisine to sauerkraut.

Mineral, spring and boiled water is widely available. Yunnan brews several beers, with *Tsingtao* and *Pabst* also available. Local brews include Kunming's very decent Bailongtan, Dali Beer from the town of the same name, and an unusual line in prickly pear and honey beer from Mengzi. Alcoholic drinks such as *baijiu* and *qingjiu*, made from corn, can be quite potent. *Chingkojiu* is distilled from barley. Lijiang's *yinjiu* is a dark, sweet, sherry-like wine made from sorghum, honey, barley and spring water. It is stored in ceramic jars. Papaya and plum wines are excellent, though cloyingly sweet.

Tea is often served free in restaurants. Almost all hotels provide guests with a thermos flask of hot water and tea bags. Muslim restaurants sometimes serve their Eight Treasures tea, consisting of crystallised sugar, nuts, dried fruit and seeds – an unusual and refreshing taste.

PUBLIC HOLIDAYS AND FESTIVALS

Offices and businesses close during official national holidays. During the time of the Chinese New Year business comes to a complete standstill. The holiday officially lasts for three days but has a big impact and it can seem that half of China is on the move. For a few days either side of the holiday all transport tends to get fully booked. If you are on an organised tour then this won't affect you but otherwise you should aim to be somewhere you like, because the chances are you won't be leaving there for a while!

National holidays

January 1 New Year's Day
January/February Chinese New Year. Between three days and one week. Next dates will be January 24 2001, and February 12 2002.

March 8	International Women's Day.
May 1	International Labour Day.
May 4	Youth Day.
June 1	International Children's Day.
July 1	Birthday of the Chinese Communist Party.
August 1	Anniversary of the Founding of the People's Liberation Army.
October 1	National Day. Celebrates the establishment of the PRC in 1949. Can last up to five days.

Non-official holidays also enjoy great popularity as ancient traditions and customs are once more being revived. The most common ones, which follow the lunar calendar, are as follows:

February/March Lantern Festival. Paper lanterns are paraded through the streets and hung out in parks and public spaces making a very colourful specatcle, often accompanied by other celebrations such as lion dancing and family picnics. Next events will be held on February 7 2001 and February 12 2002.

March/April Guanyin's birthday. Guanyin (the goddess of mercy) is a widely worshipped deity throughout China and the East; she is also known as Avalokitesvara and her image can be found in many temples or specific shrines to her. Next events will be held on March 13 2001 and February 12 2002.

April Qing Ming Festival. This is when Chinese people pay their respects to their ancestors. Grave sites of departed relatives are swept, tidied and paper offerings burnt for the deceased.

June Dragon Boat Festival. Dragon boats, narrow hulled long wooden craft, are raced by competing teams of paddlers all over China commemorating the death of a 3rd century BC official, Quan Yu, who drowned himself in protest at the corruption of his government. Dragon boat festivals are usually very lively, fun events and fall on June 25 2001 and June 15 2002.

August Festival of the Hungry Ghosts. For superstitious Chinese this is a time when spirits are said to walk the earth. August 19 2001.

September/October Mid-Autumn Festival. Also known as the Moon Festival, this commemorates an uprising against the Mongol Yuan dynasty, when secret messages were passed between conspirators in cakes. Moon cakes are sold everywhere and fireworks also let off. Next dates October 1 2001 and September 21 2002.

Minorities are now being encouraged by the central and local governments to celebrate openly their heritage and diversity through reviving traditional festivals. Such festivals are a good vehicle for attracting tourist money. Yunnan has become a showcase of countless ethnic celebrations that mirror the extraordinary diversity of its inhabitants. Each minority has its own festival and these are the best times to see people in their traditional dress worshipping, dancing, singing and celebrating with feasts of their native foods and religious offerings. Some of these festivals may have been changed beyond recognition from their original forms but overall the authentic celebration of ethnic identity and pride that these festivals represent shows that minority nationalities continue to thrive in Yunnan and have overcome the damage and conformity imposed on them during the Cultural Revolution.

The origins of the festivals vary greatly but broadly speaking it can be said be said that there are four different types of festival: religious, such as the water-splashing festival of the Dai; commemorative, such as the torch festival of the Yi and sword pole festival of the Lisu; festivals connected with farming activities like the rice-tasting festival of the Zhuang and Miao; and entertainment and trade occasions such as the Raoshanling of the Bai and horse-racing festival of the Tibetans. Some ethnic groups share the same festivals but celebrate them in different ways and for different purposes. The torch festival is a good example, as it is celebrated by the Naxi, Yi, Bai, Hani, Lisu, and Pumi, but all for varying reasons. The Yi Torch Festival commemorates a victory over their enemies, whilst the Bai people's celebration is in memory of a legendary figure.

Some festivals, such as the water-splashing festival of the Dai in Jinghong and the third month fair in Dali, have become well known, attracting crowds of Chinese tourists and overseas visitors.

But the sheer number of festivals in Yunnan, and the fact that many happen in winter when the crops have been harvested and there is leisure time, means that many remain unattended by foreigners. It is still possible to run across lively celebrations, even in the most tourist-oriented towns such as Dali, where you will be the only outsider and more often than not made to feel very welcome.

The following are a selection of some of the many colourful festivals on offer in Yunnan throughout the year; Xishuangbanna and Dali prefectures tend to hold the most. Ask at the local CITS, a traveller's café or your hotel to find out what is on locally.

January 30	Trekking the Flowery Mountain. Honghe and Wensha. Miao.
February 8	Herding God Festival. Yongning. Mosu.
February 11	Kitchen God Festival. Lanping. Pumi.
March 6	Sword Pole Festival. Tengchong and Nujiang. Lisu.
March 26	Singing Festival. Shibaoshan, Jianchuan. Bai.
April 11	Black Dragon Pool Fair. Lijiang. Naxi.
April 30	Wheat Brew Festival. Throughout the north and northwestern parts of Yunnan.
May 23	Lisu Ancestral Rites. Ninglang. Lisu
May 30–31	Horse Racing Fair. Zhongdian. Tibetan.
June 7	Festival of the Blue Banners. Heqing. Bai.
August 2	Tawpeu Communal Feast. Lijiang. Naxi.
August 28	Torch Festival. All Bai, Yi and Naxi regions.
September 4	Devil Festival. Luxi. Zhuang.
September 30	New Rice Festival. Honghe. Hani.

October 5	Offerings to the Sun and Moon. Lincang. Lahu.
October 5	Mid-Autumn Fair. Shaping. Bai.
November 19	Posting Oxen Horns. Jingping. Miao.
December 4	Panwangjie. All Yao villages.

INTERACTING WITH LOCAL PEOPLE

The extraordinary diversity of peoples within Yunnan, each with their own distinct traditions and social customs, raises the question of how easily a visitor can interact with and get to know the people of this region. Now that travel restrictions have been eased and more and more of the province is open to visitors there is tremendous scope for visiting and interacting with previously isolated peoples who have had little or no previous contact with foreigners. With the revival of ethnic identity and traditional festivals over the past 20 years there are great opportunities for memorable and meaningful encounters between locals and visitors. Unfortunately it sometimes seems that the complex mosaic of cultures that goes to make up Yunnan is rarely appreciated and understood by the mass of tourists which now descends on the popular sights of the region. The unique cultures that are the very essence of Yunnan run the danger of being turned into mere curiosities and sidelined in their own towns and villages by an onslaught of tour groups whose only interaction with a local is through a camera lense. Cultures become commercialised and trivialised to postcards, trinkets and souvenirs. But, if you are prepared to be adventurous and make the effort to learn something about the cultures, there is still much scope for learning and interacting with people in Yunnan .

Generally speaking the people of Yunnan are very welcoming to visitors and ready to show their traditional hospitality. The reception you get varies from group to group and town to town, reflecting differences in culture and lifestyle.

Of the minority peoples the Naxi were among the first to throw open their doors to foreign visitors and welcome them in and as a result have long since become accustomed to foreigners in places like Lijiang, Shigu, Baoshan and Baisha. The Naxi fondness for acquiring knowledge and learning has perhaps inspired their readiness to interact with foreign guests and it is easy to strike up conversations with people in these towns, for there many accomplished English speakers. Another people who have become accustomed to foreign visitors are the Musuo who live around Lugu Lake for, despite the relative isolation, they receive a steady flow of travellers who are encouraged to stay with locals. So the regular interaction between the Musuo and visitors has allowed them to learn something of their guests and the outside world. The Tibetan people of the far northwest have had far less exposure to outsiders and are generally shyer, though you could be forgiven for thinking this wasn't the case in Zhongdian where it seems that everyone in town will call out 'hello' to you. Tibetans are actually very hospitable people and it is not dislike that holds them back but simply the language barrier and lack of experience in meeting foreigners. The Yi people are even more reserved and can seem positively hostile if you intrude upon their villages. They also dislike having a camera pointed at them and will often turn or run away, even if you have first asked permission for a photograph. The best way to interact with some of the shyer hill tribe peoples is to be introduced by someone of their own nationality, such as a guide. Quite often these seemingly aloof people are incredibly welcoming and hospitable once you have been introduced to them in a familiar manner. It is not a lack of good will that stands between local people and visitors in Yunnan, only an ignorance of one another's customs and habits.

Local people are often eager to learn about the foreign guests in their midst, but it is a lack of knowledge of foreign ways and habits and uncertainty as to how they should behave that deters them. Basic Chinese is spoken and understood almost everywhere so you can get by with a limited amount of Chinese and this will certainly break the ice. But if you really want to gain some respect from the minority peoples then you should try to learn something about their cultures. This might be as simple as knowing the significance and story behind a festival you are attending or understanding the rites being performed in a ritual. If you are invited into someone's home try to learn and observe the traditional codes of hospitality. Above all, if you get the chance to learn some words of a local minority language then this will show that you have made an effort to honour and understand the culture of your hosts. China's minority peoples have long lived in the shadow of their giant neighbours the Han Chinese, and generally perceive that the Han and any other people of technologically advanced nations feel superior to them. If you make the effort to learn about and respect their local cultures and customs then you overcome this feeling and open up the way for real interaction and friendship.

Some dos and don'ts of social interaction

The following are general rules of behaviour that can apply with any peoples in Yunnan or China as a whole:

Face

Never show any public displays of temper when dealing with people, even though your patience may be often stretched to the limit. Getting angry will rarely get you what you want and more often than not will damage your cause. If you have been given bad service or a refusal then you should politely continue with your request, explaining patiently and smiling all the while. If someone has given you a flat refusal the best tactic is to offer them some kind of excuse to change their minds, otherwise they will not be able to change their decision without losing face. The concept of face is extremely important to Chinese people and it is vital that you do not try to force someone to back down publicly from their stated position. Face can best be described as an idea of self respect and status. In a dispute a negotiated compromise is always preferable to trying to force an apology or admission of error, thereby saving someone's face.

Invitations

If you have the opportunity to get to meet Chinese people personally you will find that their hospitality knows no bounds once you are known and accepted into their family or social circle. If you are invited to dine or stay with someone your hosts will be unfailingly kind and attentive to your perceived needs, sometimes embarrassingly so. Given the disparity in incomes you should always be aware that this hospitality can be a big drain on a family's resources and try to reciprocate in kind. If you are taken out for a meal or given a gift then ensure that you return the favour in kind; though you may be met with polite refusals you should insist upon having your turn. Similarly if you are visiting someone's home for a meal then bring a present with you; this could be a basket of fruit, a bottle of spirits or something from your home country. The Chinese way is not to make a big fuss when they are given a present but to try to return the favour in kind.

Eating and drinking

Chinese people enjoy a very different way of dining and drinking from Westerners and the idea of a quiet, candle-lit dinner for two or the slow sipping of a drink is not their style at all. Although Western-style restaurants are making inroads in the cities, the Chinese ideal for a restaurant is an informal, glaringly bright, neon-lit affair with lots of noise and activity. You will often find groups of diners in such restaurants involved in noisy drinking games with the volume getting progressively louder with each successive drink. Drinking takes the form of toasts with everyone joining in, especially when it is spirits that are being drunk. The most common toast is *gan bei*, the equivalent of 'cheers' or 'bottoms up'; it translates as 'dry cup'. Don't be shy in proposing your own toasts to the food, company and hospitality of your hosts.

You will always be served tea at a meal and whenever you take a sip you will find that your glass is refilled as it is considered bad form to leave a guest with an empty cup or glass. If you don't want any more of what is being offered then it is best to leave your glass full. Once the meal is under way there are a few points to observe. It is quite acceptable to eat noisily and slurp your noodles, as you will have probably noticed from the other diners. Also you can drink soup straight from the bowl or pick up a bowl with one hand and eat close to your mouth, as is the style with rice eating. Avoid waving your chopsticks around while speaking and do not stand them upright in your bowl, as this has connotations of bad luck. Meat and fish is often served on the bone and you should separate the flesh from the bone in your mouth and then put the rejected bones on the table next to your plate. Try to avoid overfilling your bowl with food and eat all that you have put in, but at the end of a meal leave a little food, or you will give the impression that your hosts have not provided enough. Avoid sneezing or blowing your nose at the table as this is considered very impolite. Meals tend to come to an end quite quickly in that people don't hang around the table once the meal is finished.

Although it might seem like a complicated affair, dining in China is a very informal and enjoyable experience and, if you forget to observe the conventions mentioned above, your Chinese hosts will be understanding and make allowances for you as a foreigner.

Some points of etiquette with minority peoples

Different ethnic groups have their own peculiar proscriptions and social taboos and generously make allowances for foreigners who unwittingly fall foul of these customs. The following is a selection of social customs which it might be useful to be aware of when you are interacting with minority people.

* Do not touch the heads or head ornaments of children, young monks and young girls.
* Take off your shoes when entering a main temple or someone's house, unless others are wearing their shoes.
* If staying in a Dai peoples' house overnight, you should not place your head toward the host's bedroom; instead you should place your feet in that direction. Avoid stepping over the feet of any women in the house.
* When someone hands you a bowl of rice it is polite for you to receive it with both hands. Try not to overfill your bowl with too much rice.
* Avoid even mentioning pork when eating at a Muslim restaurant.
* Do not step on, or touch, any religious symbols, objects or shrines.
* It is not considered acceptable to give gifts or ornaments to young girls.
* Take off your hat when entering a house or temple and avoid whistling inside.
* It is not acceptable to talk about any topic related to sex.
* Don't step over the triangle frame on a fire. Never use the triangle frame to hang your clothes or rest your feet.
* When someone proposes a toast to you it is best either to drink a mouthful or at least have a sip as it is regarded as impolite if you refuse to do so.
* When you feel that you have had enough food or drink, the polite way to tell the person who is intending to fill your bowl is to say 'I have had enough' or to point to your stomach and indicate that you are full. Avoid an outright refusal or saying 'I do not want it'.
* Never sit in the middle of an entrance threshold.
* Do not pick up a young baby when you enter a room.

PHOTOGRAPHY

Travel and photography are old companions. French photographers with daguerreotypes were roaming the Pacific as early as 1841; Maxime du Champ, in the company of Flaubert, embarked on a two-year Grand Tour of the Middle East in 1849, focusing his camera on such attractions as the Temple of Baalbek and the Colossus of Abu Simbel. Fox Talbot, making sketches of Lake Como in 1833 using a camera obscura, a device which allowed an image to be projected but not fixed, anticipated the advantages of photography when he wondered if it would be possible or not 'to cause these natural images to imprint themselves durably'. By the 1870s the British photographer and traveller John Thomson had already broadened photography's portfolio to include the documentary study with his books *Street Life in London* and *Illustrations of China and Its People*.

The failure rate of photographers like Thomson, just how many glass plates they tossed into the Ganges or left behind in the Hindu Kush, will never be known. The modern photographer has the advantage of being able to travel light without a Victorian checklist that would have included such items as oak tripods and developing buckets. That doesn't mean that travel photography is a pushover. Many people delude themselves into thinking that the journey, if interesting enough, will provide first-rate pictures as a matter of course. Another popular misconception is that by taking 20 or 30 rolls of film with you on a trip you are bound to get good shots, or that by going to somewhere like Yunnan, a place that seems an instant feast of colour and light, you will automatically succeed. Photography doesn't work like that. Nor does the so-called 'machine-gun' approach to photography in general, whereby several pictures are taken in quick succession in the hope that one brilliant image will emerge.

While there is certainly an element of luck involved in being in the right place at the right time, in having the right lens, film speed and available light to co-operate with the shot, ultimately the key to getting good travel pictures can be described in one word – composition. Curiosity, a pair of itchy feet and a bit of imagination can overcome most technical problems, but there are a few points worth bearing in mind when visiting terrain as varied as Yunnan.

Good travel photos are the result of good trips, usually carefully planned ones. This is not to say that serendipity, or a random, unplanned itinerary, cannot provide great photo opportunities, but knowing where you are going and what you want unquestionably helps. People who know that they are going to Bhutan to photograph monasteries, Yunnan for the flora, or Havana for the vintage 1950s cars, usually get what they want.

Read as much about the destination before the trip as possible. While travelling pick up local publications which are often more up to date. Planning also applies to equipment and materials. Given the photo opportunities that places like Yunnan offer to the keen eye, taking a camera along with you on a holiday is almost mandatory. Always keep your equipment dust and humidity-free by 'opening up' the body and removing the lens at the end of the day for an inspection and cleaning. Add a couple of packets of silicon crystal, a bottle of cleaning fluid and a cloth or packet of lens tissue to your camera bag and your gear should be safe.

For serious photographers, or travellers who insist on high quality, the choice of which film to take with you is best made before you go on a trip rather than after. China's best make of film is the Lucky brand, but there's no real need to use it. Kodak, Fuji and Konica ASA100 and 200 colour print film can be bought in most cities at prices slightly lower than in Europe or the States. Fast film ratings at ASA400 are usually more expensive and difficult to find. Slide film is more difficult to get hold of but is available in Kunming, Dali and Lijiang. The choice of speeds is more limited than you would find in the West so try to bring an adequate supply with you if you require a range of different speeds.

Because of the geographical diversity of Yunnan, from steamy jungles to crisp Himalayan peaks, it is best to have various film speeds at hand. Black and white film is easy to come by, but again, don't expect to find some like Ilford's ASA50-rated Pan F. China certainly lends itself to monochrome and many of the best photos I have seen by Yunnan photographers have been black and white prints. Lithium batteries are easily available but it is always worth bringing along a spare set.

There are various restrictions on photography in Yunnan, but the extent to which they are enforced varies from region to region, person to person. Officially, you are prohibited from photographing military complexes, harbours, airports and railway terminals. Technically, you are not supposed to take pictures from airplanes, though nobody has ever stopped me. Bridges are also off-limits but, again, it depends on the sensitivity of the site. Nobody is going to object to you photographing the old chain bridge at Shigu, for example. Archaeological sights, some grottoes and temples also restrict photography on the basis that you will then buy their postcards.

Most Chinese people dislike having their photo taken unless you ask permission. In the latter case you're likely to end up with some very wooden shots. If you are trying to take candid shots, be cautious. If somebody is kind enough to pose or not object to a candid shot, it is a nice courtesy to take their address and send on a picture. People, especially in rural areas, really appreciate receiving photos by post a few weeks later.

Accidents usually occur when film is exposed to excessive heat or continuous warmth – the type you get if you leave your rolls in a bag sitting over a bus engine or wheel well – or sudden changes such as a long hot drive followed by an over-cooled hotel lobby. Most problems with exposed film come from direct contact with warm surfaces, something that can be avoided by providing ventilation like an open window, when travelling.

Lead-laminated bags, though by no means infallible, are useful as storage containers and also for passing through X-Ray machines. Most equipment used in international airports these days is said to be film-safe but I'm not completely convinced and always insist on passing a tray of film around them for hand inspection. Meant primarily as an X-Ray screen, they also help to keep film cool and stable. If you are storing your film in a hotel room, check during the day that your air-conditioning or ceiling fan has not been switched off while you were out. Note that keeping film in a fridge is only a good idea if you are transferring it into a cool transitional stage before putting it in for development. If it is going back into a hot, brothy atmosphere, expect trouble. An air-conditioned photographic store stumbled upon in the daytime can easily become a steamy, moss-breeding jungle by night as shop staff switch off coolers before returning home.

Unlike aging groceries in your fridge, film gives no obvious clues to whether it is still usable until it is too late. When film gets old it deteriorates in its own way, losing sensitivity which results in, among other things, unwanted graininess, peculiar colour shifts, lower rather than higher contrast, and colour blending which can give the image the appearance of a double exposure. How old then, is too old for your film? Surprisingly, the expiry date is not something you need to be too exacting about. Unused film, when kept in its case and not over handled or exposed to too many temperature changes, should last up to six months beyond the printed date. Film, once in the camera, is far more fragile, especially when your machine is in direct sunlight or humidity.

Strategies for taking good travel photographs, once you have established that your equipment is up to the task, are legion. A rather calculated way of choosing good subjects for travel shots, one recommended by several how-to style photo handbooks, for example, is to buy postcards of places of interest, main sights and attractions. This is actually not such a bad idea as it sounds as it gives you something to match or, hopefully, improve on as well as giving you an instant shortlist of worthwhile potential photo sites. No two photographs in any case, even if taken from an identical angle, will ever be the same. Most of us prefer a more unscripted approach, but postcards do have their uses.

Don't be despondent if you think you are not getting the shots you should be. There's always another picture around the next bend of the road. When asked once which of her images was her favourite, the American photographer Imogen Cunningham wisely replied, 'The one I'm going to take tomorrow.'

GIVING SOMETHING BACK

There are many needy people in Yunnan. You can hardly fail to notice the destitute, brutally disabled, or terminally unemployable individuals without families or relatives – a severe handicap in China – who receive little or no help from the woefully inadequate welfare safety net provided by state. These are people you might wish to support in some modest financial way, though you should be aware that giving money directly to people can bring its own problems and should definitely be avoided with children. Targeting foreigners for begging becomes a habit that is reinforced every time you give. Concerned international organisations, with the approval of the Yunnan provincial government, are also doing their bit to alleviate misery, and raise standards of hygiene and levels of health care.

Australian Red Cross and Yunnan Red Cross have been collaborating since 1994 on youth peer education and HIV prevention. Essentially this project aims to train young people in the skills necessary to run HIV/AIDS workshops for other young participants. Young people have been targeted because over 50% of all new infections are among people under 25 years of age.

Project staff provide five days of training for Youth Facilitators aged between 15 and 30. The course includes basic medical training, and HIV/AIDS and facilitation skills. Members then work in teams of two or more, presenting two-day workshops for other young people on HIV/AIDS awareness. They are then expected to disseminate the information and experience they have gained to their families, friends and colleagues. Courses have so far been held in Kunming, Qujing and Simao prefectures, with more planned for the future.

Contaminated blood, careless sexual habits and peer pressure are common reasons for HIV/AIDS transmission the world over. So why did the organisers choose Yunnan? A major factor is clearly its proximity to the opium growing areas of the Golden Triangle and its key position astride some of Asia's most important drug trafficking routes. There are in excess of 40,000 identified hard drug users in Yunnan, over 70% of whom are heroin abusers, a figure that is acknowledged to be only the tip of the iceberg. Offenders are incarcerated in re-education camps and subjected to vigorous 'physical, psychological and moral re-training'. Methadone is not prescribed. Addicts go cold turkey, an ordeal that is slightly ameliorated by the use of Chinese herbal medicines. One of the groups most highly at risk from both narcotic and sexually contracted AIDS in Yunnan are truck drivers, particularly those on the cross-border routes that run from Burma into Xishuangbanna and onto Luang Prabang and Phonsaly provinces in Laos. There are many other areas that could reach potential epidemic levels. While looking for a possible community care model – an HIV 'at risk' village in western Yunnan – members of the project questioned the headman. Quizzed on the social habits of young people in his Muslim village, he expressed outrage when the subject of drinking and sex came up, but when asked if the younger villagers injected themselves with heroin, he was more tolerant, explaining that there was no specific stricture against it in the Koran.

How can travellers help the scheme, its small team of workers and gain some first-hand insights into the work of the Yunnan Project into the bargain? Project Manager Audrey Swift insists that, however busy they are, their head office opposite the Yan'an Hospital in Kunming always welcomes visitors. Interested parties are also free to attend information workshops which are held periodically at different venues throughout Yunnan. Although funding for the main project is assured for the time being by AusAID, once a community village is set up and running donations to be used at the local, grassroots level will be gratefully accepted at the Kunming centre.

For more information on the Yunnan Project contact Audrey Swift at Room 614, No 246 Renmin East Road, Kunming, Yunnan PRC 650051; tel: 86 871 312 5624; email: hivyrc@public.km.yn.cn.

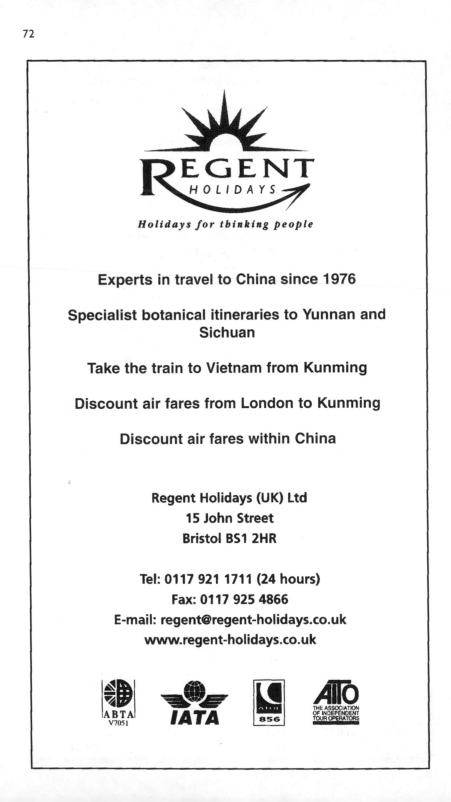

Part Two

The Guide

Kunming 昆明

'...in Chinese terms prosperity always spelled pollution. That was how I felt until I reached Yunnan.'

Riding The Iron Rooster, Paul Theroux

HISTORY

Kunming and the Lake Dian area were home to Yunnan's earliest inhabitants and the cradle of its first civilisation. Bronze Age artefacts discovered in tombs around Lake Dian hint at the existence of a well-developed culture, one that could produce paintings, musical instruments, weaponry and well-crafted ornaments and accessories. Chinese military expeditions explored the area as early as China's so-called Spring and Autumn Period (722–481BC), and the Kingdom of Dian was centred relatively close to the present-day city of Kunming.

Although a prefecture, Yizhoujun was established in Kunming in 109BC, the town was dismissed as a remote settlement at the edge of the Chinese empire, a place of little significance until the 8th century when the armies of the Kingdom of Nanzhao seized the town and made it their eastern capital. When the Mongol armies passed through in 1274 the town, then known as Yachi (Duck Pond Town), had begun to profit from its proximity to caravan routes between China and Europe. Marco Polo, visiting the city at this time, found a flourishing mercantile centre. Awash with goods and livestock, trade was conducted with cowry shells as currency. Polo, always wide-eyed and receptive, was intrigued by the hustle and bustle of the place but also its cosmopolitan blend of people, noting that: 'In it are found merchants and artisans, with a mixed population, consisting of idolaters, Nestorian Christians and Saracens or Mohametans.'

The Ming, who occupied the city in the 14th century, extended its parameters, built fortified walls and made several defensive and infrastructure improvements to Yunnanfu, as the city was renamed. Kunming's closer ties with China were a mixed blessing in the centuries to follow. Manchu armies invaded the province in the 1650s, dislodging the last of the Ming.

The Muslim rebellion of 1858 had disastrous consequences for Kunming. The leader of the Muslim rebels, Du Wenxiu, the self-styled Sultan of Dali, ransacked the city on several occasions, destroying many of its most important and prestigious public and religious buildings until the rebellion was finally, and brutally crushed in 1873. Quick to take advantage of the ensuing chaos, Kunming found itself uncomfortably close to the encroaching ambitions of Britain and France who, already coveting the prospect of colonies in Burma and Indochina, were keen to exploit the mineral and forestry resources of Yunnan. Concessions prized from a weakening Qing dynasty opened Kunming, Simao, Mengzi and Hekou to foreign trade by 1900. In 1911 the Kunming-Haiphong railway, a project that took 13 years and, if we are to believe the Chinese official version of its construction, many thousands of labourers' and coolies' lives to complete, was opened, connecting the city for the first time with Vietnam.

Kunming's modern phase, its expansion and development as an important commercial and industrial centre, began with the Japanese invasion of east China in the late 1930s, a run-up to World War II. Funds from wealthy east coast refugees helped to build up Kunming's manufacturing base and put it on the resistance map. As a supply depot for the relocated Chinese government in Chongqing and as a base for Anglo-American forces supplying Nationalist troops in Yunnan and Sichuan, important equipment and materials passed along the Burma Road, or were flown in by American pilots – members of the volunteer Flying Tigers – to Kunming.

Kunming, like every Chinese city, suffered from the violence and insanity of the Cultural Revolution. A handful of old or culturally important buildings that had survived the ferocity of the Muslim rebellion were either destroyed or vandalised, and several people, including the mayor of Kunming, were tortured to death by Mao's goons. Even clothes mannequins whose features bore any resemblance to Westerners, were dragged out of shop windows and torn to pieces.

The provincial capital today presents a very different picture to the visitor. Covering an area of 6,100km^2 Kunming is divided into four urban districts and eight counties, with a total population of 3.3 million people. The city proper has a resident population of about one million. Known as the City of Eternal Spring because of its mild climate and profusion of flowers and plants, the city, sitting at a comfortable altitude of 1,891m on the Yunnan–Guizhou Plateau, surrounded by green mountains on three sides and Lake Dian to the south, is just the sort of place where many Chinese urbanites would like to live but few actually do.

Industrial complexes outside the city centre have made Kunming an important manufacturing centre, exporting textiles, chemicals, steel, machine and electrical equipment parts, and processed and natural foods. Tourism and foreign investment in the 1980s have increased the city's wealth and created an air of calm prosperity. Towering office blocks, new housing projects, and broad streets with wide pavements confirm the impression of a clean and efficient city.

Sadly, the old quarters of Kunming, the city's wooden houses, with their balconies and shutters, and many of the traditional artisan centres have been razed in the name of progress and better amenities. There are plenty of compensations though, and this vibrant city remains a highly enjoyable place to spend a few days organising your itineraries. Its department stores and specialised shops offer a tremendous range of Chinese, local and imported goods, and the city boasts some of the best restaurants, coffee shops and tea houses in Yunnan.

Not all of its tree-lined avenues and quaint lanes have disappeared, and many street and night markets continue to thrive. A handful of old streets, replete with wooden shop-houses and small, neighbourhood parks and Chinese gardens can be sought out without too much difficulty, where the elderly still gather in defiantly traditional groups, wearing their blue jackets and Mao caps, to smoke their wood-brass pipes, listen to storytellers and folk singers, or practise on musical instruments that look thoroughly gnarled and ancient. Traditional masseurs and ear-wax cleaners continue to ply their trade along the main thoroughfares. Fresh fruits and vegetables pour into the city every morning from the surrounding countryside, and the city's few temples and pagodas, foreign villas and legations evoke, in the quiet moments and spaces between the roar of traffic, neon-strung skyscrapers and giant video screens advertising Coca-Cola and Canton pop, the mood of a bygone age. This can still be sensed in the native hospitality and good manners, the small courtesies extended to visitors.

GETTING THERE AND AWAY

Kunming's superb international airport, with a domestic terminal at an adjacent ground floor level, was completely modernised in 1999 and has been in operation for some time now. Passengers departing on international flights are required to pay a Y100 'construction fee' – the equivalent of airport tax – while domestic passengers pay Y50. Luggage trolleys in the arrival hall cost Y2. In the middle of the arrival hall there is a tourist information desk where you can buy maps, but the staff speak only limited English. There is also a touch-screen information machine located there, which among other things, gives information in English on flight arrivals and departures. There is a bank for changing money on the first floor of the departure hall on the left-hand side.

Just outside the arrival hall there are regular CAAC buses which can drop you off at various destinations in the city; ask at the information desk for the relevant bus. The cheapest option is to take a No 52 bus from the exit of the small street on the roundabout across from the airport. The fare is just Y2 and recorded announcements for stops are made in both English and Mandarin. The taxi rank is located to the left-hand side of the exit. The meter starts at Y8 and it is only a short ride along a new highway to the city. Expect to pay about Y14 to the hotels and bus station on Beijing Lu and Y20 into the city centre. Many of the large hotels have a free shuttle bus service and pick-ups can be arranged by request if you book a place 24 hours in advance.

If arriving by train from elsewhere in China you will come into the main railway station at the southern end of Beijing Lu. Trains from Vietnam and the stations along this line come into the smaller north railway station. There are a number of hotels within walking distance of the main station on Beijing Lu;

alternatively, if you have a lot of luggage, a cab from the station to any of these hotels will cost the basic fare of Y8. If you are going further into the city a cab will cost around Y10–12 from the station to the city centre. A No 23 bus runs from the main railway station to the north railway station and is handy if you are heading for the area around the Camellia Hotel. Jump off at Dong Feng Dong Lu and walk eastwards for a block-and-a-half to reach the Camellia. Many long-distance buses arrive and depart from the south bus station close to the main railway station on Beijing Lu, so the main modes of transport apply from here as well.

As Kunming forms the nucleus of the province's transportation system, moving on from the city is very easy. Domestic flights leave from the new airport terminal and Kunming is well connected, with air services to most popular destinations. There are daily flights to Jinhong (Y520), Lijiang (Y420), Baoshan (Y370), Xiaguan (for Dali, Y320), Mangshi (Y530), Simao (Y390) and a four-times-a-week service to Zhongdian (Y560). Though there has been much talk of an airport at Deqin this has yet to materialise. Tickets can be booked through CITS and local agents in Kunming. For more information on flights see the 'Getting there' information at the beginning of each chapter or the air travel section in Chapter 2. Kunming also has excellent air links with most major cities in China and again these should also be booked through a local agent rather than from the airline which is more expensive.

The rail network within Yunnan is fairly limited but the service is slowly improving with the opening of the Kunming–Xiaguan line and the new service to the Stone Forest. Trains for Kaiyuan, Jianshui, Shiping Geiju, Hekou and onwards to Vietnam all depart from the north railway station. (Don't attempt to reach Hanoi unless you have the correct visa with 'Hekou' stamped on it as the point of entry.) The ticket office is located in the northeast corner of the station. Trains for Hekou leave at 14:45 and take 19 hours; the fare is Y210 for soft sleeper. A 22.40 train follows the same line but branches off at Kaiyuan for the towns of Jianshui and Shiping. Chuxiong and Xiaguan (for Dali) are also served by an overnight train from this station. No 262 from Kunming to Xiaguan takes approximately ten-and-a-half hours and departs from Kunming at 22.10 every evening. A berth in a comfortable soft sleeper compartment costs Y150 or Y90 if you want to brave the hard seat carriage.

The new express train to the Stone Forest leaves from the main railway station at the southern end of Beijing Lu. Connections onwards to other cities in China depart from the main railway station. Destinations include: Beijing, (daily; 48 hours), Chengdu (three a day; 21 hours), Guangzhou (twice a day; 48 hours), Chongqing (twice daily; 23 hours), Gulin (twice daily; 30 hours), Guiyang (five daily; 12 hours), Nanning (daily; 16 hours), Panzihua (three a day; six hours) and Shanghai (twice daily; 60 hours). Tickets for sleepers and hard seats are sold at the No 12 window at the main railway station, except for the Stone Forest train which has its own ticket window on the east side of the building. Tickets for sleeper trains can be purchased up to three days in advance. To save hassle it is worth paying a little extra and getting one of the tour agencies to book your rail tickets for you, particularly if you want soft sleeper.

The bus network out of Kunming is unlimited and there are a couple of different stations in the city that serve various destinations. You should first try the main long-distance bus station located on Beijing Lu near the main railway station. The ticket office here sells standard, express and sleeper bus tickets all over the province. The following are some sample prices and journey times:

Baoshan   sleeper bus Y130, 15 hours
Dali/Xiaguan standard bus Y60, 8 hours; express Y110, 5 hours
Geiju   standard bus Y40, 6 hours; express Y70, 4½ hours
Lijiang   standard bus Y95, 13–14 hours; express Y170, 8–9 hours; sleeper Y130, 12 hours
Jianshui   standard bus Y33, 6 hours; sleeper Y45, 8 hours
Jinhong   sleeper bus Y170, 18 hours
Kai Yuan   standard bus Y32, five hours
Ruili   sleeper bus Y180, 22–24 hours
Tonghai   standard bus Y20, 3–4 hours

Please note that with the longer journeys the times are average (and ideal) times and may sometimes take a lot longer than this. If you are in any way restricted for time you would be best avoiding the extended bus journeys to places like Jinhong and Baoshan and advised to take a plane instead.

Useful numbers

Rail enquiries   316 2321
Long-distance bus station   316 4778
Airport information   313 3216

Kunming to Lhasa

One of the most interesting travel options out of Kunming if you can arrange it (and if the authorities are still giving the nod to the idea by the time you read this), is the overland route by four-wheel drive into Tibet and on to its capital Lhasa. Most travellers fly there, after obtaining the correct documentation, from Chengdu. A more interesting alternative is to join a small, authorised tour through a Kunming-or Lijiang-based travel agency.

Toyota land cruisers are used to coping with the rough terrain. It takes a full ten days to reach Lhasa from Kunming, stopping off or passing through Dali, Lijiang, Zhongdian and Deqin on the Yunnan side before crossing the border into Tibet and heading for Markham, Bhagda, Rangwin, Bayi, Gyamda and eventually Lhasa. Accommodation is generally in Tibetan homes, roadside hostels or in tents. Food is provided at wayside restaurants or cooked in an open fire at the roadside. If you decide to join one of these tours you will need to come equipped with all-weather clothing and be in fairly good physical shape. You can expect to pay something like US$2,000 all told. Yunnan Exploration Travel Service at 73 West Renmin Lu (tel: 0871 531 2283; fax: 0871 531 2324; email: travelguide@km.col.com.cn) have the most experience with this kind of trip. They also run the more local Yunnan Adventure Club travel agency from the same address. Another very reliable operator that offers overland trips to Lhasa and the border areas of Tibet is Haiwei Trails who are based in Lijiang (tel: 01350 888 6126; e-mail: haiweitrails@chinamail.com; web: www.haiweitrails.com).

GETTING AROUND

There are few outstanding monuments or landmarks in Kunming to help you negotiate the city, but its zoning and street layout, at least in the city centre, is fairly straightforward. Kunming's bearings are its major roads, particularly those that run along a north–south, east–west axis. Beijing Lu runs for 5km in a north–south direction, crossing the eastern edge of the city. The roundabout that forms the intersection between Dongfeng Dong Lu, and Zhengyi Lu might be called the city centre proper. Here you will find a concentration of department stores, cinemas, discos, karaoke venues and Kunming versions of fast food. Mercifully, it is a short walk from here to the old trade quarter between Zhengyi Lu and Wuyi Lu, with its humming street and bird markets, old residencies and cubby-hole restaurants. Dongfeng Xi Lu is the western counterpart of Dongfeng Dong Lu. The street becomes Renmin Xi Lu as it leaves the city, the first step in the past on the old Burma Road. Most Kunming sights are north and west of the centre, close to Green Lake (Cuihu) Park, the university and Dongfeng Xi Lu. A ring-road, Huancheng Dong Lu, encloses the city centre.

The long-distance bus and main train stations are 500m apart from each other at the southern end of Beijing Lu, the terminal of the less used North Station at the other end of the road. A small number of long-distance buses depart from the western bus station on Renmin Xi Lu, but this mostly serves local Kunming routes.

Although some of the main roads can seem long and straight, the city is fairly easy to get around on foot. Some hotels rent bicycles which is also a good option. Otherwise there are plenty of local buses.

PRACTICAL INFORMATION
Maps

You can pick up the English-language *Kunming Tourist Map* for Y2.5 at the airport. The more detailed maps tend to be written in Chinese. The Foreign Languages Bookstore along Qingnian Lu has a spotty selection of maps but you can sometimes be lucky. Again, it is pot luck but you occasionally see people hawking maps to travellers on the street. Museums also occasionally stock maps. There is a good 3D artist's map, entitled *A Bird's Eye View of Kunming*, which covers all the area within the second ring road and has all the major streets and buildings written in English. As most of the major buildings are featured it is quite easy to navigate your way around the city with this map. You can buy it from most hotels and street vendors for Y3.

Tourist information

There are several tour operators in Kunming who can act as a source of information on local sights and tour options. CITS have several branches attached to the larger hotels. The head office at 285 Huancheng Nan Lu (tel: 313 4019) is probably the best place to make arrangements; ask for Ms Shirley Du who is particularly helpful. Other CITS offices can be found at the Golden Dragon Hotel (tel: 355 6361) and the King World Hotel on Beijing Lu (tel: 313 8888). Office hours are 08.00–22.00. The travel agency attached to the Kunming Hotel is also useful for booking plane and train tickets (tel: 316 3784). The best budget option is the Camellia Hotel travel agency, which seems to have the most reasonable prices for tours and tickets. There is also a travellers' information board at the Camellia, which is a good source for updated news and travellers' tips when you first arrive.

Visa extensions and consulates
If you require an extension of your visa you will have to go to the Foreign Affairs Branch of the Public Security Bureau (PSB) for extensions of between 15 days and one month. The PSB office, located in a small alley off Beijing Lu, is open 08.00–11.30 and 14.30–17.30.

Burma, Laos and Thailand have consulates in Kunming which can, depending on the prevailing political winds, issue travellers with visas for overland crossings into their countries. They are located at the following addresses.

Burma (Myanmar) 3rd floor, Building Three, Camellia Hotel; tel: 317 6609
Laos 2nd floor, Building Three, Camellia Hotel; tel: 317 6623
Thailand Next to Kunming Hotel; tel: 313 8888

Money matters
Money can be exchanged at the Bank of China in the airport or at its city address at 488 Renmin Dong Lu, but it is often easier, and the hours are more traveller-friendly, to do this at a large hotel. They all offer about the same rates. The Camellia, Kunming, Green Lake, Holiday Inn and King World are the best bets. If you do decide to opt for the state bank, its opening hours are 09.00–11.45 and 14.30–17.30. There is a second branch of the Bank of China on Qingnian Lu which has a convenient, well-marked foreign exchange counter.

Post and telecommunications
The large Post & Telecommunications Office is located on the corner of Dongfeng Dong Lu and Beijing Lu. The International Post Office is along Beijing Lu, on the left side as you walk towards the bus station. They both have an excellent poste restante service. Post office hours are 08.00 to 20.00. Telecommunications services are generally open from 08.00 to 17.00.

The area code for Kunming is 0871.

Email/internet services
Camellia Hotel 96 Dong Feng Dong Lu. The business centre has internet access for Y10 an hour.

Dove E-Mail 47 Wen Ling Jie. Between Green Lake and Yunnan University, near Teresa's Pizzaria. Tiny, hole-in-the-wall place run by a friendly bunch of people. Also has limited tour guide and travel service.

Hasan's 42 Wenlin Lu. A small bar and internet café.

Sophie's Business Centre 62 Dongfeng Lu East. Internet, ticketing and tourist information services.

Medical services

The foreigners' clinic on the first floor of Building No 6 at the Yan'An Hospital offers the best service for travellers. The hospital is on Renmin Dong Lu; tel: 317 7499, ext. 311.

Shopping

China is in the throes of a people's consumer movement which is not limited to a three- or five-year plan, a proliferation of every kind of goods conceivable. Ration books, tourist-only 'Friendship Stores' and off-the-peg Mao suits are a thing of the past. Those who run private shops or work in Kunming's hangar-sized department stores are no longer labelled 'profiteers'. To shop is truly glorious.

Kunming shops, departments stores and street markets are a digest of all the goods available around the province. Minority goods are popular not just with foreigners, but also the increasing number of Chinese tourists who are descending on the city. Tribal wares include a whole range of embroidered tunics, shoulder bags, headdresses, shoes and slippers, hats, capes, aprons, dresses, and appliquéed baby carriers. Indigo batik cloth from Dali and other places is made into tablecloths, bags and napkins. You can also find Chinese silk products.

You are unlikely to find any real bargains in antique shops as the Chinese are extremely sharp when it comes to assessing the value of such things, but you can pick up genuine porcelain items, chops (personal seals), ink stones, silver jewellery and snuff boxes, coins, stamps and occasionally, old scrolls and woodblock prints if you are lucky.

Cooking utensils, especially *huoguo* (copper) and *qiguo* (ceramic) steam containers used for making chicken hotpot, are a good buy. Yunnan's many varieties of tea can be bought in teahouses, department stores and at open markets. Dried mushrooms and Yunnan ham, a delicious, slightly sweet meat that can be taken home tinned, are popular souvenirs. *Pu'er* is Yunnan's best known export tea but there are dozens. Highly recommended are Yunnan black tea, *Tuo*, *Dabaicha* and *Dianlu*. Yunnan coffee is also excellent. Traditional Chinese medicines are widely available. Many people swear by them but you will need some help from a local if you intend to explore Yunnan's complex pharmacopoeia.

Bookshops are a good place to stock up on local publications in English, pick up maps, calendars and examples of calligraphy. The Foreign Language Bookshop along Qingnian Lu has a decent selection of English titles, especially on minority cultures, local history and children's folktales. The larger Xinhua Bookshop is beginning to stock more English books as well.

Street markets are where the really cheap goods are to be had, though you can't expect any form of guarantee or warranty on a watch, blouse or pair of thongs bought here. Prices are completely negotiable though, and with discounts of up to 30 or 40% on goods which are already considerably cheaper than at home, shoppers rarely get ripped off. There are some excellent markets in the backstreets between Huancheng Nan Lu and Jinbi Lu, in Kunming's old quarter between Zhengyi Lu and Wuyi Lu, and in the side streets off Dongfeng Dong Lu as you walk in the direction of the Camellia Hotel. Look out for temporary markets that spring up for a few weeks on housing blocks in the city centre that have been cleared for redevelopment.

Nature notes

Kunming enjoys one of the most temperate and even climates in China, a fact reflected in its all-year round flora. Its designated city flower is the *Camellia yunnanensis*, a species that is indigenous to the province. Kunming itself boasts over 400 flower types. Among the more common varieties are azalea, primrose, jasmine, *Primula malacoides* and various varieties of cactus. Ornamental flowers, at least one of which is in bloom at any given time throughout the year, include orchids, begonia, magnolia, hydrangea, chrysanthemum and tree-peonies. The most common fruit trees in the Kunming vicinity are plum, apricot, cherry, pear and peach, though you will often see tropical fruits like mango and lychee in the markets of Kunming.

The Yunnan Natural Forest Center (part of the grounds of the Golden Temple) is located in the northern suburbs of Kunming and is worth a visit for its abundance of trees and birds. The Yunnan Wildlife Collecting Center, a reserve for breeding and conserving wild animals, is here in the middle of a forest. The centre, which is trying to promote a much-needed awareness of wildlife protection by saving rare or endangered species, provides an opportunity to view such animals as binturong, red-necked cranes and the Malayan bear. Apart from the odd sparrow, duck or snake glimpsed along the shores of Lake Dian, the only other fauna in a natural habitat you are likely to come across is in Kunming Zoo.

WHERE TO STAY

Kunming experienced a hotel boom in preparation for its Expo '99 flower and plant festival. There is now a bigger and better range than ever before but don't expect to find any outstanding bargains in the provincial capital. There is virtually no guesthouse or pension-style accommodation for travellers, leaving only hotels. Most of these are conveniently located within the city centre, largely along or within walking distance of the long Dongfeng Dong Lu Road and its extensions. Many hotels offer significant discounts from the rack rates in low season, so it is always worth enquiring of any specials. Also be aware of the 15% service charge that is commonly added to your bill.

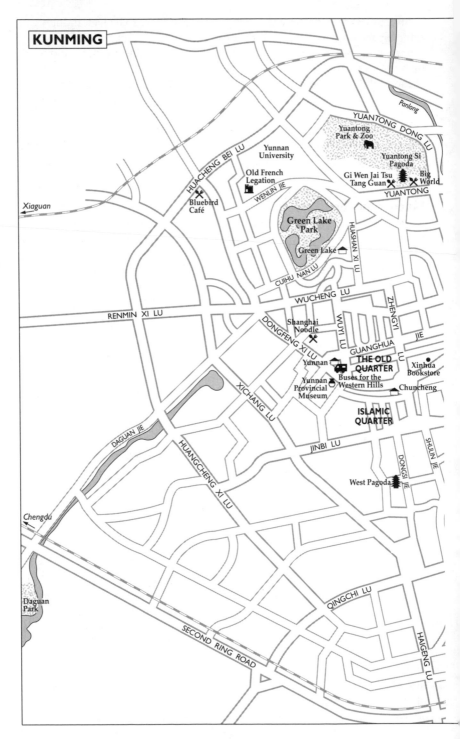

Above Springtime near the ancient village of Baishan in northeast Yunnan

Below The old Tibetan quarter of Zhongdian

Above Yunnan markets are full of interesting herbs, spices and condiments

Below Durian fruit in a Ruili street market

Below right A Bai woman selling incense sticks

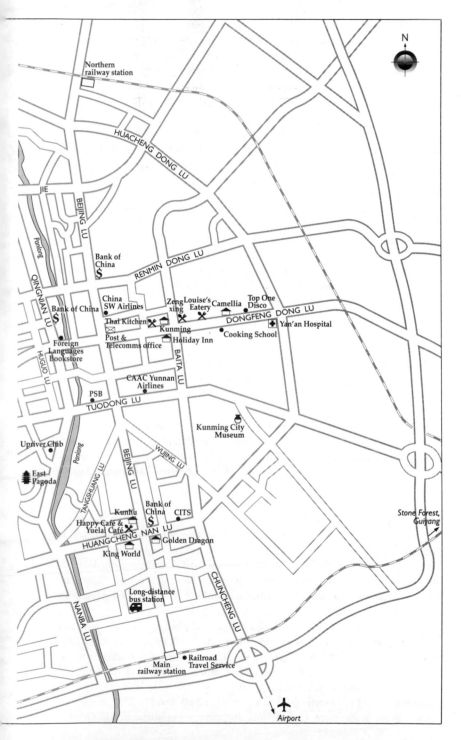

Camellia Hotel 96 Dongfeng Dong Lu; tel: 316 2918; fax: 314 7033; email: chbg@public.km.yn.cn. Long popular with backpackers for its cheap dormitory rooms and travel services, the 2-star Camellia tries to please everybody. It has 200 standard and luxury rooms, a restaurant, coffee shop, bar, shops, business centre and entertainment facilities. Their travel agency can arrange plane and bus tickets, as well as packages and tailor-made expeditions. Beds in 20-person dorms Y30, small standard Y140, standard Y220, small suite Y270.

Chungcheng Hotel Dongfeng Xi Lu; tel: 316 3271; fax: 316 4191. One of the best deals in Kunming, this centrally located hotel, also known as the Spring City Hotel, has comfortable, clean, spacious rooms with TV, hot baths and showers. Friendly staff who speak reasonable English. Has a popular restaurant. 72 rooms. Standard doubles Y168, twins Y190, suites Y220.

Golden Dragon Hotel 575 Beijing Lu; tel: 313 3015; fax: 313 1082; email: gdhotel@public.km.yn.cn. The Golden Dragon is a four-star establishment used mainly by Far East tour groups. The rooms are of a reasonably good standard, but it is quite a soulless place and the service is indifferent. On the bright side there is a good range of facilities including swimming pools and a private cinema screening Western films each evening for guests. Rooms start at $88 for a single/double.

Green Lake Hotel 6 South Cui Hu Lu; tel: 515 5788; fax: 515 3286; email: glhbed@public.km.yn.cn. Probably the best choice of the upmarket hotels if you're staying for more than a day in Kunming. What makes this hotel so appealing is its location in the quieter part of town, close to Cui Hu Park and away from traffic noise. This smart, four-star hotel makes a very comfortable retreat from which to explore the city. The service and rooms are faultless and those at the back of the hotel have a view over nearby Cui Hu Park. Singles/doubles start from Y588.

Holiday Inn Kunming 25 Dongfeng Dong Lu; tel: 316 5888; fax: 313 5189. All the usual facilities of this famous chain. Good for a splurge or in if there is a sudden room shortage, but generally not for the independent traveller. Has one complete floor of restaurants open to public. A little pricey but makes a good change with Thai, American, European, Chinese as well as Yunnan food choices. 242 rooms. Standard US$96, superior $115, suites $181–488.

King World Hotel 98 Beijing Lu; tel: 313 8888; fax: 313 1910; email: kwhotel@public.km.yn.cn. The King World is a comfortable, modern four-star hotel located in the business district, within walking distance of the southern rail and bus stations. The service here is friendly and efficient, and facilities include several restaurants, one of which, the revolving restaurant, stakes its claim as the highest above sea level in China. Other amenities include a bowling alley and traditional Chinese medicine shop. Rooms are fairly standard but represent good value, with prices starting from $58.

Kun Hu Hotel 44 Beijing Lu; tel: 313 3737. A good place to stay if you have an early bus or train to catch as it is just a couple of minutes' walk from the stations. Simple, unpretentious rooms. A little English spoken but not much. Reasonably clean, good security. Because of location it can be noisy. Dorm beds Y30, standard rooms Y80, doubles Y90, doubles with bathroom Y130.

Kunming Hotel 52 Dongfeng Dong Lu; tel: 316 2063; fax: 316 3784; email: kmhotel@public.km.yn.cn. One of Kunming's original upmarket hotels. Good central location. Has more facilities than you will probably have time for, including various restaurants and bars, a business centre, ticketing service, sauna, bowling alley, a tennis court and indoor pool, as well as the inevitable karaoke rooms and billiard tables. 400 rooms. Singles/twins Y560, suites Y1,599–2,519.

Railroad Travel Service In front of main railway station; tel: 351 2166; fax: 351 3421. Clean and well located for the station. Has quite decent doubles with bathrooms for Y190 but not much choice of room types.

Yunnan Hotel 83 Dong Feng Xi Lu; tel: 313 7667; fax: 316 7906. Centrally located but mediocre three-star hotel, whose main attraction is its proximity to the old quarter and provincial museum. Rooms and facilities are OK and conform to the standard blueprint to which all three-star hotels in China seem to have been constructed. Double rooms start at Y220.

WHERE TO EAT

Kunming is teeming with restaurants, and many local specialities as well as Chinese and Western options are available. Typical Yunnan foods readily available in Kunming are the classic 'Across-the-Bridge-Noodles', *huotui*, a strong, slightly sweet cured-ham, and steampot chicken casseroles stewing in medicinal herbs. The back lanes and small roads north of Dongfeng Xi Lu have clusters of cheap restaurants and street stalls selling casserole hotpots, soda bread and grilled cheese. The bakery-cafés and coffee shops along Beijing Lu are good breakfast stops. Kunming's small Muslim quarter is a fascinating place to eat as the ingredients are often displayed on the street or, like strips of wind-dried beef, hung from doors and eaves. This is the place for spicy noodles, winter mutton stews and goat's cheese served with nuts and raisins. The lanes of the Old Quarter around the Market of Flowers and Birds, is crammed with small restaurants, and very clean, white-tiled Chinese canteens, as well as stalls selling morning *baba*, fried sticks of batter, and bottles of yoghurt. Kunming has its own brewery but other Chinese and foreign beers are readily available.

Big World Restaurant A few metres east of the Yuantong Temple. A smart restaurant popular with well-to-do locals. Specialises in seafood, but also has Across-the-Bridge-Noodles and some other Yunnanese dishes.

Blue Bird Café At 69 Dongfeng West Road, near the university. Popular with travellers and expats as well as Chinese. A good selection of Western-style food, sandwiches and pizzas as well as crêpes and bakery food. Has Chinese and Yunnanese dishes but not very authentic. A good ambiance, a wooden interior with hand-crafted textiles and objects.

Chungcheng Hotel Dongfeng Xi Lu. Well known for its dim sum breakfasts, also has an excellent, eat-as-much-as-you-like Chinese lunchtime buffet for a mere Y10.

Cooking School Dongfeng Dong Lu. Just opposite the Camellia Hotel. Not a bad place if you are on a low budget and like Chinese food. The students here prepare passable food, though some hungry travellers have complained about the size of the portions.

Gi Wen Jai Tsu Tang Guan Next to the Yuantong Temple. A superb vegetarian restaurant. Menu in English. Two-floor restaurant with private cubicles on upper floor.

ACROSS-THE-BRIDGE-NOODLES

The province's best-known dish owes its origins to a colourful story originating from medieval southern Yunnan. A Qing dynasty scholar looking for a conducive spot to prepare for the imperial examination, confined himself to a small island on a lake in Mengzi County. The studies were marred by one thing – food. By the time his wife reached him across a long bamboo bridge, his noodles were always cold. One day she discovered by accident that by pouring a thin layer of oil over the broth, it would stay hot. She could then place the slices of meat and vegetables in the soup once she reached the island. In this way *Guoqiao mixian*, or Across-the-Bridge-Noodles, came into being, and the student was able to pass his exams.

The dish has been considerably refined since then, but the basic idea remains unchanged. A piping hot broth, made from chicken, spare-ribs and duck is placed on the table alongside several side dishes. Typically, slices of raw chicken, ham, liver, fish and pork tenderloin cut as thin as butterfly wings, with spinach, onions, chives and other seasonal vegetables, plus a few drops of chilli pepper and sesame oil, complete the picture. Fingers should not come into contact with the broth which is in a sizzling hot cauldron. Ingredients are placed into it with a pair of long chopsticks.

It's best to eat this fun do-it-yourself dish in Kunming where there are dozens of restaurants specialising in Across-the-Bridge-Noodles.

Specialises in so-called 'imitations of meat' dishes like coconut-flavoured green rib bones and diced jade meat, 'imitations of seafood', including sea cucumber rolls, and 'milk' dishes like water-fried cheese. Nutritious, elegant and novel; also quite cheap.

Happy Café & Yuelai Café Bottom end of Beijing Lu. Two restaurants in a row of similar establishments that all have terraced tables. Cheap, well-prepared food with a good view of life along busy Beijing Lu. Good all-round selection but the steampot chicken dishes and soups stand out.

The King World Hotel revolving restaurant The King World Hotel on Beijing Lu. The revolving restaurant offers a wide selection of Chinese cuisine styles; the food is interesting and the service good but of course the real draw here are the superb views over the increasingly neon clad 21st-century cityscape of downtown Kunming. Worth a visit purely as an experience in extreme contrasts if you've just arrived from prolonged travels in the countryside.

Lan Bai Hong 44 Cultural Lane, off Wenlin Street. A newish French bakery, tea and coffee house run by a French couple. There are no croissants or baguettes but plenty of good cakes, pancakes, and crêpes, and well brewed Yunnan coffee. Nice decor. Very relaxing place popular with students, intellectuals and those wanting to practise their French.

Louise's 24 Eatery Next to the Camellia Hotel on Beijing Lu. A good place to head if you've arrived late into Kunming or fancy a late-night bite when everywhere else is closed. An extensive selection of local and Western dishes on offer, including some very palatable attempts at Mexican fare and iced beer glasses to match.

Shanghai Noodle Restaurant 73 Dongfeng Xi Lu. A cheap, working-class place that has fine chicken steampots in addition to the eponymous noodles. If the restaurant is still there by the time you read this – it's the type of old place that has 'Condemned' written all over it – it's a fairly non-descript, yellowish coloured building.

Ten Fu's Tea Renmin Zhonglu. Just by the footbridge. The Ten Fu is a good, representative example of the dozens of tea houses to be found in Kunming. A very sophisticated shop. You can sample various teas, watch the little rituals that go into their making, and buy leaf and small ceramic tea sets.

Thai Kitchen 145 Dongfeng Dong Lu. A nice change from Chinese and Yunnanese food, the dishes here are a bit pricey but worth it. Authentic Thai food. Recommended are fried pandanus leaf chicken, Thai satays, green, yellow and red curries, and the seafood congees. There are also a few dishes, like sea-blubber and pig's knuckle salad that might be more to the taste of Chinese customers. Expect to pay Y40–50 for a meal without drinks. Impeccable service. Menu in English.

Upriver Club 7 Hou Xin Road. A trendy bar, restaurant, tea and coffee house with prices to match, the club is located in a nicely renovated, lovely old French villa. It is managed by a group of well-known Yunnanese artists and has two good galleries with exhibitions that change regularly, and an art bookshop. A pleasant place to hang out.

Zeng Xing Restaurant Just off Dongfeng Dong Lu near the footbridge before the Camellia Hotel. A good general selection of Chinese dishes with a menu in English. A cheap restaurant that serves large helpings of everything. A good place to sample Across-the-Bridge-Noodles in Y10, Y20 and Y30 sizes. The Y10 is more than large enough for one person.

Entertainment and nightlife

Kunming's nightlife scene is fairly straight-laced compared to China's east coast cities. For most travellers, lingering over a good meal, a few drinks in a restaurant, and then wandering in one of the big parks or open gardens where a few impromptu nocturnal pastimes like singing, dancing and storytelling are held, is about it for the evening.

A few bars have Western-style live music, mostly pop and soft-rock covers, and there are a number of other watering holes that sustain a growing expat drinking crowd. Like everywhere these days in Asia, karaoke rules. If you like crooning to old Neil Sedaka, Beatles and Dusty Springfield backing tracks, or having a bash at following the melodies of Canto Pop, you'll be in your element. Discos often accommodate karaoke customers. **Top One Disco** is not a bad place for travellers as everyone seems to speak English, including the blond-wigged Chinese waitresses. It's a lively spot with lots of theme nights. It is straining itself a bit to be trendy, claiming to offer the newish fads in club music. You won't hear much ambient, trance or hip-hop here, but the music's some of the best in town. The **Kunming Hotel Disco** is another option. The right side of the disco plays techno, the left a softer blend of music. **Geli Kongjian**, in the busy Kundu bar area to the south of Dongfeng Lu West, is

Kunming's attempt at far-out, bizarre entertainment. Behind the club's beer terraces, up on the second floor, you'll find an arena for live bands, jugglers, plate-spinners, acrobats, comedians and scantily-clad dancers.

The **Journey to the East Café** up·near Yunnan University gets rave reviews from foreign students living here as a source of information on what's going on around town. **Wei's Place** along Huancheng Nan Lu has Western music evenings. **Brewhaus Hans** on Tuodong Lu, near the Kunming City Museum, has a second-floor restaurant, a brewery pub and live music. The upmarket **Upriver Club** has an excellent bar and outside drinking area. You can also watch videos here. The **Hot Spot**, in the bird and flower market, is run by an English-speaking guy called Michael who puts on the odd 'reggae party' and other theme evenings. The **Rum Bar** at 12 Cuihu Road North, hosts a lively scene during its 17.00–19.00 happy hour. They also serve fairly good Mexican food and pub grub. The drinks are cheap and the company usually good at **Katty's Bar** at 40 Wenlin Lu, where they also have pub snacks. The **Yoko Ono Bar** at 88 Cuihu Lu South, near Green Lake, is a friendly place with one of the best collections of Western music in Yunnan.

Foreign films shown in cinemas are usually dubbed, but you might check at the row of cinemas near Nanping Jie. There is an informal International Film Club which shows recent Western movies. Enquire at the Golden Dragon Hotel to find out if it is still going.

Check at the CITS office for a list of upcoming **theatre** or **dance** performances. These are mostly of the ethnic minority type, but there are also travelling opera troupes and acrobatics sometimes. Performances often take place at the **Arts Theatre** on Dongfeng Xi Lu. For an idea of what's going on in Kunming grab, if it is still in business, a free copy of KMS (kunmingscene@hotmail.com), a useful bi-monthly events magazine available at expat bars, restaurants and hotels like the Camellia.

WHAT TO SEE
Green Lake Park
Entrances in Cuihu Nan Lu and Cuihu Bei Lu. Open daily 06.30–21.30. Y2.
Although he found its go-kart track, drained ponds, children's football field and 'pathetic circus' whose star attraction was a 'tortured-looking bear pacing in a tiny cage' (this seems to have disappeared since his visit), Paul Theroux's favourite place in Kunming, was Cuihu, the Green Lake Park.

Originally a marshland on the outskirts of the town, the park is now located in the central to northwestern section of Kunming. The Emperor Kangxi had the swamp drained and turned into a pleasure garden with causeways, arbours and a main pavilion. The park is divided into four sections: the 'Spring Pavilion' in the northeast, the southeastern 'Water and Moon Verandah', the southwestern 'Calabash Island', and the central, 'Lake Pavilion'. Despite some tacky attractions like paddle boats and a pirate ship permanently moored in the lake, the park's pavilions, tree-lined embankments and lotus pond are attractive.

It is worth the Y2 entrance fee just to see the locals who turn up in the early hours to work out, practice *tai chi chuan*, show off their birds and enjoy social dancing. You can hear traditional storytellers, amateur opera singers and instrumentalists giving impromptu performances any day of the week, but weekends are especially lively. Families turn out in force, and there is an informal English Corner every Sunday. The park offers added interest during the Chinese New Year, and the Lantern Festival in late August/early September when decorated paper boats are lit with candles and launched across the lake.

An enchanting addition to the park's natural attractions is the appearance every winter of large flocks of red-beaked seagulls who fly in every November, making temporary nests around Dian Lake until March or April. The birds first appeared mysteriously in 1985 and have been making their shelter here ever since.

The old French Legation
While you are at the park, check out the old French Legation just opposite, an orange-yellow colonial period building that looks like a Franciscan seminary. It is one of the most beautiful buildings in Kunming with a massive, largely untended courtyard at the centre. Nobody seems to mind if you nose around the grounds. The quadrangle of buildings can be entered when exhibitions are held there. Hopefully this is a heritage site that will avoid the wrecker's ball.

Yuantong Si Pagoda
Yuantong Jie. Open daily 08.00–17.00. Y10.
The Ming and Qing period Yuantong Si, one of Yunnan's foremost Buddhist temples, is also an important pilgrimage spot. The temple, sitting at the foot of Yuantong Hill a short distance northeast of Green Lake Park, was founded in the 8th century and then further enlarged in 1320 under the Mongols. The original Ming gateway on Yuantong Jie is an impressive entrance to the garden processional down to the temple and its pond.

There always seems to be something happening at the temple. Large groups gather here to make offerings, attend seminars and to enjoy the subsidised meals at the temple's vegetarian canteen. The precincts of the pagoda, full of potted plants, the clanging of gongs, rehearsals of temple music, and a constant stream of devotees who come to light incense and offer prayers, have a nicely weathered, well-used feel. You can repair to the café near the pond and enjoy a cup of green tea while taking in the swirl of activity.

An **Octagonal Pavilion** and **Great Hall of the Buddha** are connected by a bridge over the central pond. The two main pillars of the hall are carved with dragons, a reference to a legend relating how the temple and monastery here were first built to pacify a dragon that lived in the pond. The grounds have an eclectic, religious theme park aspect. There's a Thai-style temple at the back of the main hall with a superb marble statue of Sakyamuni donated by the King of Thailand, that was built to accommodate the growing number of Thai tourists to Yunnan. A Tibetan chapel stands over on the east side and **Putuo Rock**, a cliff carved with ancient poems and wise sayings, lies behind the main hall. Entrance to the temple, as a sign outside declares, is free for children 'Under One Meter'.

BRONZE DRUM CULTURE

The making of bronze drums, an art form that originated in Yunnan, dates back over 2,700 years. Drums were used as musical instruments, but also in sacrificial and other rites which symbolised the power of the ruling class or clan and their nobles. Among certain Southeast Asian minorities bronze drums remain an important ritual element, a possession that increases the prestige of the tribe.

Bronze drums are still used in some remote villages of Yunnan, serving as an auspicious presence at festivals, weddings and funerals. The bronzes are suspended from frames like heavy bells or gongs, and carried with great dignity.

The Dian bronzes on the second floor of Kunming's Yunnan Provincial Museum, a collection dating back to the Warring States Period, were excavated from tombs located on the shores of nearby Lake Dian. Intriguing figurines are soldered on to the drums. Many, like dioramas of village life, depict families, their homes and chattels. Others show villagers sacrificing oxen or wrestling. Another shows an ox and a tiger in a death struggle, and a house transformed into the shape of a coffin, a momemto mori. Some of the best examples of bronze drums are those used as storage jars for cowries, a white shell widely used throughout Southeast Asia at one time as decorative accessories stitched into clothing and as a currency.

There are estimated to be roughly 2,300 bronze drums remaining in Yunnan. Among over a thousand bronze-ware objects discovered in 1975 in tombs at Wanjiaba, 3km south of Chuxiong City, five remarkable bronze drums were found. Radio-carbon dating established them as the world's oldest bronze drums discovered to date. Based on the find, Chuxiong District may prove to be the cradle of Asian bronze drum culture.

Check out the shop to the right of the temple's ticket booth. It is crammed with all the paraphernalia necessary for making the correct offerings, including a colourful selection of incense. Fans of high kitsch will love its shelves of plastic statues. Some of the Gianyin and Confucius figures are two or three feet high and have electric bulbs inside them. The beaming, roly-poly Buddhas look as if they have taken the goverment's injunction to grow prosperous, literally.

Yuantong Park and Zoo

Entrance at corner of Yuantong Jie and Qingnian Lu. Open 08.00–17.00. Y10.
A minute's walk from the Temple, the 26-hectare grounds of Yuantong Park are spread over the slopes of a spiral-shaped hill and include Kunming Zoo. The park has fine displays of flowers and trees. There are four main gardens with flowers blooming at all times of the year. Except on weekends when the park is crowded with families and another gathering of the English Corner, the

park validates Kunming's epithet as the 'City of Eternal Spring'. Flowers and trees blossom in all seasons: Oriental and Japanese cherry in early March, rhododendrons in summer, chrysanthemums in autumn, and camellia, plum and cassia during Kunming's mild winters.

As Chinese zoos go, Kunming's could be worse. There are over 100 species of animal here including tigers, wild buffalo, elephants and a mandatory panda or two. Species indigenous to Yunnan include wild oxen and butterflies from Xishuangbanna, peacocks from Mengna and black-tail pythons. Chinese zoos are usually gloomy places, the bane of animal rights groups. One of the English handouts here seems to think it is all good fun though, writing that 'the happy creatures on Monkey Mountain laugh everybody out of their life's troubles'. Judge for yourself.

There are a set of pavilions in the zoo supposedly built to reflect all the different styles of architecture throughout Yunnan province. There are good views of the city from the top of a hill here.

Yunnan Provincial Museum
Junction of Dongfeng Xi Lu and Wuyi Lu, 500m west of the centre. Open Mon–Thur 09.00–17.00, Fri 09.00–14.00. Y15.
The museum, housed in a grand Soviet-style building, has been recently reorganised and spruced up to good effect. The ground floor is divided into two sections, left and right of the main entrance. The left gallery, entitled 'Yunnan, A Mysterious Region', consists of daily objects used by farmers and ethnic minorities as well as some interesting cultural artefacts. The production tools, wooden farming implements, hill tribe textiles, religious objects, *dongba* scripts, musical instruments and an excellent photo display on Yunnan's ethnic groups are well labelled and displayed in a spacious setting. (For more information, see box on *Dongba scripts and paintings*, page 156.) The hall to the right, featuring precious gifts to provincial leaders from world dignitaries like Ronald Reagan and Queen Elizabeth, can safely be passed over.

The second floor features the important Exhibition of Ancient Chinese Bronze Drums. It is worth a visit to the museum just to see this rare collection alone. The exhibition in the left hall, entitled 'Yunnan's Ancient Buddhist Art', has some fine pieces. Supplementing the Buddha bronzes are statues of Guanyin, Goddess of Mercy, wooden figures of Vajra, Manjusri, several Bodhisattvas, and a small collection of Sanskrit bricks.

Kunming City Museum
Near the Sports Stadium on Tuodong Lu. Open Wed–Sun, 10.00–16.00. Y10.
Although the displays here pale against those at the Yunnan Provincial Museum, this might be an option on one of Kunming's many rainy days. It is quite instructive though, with reasonably well-plotted exhibits tracing the history of the Lake Dian region through replicas of excavation sites, Bronze Age tools and other artefacts, and a display on the evolution of humans from the earliest times to post Liberation. The second floor features a number of scale models of dinosaurs.

The old quarter

Inside the quadrangle formed by Dongfeng Xi Lu, Wuyi Lu, Renmin Zhong Lu and Zhengyi Lu.

There is no historical precedent for calling this the old quarter. It simply happens to be one of the only inner city districts of Kunming to have salvaged a few original streets, to have a decent community of old timers, and a number of excellent street markets and small, traditional shops. The fate of the area, like everywhere in China, hangs in the balance but, providing that it can prove its value as a vibrant marketplace and tourist attraction, it may survive.

The area is a real delight to walk around, with old family-run shops selling everything from dwarf plants, herbs and cheaply manufactured T-shirts, to

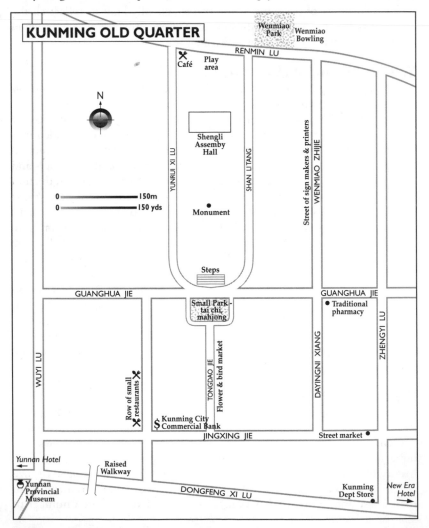

Buddhist paraphernalia for funerals and memorial rites. Look out for a superbly preserved and well-supported **Chinese pharmacy** at the corner of a street to the left of the entrance to the bird market. There is a small park with the mandatory rockery here worth a look. Old folk come here to play mahjong, and go through fitness and tai chi exercises in the morning. The **Market of Flowers and Birds**, as it is called, is a fascinating area of cubicles, shops and narrow stalls selling sundry objects, not just birds and flowers. The lanes are overhung with trees and surrounded on all sides by old wooden houses. This is the place to find bonsai plants, wood carvings, vials of ginseng, marble eggs and vases, jewellery, and jade. Look out for a tiny teahouse patronised by locals who sit out on the terrace in their fading Mao suits, smoking long-stemmed pipes. The market area is a good place to get a cheap breakfast of *baba* (sweet, flour-based pancakes), yoghurt and Yunnan coffee at one of the local cafés or from a stall.

Eastern and Western Pagodas
Vicinity of Jinbi Lu. Open daily 09.00–18.00. Y1.
Strange projections among the jumble of apartment blocks, street stalls and shops of the Jinbi Lu district, the 13-storey Eastern (Dongsi Ta) and Western (Xisi Ta) Pagodas date from the Tang dynasty and are Kunming's oldest surviving buildings. The pagodas receive only a trickle of visitors apart from the regulars who come to meet friends, read, play mahjong at the generously provided marble tables, or sip from the sealed jars of green tea everyone seems to carry.

The pagodas were built by a highly accomplished artisan called Weichi Chingde in the early 9th century. The whitewashed brick columns support four copper roosters on the top. The lovely 40.5m Eastern Pagoda has an impressive set of semi-circular stairs around its base and a stele (inscribed stone monument) describing the history of the two pagodas.

Incantation Pillar
120 Tuodong Lu.
If you can find it, tucked away in the garden of the Cultural Relics Administration building in southeast Kunming, the so-called Incantation Pillar is a curious sight. The 6m-plus pillar, carved with over 260 brilliantly sculpted figures of Buddha, disciples, celestial creatures and a figure of Vaisravana, standing in a complex mix of Brahmi scripts and esoteric iconography, appears to be some kind of cultural digest, a comment on the type of Buddhism practiced in Western Yunnan during the Dali Kingdom Period (937–1253). If you are refused admission to the garden by some obstreperous factotum from the adjoining office, insist on your rights as a visitor, or whatever else you can think of, to see this weirdly opulent sight.

Kunming mosques and Muslim quarter
Funds seem to be less forthcoming for the city's mosques than its temples and pagodas which have benefited from several recent renovations. Kunming's most revered mosque, the 440-year-old Nancheng Ancient Monument, was demolished several years ago. Perhaps they got some funds from a generous

YUNNAN IN PHOTOS

Given the restrictions on freedom of expression in the doctrinaire China that existed until recently, Yunnan has a surprising number of good photographers. The title of Xu Jinyan's first book, *Stories of Yunnan*, is apt for a colour photographer who has spent over 20 years scouring the far corners of the province in search of images that describe daily life but in an unusually arresting manner.

Zhang Tongsheng, a member of the Society of Worldwide Ethnic Chinese Photographers, has had several exhibitions in his homeland and abroad. In his latest book, *The Old Town of Lijiang*, he explores the monochrome possibilities of photography, producing exquisite prints that do justice to the changes of tone and light that characterise the ancient back alleys, Tibetan houses and cobbled-streets of that city.

One of the most gifted photographers is the self-taught Wu Jialin. Wu's work can be compared to the great French masters of surreal and documentary realism such as Cartier-Bresson and Robert Doisneau. A chance meeting in fact, with Marc Riboud, a world renowned French photographer, led to Wu's wider exposure, exhibitions, and the publication of the superb *Mountain Folks in Yunnan: Selected Photographs of Wu Jialin*.

One of the most unusual collections of photos on Yunnan is by a Frenchman who died in 1935. Auguste Francoise came to Yunnan in 1898 as consul general of the colonial French government with the task of

benefactor in the Middle East. The replacement put up in 1997, a spanking new version covered in clinical-looking white tiles and topped with a set of detergent-green domes, is said to house a business convention centre on one of its floors. If you want to see this oddity it is at 51 Zhengyi Lu, just behind the Kunming Department Store.

There is an older, more modest mosque between Chongyun Jie and Huguo Lu, just a few minutes away. The mosque is quite well preserved. Remove your shoes and, if you are modestly dressed, you can enter the prayer hall which, like the mosque itself is a interesting blend of Chinese and Arabian styles. The Islamic quarter here, concentrated into a few back streets that will hopefully survive the city's modernisation push, is one of the best places in Yunnan to eat Muslim halal lamb and beef specialities. The atmospheric old cafés and street-front restaurants – notice the weeds and tufts of grass sprouting between the ancient roof tiles – can hardly have changed since they were first built.

Tanhua Temple and Park

Beyond the railway tracks off Renmin Dong Lu. About 4 km from the city centre.
Time permitting, Tanhua Temple and gardens, located in the east of the city, are worth seeing. Despite lots of renovations over the years the core buildings date back to 1634 when they were first built. The garden at Tanhua Temple

overseeing the construction of a narrow-gauge railway linking the Vietnamese port of Haiphong with Kunming. Francoise brought seven cameras and numerous glass negative plates with him. Before returning to France in 1904 he had taken tens of thousands of photos, very few connected to railway construction. In his extraordinary images a near-feudal China – wealthy women in bound feet, beggars and minority peoples in rags, the heads of criminals displayed in baskets, a governor in his best finery – is captured in a stark and vivid realism. There are insights too. In one image, Yunnanese generals, in an uprising against foreign influence, pose for the photographer. Their archaic suits of armour and knives mottled with traces of red blood, a pouch of arrows looking pitiful against the modern arms and cannon of the foreigners, are eloquent reminders of how emaciated China, the country that invented gun-powder, had become.

Few people knew about this important collection until two men from Kunming, Yin Xiau and Luo Qingchang, travelled to France and met Francois' grandson. Rights to copies of 650 of the originals were bought and an exhibition entitled Echoes from Another Century, toured China in 1999. I saw the exhibition a year later when it was held at the old French Legation building in Kunming. Keep an eye open for it: it is well worth seeing.

Also look out for the monochrome pictures of Bert Krezyk, an American photographer whose pre-war images of Yunnan are on permanent display at the Yunnan Provincial Museum.

was regenerated by a well-known abbot celebrated for his gardening skills called Yingding at the beginning of the 20th century.

The name of the temple comes from 'tanhua', meaning epiphyllum tree, a species of the Yunnan magnolia. Also known as 'Buddha's Flower', the flower, which only opens for a brief spell before withering, is synonymous with the evanescence of life, its transitory state. The tree is also said to bring luck. Look out for a loquat tree in the backyard which is supposed to have been planted by Lan Mao, a famous Ming dynasty doctor and scholar. The gardens also have cypress, azaleas, magnolia and a lotus pond. There are several Chinese rockeries in the park as well. Call me a philistine, but this is one art form that's lost on me. Where the Chinese visitor will see sublime landscapes, visions of triple-tiered, celestial kingdoms, I've never been able to see more than a pile of artlessly glued building rubble.

SIDE TRIPS FROM KUNMING
Lake Dian and Daguan Park
3km southwest of Kunming. Bus No 4 from Yuantong Temple.
Daguan Park is at the northern end of Lake Dian and is a good introduction to this particularly lovely, though now wretchedly polluted, body of water. Countless fishing villages and farms cling to the lake shore, especially the flat eastern side. The southern section of the lake is industrialised and best left

alone. Stretching to a length of 40km, the 340km² lake is the largest in Yunnan. The fishermen here use single-sail, incredibly romantic looking mini-junks called *fanchuan*. Boats used to transport rock from lakeside quarries have three sails. These lateen vessels, with their billowing canvas sails and bamboo masts look like smaller versions of the junks you often see in Hong Kong travel brochures but rarely get an actual glimpse of. Sadly the boats are fast disappearing, but you should still be able to see several on a day trip to the area.

Emperor Kangxi had Daguan Park built in 1690. Ornamental bridges and willow-lined causeways converge on Daguan Pavilion. With its children's playground, plant nursery, rowing boats and pavilions it feels like a pleasure garden or amusement park. Daguan means 'grand view', a promise the 60 hectare grounds keep. A famous poem, by the Qing dynasty scholar Sun Ranweng, is inscribed at the entrance. The couplets, obligingly translated into English, praise the beauty and serenity of the lake and Kunming's victories in battle, but end on a melancholy note, commending the enduring qualities of the lake:

> 'What alone remains through eternity are the twinkling lights of the
> fishermen's boats, the lines of wild geese in the calm autumnal sky, the
> ringing bell of a distant monastery and the frost that stealthily sets upon the
> lake's shore.'

A walk in the Western Hills

The Western Hills, also known as the Green Peacock Mountains, stretch for over 40km along Lake Dian's western shore, offering some of the best scenery in the area. A treasury of temples and historical monuments can be found in the forests and slopes of the Western Hills, and its peaks offer fine views of Lake Dian and the Yunnan plain beyond. You can take a micro-bus from the forecourt of the Yunnan Hotel to reach the hills or hop on bus No 5 outside the Kunming Hotel. You'll have to change at the Liangjia terminus to a No 6 bus to complete the journey to Gao Qiao Station at the base of the range.

From the station walk along the road for 2.5km until you reach **Huating Temple**, Kunming's largest Buddhist complex. Huating dates from the 11th century, but additions and renovations have changed the original structure considerably. The setting in a garden with an ornamental pond and several white stupas is exemplary. Inside the main hall, statues of the Kings of the Four Directions wear armour used by warriors over a millenium ago. The huge Buddha figures in the main temple, gilded and with blue hair, are arresting. The walls at the side are covered with a rich and weird melange of folk characters. The images (one hilariously depicts a holy man with eyebrows drooping to his knees) seem to have been created as a counterpoint to the contemplative and solemn Buddhas. The 500 arhats, or disciples of the Buddha, can be seen at the Bamboo Temple (see box *Li Guangxiu's Outrageous Art*, opposite).

Continue walking along the road outside the temple as it ascends for 2km. When you see another road bearing sharp right, turn, and a few moments later you will reach **Taihua Temple**. The setting, in a deep forest with a garden full of camellias and magnolias, is charming. There are also great views from

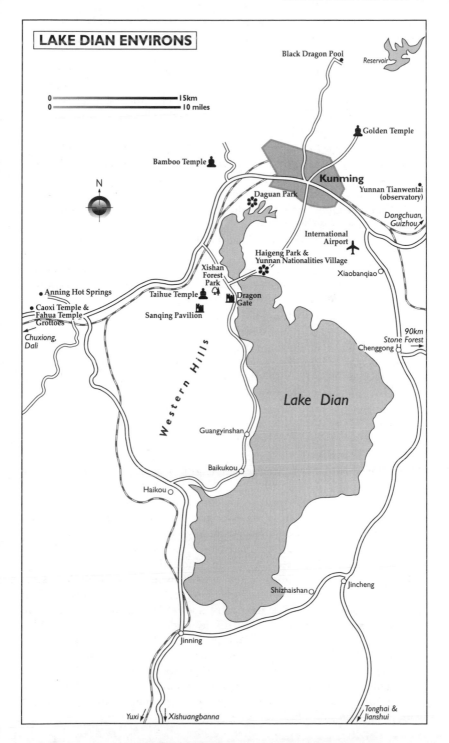

LAKE DIAN ENVIRONS

0 ———————— 15km
0 ———————— 10 miles

N

Black Dragon Pool

Reservoir

Golden Temple

Bamboo Temple

Kunming

Yunnan Tianwentai
(observatory)

Daguan Park

Dongchuan,
Guizhou

International
Airport

Haigeng Park &
Yunnan Nationalities Village

Xiaobanqiao

Anning Hot Springs

Xishan
Forest
Park

Taihue Temple

Dragon
Gate

Caoxi Temple &
Fahua Temple
Grottoes

Sanqing Pavilion

90km
Stone Forest

Chuxiong,
Dali

Chenggong

Lake Dian

W e s t e r n   H i l l s

Guangyinshan

Baikukou

Haikou

Jincheng

Shizhaishan

Jinning

Tonghai &
Jianshui

Yuxi   Xishuangbanna

here over the tree-line across the lake. Taihua is dedicated to the ever-popular Guanyin, Goddess of Mercy, and deliverer of sons to barren parents. The first temple at Taihua was built in 1306.

Roughly halfway between here and the next sight (the **Sanqing Pavilion**, a distance of 2km) you will notice an atmospheric old cemetery, its tombs and grave markers covered in moss and leaf mould. This is the resting place of Nie Er, the talented young musician who composed the Chinese national anthem. Nie Er died at the age of 24 when his boat sank off the coast of Japan in 1936. See Chapter 14, *Nie Er Memorial Resort*, page 266.) The road ends at a flight of steps leading up to Sanqing Pavilion, and what many people regard as the climax of a trip to the Western Hills. The complex of temples, pavilions and halls here stand between Luohan and Guibang mountains, the highest points in the hills. Sanqing dates from the 14th century when it was built as a summer palace to accommodate a Mongol prince. In the 18th century the pavilions were turned into a Taoist shrine. The teahouse here has exceptional views of the area and lake below.

For an even finer view, keep trekking up a stone path from the pavilions until you reach a collection of caves and grottoes called the **Air Corridor**, a shelf chiselled out of the rock face. The end of this extraordinary eyrie enlarges after you pass through a stone gate with the characters *longmen* (dragon gate) inscribed on it. Work on **Dragon Gate** began when a Taoist monk called Wu Laiqing, motivated by sheer devotion, started hacking his way up the cliff in 1781. The work, which involved hanging perilously from ropes while attacking the cliff with hammers and chisels, was completed in 1853. Dragon Gate stands at an altitude of almost 2,500m. The views from the ledge and the rock shrine called the Attainment of Heaven Cave, are superlative.

Bamboo Temple

12km northwest of Kunming. Regular micro-buses from outside the Yunnan Hotel cost around Y10. Temple entrance Y10.

According to legend the temple was founded after two princes were led into the depths of a forest by a magical rhinoceros where, before they vanished into a purple mist, they were vouchsafed the vision of monks holding bamboo staves. A grove of bamboo sprouted where the monks had stood, the site where the brothers dedicated a temple to honour them.

The present temple buildings date from 1280 when Kublai Khan held sway over the area. A stone stele near the temple's main hall is inscribed in Mongolian script. Look inside the main Buddha Hall and you will find three impressive statues: one of the Medicine Buddha, another of Amitabha, Buddha of the Western Paradise and, in the middle, the historical Buddha, Sakyamuni. The temple's pleasant forecourt has several tables where you can sit and enjoy, when there are no tour buses around, the tranquillity of the place. There are two 450-year old cypress trees in the courtyard. The reason most visitors come to the temple is to view its amazing 500 arhat figures, the work of Li Guangxiu, a brilliant sculptor from Sichuan.

LI GUANGXIU'S OUTRAGEOUS ART

Li Guangxiu, the brilliant, mercurial Sichuanese sculptor seems to have upset quite a few well-placed conservatives with the unveiling of his 500 *luohan*, or arhat (disciples of the Buddha) statues at the Bamboo Temple. A traditional folk art rarely found inside a temple, these extraordinary clay figures by the master and five of his student assistants were executed between 1884 and 1890 while Li Guangxiu was directing the restoration of the temple. If he had sculpted entirely from imagination or along the lines envisaged by the abbot who commissioned the work, there would have been no outcry, but many of the life-like figures were modelled after real people.

Li Guangxiu instructed his workers to make the arhats in the upper and lower tiers of the two halls where the figures are displayed, stand. The most arresting figures, the ones on the middle shelf that most transfix the visitor, were probably sculpted by Li Guangxiu himself. Each represents a Buddhist virtue, or failing. The manner of the sculptures, merciless characters, are what makes these realistic fluid figures quite unique. Whether naked or draped in silk brocade, their facial expressions and gestures are what stand out. One figure, a monk, holds a coronet; others clasp pomegranates, lotus stems, or feed greedy eyes on a bruised peach; a man baits a pet monster; another, with hands longer than his body, attempts to reach the moon with the help of a magic instrument. Little wonder that, after Li Guangxiu's surrealistic collection was displayed, the master quickly vanished.

Locals believe that if you start counting your own age from any point along any given row, you will arrive at the arhat which most accurately embodies your character and inner self. You may not like what you find.

Black Dragon Pool

17km northwest of Kunming. Bus No 9 from the north railway station.

A restored Ming dynasty temple is the centrepiece of Black Dragon Pool, a wooded parkland in pleasant but somewhat lacklustre surroundings. It is definitely on the tourist map, its former reputation as one of Yunnan's foremost Taoist centres, preceding it. The views of encircling mountains at least are rewarding.

The name comes from a legend, according to which ten malicious dragons lived in the pool. In the year AD750 (Chinese legends are often historically specific) the scholar Lu Dongbin set out to slay the dragons. After killing nine, one reformed dragon was left in the pool to live a life of greater service to mankind. The temple overlooks the pool and is stacked up on three separate tiers.

The **Kunming Botanical Institute**, just few minutes walk from the temple, is in some ways a more rewarding sight, with over 4,000 species of tropical and sub-tropical plants collected from all over Yunnan growing in its gardens and greenhouses. Highlights are the Yunnan pines, azaleas, camellias and rhododendrons.

The Golden Temple

11km northeast of Kunming. Bus No 10 from north railway station. Y20.

Located in a pine forest at the top of Phoenix Song Mountain, the Taoist Golden Temple stands on a terrace of Dali marble at the end of a flight of stone steps that pass through four Heavenly Gates. The original temple, commissioned in 1604 by the governor of Yunnan to honour the Taoist god Zishi, was transported to Jizushan (Chicken Foot Mountain) in Western Yunnan.

Like its predecessor, the current building, which dates from the Qing dynasty, is actually made of copper, not gold. Standing 6.5m high, the temple weighs over 300 tons. The grounds make a pleasant place for a picnic, but if you don't bring your own food there is a teahouse and noodle shop. Look out for a 600-year old camellia tree which blooms into hundreds of red flowers in February. There is a three-storey tower behind the temple which houses a 14-ton bronze bell made in 1432. When it's rung you can hear the sound all over the mountain.

Horticultural Exposition Garden

Not far from the Golden Temple are the gardens created for Kunming's 1999 World Horticultural Exhibition. Set in 218 hectares, the landscaped gardens are worth a look if you happen to be visiting the temple. There is a Chinese Hall and a greenhouse displaying tropical to cold zone and mountain plants and a Science Hall featuring advanced horticultural technology. The International Hall focuses on horticultural samples from around the world. The Outdoor Exhibition area is also interesting with thousands of varieties of plants, including orchid, herb, bamboo and potted plant gardens. There is also an 'authentic' tea plantation if you don't have a chance to see the real thing in Xishuangbanna or elsewhere.

Yunnan Tianwentai (observatory)

10km east of Kunming.

Impressive views across the Yunnan plain, Lake Dian and the Western Hills can be had from the Yunnan Observatory on Phoenix Hill. The observatory, with a collection of laboratories, a satellite tracking station, and viewing domes with some of the best high-powered optical telescopes in China, is run by the Chinese Academy of Sciences. If you would like to visit the observatory there are guided day-time and night-time planetary viewing tours conducted throughout the year. For more details you might check at the CITS office in Kunming.

TRIPS AROUND LAKE DIAN

Haigeng Park and Yunnan Nationalities Village

10km south of Kunming. Bus No 44 from the street north of Kunming Main Railway Station. Y40 entrance to Nationalities Village.

The name Haigeng is known to Chinese people because of an Olympic stadium and village nearby where athletes come to train. The Yunnan

Nationalities Village has eaten up a large chunk of Haigeng Park but there is still a green, willow-lined esplanade and picnic area beside the lake with good views across the water towards the Western Hills. Its forlorn amusement park gets less visitors these days, its empty roller-skating rink, paddle boats, rusting roller-coaster and boarded-up restaurants mocking its local epithet as the 'Riviera of Kunming'. The beach is still there though, and the grounds are still a good place to retreat from the crowds and find a quiet picnic spot.

The Nationalities Village next door is an attempt to represent the life and micro-cultures of Yunnan's 25 different ethnic groups. Anthropologists and sociologists generally concur that, if you transplant an ethnic person from his or her customary habitat, they will somehow lose their vitality, their zest for life. Members of ethnic minorities working in the sample villages at the park have been dragooned into acting out their ethnicity in a rather listless pageant of dances, musical performances, excerpts from their festivals and displays of craft work. Ostensibly set up as a 'site for the conservation, promotion and dissemination of the traditional cultures and exemplary customs of the ethnic peoples of Yunnan', the site has rapidly degenerated into an amusement park and picnic area for Chinese families and a handful of foreign tourists. The Disneyesque quality of the gardens at the village, understandable perhaps in theme parks which are historical recreations, seems oddly out of place in what is trumpeted as a tribute to real people.

The sensation of being there to ogle at ethnological exhibits is reinforced by the presence of signposts in Chinese and English which appear, in much the same way that botanical plants are labelled, at the entrance to each village. To make matters worse, it is a relatively expensive experience for the visitor. In addition to the main entrance fee, extra levies are charged for playing 'ethnic games', and attending some of the song-and-dance performances.

Some of the groups of young men and women I encountered at the village, a confident, urbanized swagger about them, were a little too worldly to convince of their ethnic origins. It is the women in the end who give the game away. Several, attractively attired, unusually tall and wearing good leather shoes and quality wrist watches, convey the impression that they are taking part in a sequence of costume changes. Their complexions and meticulously applied cosmetics are closer to the faces of Air Yunnan flight attendants than the region's ethnic peasantry. 'Some of them really are from villages in places like Xishuangbanna, but a lot of them are students brought in from the university', a Chinese-American tourist with a sceptical look in his eye informed me: 'They're part-timers!'

If you think you won't have time to visit a real ethnic village, then a day here may be worth the effort.

Xiaobanqiao

12km southeast of Kunming.
Xiaobanqiao's **Sunday market** is a lively country event well worth attending. Peasants from villages in the region descend on this market town to sell their wares and enjoy the bonhomie of the market. Stalls extend along the main street but also along the side lanes and alleys. Besides the usual vegetables and

poultry, there are plenty of local handicrafts to barter for. You can cycle here without much trouble as the way, directly south of Kunming, past the airport on the road to Chenggong, is mostly flat.

A circuit of the lake

The road beyond Xiaobanqiao passes through a belt of orchards along the east coast of the lake where pears, peaches, apples and *baozhuli*, the locally produced pearl pear, are grown. Near the town of Chenggong, there is a fabulous flower market at the village of Dounan well worth visiting any day of the week. The **Dounan flower market** has steadily grown over the years. Today there are over 1,000 stalls supplying private customers and wholesalers in this fragrant village. **Chenggong** itself has been an important market centre for well over 700 years. A Yuan dynasty chronicler mentions the town having 'markets that are crowded with Han and tribal peoples; a place where shells are used as currency'. The old market is still there, as busy as ever.

Continuing some 14km south along the east shore of the lake you will come to the market town of **Jincheng**, a good place to stop for lunch or to relax at one of its teahouses. Jincheng is the departure point for trips to the archeological site of **Shizhaishan**, a hill 5km west of the town. Forty-eight Bronze Age tombs stuffed with treasures were unearthed here in 1955. Passing along the more industrialised southern rim of the lake the next town of note is **Jinning**, birthplace of the 15th-century naval explorer Zheng He (see box in *Chapter 1*, page 8). Also known as the 'eunuch admiral', he was a Muslim. Muslims still live in this area alongside a mixture of Han and ethnic Yi. Zheng He Park on Yueshan Hill has a museum and mausoleum dedicated to He. The first floor of the museum contains rubbings from steles describing He's accomplishments. The more interesting second floor houses some of the goods He traded, such as Ming pottery, on his seven voyages to Africa and southeast Asia.

Following the road north along the lake leads to the unprepossessing town of **Haikou**, an industrial blot on the surrounding landscape. Pass through here and head for **Baikukou**, where there is a health resort in an imposing stone mansion owned by a former mayor of Kunming. Attractive grounds and gardens surround the mansion. Behind the sanatorium there are caves among the eucalyptus and pine woods. If you continue north along the shore you will see a ruined pagoda standing on a promontory above the lake. Behind the pagoda is the small Ming temple of **Guangyinshan**. Dedicated to Guanyin, the Goddess of Mercy, the temple is well tended. Worn stone flags, hanging silk banners, wisps of incense and the sandaled feet of the few monks and nuns that look after the temple are atmospheric. If you walk down to **Guanyin Ta**, the ruined pagoda, there are fine views across the fields of the lake and mountains.

Further afield
Anning Hot Springs
40km southwest of Kunming.
Chinese hot springs are a bit of a shambles when compared to their more graceful counterparts in Japan but if you have never had your skin wrinkled in

this way or been near-parboiled, it is worth giving it a go. The thermals here, located about 8km north of the town of Anning, are situated on the legendary Burma Road, the revitalised transport artery that runs east-west between Kunming and over the border and on to Mandalay.

The waters hit a temperature of 42–45°C. The springs contain a bucolic mix of Magnesium, calcium carbonate and sodium. Their curative powers are said to alleviate arthritis, skin diseases and various gastric disorders.

Caoxi Temple and Fahua Temple Grottoes

2km south of Anning.

If you are in the Anning area you shouldn't miss a chance to visit Caoxi Temple or the nearby Fahua Grottoes. The temple is important because it is the only building in the Kunming region to have survived from the Song dynasty (AD960–1279). There are several Song period wooden statues inside the main hall that miraculously escaped the rampaging of the Red Guards. The central Buddha image, the Sakyamuni Buddha, is the focus of interest during the night of the Mid-Autumn Festival, when a beam of light is said to pierce a small hole in the temple's roof, striking for a moment the statue's forehead and bathing it in an ethereal light.

The Fahua Temple Grottoes, a Song dynasty rock temple, are 5km east of Anning in the rockface behind the village of Xiao Taohua Cun. The carvings in the rock here date from the 13th and 14th centuries. The first set of carvings depict 18 arhats, or holy men, the second scenes from the Jatakka, tales that describe the early life of the Buddha. There is also a large, reclining Buddha, and statues of Guanyin and the bodhisattva Dizang. Very few foreign visitors come here.

The Stone Forest

126km southeast of Kunming. Y33.

Shilin 石林, the so-called Stone Forest, an 80-hectare area of karst limestone pillars, needles and crags, is one of the main sights of Yunnan for Chinese tour groups. An ocean seems to have once existed in the area, probably during the Permian period some 270 million years ago. As the waters withdrew they left a limestone seabed that rose to the surface. Like the weird and wonderful tufa rock formations at Capadoccia in central Analtolia, erosion by wind and rain sculpted the stone into its present petrified forms. From a distance it certainly does look like a petrified forest.

A popular Yunnanese legend has it that a character called Ahei, rescuing his beautiful sister Ashima from the clutches of a wicked magician, fled into the forest for protection. The evil warlock released a flood that flushed Ashima out from the rocks, eternally separating her from Ahei. Her spirit returned to the forest in the form of an echo. There is a formation in the forest said to resemble her. The Chinese, who love to interpret nature in romantic images, have had a field day at Shilin. You will find pinnacles bearing names like the Great Waterfall, Weird Wind Grotto, Phoenix Preening its Wings, and Everlasting Fungus, titles suggested by the shapes of the formations.

The place would be incredible if there weren't so many people clambering along the paths, climbing up and down stone steps to pavilions, or having their photos taken with their guides or against rocks incised in red paint with couplets, famous sayings and flourishes of calligraphy. Spotlessly turned-out guides, mostly young women from the local Sani minority, lead large tour groups around the maze of rocks, obstructing the pathways that wind through the densest parts.

It is easy enough though, to escape from the main area into open farmland where the formations are smaller but just as interesting, the setting more natural. Several gravel paths spiral out from a pedestrian road that circles the park. The northern section of the forest abuts a large lake with a small Sani settlement called Wushu Cun, meaning 'Five Tree Village'. It's a bit commercialised, but a step removed from the rampant tourism of the forest proper. Continue south of here and you'll find less spoilt villages.

A word of warning though: it can be very difficult to find your way out of the Stone Forest. The complex maze of narrow paths and stairways can defeat even the keenest sense of direction and many travellers have been known to emerge fairly exhausted after a couple of hours of wandering around its labyrinthine interior. If you have any doubts about your ability to negotiate this maze then you should consider hiring one of the local Sani guides to show you around.

Although you can easily cover Shilin in a day trip it is more interesting to stay overnight, wander the blissfully empty forest in the moonlight, and explore other options in the area the next day. There is an even larger stone forest called the **Fungi Forest** 12km northeast of Shilin well worth exploring. **Dadieshui Waterfall**, Yunnan's largest waterfall, **Moon Lake** and a number of fascinating grottoes are only 15km away. If you decide to stay overnight you can attend one of the Sani dance and music performances put on by hotels in the area. These cultural digests are surprisingly lively and usually get the thumbs up from travellers expecting the worst.

A new introduction to Shilin is the high-tech sound and light show which starts around 21.00 each evening at the outdoor stage in front of the Lotus Pond. The legend of Ashima is told by characters projected on to a giant water screen with a sophisticated laser-show accompaniment. This new addition completes the picture of commercialisation at Shilin, but nonetheless it is suprisingly good, even if all the dialogue is in Chinese. Entrance to the show is Y70.

The highlight of the Sani year, if you are lucky enough to be around at the time, is their **Torch Festival**, which takes place in late July or early August with displays of wrestling, music, horse-racing and bullfighting. The climax is a magical torch-lit parade through the Stone Forest to the accompaniment of lutes and elephant drums.

Getting there
The best way to reach the Stone Forest is on the fast new express train that leaves from the South railway station on Beijing Lu each morning. The platform for the Shilin train is on the left-hand side of the main terminal building where you will find a separate ticket counter, underneath a green sign board.

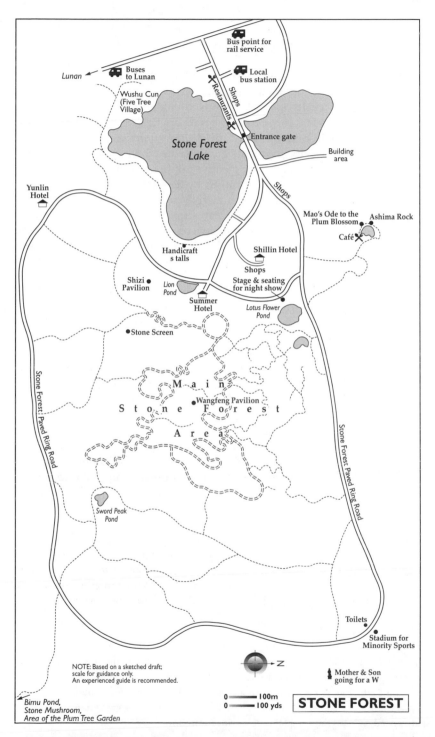

Lunan

Buses to Lunan

Bus point for rail service

Local bus station

Wushu Cun (Five Tree Village)

Restaurants

Shops

Entrance gate

Stone Forest Lake

Building area

Shops

Yunlin Hotel

Mao's Ode to the Plum Blossom

Ashima Rock

Café

Handicrafts talls

Shillin Hotel

Shops

Shizi Pavilion

Lion Pond

Stage & seating for night show

Summer Hotel

Lotus Flower Pond

Stone Screen

M a i n

S t o n e   F o r e s t

Wangfeng Pavilion

A r e a

Stone Forest Paved Ring Road

Stone Forest Paved Ring Road

Sword Peak Pond

Toilets

Stadium for Minority Sports

NOTE: Based on a sketched draft;
scale for guidance only.
An experienced guide is recommended.

N

Mother & Son going for a W

0 ▬▬▬ 100m
0 ▬▬▬ 100 yds

STONE FOREST

Bimu Pond,
Stone Mushroom,
Area of the Plum Tree Garden

Tickets cost Y55 and the comfortable new train, No 201, departs at 08.28, arriving into the Shilin station at 09.55. From here you board a bus for the short ten-minute journey into Shilin itself where you are dropped off close to the entrance to the Stone Forest. If you buy your entrance ticket for the Stone Forest on the train then it includes the price of this bus ride as well. The return train departs at 15.54 from the Shilin railway station, arriving in Kunming at 17.21. The views from the train are excellent, as it passes lakes, mountains and stony outcrops which mark the beginning of the Stone Forest region. The only real drawback to the train is the ethnically attired attendant who sings with a microphone for the first half hour of the journey.

Alternatively there are tours organised by the Camellia Hotel. You'll have to endure a mandatory stop-off at a marble emporium and souvenir outlet but it is far better than the major cave-exploring, shopping distractions factored into the standard tours organised by other travel agencies in Kunming. The trip by minibus should take about three hours all told and costs Y40. Direct buses also leave from the long-distance bus station at 07.30 and 08.40, and cost Y18.50.

There is also the option of hiring your own private car and driver, offered by CITS Kunming for Y350 for the day. Certainly if you wanted to explore some of the other Stone Forests in the region or attractions en route then this could be worthwhile.

Buses from Kunming pull up near the entrance to the forest where there are several stalls selling pretty ordinary-looking Sani handicrafts. The food stalls are more interesting with charcoal-grilled and clay-baked duck, pigeon, pheasants, noodles and baked breads on offer. Getting back to Kunming is simple. Buses wait near the entrance and, when they are full up, leave. The last bus departs between 14.30 and 15.00.

The Stone Forest can easily be incorporated as part of an onward journey or circuit to other towns and attractions that lie south of Kunming, such as Jianshui and Tonghai. There are regular mini-buses from Shilin to Lunan, from where you can catch an onward connection. Buses for Kaiyuan can be picked up from the main highway just before the town of Lunan. If you walk up the highway on-ramp and stay on the right-hand side of the road, there are fairly regular minibuses which can be flagged down. The fare to Kaiyuan is Y20 and the journey takes only around two-and-a-half hours on a surprisingly good highway. Once you reach Kaiyuan there is the option to continue on by bus to the railhead at Geiju or transfer by taxi (Y3) to the other bus station for the journey to Jianshui, which takes around two hours and costs Y11.50.

Where to stay and eat

Stone Forest Hotel Located off the entrance road, close to the lake; tel: (0871) 771 1405; fax: (0871) 771 1414. Although there is not a great deal to differentiate between the hotels on offer at the Stone Forest, this is definitely the smarter of the three options as the rooms and service are superior and the surrounding grounds more attractive. There are two restaurants here but the opening times are erratic. Rooms are priced at Y250 for a single/double with bathroom.

Summer Hotel Located close to the lake and Stone Forest Hotel; tel: (0871)771 1088. Reasonable rooms but the building itself is characterless with nothing to recommend it. A single/double with bathroom costs Y300.

Yunlin Hotel Located further along the Stone Forest ringroad; tel: (0871) 771 1410; fax: (0871) 771 1409. Situated in a quieter part of the Stone Forest away from the hustle and noise of the main entrance area and therefore a little more atmospheric than its neighbours. The hotel is listed as a three-star and has facilities which include a swimming pool, but it has seen better days and the rooms and décor are shabby. There are actually two buildings which constitute the Yunlin; the newer building is further away from the direction of the Stone Forest entrance and is a better choice. A single/double with bathroom costs Y250.

Eating can be a bit of a problem if you stay on at the Stone Forest; in the evenings the hotel restaurants seem to be closed unless there are large tour parties staying. There are some small restaurants on the road leading to the main entrance but the selection is limited and menus are printed in Chinese only. It is worth checking around the various hotel restaurants if the one you are staying in happens to be closed, but even if you are lucky enough to find somewhere open don't have high expectations of the food.

Lunan 路南

10km from Shilin.

Lunan is a market town not far from the Stone Forest well known for its excellent Wednesday and Saturday **markets**. Colourful Sani women in minority dress plus a host of tractors, mules and bicycles converge on the town to buy and trade. Coming out of the Stone Forest if you proceed to the top of the main street and turn left you will find mini-buses that take you into Lunan for Y2. Alternatively you could jump on a motorbike taxi for the 15 minute ride to town. They leave from the souvenir stall area in front of the entrance to the forest and shouldn't cost more than about Y10.

Luxi 泸西

80km from Shilin.

Although only a little over 200km from Kunming, few travellers seem to make it to Luxi. This under-populated county spreads across a highland plateau of mixed topography: part plain, mountain, ravine and hills. Its mountains, extensions of the Wumeng Range, are rich in coal, as well as zinc, manganese, iron and cobalt. Timber products and rare medicinal herbs are also prized. Tobacco is an important cash crop in this well-endowed region, but it is Luxi's red peppers, hanging to dry from walls, roof eaves and bamboo frames, that you are most likely to notice. Many of its inhabitants are minority peoples, the Zhuang, Hui, Yi, Dai and Miao forming the largest groups.

There are few tourist sights to see in the town itself, but several excursion points in the suburbs or a few kilometres beyond. At **Shidong**, to the west of Luxi, are a number of excavated Han dynasty tombs. Several items, including spearheads, bronze axes, and picks have also been found. The well-known

Hexagonal Pavilion on Xiushan Hill in the northeast of town, is close enough to justify a look. Built during the Ming dynasty, the 25m-high pavilion is built of wood and is situated in a pleasant wooded part of the hill.

Luxi County's best known attraction is the **Alu Caves**, named after a local tribe that once inhabited the area. Less than 3km from the city, the caves are divided into four sections: the Biyu, Yuzhu and Luyuan Caves, and the subterranean Yusun Stream. They run for 3km through tunnels and grottoes of karst limestone. The Chinese have christened each formation with a fanciful title. You may have trouble recognising which rock shape is the 'three elephants racing across a plain', 'the old tortoise peering up at the moon', or the enigmatic 'King of Wei reviewing his soldiers'!

There is only one bus a day to Luxi from Kunming's main bus station, departing at 14.00, but there are a number of minibuses leaving from the railway station and eastern bus station. If you are staying overnight at the Stone Forest you can easily catch a bus for Luxi from the small bus station off the main entrance road to the forest. Or alternatively proceed to Lunan and catch one from there.

Qujing 曲靖
157km northeast of Kunming.
One of the most important industrial and market cities in eastern Yunnan, Qujing is a convenient stop for travellers heading for the border with Guizhou and on to Guiyang or Guilin. Sizable numbers of Yi, Hui and Miao live in the vicinity of the city which occupies a broad plain sitting at an altitude of 1,880m. The city has been a crossroads for over 2,000 years. It was also a key stop on the Imperial Post Route. A 20km section, the famous Five-chi (*chi* is a measurement equal to about 33cm) Post Route, one of China's oldest surviving roads, can still be seen between Yanfang and Songlin, about 30km north of Qujing. Later on, Qujing became an important station along the Southwest Silk Road.

Douge Pavilion, a late Ming construction located near the city's East Gate, is an interesting sight as it is made almost entirely of compacted clay and timber. The imposing structure is 13m high. Qujing has a number of pleasant parks. The most accessible is **Unicorn Park**, in the centre of town. **Forest Park**, is on Liaokuo Mountain at the western edge of the city. This is where the founder of the Ming dynasty, the emperor Zhu Yuanzhang, rounded up the last of the Yuan forces.

Some 47km north of Qujing is the much visited source of the Xi Jiang, better known as the Pearl River. The spring seeps from a crack in the eastern face of the Maxiong Mountains where a holiday resort has been built.

There are several buses every hour to Qujing from Kunming's main bus station, the first leaving at 06.50. The road is good so it doesn't usually take more than four hours. If you prefer trains, this is a chance to use the Kunming-Guiyang line which stops at Qujing. The first train, No 212, departs at 09.58.

Kunming to Xiaguan

'It was a sunny day. The villages through which we passed were of mud and mud-brick. Gone was the drab concrete of Kunming. The hills had bamboo groves, and crops of rice, maize and tobacco.'

A Traveller in China, Christina Dodwell.

The 390km stretch of the Burma Road that runs from Kunming to Xiaguan, before swerving west and heading for the border, is seldom explored by foreigners disinclined to get off buses bound for the rumoured delights of Dali and Lijiang. If you have the time however, there are several spots to recommend themselves on or close to this route that include lively market towns, important Neolithic sites, Taoist and Confucian temples and, at the extraordinary Yuanmou Earth Forest, a stranger and far less visited sight than even Kunming's Stone Forest.

The journey from Kunming to Xiaguan is beautifully scenic as the highway twists and turns its way through numerous hills and steep river valleys. The views are at times reminiscent of a painting with idyllic-looking traditional villages tucked away among green hills surrounded by bamboo groves and terraced fields. If you have just arrived in the province then this journey is well worth undertaking for an unforgettable first look at the Yunnanese countryside.

Nature notes

The climate of this region is of the northern, sub-tropical monsoon type, meaning that it embraces cold, temperate and warm-to-humid climates, having dry winters and wet summers.

Chuxiong County has a great variety of flora, its warm valleys and vegetation belts supporting moist, evergreen broad-leaf forests. Common tree varieties are yew, gingko, red camphor Yunnan pine, walnut and mulberry. Edible fungi are common in the mountainous regions and, among the blooms and flowering shrubs of this area are honeysuckle, magnolia, camellia, azalea, and various types of hibiscus. There are said to be over 500 species of medicinal plants.

Forests account for slightly over 30% of the land mass of this area, the cover and protection it affords helping to support tufted and river deer, golden cats, the rare red pheasant, grey lear monkeys, muntjacs, bears and pangolins. Claims that there are still tigers and leopards in the region are difficult to substantiate.

CHUXIONG 楚雄

185km west of Kunming.

Chuxiong, the administrative capital of the Yi minority, is the main stop on the Kunming to Xiaguan road. Inhabited since the time of the Zhou dynasty, Chuxiong is also known as Lucheng, or the Deer City, a name which may have come from the Yi language. A Yi legend tells how a deer descended from heaven and, running around the periphery of what would become the original enclosed city, outlined the boundaries of Lucheng.

Topographically the city resembles a climatic slide-rule or spirit-level, high in the northwest, inclining to the southeast. Locals quip that 'four seasons co-exist in one city'. The city also has large numbers of Hui and Bai. The Yi celebrate their version of the Torch Festival on the 24th day of the sixth lunar month with a colourful fair, night markets and performances of songs and dance.

Getting there

Being on the Kunming to Xiaguan route, Chuxiong is served by dozens of buses throughout the day. A stream of them depart from Kunming's main bus station from 07.00 onwards. The journey from Kunming to Chuxiong takes approximately three hours by bus. With the exception of the express buses, which bypass Chuxiong, any Dali-bound bus should drop you there. The Kunming–Xiaguan rail line also stops at Chuxiong; the journey takes approximately four hours but at the time of writing the only service was an overnight train departing Kunming at 22.10 and arriving inconveniently in the early hours, but this situation could soon change.

The area code for Chuxiong is 0878.

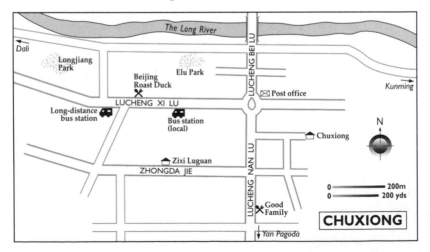

What to see

Chuxiong is known to the Chinese because of its high-quality **silver jewellery** which can be viewed in its markets. The town has a number of good parks displaying some of the region's flora. Live performances of Yi music and dance sometimes take place at **Longjiang Park** in the northern part of this fairly small city. **Elu Park** is Chuxiong's second largest green space. Built at the top of a mountain in the western section of town, this has the best views of the surrounding countryside. The park is well known for its camellias, attracting thousands of admirers from all over the country. The Ming dynasty **Yan Pagoda** lies a little south of town. After collapsing during the Qing dynasty, the seven-tiered brick building was rebuilt in 1710. It was completely renovated in 1982.

Side trips from Chuxiong
Wanjiaba and Lufeng excavations

Just south of the town of Chuxiong, an important collection of bronze drums was found in the southern suburbs of Wanjiaba. The drums, the oldest to be discovered in Asia, are now in the Yunnan Provincial Museum (see *Bronze Drum Culture*, page 92). Although there isn't that much to see you can still visit the site.

About 80km east of Chuxiong, closer in fact to Kunming, are the excavations at Lufeng, an important archeological site. Bone shards from two dinosaurs, fragments of fossils and other valuable finds have been unearthed here and the consensus is that more remains.

Zixi Mountain
20km west of Chuxiong.

This was the mountain peak, as every Yunnanese schoolboy and girl will tell you, where Gao Liangcheng, a Prime Minister serving the Dali Kingdom, retired after a successful life of officialdom. The tireless Gao devoted himself to overseeing the building of some 100 Buddhist temples, monasteries and nunneries over the 12km-long range.

Only **Ziding Temple** remains. The slopes of the range are a pleasant place to wander, covered in tall trees. Apart from the solitary temple, the range is known for a famous 600-year old camellia tree that has a 2.76m girth. There are also said to be two flocks of wild peacocks strutting around the range.

Dayao
100km northwest of Chuxiong.

The main reason for visiting Dayao is to view its **White Pagoda**, a rarity among Tang dynasty design. The weirdly shaped structure's other name is the 'Inverted Bell Stick Pagoda', an apt description.

The 18m-high, solid brick structure has an octagonal platform, a central octagonal pillar, and is topped with the so-called inverted bell shape. A large crack in the upper level was caused by three strong earthquakes that have hit the pagoda and its foundations on Baita Mountain.

Thirty minutes' drive west of the White Pagoda, is a Confucian temple at **Shiyang**. Its bronze statue of the sage is said to be the oldest of its kind in China.

Yuanmou Earth Forest
100km north of Chuxiong.
Some visitors who make it to the Yuanmou Earth Forest, which extends through the villages of Huxi and Banguo, are more impressed with this natural wonder than Kunming's much lauded Stone Forest. There are certainly far less tourists here, although that may just be a question of time. The most concentrated area of clay and sand forms that make up the weird and wonderful earth forest, covers roughly 50km^2.

The cathedral-like pillars and spires that line the banks of the Dongsha River create a strange impression as they change colour throughout the day according to the prevailing light, like a miniature Grand Canyon or Colorado River Valley. The Chinese have given these striated formations suitably odd names like 'shooting asparagus', 'exposed barricades', and 'warriors in helmets'. If you have a chance, this is a must.

The forest lies to the west of the main road, but there is no public transport there. You can either hop off the Xiaguan-bound bus and hitch a lift, or arrange your own private transport.

XIAGUAN 下关
Unless you take the new highway that runs to Dali, the road from Chuxiong to Xiaguan is mountainous until it reaches the wide Changyun Plain. There is an old World War II airstrip here, the remnant of a strategically important supply route in the struggle against the Japanese invaders. More mountains rise from the plain before you cross into the Dali Bai Autonomous Region, roughly 400km west of Kunming.

Xiaguan is an important transportation hub, sitting at the junction of the vital east–west Burma Road route and roads to Dali, Lijiang and further north. Xiaguan is also called Dali Shi (Dali City), as it is the capital of the Dali Prefecture. This gives rise to much confusion among foreigners who think they have already arrived in Dali. Dali, in fact, is another 15km on. The city is situated at the southern end of Erhai Lake. Although there is not much to delay you in Xiaguan itself, there are one or two sights worth seeking out if you happen to find yourself in limbo there, or staying overnight on the way to or from Kunming or elsewhere.

Getting there and away
Xiaguan has its own airport, often referred to as Dali airport, which serves both Xiaguan and passengers bound for Dali. It is a handy addition to the infrastructure of the area with daily flights to and from Kunming. The one-way fare is Y320 and can be booked through any CITS branch or other travel agency. The flight time from Kunming to Xiaguan is just 30 minutes. Flights leave from Kunming airport at 07.40 and 08.10 and from Xiaguan to Kunming at 08.40 and 09.10.

THE YUNNAN-BURMA HIGHWAY
Marco Polo knew the route as the Southern Silk Road, a trading corridor that extended from the markets of the Han empire as far as Rome. Known in a later age as the Tribute Road, after China annexed large areas of eastern Burma in the 17th century, the highway was abandoned during the Qing dynasty period as the country tried to isolate and immunise itself against outside influences.

A vital east–west route from China was not to exist until the national crisis of the 1930s. On the basis that a transport route could be established in the same way as the Southern Silk Road had been 2,000 years before, the Chinese government, driven from their power bases by invading Japanese forces, turned towards British India for help in building a new supply route. Three hundred thousand labourers and coolies equipped in most cases with only the most primitive of tools, slaved in inhospitable, sub-tropical conditions to complete the 1,100km road, to connect it in the east with an existing link between Xiaguan and Kunming, and to the west with the British railhead at Lashio in Burma. For a time, the legendary Burma Road was China's only means of contact with the Allied Forces. With the fall of Lashio to the Japanese however, the road fell into disuse.

In the new mercantile China, fresh uses have been found for the road which now stretches for 910km between Kunming and the frontier crossing into Burma at Wading. Known as the Yunnan–Burma Highway, China's hungry entrepreneurs are making sure that the road stays open this time.

There is a limited number of destinations covered by Xiaguan airport and at present the only other flight within Yunnan is to Jinhong in Xishuangbanna. The Jinhong flight takes 70 minutes and operates on Tuesday, Thursday and Sunday. The airport is located 15km from Xiaguan and there is an airport bus that takes you into town for Y10 or alternatively the local No 7 bus. Taxis are also available. If you are heading to Dali from the airport expect to pay about Y50 for the 40-minute taxi ride or catch the No 7 bus into town and then change to a No 4 bus.

Other routes are likely to be added, so check out any new itineraries. I flew from Jinghong to Xiaguan on my way to Dali, which was a tremendous time-saving compared with the bus.

There is the option of an overnight sleeper train, No 262 from Kunming to Xiaguan (and vice versa), that takes approximately ten and a half hours and departs from Kunming at 10.10 every evening. A berth in a comfortable soft sleeper compartment costs Y150 or it costs Y90 if you want to brave the hard seat carriage. The railway station is located at the eastern end of Xiaguan on Dian Yuan Lu, the No 1 bus will take you from the station into the centre of town. In Kunming the train leaves from the northern terminus on Beijing Lu.

Tickets for the train and plane can be purchased from CITS or the Camellia travel agency in Kunming and Xiaguan and any one of the many ticket agencies in Dali.

Xiaguan's two bus stations are on the same street, and quite close to each other. The main bus station is the one closest to the Dali Hotel. Most people just transit in Xiaguan. All Dali-bound or exiting buses will stop here, even those using the new super highway. The two depots serve a wide range of places in Yunnan between them and it is worth checking at both to see which has the best departure time to suit your destination. From here you can catch buses to Lijiang (three hours express), Baoshan (six hours), Zhongdian (ten hours), Mangshi (12 hours), Ruili (15 hours) and Jinhong (32 hours). To catch a bus to Dali exit on to the main street and the local No 4 bus will take you there in 30 minutes. There are frequent buses throughout the day to Kunming with various classes of vehicles on offer, ranging from the comfortable new air-conditioned Volvo coaches, which have videos and free water on board, to decrepit East European-made sleeper buses which have an abysmal record of breakdowns en route and should be avoided. Prices range from Y60 for a normal bus, which can take from eight to ten hours to Y110 for one of the luxury express coaches can do the route in five hours.

The area code for Xiaguan is 0872

Where to stay in Xiaguan

Jingpeng Hotel Near the main bus depot; tel: 217 4933. Typical of the new, slightly ostentatious Western-style hotels that have sprung up in town. Luxury doubles with air-conditioning, satellite TV and phones quite reasonably priced for Y200.

Keyan Hotel Next to the bus station; tel: 212 5286. A good choice of rooms, all reasonably priced and clean. Y100 for singles and doubles, beds in triples or quads for Y20–50.

Manwan Hotel Canglang St, a couple of minutes walk from the train station; tel: 218 8188; fax: 2181739. The Manwan is billed as the only four-star hotel in Xiaguan; the rooms, however, are nothing special but adequate enough. Facilities include restaurants, shops and a bowling alley. Prices for a single/double are Y320.

Xiaguan Hotel Opposite the bus station; tel: 212 5579. Good value with clean, spacious rooms: doubles for Y200.

Apart from the bus stations, most of the half-acceptable eateries are in the hotels. Xiaguan has a reputation for being the worst place – perhaps because it is a truck stop for most people – to eat in Yunnan.

What to see

Though largely a commercial and industrial centre, Xiaguan is not without the odd beauty spot. **Erhai Park** is its best known attraction, a spacious place with good views of **Erhai Lake** and the possibility of boats and excursions from its pier.

A park called the Ten Thousand War Victims Pit, is located at **Tianbao Park** near the Black Dragon Bridge. The pit holds the remains of soldiers who were killed in battles aimed at bringing the Nanzhao Kingdom to its knees. The park is situated on a hill with good views of the city.

Snake Bone Pagoda
3km north of Xiaguan on the road to Dali.
The Snake Bone Pagoda is part of the Baoling Temple, situated in Yangping Village. The temple was built to house a statue of a local who, according to legend, saved Erhai Lake and the locality from the tyranny of a demon-king, one of the many who seem to have terrorised the ancient Chinese mind. The story relates how the man tied sharp knives to his body and then plunged into the lake, allowing himself to be eaten, the sacrifice also destroying the demon.

Any bus bound for Dali will drop you there, and the temple is walking distance to the west of the road.

Xiaguan Hot Spring
Southwestern suburbs of Xiaguan.
If you have a spare hour or two, a walk or motor-tricycle trip to this mini hot spring resort is a pleasant way to pass the time. Bathtubs have been placed under small waterfalls to increase the pleasure and ease out the aches and pains of those, mostly locals, who use the thermals.

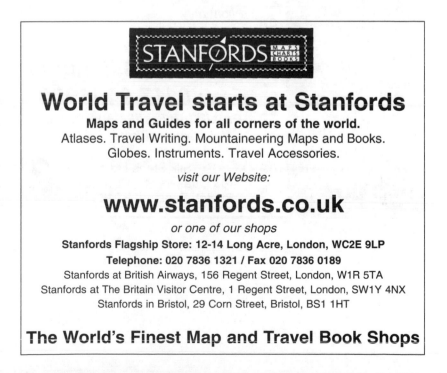

118

Dali 大理 and Erhai Lake

'...before I got to Xiaguan I had never seen an electric light. An old women asked, "Is there a god in Heaven to control the electricity, like the Fire God and the Water God?"'

Mr China's Son: A Villager's Life, He Liyi.

Despite Dali's growing fame and its popularity among independent travellers, the city still has a rural feel to it. Cafés along Huguo Lu may be wired up with email services but ask if you can use the toilet and you will be politely given directions to the nearest public WC. It's easy to see how a town with internet facilities but restricted plumbing has become so popular with shoestring travellers and among the older 'backpackers with credit cards', how the ancient city has become both cultural resort and convalescence. Nestled beside the blue waters of Erhai Lake, along a green valley that shadows a range of marble mountains, Dali offers travellers some of the most comfortable and convivial guesthouses in China, excellent food and an extraordinary choice of travellers' cafés where notes can be compared, anecdotes swapped, warnings issued. Ultimately, Dali's appeal (the same might be said for the whole of Yunnan) lies in its ability to vitalise the battered traveller. After a cup of Snow Tea and a session with a local masseur you will feel suitably relaxed to explore Dali's excellent cafés and local cuisine. April to June is an excellent season for visiting Dali, with sunny days and slightly cool evenings. The summer proper is also good with clear days and a high sun count. Autumn is crystal clear during the day but the nights can be cold. A fairly high altitude means snowfall in winter and occasional transport problems.

HISTORY AND ORIENTATION

Dali is the homeland of the Bai, one of the largest and most prosperous minority nationalities in Yunnan. Dali was once the independent capital of the powerful 8th-century Nanzhao kingdom. While the Tang dynasty ruled in China, the armies of Nanzhao, with the aid of strong Yunnanese horses, expanded their independent kingdom into parts of present-day Burma, Thailand and Laos. Horses are still traded in Dali. The kingdom came to a bloody end in AD902 when the heir to the throne and all the key members of the royal family were murdered by the chief minister, plunging the realm into decades of chaos. A coup organised by an official in AD937 heralded three centuries of relative stability as Nanzhao became the Kingdom of Dai. The kingdom's prosperity continued until 1253 when Kublai Khan's armies conquered the region and Dali became a remote but important outpost in the Mongol's vast military empire.

Capital of the Dali Bai Autonymous Prefecture, the name Dali refers to both the newer, administrative city of which Xiaguan is a part, and the old granite stone town called Dali Old City. The old city runs between the two recently restored north and south city gates, but can also be measured by glancing at two sets of pagodas which act as distance posts: Yita Si in the south and the magnificent Dali San Ta (Three Pagodas) complex to the north. The town forms a neat grid of streets between the lakeshore and the main road that runs north-south along the foothills of the Cangshan mountain range. The main east–west, north–south roads are the mostly traffic-free Huguo Lu, (referred to by locals as the 'foreigner's street') and Fuxing Lu. Souvenir shops and travel agencies along Huguo Lu usually have a good selection of maps of the town and Erhai Lake. Some cafés also stock maps and books on the area.

GETTING THERE AND AWAY

The competition between bus companies to get customers for the Kunming to Dali run is fierce. There are many daily buses from Kunming, starting from the long-distance bus station as early as 07.00. There are also plenty of night sleepers. The journey takes about nine hours, but may be subject to delays and breakdowns. A special, luxury, air-conditioned bus leaves Dali once a day in the morning and does the journey in five hours using the new Kunming to Dali Highway. There are two buses: the 09.30 deluxe super express is a Daewoo bus, the 10.30 a Volvo. Both are non-smoking which is a nice change, and cost Y100 and Y110 respectively. Despite what the travel agents tell you about this bus being non-stop, it does in fact make a 30-minute stop in Xiaguan and another at a service area with a restaurant and souvenir shops. There are also more express buses that depart from Xiaguan throughout the day. If your bus from Kunming terminates at Xiaguan then you can catch the local No 4 bus to Dali from outside the bus station for Y1.5. Most buses go via Xiaguan, pulling into the main long-distance station near the Dali Hotel. Some buses also terminate outside the Cangshan Hotel. The No 4 bus stop is located near here. Buses depart from here throughout the day for Dali.

When it comes to moving on from Dali there are excellent travel options to all parts of the province including far away destinations like Jinghong in Xishuangbanna and Ruili on the wild frontier with Burma. There are daily flights each morning from Xiaguan to Kunming with Yunnan Airlines; these take 30 minutes and can be booked for Y320 through CITS or other ticket agencies. Flights also operate to Kunming in the evenings on some days, but check with a local agent for up to date timings as this is not as reliable as the morning service. There are also three flights a week operated by Yunnan Airlines between Xiaguan and Jinhong on Monday, Tuesday and Thursday. The flight takes 50 minutes and costs approximately Y680. This is one of the most time-saving flights you can take if you intend to incorporate a visit to Xishuangbanna as part of your travel plans. It is best to look around and compare prices as they vary considerably. You can get tickets at the standard price at the Dali passenger service ticket office along Boai Lu.

There are daily Air Yunnan and Air China flights to the airport at Xiaguan where you can then catch a taxi or bus. The journey takes about 40 minutes. Taxis are much easier. They charge Y50–70 for the ride. The new express train between Kunming and Xiaguan is another option. The line suffered some serious damage in 1999 due to flooding which looks as if it might be an annual problem during the rainy summer months.

GETTING AROUND DALI

Dali, with its old stone streets, ox-blood coloured shop and tea houses, museum gardens and street markets, is made for exploring on foot. Bicycle rentals are cheap. Ask around the guesthouses where they usually charge about Y8 for the day for a Chinese model, a bit more for mountain bikes. Buses also run up and down the lakeside taking visitors to the Monday market at Shaping and villages inhabited by the local Bai minority. Fishing and cruise boats ply the lake offering endless possibilities for independent travel. Horse-carts around the lake or to specific villages are another option.

PRACTICAL INFORMATION
Post and telecommunications

The post office is a large building on the corner of Huguo Lu and Fuxing Lu. The office is efficiently run and most of the staff speak English. This is the best place to make international calls. You pay a deposit, the call is made from a private cabin, and then the difference is handed back to you. There is no service charge as the calls go direct.

The area code for Dali is 0872.

Email/internet services

MCA Internet Coffee Huguo Lu; email: sales@yunnanhotels.com. Run by the same people who have the MCA Guesthouse. Reasonable rates. Recommended.
Yunnan Café Huguo Lu; email: lxf@public.km.yn.cn. Has email/internet service on the second floor. Helpful service.
Mr China's Son email: dalihely@public.km.yn.cn. Email service located in the café. The email service is free for customers.

Money matters

You may be approached by the odd money changer on the street but it is wiser to exchange foreign currencies at the Bank of China just up from the post office along Fuxing Lu. There is a second branch on the other side of the road. The bank is open for exchange from Monday to Friday. The Industrial &

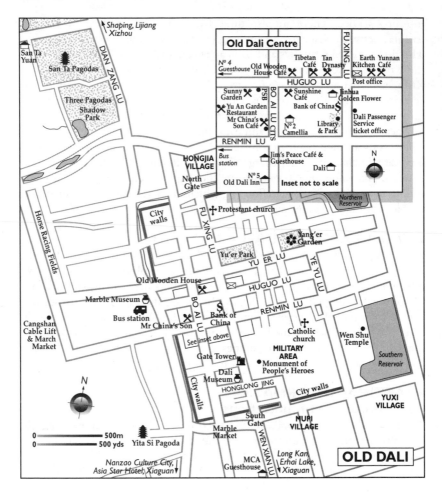

Commercial Bank on Huguo Lu can also change money and travellers' cheques. This bank has the advantage of being open until 21.00.

PSB office

As one of Yunnan's major travel centres, visitors may wish to get their visas extended here before venturing off into the wilds of the west near Burma or the Tibetan northwest. The people at the office along Huguo Lu are friendly enough and can usually issue you with a first extension without much fuss.

Nature notes

Dali's splendid topography, situated between deep blue Erhai Lake, the monasteries and hermitages of Cangshan (Azure Mountains) range, and the upper reaches of the Mekong River, has been a subject for Chinese poets for centuries. The lake has always been central to the Bai people's way of life. The ear-shaped lake (er means ear in Chinese) extends to 41km in length, its width varying between 3km and 9km. Part of the Mekong River drainage system, the lake is fed by the Xier River whose waters are swollen by the melted snow and glaciers of Tibet.

Erhai is the seventh largest freshwater lake in China. Deep and well stocked with fish, the lake is seen as a symbol of providence by the Bai people of Dali. The lake contains over 40 different kinds of fish. These include some unusual species like the so-called 'bow fish' a variety of edible carp that places its tail in its mouth, then releases it to shoot into the air. Fishermen at the lakeside village of Haiyin specialise in night fishing for the mysteriously named 'green fish' which can reach a weight of 40kg. Unfortunately, the presence of the schistosomiasis (bilharzia) parasite makes the water unsafe for swimming.

The Cangshan range stands behind Dali like a marble screen. The range consists of 19 granite peaks, some of which are over 4,000m high. Eighteen mountain streams rush down the sides of the range, irrigating fields and

THE BAI

The majority of the 1,340,000 Bais inhabit Dali Bai Autonomous Prefecture, with a scattering found in Lijiang, Lanping, Yuanjiang and Kunming. There are also Bai communities in parts of Sichuan and Guizhou provinces. The name *Bai* means 'white', a colour they identify with nobility.

The Bai are among some of southwest China's most advanced agronomists. Bai ancestors lived around the Erhai Lake area 4,000 years ago, cultivating rice and other crops. The Bai began to experiment in dairy production during the Ming period, mostly dairy cow husbandry. Milk and curd became the mainstay of the Bai income during the Jiaqing and Qing eras. After the founding by Bai aristocrats of the Nanzhao kingdom, the cultivation of rice was extended, and wheat, millet, and broomcorn production increased. It was at this time that the Bai developed the Cangshan water conservation project, bringing fresh water to thousands of hectares of arable land. The hard working Bai access the lake freely, using nets to catch fresh water fish, conch, shrimps, edible weeds and water chestnuts.

The most economically successful of all Yunnan's minority nationalities, the Bai have a long history and advanced culture. Known for their fine wood carving, marble and stone work, the Bai, relatives of the Tibeto-Burmese Yi, have been literate in Chinese for far longer than most of the province's other ethnic groups. Belonging to the Sino-Tibetan language group, they have no written script. Several Bai tracts and theses penned in Chinese, particularly on the subjects of astronomy and medicine, are regarded as classics. Bai opera, known as *chuichui*, combines narrative signing with folk music and dance. Although predominantly Buddhist, the Bai's syncretic tendencies have supported a polytheism that even includes elements of Catholicism.

replenishing the lake. Cangshan supports a highly varied range of vegetation. Over 3,000 species of plants thrive here. Most are shrubs, grasses and evergreen coniferous trees. There are valleys and highland plateaus up on the range where cattle graze. The area blooms with native rhododendrons, yellow alpine azaleas and gentian flowers. The green of the grasslands pastures, pine and fir forests, and moss is refreshing. Black-necked cranes, Chinese copper pheasants and the rare blue-tailed salamanders, also make this their home. There are vultures and snakes up on the range as well.

Dali was known for its trade in winter opium until the 1930s when the government banned the practice. Don't be surprised if you are approached on the streets by local Bai women selling *ganja*. Dali is only a few kilometres from the Burma Road, Yunnan's main east–west route, a notorious smuggling corridor that runs directly into the Golden Triangle. These days the lake valley is sown with rice, beans and wheat in the summer and autumn, and yellow rape seed between.

WHERE TO STAY

Unlike other parts of Yunnan, Dali has been on the independent traveller route for several years, which explains why there are so many good guesthouses and inns, but relatively few conventional hotels. Backpackers on really slim budgets and shrinking waistlines have always found Dali the perfect place to recuperate after long-haul travel through less visitor-friendly parts of China. The guesthouses are numbered, but also have names. There are usually touts working for the various establishments waiting to intercept travellers as they get off the buses.

Asian Star Hotel Dian Zang Lu in the southwest suburb of the city; tel: 267 0009. This massive new four-star addition to Dali stands out a mile, particularly at night when it is lit up like a Las Vegas casino. The hotel offers the only luxury lodgings in the city, with an enormous, impressive lobby that seems quite out of place with its surroundings. The hotel has 310 good-quality, tastefully furnished rooms, with good views either over Erhai lake or the Cangshan mountains to its rear. The usual facilities of a four-star hotel are on offer, with both a Chinese and Western-style restaurant, a business centre and a health club. The centre of Dali is a 15-minute walk away, as a result of which the hotel feels a little isolated from the action and atmosphere of the city. A single/double room costs Y560 including breakfast.

Dali Hotel Fuxing Lu; tel:267 0386. The hotel has seen better days but the rooms are quiet, spacious, and clean. All have attached bathrooms. A good deal for couples. Has large stone courtyard. Double rooms are graded into Y110, Y200, and Y240 depending on size and condition.

Jim's Guesthouse 57 Boai Lu; tel: 267 1822; fax: 267 0188; email: jimguesthouse@hotmail.com. A small, well-managed place, that also has a café serving good Tibetan and Bai dishes. Jim (real name Jin Che) is also a reliable tour manager. Bed in triple Y10, large and medium sized doubles with bathrooms Y80.

Jinhua Hotel Fuxing Lu; tel: 267 3343; fax: 267 3846. Also known as the Golden Flower Hotel, the Jinhua is a bit of an anomaly in otherwise quite tasteful Dali. Its state mausoleum appearance, with everyone dressed in minority costumes, is distinctly unsettling. It has to be said, though, that its 58 standard double rooms and four luxury suites are exceptionally clean and comfortable. Prices start at Y260.

MCA Guesthouse Just outside the south gate on Wan Xian Lu; tel: 267 3666. A long-established backpacker favourite and the only place with a swimming pool in Dali. Its common area and bar make this a good choice for socialising, but the rooms are nothing special. Bike rental, book rental and email service are available here. Dorm beds start from Y10 and doubles with bathroom from Y100.

Old Dali Inn (Guesthouse No 5) 51 Boai Lu; tel: 267 0382; fax: 267 5360. This inn is one of the most popular in town, partly because of its excellent service, and friendly and willing staff, but also because of its very reasonable rates and choice of rooms. Bai-style brick cottages, the most expensive options, are ranged around a courtyard with a central gazebo hung with flowers and potted plants. It has a nice restaurant and breakfast room. The downside of the inn is the endless background of soft-rock tapes and the disco party they throw every Saturday night. The cottages are great value though the plastic rococo mirrors, frilly duvets and flowery headboards make the rooms feel like Cinderella's crypt. Only the cottages have private bathrooms. Other guests use public showers. Hot water is always available. Dorm rooms (four beds) Y15, single room Y30, double room cottages Y50.

Red Camellia Hotel (No 2 Guesthouse) 32 Huguo Lu, also with an entrance on Bo Ai Lu; tel: 267 0406; fax: 267 0309. The first hotel in Dali to accept foriegners, the Red Camellia is showing its age and is badly in need of a facelift. Its central location is now its sole chief advantage. Dorms beds are available from Y12 and double rooms are Y200.

Santa Yuan Hotel Behind the three pagodas, about 1km from the north end of town; tel: 267 5962; fax: 267 6520. A reasonable three-star hotel, in a modern building with courtyards built in a traditional style. The rooms are the usual three-star standard – fairly basic but clean and adequate. The hotel restaurant serves both Western and Chinese food and the service is friendly. The views over the mountains and pagodas next door are excellent but the distance from town is its main drawback. There is, however, a hotel shuttle bus which operates fairly frequently to compensate for this. A single/double room costs Y290.

Yuan Garden Hotel (No 4 Guesthouse) 4 Huguo Lu; tel: 267 2093. At the top, quiet end of Huguo Lu, a green and leafy place with a nice courtyard, pools, a raised, terrace restaurant and some sophisticated touches like pavilions and an art gallery. Has a good travel service office. The laundry service is free. 24-hour hot water. 5–6 bed dorms Y10, 3-4 bed dorms Y15, singles Y30, doubles Y50, standard Y100.

WHERE TO EAT

Dali is by far one of the easiest places in Yunnan to have a good meal. Restaurateurs and café owners seem to know what travellers are looking for and have developed nice menus that combine local treats with familiar dishes. Cafes often go out of their way to create a relaxing and attractive ambiance, taking some care with decor, reading materials, music and homely furniture. The food is generally tasty, cheap and inventive. Several travellers have left behind their own recipes and preferences are often reflected on the menus.

The majority of cafés are concentrated along the upper part of Huguo Lu and along Boai Lu, but there are several other streets, many of them with modest, often grubby-looking local eateries that can produce surprisingly good food and friendly service at short notice. Note that descriptions can be deceptive. An English breakfast may turn out to be an omelette served with fried vegetables, a side dish of apple and papaya, and a glass of fresh guava juice. Cafés try hard to please and get your return custom in what is probably an over-subscribed sector, but don't always get it right. Many of the cafés also double as local travel agencies, offering one-day sightseeing tours, special excursions by boat, hiking, horse riding and the like. Options are often written on the menus. They can be a cheap and time-saving way to get around.

Dali Old Wooden House Café Huguo Lu. A popular restaurant with an extensive menu. Can be difficult getting served in the mornings when there are hiking groups at the tables. Highly regarded menu includes such local specialties as Yunnan ham with fried broccoli, Erhai Lake fish in casserole, wood-ear salad and the enigmatic 'fried three things'. The Ancient Music Teahouse, a stone courtyard with a covered stage where you can sit and sip tea or attend classical concerts in the evening, is attached to the café.

Earth Kitchen Huguo Lu. A family-run restaurant that has nice veggy soups and brown breads with walnuts and sunflower seeds. Despite the name it's not a vegetarian restaurant. Has a sixties, 'purple trail to Asia' atmosphere. Mongolian beef with ginger and onions, or chicken with lychee, washed down with 'earth sunshine tea' recommended. The café sells batiks and delicate, hand-made cards.

Happy Café Boai Lu. A Nippon backpacker hang-out recommended in all the Japanese guidebooks. Japanese and Western dishes.

Jim's Peace Café 57 Bo Ai Lu. Having been one of the original Dali cafés to open back in 1985 the Peace Café has become something of a legend and Jim remains as friendly and interesting a host as you could hope to meet. His famous 'No 1 whisky', made from local herbs and roots with supposedly medicinal properties and a superb mellow taste, is a good enough reason alone to spend time here. Combine that with a laid-back atmosphere, good music, food, excellent tours and information and it is easy to see why it is still a perennial favourite on the Dali scene.

Lucy Café Huguo Lu. A newish café run by a friendly family. Chinese and Western meat and fish dishes. Serves Bai 'Three Courses Tea' set. You can drink refreshing, potable water from the family's spring in the back garden here where most of the cooking goes on.

Mekong River Culture & Art Centre 7000 Wen Xian Rd. This interesting new addition to Dali could be well worth checking out if you plan to spend some time here. The building itself is constructed in a traditional style, with an attractive Chinese garden adorned by rock sculptures. The cultural centre offers short and long courses in a variety of Chinese traditions; classical and modern art, calligraphy, Chinese language, music and Tai Chi. Their speciality is the cultures of the Mekong River. The café, restaurant and bar also prepares good Chinese, Bai and Western dishes.

Mr China's Son Boai Lu. Billed as a 'Cultural Exchange Café' this extraordinary place is run by the writer He Liyi whose books, translated into English, are available over the counter here. Lots of information printed up on local sights, dos and don'ts of Dali, and other resources. Has email/internet service. Good food and a chance to meet other travellers as well as chat with Mr Liyi and his son whose English is impeccable. Mr Liyi was the first Bai in recorded history to go abroad and his life story is a remarkable one that reflects the turmoil and changing fortunes of the country at large. It is well worth buying a copy of his book *Mr China's Son* for an unrivalled account of how the momentous events and policies of the last 30 years in China translated at a local level in Yunnan. Mr Liyi has permission to reproduce some of his books in Yunnan and usually writes a generous personal introduction to each copy.

Oriental Café Off Huguo Lu. A newish venture in a small cul-de-sac opposite the Dong-ba Gallery, specialising in minority dishes from all over Yunnan. A good chance to sample dishes from places you will not have time to visit. The Dali spring rolls, and bamboo chicken and fish items are especially good.

Sisters' Café Boai Lu. This café has an extensive, 22-page menu that includes Western, Chinese, Japanese and local food. The best local dishes may be the oiled lake fish in casserole, and fried spring shrimp with Dragonwell Tea. Has a fine tea listing, with the local 'Three Courses Tea' on it. The maize, papaya and wheat wines are also worth indulging in.

Sunshine Café Huguo Lu. A comfortable place to pass the time over a meal or writing postcards at the table under the skylight. Friendly staff, a good collection of teas, Tibetan and local dishes. Has a small garden at the back.

Tibetan Café Huguo Lu. One of the oldest restaurants along the Huguo Lu strip, this has a good all-round selection with good vegetarian choices. Don't expect authentic Tibetan dishes and beverages here, though the *tsampa* and yak butter tea breakfast is close. The 'Tibetan cocktail' concoctions, with names like 'Mysterious Tibet' and 'Tibetan Pastoral Song', are pure inventions. The peanut vegetable soup is delicious and the Tibetan Café ranks as one of the best places to try some traditional Bai dishes.

Tan Dynasty Huguo Lu. A small but elegant place with inside/outside tables. Strong on meat dishes. Look out for the spicy Sichuanese chicken and pineapple sweet pork dishes. Its Dali favourites are the stone hotpot fish and tofu treats, and the deep-fried Bai cheese. Also Chinese and Western dishes. A couple of street tables with fresh flower arrangements are pleasant for mid-morning coffee.

Yunnan Café Bottom end of Huguo Lu. Everyone has a favourite café in Dali. Discerning travellers often elect the Yunnan Café as a place to relax in civilised surroundings that include what is unquestionably the best selection of new, secondhand and library exchange books in Yunnan (including many hard-to-find titles on Yunnan subjects), an upstairs sun-deck, email and internet facilities, and a well-stocked bar. Dali-born Helen Wang and her partner speak disarmingly fluent English, provide excellent company and can advise on local sights. Western and indigenous food is served along with a selection of vegetarian dishes. Hearty muesli, fruit and yoghurt breakfasts, with honey-tea or well brewed Yunnan coffee is recommended as a good way to start the day.

FESTIVALS
Most festivals in the Dali and Erhai Lake area, including Xiaguan, are held by agreement between February and October. Besides the Chaohua Festival

DALI'S THIRD MOON FAIR

However secular or earthy they may seem to the traveller, Yunnan's festivals, celebrations and fairs usually have a religious origin. According to legend, Guanyin, the Goddess of Mercy, is said to have paid a visit to the Kingdom of Nanzhao and preached in the Bai language. Sanyue Jie, the Bai people's great Third Month fair, an annual five-day event which takes place on a piece of open ground near Dali's west gate during the third lunar month (April or early May), began over a thousand years ago as a gathering of monks, holy men and Buddhist disciples who met annually to offer prayers, fast and instruct the lay people. As the event became an established annual festival and spiritual workshop, a flourishing trade sprung up to serve the needs of devotees.

Today, because of a scarcity of accommodation, an encampment of tents and trading booths appears each spring like a bivouacking Mongolian army with dancing, singing and wrestling entertaining the thousands of visitors who attend the fair. Mountain tribes and merchants from all over China descend on the Dali Plain for five days of glorious commerce. Livestock and tea are important commodities at the fair. Yunnanese horses, still highly regarded, are also traded at the fair. Bare-back races, designed to show their speed and strength, take place each day.

For the Chinese, the most important aspect of the fair is the lucrative trade in rare herbs and medicines collected by Tibetans from isolated mountains along the Yunnan borders.

(The **Pilgrimage to Flowers Festival**) in the middle of the second lunar month, an event in which the flower growing and loving people of Dali bedeck houses and streets with potted plants and flowers, there are three main events that most attract visitors. The first is the **Third Moon Fair**, a spring festival that attracts some of the largest crowds of any festival in Yunnan.

The Raosanling, or **Three Temples Festival**, is a movable event usually held in late May. Participants tour three important temples in the region on foot, starting with a procession from the town's South Gate, and proceeding to the foot of Mount Wutai, home to Shengyuan Temple. Celebrants stay up late, walking the next morning to Jingui Temple on the lake. The third day takes them to Majiuyi Temple and back to Dali. The whole proceeding, with music, dance, feasting and the imbibing of more than a little local wine, is more merry than devout, although prayers are offered along the way.

July's **Torch Festival** is a mostly nocturnal event but no less colourful than the above festivals. Burning torches are carried through villages and fields, dragon boat races and fireworks displays held. Some of the Dali cafés organise tours to lakeside villages that are known to be especially jubilant in the celebration of the torch festival. The **Mr China's Son Café** organises a more refined party, hosted by the venerable Mr He Liyi.

Besides the larger festivals there are numerous small festivals held in Dali on a regular basis and if you happen upon one of these local affairs they can be extremely lively. For instance, every neighbourhood temple has its own feast day and these celebrations can attract a crowd of thousands of Bai people, who joyfully and noisily mark the day with firecrackers, singing and offerings. Foreigners are generally made to feel very welcome at these gatherings and they provide an excellent insight into the richness and exuberance of the Bai culture.

TRADITIONAL MASSAGE

Chinese masseurs have been perfecting their techniques for centuries. Traditionally many were blind people who roamed the streets playing a flute to announce their arrival. Dali is a good place to experience a traditional Chinese massage. The **Yueda Health Care Traditional Massage Service Centre** on Boai Lu is recommended. Some of the masseurs there are mute. They will show you a list of categories to choose from. The fees are graded according to the part of the body and time involved. An 'acupoints and head' massage will cost Y15 and last 10 minutes, a full, one-hour body massage will come to Y70. They use pleasant-smelling ointments and unctions.

Dr Mu Qingyun, a Naxi therapist who has a clinic above the Yunnan Café, is a highly recommended specialist. His techniques are based on traditional methods of applying energy to specific nerve meridians, blood vessels and clusters of muscle. A whole body massage costs Y60.

A caveat: unlike Thai or herbal massage, Chinese methods are very strenuous, involving extensive mauling, rubbing and scouring of the skin which can feel quite painful at times especially if you have even a touch of sunburn.

WHAT TO SEE
Dali Museum
Fuxing Lu. Near the South Gate. Open Tue–Sun 09.00–17.00. Y4.
The Dali Museum, though small, is well worth a look. The building itself is of historical interest as it is the remains of the general headquarters of Du Wen Xiu one of the leaders of the Muslim uprising of 1856. Du Wen Xiu was known locally as the 'Generalissimo' and his headquarters as the 'Forbidden City'. The main drawback to the museum is that exhibits are not labelled in English, but an explanatory leaflet can be picked up from the entrance booth for Y3 that details the main pieces.

On the ground floor you can find Neolithic axe heads and potsherds, ancient farming implements and bronze swords from the Han dynasty period (207BC–AD220), among a slew of other objects that include cowrie shells and a stone Buddha from the 10th century. There are a number of interesting Buddhist statues and other pieces that date from the era of the Nanzhao kingdom, which was based in Dali. The giant bronze bell which hangs outside in a pavilion, close to the forest of Steles, came from the bell tower of Dali and produces amazing reverberations that last for several minutes when struck.

The upstairs section of the museum contains wooden sculptures of bodhisattvas, cremation jars, seals, bronze mirrors, ritual objects and tomb figurines, quite a mixture all told. Be sure to visit the calm and quiet courtyard at the back of the museum where there are some valuable Yuan and Ming period steles. The gardens here are planted with bougainvillea and lantana. The small pavilions are a pleasant place to sit or read.

North and South Gates
Fuxing Lu. Y4 to climb gates.
The pedestrian, shop-lined processional of Fuxing Lu is dignified by two impressive gates at its northern and southern ends, remnants of the four original gates that guarded the city in the late 14th century. The gates are in remarkably good shape after some recent renovation work and sections of the original battlements can also be seen.

You can climb to the upper levels and sign the visitor's books. There are good views from the temples at the top and you can sometimes hear local ensembles using the rooms or shaded areas under the roof eaves for practicing traditional music. The other traditional structure in the middle of Fuxing Lu, close to the museum, is the old Drum Tower that signalled the close of the city gates each evening.

Ecclesia Catholica
6 Xin Min Lu.
Dali's Catholic church, tucked down a side street that runs down to the lake, is an extraordinary, whimsical mixture of Tang dynasty tiled roofs, wooden transoms, and painted gables, surmounted by a whacking great cross, an attempt at winning over a reluctant flock perhaps.

The church was built in 1938. The interior is high kitsch with a marble altar, tacky posters and figures of the baby Jesus floating from the rafters in the form of cardboard mobiles. The ceiling is surprisingly beautiful, stars and suns against an eggshell-blue firmament. The air is damp inside, but there does seem to be a small congregation of sorts. How the place survived being dynamited during the Cultural Revolution is a mystery. The kind people who look after the place are happy to fetch the key and open the church for you. There is a red cross donation box behind the pews which you might like to drop something into.

The history of Protestantism in Dali goes back to the early 1880s when a number of missionaries came here as preachers. Among their more useful good works was a hospital run by American and British doctors. A Protestant Church can be found at 576 Fuxing Lu. It is a bit plain after the Ecclesia Catholica. The structure is not the original 1913 one, but the bell comes from the first building. A small gathering of people collect here every Sunday morning to keep the faith.

Dali marble factory
Dali marble is so highly regarded throughout China that the word for marble in Chinese is *dalishi* – Dali stone. Dali's marble factory, located near

the South Gate, is the best known of over 30 such places in China. Great gouges in the Cangshan range testify to over 1,200 years of quarrying in the area. Many visitors mistake all the dust that lies across some of the mountains for snow.

The factory is open for tours, an option that may be more interesting than buying a marble souvenir yourself. Many of the ancestors of the men at the factory were also marble workers. If you want to see some more natural masterpieces, the **Wang Yongling Marble Museum** near the entrance to Dali March Fair Market, has a vast collection of marble art.

Huge amounts of marble are exported from Dali to places like Hong Kong and Japan. If you wish to buy a marble object, the street markets and shops in Dali are full of them. Most foreigners refrain but there are some nice pieces if you look carefully: fine-grained slices of stone that resemble mountain scenes and waterfalls, and marble eggs that make good paperweights. Just outside and to the right of the South Gate there is also now a small market that specialises in marble products.

Nanzhao cultural city
Open daily 09.00–18.00. Y60.
This fairly recent addition to Dali is located five minutes' walk beyond the South Gate in the direction of the Asian Star Hotel. The Nanzhao cultural city is a recreation of the arts and culture of the Dali-based Nanzhao kingdom. The building's architecture is supposed to resemble a rather grandiose Bai residence from the Tang Dynasty. Inside are numerous wax statues of Nanzhao kings, generals and courtiers and a recreation of an old Nanzhao street during the March Fair.

A Nanzhao music and dancing palace puts on displays of traditional song and dance while serving Bai-style food and the three-course tea ceremony. Better than many of the contrived ethnic experiences in China, it makes for a pleasant enough afternoon for anyone with a genuine interest in the Nanzhao era but it's hard to overcome the artificial feel of such places.

BEYOND THE CITY LIMITS
Zhonghe Temple
Directly southwest of Dali on Cangshan range. Y2.
You can reach Zhonghe Temple on foot in about one hour, following paths and other trekkers up the mountainside behind Dali. The views of Dali and the Erhai Lake as you wend your up through eucalyptus and cedar woods and past ancestral tombs, are outstanding.

There are no signposts to direct you up the hill but basically, if you keep going from the small bridge on the road, a little north of town, and follow virtually any of the paths that wind upwards, you will get there eventually. As you pass by the cemeteries you might see the 4m-high **Shizu Stele**, an inscribed tablet placed here in 1304 to commemorate Kublai Khan's conquest of Yunnan. At the temple you can enjoy noodles or a pot of tea at one of the cafés there which offer more stupendous views. The last time I visited they were just about to open a hotel

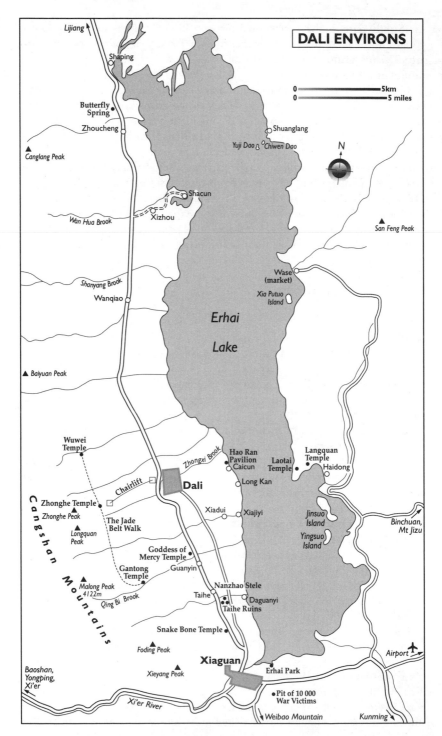

DALI ENVIRONS

0 ————— 5km
0 ————— 5 miles

N

Lijiang

Shaping

Butterfly
Spring

Zhoucheng

Canglang Peak

Shuanglang

Yuji Dao Chiwen Dao

Shacun

San Feng Peak

Wan Hua Brook

Xizhou

Shanyang Brook

Wanqiao

Wase
(market)

Xia Putuo
Island

Erhai

Lake

Baiyuan Peak

Wuwei
Temple

Zhongxi Brook

Hao Ran
Pavilion

Caicun

Laotai
Temple

Langquan
Temple

Haidong

Chairlift

Dali

Zhonghe Temple

Long Kan

Zhonghe Peak

The Jade
Belt Walk

Xiadui

Xiajiyi

C a n g s h a n

Longquan
Peak

Jinsuo
Island

Binchuan,
Mt Jizu

Goddess of
Mercy Temple

Guanyin

Yingsuo
Island

Gantong
Temple

M o u n t a i n s

Malong Peak
4122m

Qing Bi Brook

Nanzhao Stele

Taihe

Daguanyi

Taihe Ruins

Snake Bone Temple

Foding Peak

Xiaguan

Xieyang Peak

Airport

Baoshan,
Yongping,
Xi'er

Erhai Park

Pit of 10 000
War Victims

Xi'er River

Weibao Mountain

Kunming

next to the temple. Details of room rates were not available, but it might be worth checking. The views from the rooms were superb.

The Zhonghe Temple was built in the Ming Dynasty but nothing now remains of the earlier buildings. The temple was also once honoured by being made the subject of an epigraph by the Qing Emperor Kangxi, who wrote, 'Yunnan cloud flies over its roof.' Zhonghe Temple observes both Buddhist and Taoist rituals, which can be evidenced in its various halls.

The Jade Belt walk

The Jade Belt refers to the band of cloud that sits below the summits of the Cangshan mountain range for much of the year, particularly in the late summer and autumn. This band of cloud, also known locally as the 'Waiting for husband cloud', sits motionless and looks like a belt around the middle of the mountain. The cloud can stretch for 10km and last for several days. There is a spectacular walk, known as the Jade Belt walk, which follows this same line around the mountain and runs from the Wu Wei temple in the north to the Zhonghe Temple in the south, a total of some 9km. The easiest way to access the walk is by taking the cable car up from the area of the March fair market; the cable car costs Y35 return. The trail between the two temples offers spectacular and far-reaching views over Lake Erhai and its environs. The trail itself is clearly marked and winds through forested areas and open expanses. It does have some fairly exposed sections, some of which are guarded by fencing on the outside but could still pose a problem for anyone who suffers from vertigo. It is an outstanding walk and well worth the effort if you have a couple of days in Dali. Some of the cafés in Dali also offer organised hiking tours around the mountains with guides and packhorses.

Guanyin Tang Temple
5km south of Dali.
A small temple at the foot of Mount Foding, the Goddess of Mercy Temple is dedicated, like so many others in Yunnan, to Guanyin, otherwise known as Avalokitesvara. Legend has it that when a Han army attacked Dali, Guanyin turned herself into an old lady and carried a huge stone with a single straw rope to block their advance. When the soldiers saw an old woman with such power they became afraid of what the men of the area must be like and withdrew. Later a temple was built on the stone and dedicated to Guanyin. Every 19th day of the third, sixth and ninth lunar months Avalokitesvara Day is observed here and large crowds of locals descend upon the temple for lively celebrations.

The temple has a rather gaudy new entrance gate, but within the grounds themselves are some fine examples of wood and stone carving. The legendary stone can be seen lying under a small temple in the middle of a bridged pond.

Gantong Si Temple
6km south of Dali.
This temple can be reached by taking a path that winds uphill from the back of Guanyin Tang Temple. Much depleted in size it once boasted three sub-

temples. It was a popular retirement spot for government officials who joined the temples as monks. It's still the largest religious building up on the Cangshan range and worth the hike.

San Ta (Three Pagodas)
2km northwest of Dali. Y10.
San Ta, or the Three Pagodas, is one of the most imposing sights in the Dali area. Standing between the backdrop of Cangshan mountains and the lake, the pagodas are an impressive sight at any time, their pale stone towers reflecting minute changes in the light over the lake like weather vanes. As this is one of Dali's major attractions, it's best to get there early before the tour buses arrive. Expect to find dozens of souvenir shops and stalls as well. Fortunately, most of these are confined to the lower levels beneath the steps that lead to the pagodas themselves.

The tallest pagoda of the three, called **Qianxunta**, has 16 tiers. It was constructed in AD850 and reaches a height of almost 70m. The smaller, ten-tiered pagodas behind reach heights of 42m and were built in the 11th century. While Qianxunta was being renovated in 1979 a trove of over 400 objects, including gold and silver ornaments, sutras, scrolls, unguents and copper mirrors were found in the roof of the pagoda. This priceless find is on display at a small museum just behind the pagodas.

Apart from serving as reliquaries for precious objects, the bones and ashes of saints and important religious icons, pagodas were also symbolic barriers against natural disasters like floods and earthquakes. Four Chinese characters are incised onto a marble inscription in front of the Qianxunta pagoda – *yong zhen shan chuan*, meaning: 'Subdue for all time the mountains and the rivers.'

You can walk to San Ta or hop on any of the northbound buses that go along the main road.

Nanzhao Stele
Above the main road, halfway between Dali and Xiaguan.
This historically important stone tablet records the political system and economic management that existed under the Nanzhao Kingdom, and has given historians valuable information on the demographic patterns of the area at the time. It also records in some detail Nanzhao's often turbulent relations with the Tang dynasty. The 3m-high stele is dated AD766 and stands in a pavilion picturesquely situated between the Foding and Shengying mountain peaks. A Qing dynasty scholar rediscovered and copied the inscriptions on the stele just in the nick of time. Since then locals, in the belief that the stele has curative properties, have been in the habit of chipping bits off the tablet, grinding them down and mixing the powder into their medicines.

The stele stands on the site of Nanzhao's first capital, Taihe. You can see overgrown stumps on the nearby hills which are the remains of the city wall. A grassy declivity heading north from here is the ghostly outline of the old Nanzhao highway.

Xizhou 喜洲

20km north of Dali. 3km east of the main north–south road.
You can either walk to Xizhou village from the main road or hop on a motorbike taxi, a good option on a hot day as there is almost no tree cover along the road. Alternatively some of the cafés and the CITS in Dali can arrange a visit here or you may wish to arrange a deal with a taxi.

Xizhou's fortunes were originally made in the tea trade. Wealthy tea merchants built their residences and pleasure gardens here during the Ming period. A few of these mansions still remain though they are in a fairly dilapidated condition. Today, Xizhou is better known for its craftsmen and carpenters who make the distinctive carved doors, shutters and decorative panels that grace modern homes built in the traditional style. Xizhou has a lively shopping street with a market feel to it. If you follow one of the side roads that slip down to the lake, you can visit the tiny, sheltered port of Haishe, a quaint collection of wharves wooden jetties, old boats and unspoiled inlets.

Zhoucheng 周城 and Butterfly Spring

Zhoucheng: on the main road 30km north of Dali. Butterfly Spring: 35km north of Dali.
Like Xizhou, the prosperous village of Zhoucheng, comfortably nestled between the highway and Yulong Peak, has some fine examples of local Bai architecture. New houses continue to be built in the traditional style, the carpentry and masonry exemplary.

With the exception of a few Naxi and Dai families, the village is almost entirely Bai. The people of Zhoucheng are known for their diversity and adaptability. Over the years they have turned their talents to producing noodles, toys, tie-dye cloth, sweets and copper goods, as well as farming. Zhoucheng's main square is always an interesting place to sit and watch the life of the village. There are two large fig trees there which afford shade and mark the spot where a small market is set up each day.

A trip to Zhoucheng and the market at Shaping can also include a visit to the nearby, much-overrated Butterfly Spring. Known to most Chinese because of a love story of the same name made in the 1950s, Butterfly Spring is the focus for the story of two lovers who, escaping from the intolerant, Confucian society that condemned such relationships, came to the spring and committed double suicide by drowning themselves. Their spirits, embodied as a pair of butterflies, reappear each spring.

Tens of thousands of butterflies used to swarm around the spring at this time until agricultural policies dictated the use of pesticides in the late 1950s. The spring, a sparkling pool of clear water that bubbles up in the middle of a sylvan grove, might be a pleasant spot if it weren't for the hordes of tourists and the snapping stall holders that work in the overcrowded market beside the spring.

Shaping 沙坪

37km north of Dali.
The large **open-air market** at Shaping takes place every Monday and is well worth attending. You will get a taste of the market on the 30-minute bus ride

BAI RESIDENCES

When a design is as well-tried and tested as the design of traditional Bai houses, there is not much room for improvement. The majority of homes built in and around Erhai Lake are still constructed according to traditional designs, using age-old materials, and are made to face an easterly or westerly direction as they always have been.

A typical Bai house consists of the main residence, a smaller side house, and an elegant and homely courtyard, enclosed by a so-called 'shadow wall'. The beams of these spacious, two-storey homes are made of wood. Walls made from mud mixed with chaff support tiled roofs with finials, making them resemble temples. Walls are whitewashed or covered in peach-, rust- or magnolia-coloured plaster which may be decorated with pictures and calligraphy. Private gates, graceful structures like Ming temples or miniature watch-towers, add power and a sense of privacy to the complex.

A grand ceremony is held on the day the first beam is put in place. After the sacrifice of a sheep and pigs, relatives and friends are invited to a sumptuous 'Eight Owls Banquet'. Pieces of red cloth – red is an auspicious colour – are given as presents and hung from the beam, and fire-crackers are let off.

The feature that catches the eye of most foreign visitors are the courtyards. Planted with dwarf trees, shrubs and flowers like citron and camellia, and paved with stone or pebble-mosaics, the Bai spend much of their time in these green and cool enclosures.

from Dali which will be full of women taking their produce there. The main part of the market is located in what looks like a former marble quarry.

The market sells a wide range of fruit, vegetables, spices, condiments, seeds, tobacco and bundles of dried noodles; it also has textiles, tie-dye cloth, hemp rope, minority clothes, long-stemmed pipes, a whole woven basket section, and sundry other goods for sale. Watch out for women who have stalls along the road offering you bits of fake Ming pottery. The bumpy glaze, biscuit-like firing and rather deliberate chips and gouges give the game away. If you can't be bothered to walk up to the main road for the bus to Shaping, several Dali cafés organise tours to the market that also include Butterfly Spring and other tourist spots.

The lake and western shore

It takes about 45 minutes to reach the lake shore on foot from the town centre. Bicycles do it in ten minutes. There are several ways to explore the lake. Ferries and private boats cross Erhai from several points. Ferries start to leave early and continue until gone 16.00. The routes between Longkan and Haidong, Xiaguan and Jinsuo Island, and Caicun and Wase are some of the most common. Caicun is the nearest village to Dali with regular ferry services. There are many private boat owners around the lake. Café owners usually know someone with a boat who you can negotiate a price with. The café will probably take a small percentage but then you do get their services as tour arrangers and interpreters. They can tailor special tours like cormorant fishing which takes place at certain points on the lake and is fascinating to watch. If you are hiring a bike, no-one usually objects to you putting it on board. Another alternative is to take a horse-cart around the islands. The routes are a bit limited but it is a relaxing inter-village form of transport.

Jinsuo and Xia Putuo Islands
Ferries from Caicun and Wase.
Nanzhao royalty once used Jinsuo Island (Golden Shuttle Island) as a summer retreat. The name apparently comes from the shape of the island which

DALI'S EMBROIDERED FLOWER CLOTH
The making of tie-dye, or 'spreading flowers' as it is called among Bai women, is by no means exclusive to Dali but you can't help noticing its colourful presence in the ancient city and in the market towns along the shores of Erhai Lake. The colours are actually rather limited – generally a forecolour of white on a blue or indigo background – but the attraction of these fabrics, draped over market stalls or hung to dry from walls, is immediate.

Like traditional Bai embroidery, thread-tie dyeing is a relatively old form of textile printing. Patterns and motifs may include complex designs, abstractions and more contemporary figurative elements, but often feature the outlines of plants, animals, insects, rivers, mountains and flowers. The effect may look simple but the process, involving at least five different stages of dyeing, tying, drafting and fastening, untying and washing, is a time-consuming one. The best fabrics, homespun from natural fibres like pure and hemp cotton, eschews chemical dyes in favour of stem, leaf and root extractions. Soft but durable, with dyes that seldom fade or bleed, the cloth is used in a variety of ways from sarongs and shoulder bags to tablecloths.

An increase in tourism has given a boost to the craft. The cottage industry village of Zhoucheng, between the lake and the foot of Yunlong Peak, is a good place to observe the process. To meet a growing demand for Dali tie-dye products, a dyeing factory was set up in 1984 in Zhoucheng county, employing over 5,000 women. In 1993 another factory was set up in the Dali township of Qiqiao.

Not quite a mass product yet, despite healthy exports to Europe, the States and Japan, inevitably a more shrill commercialism is creeping in, evident in a sign I saw, written in English, tacked to a tie-dye stall in Dali: 'Don't Leave Us Without A Good Buy'.

resembles the shuttle used by fishermen to weave nets. The island attracts a steady trickle of Chinese visitors, drawn by a subterranean cave complex on its eastern shore. More interesting is the north end of the island with a small fishing village, old alleys and the island's other drawcard, the **Luoyuan Temple**. Buddhist structures, destroyed, rebuilt, renovated and then vandalised during the Cultural Revolution, have a history of 1,500 years. Despite the inevitable souvenir stalls and a priest who offers to tell your fortune, the temple has been charmingly restored and is worth a look.

Putuo is close to Wase and café tours to the market there often include a sightseeing circuit of the island. **Putuo Temple** is the main feature of this tiny, rocky outcropping. Legend has it that the temple was formed by a stranded bodhisattva who forgot to construct a bridge back to the shore. The temple dates from the 15th century and is dedicated to Guanyin. The temple is noted for its imaginative roof and eaves, and its nicely restored walls which have colourful paintings of birds, flowers and animals. There is a well appointed café with a nice terrace on the island.

Near the northern shore of Erhai Lake and the village of Tianshengyin, are two minuscule islands that are a sanctuary for travellers wanting to be alone for a couple of hours or enjoy a picnic in quiet, unspoiled surroundings. Limestone **Yuji Dao** and the spoon-shaped **Chiwe Dao** as they are called, have some interesting clusters of old houses and a well-preserved pagoda.

Wase 挖色

By ferry from the pier at Caicun.
Ferry boats leave from the lakeside village of Caicun at 16.30 every day for Wase, a quiet old fishing village that has changed little over the years. Better though to join one of the half-day tours organised by some of the Dali cafés to the **Wase market** which takes place every five days.

Some people rate this a better market than Shaping. Although dozens of stalls are crammed into the village square near the quays, Wase is more of an organised street market than the rag-pickers' event at Shaping. Bai and Naxi women in national costumes and old men in Mao suits sucking on their pipes make up Wase's colourful, unhurried residents. There are a few less tourists here than at Shaping but more goods on display. The cafés opposite the village square are good places to stop for noodles or freshly prepared pancakes and yoghurt. The Yunnan Cafe organises the best hassle-free tours to Wase and usually posts them up on the wall a few days in advance. There is one modest guesthouse in Wase if you want to stay overnight. It is a 30km minibus ride to Xiaguan.

Another market well worth visiting is Wei-san, located in the mountains about an hour south of Xiaguan, next to the village of Diang Zhong (so you may see it referred to by this name as well). This market attracts large numbers of Yi and other minority people who descend from the hills bedecked in their traditional finery. The market starts around 10.00 and keeps on going until around 16.00. It's best around midday, but try to get there early to watch the people coming down from the hills by foot or on horse. Both produce and livestock are traded here, with pigs, buffaloes, horses and cows being traded; it is a fascinating and colourful scene. Jim's Peace Café is currently the only place that offers trips to this market (Y60), which takes place every ten days and is far less frequented by tourists than the markets at Wase and Shaping. Alternatively, if you prefer to make your own way, a public bus can be caught from Xiaguan local bus station.

Temples of Laotai and Langquan
Ferries from Caicun and Jinsuo Island.
Easily accessed from Jinsuo Island, Caicun or the nearby village of Haidong, Laotai and Langquan temples are probably worth a visit if you can factor them into a itinerary that includes a number of other, more interesting spots.

Laotai Temple has a rather sanitised appearance, due to what looks like a job-lot of white tiles that cover its surfaces. These are jollied up with strings of fairy lights, giving the building the impression of a Hindu temple devoted to the elephant god Ganesh. There is an impressive fresco on the ceiling of the temple. The views of the lake from Laotai are exceptional.

The name Langquan is associated with a legend which says that a beautiful princess was banished here and then turned into the statue of a stone donkey after refusing to agree to her father's plans for an arranged marriage. Statues in fact, are one of the features of this temple.

Further afield
Shibao Mountain Grottoes
Shibao is about 97km north of Dali.
Heading north from Dali in the direction of Lijiang, you will have to turn off the main road at the village of Diannan, about 9km south of Jianchuan, to reach Shaxi, the village near to the Shibao Mountain Grottoes.

The grottoes are well worth seeing if you can arrange private transport to get there or manage to hitch a lift from Diannan. Divided into three temple groupings, they contain an impressive 139 stone statues in 16 different grottoes. Shizhong, the **Stone Bell Monastery** group, has some of Yunnan's best Bai carvings, including Nanzhao Kingdom figures like the Emperor Yi Mouxun, the monk Ge Bi and the important imperial official Du Guanting. One of the grottoes contains carved images of female genitalia. Bai women who cannot give birth come here to pray for fertility.

The **Lion Pass** group are interesting as they include an entire imperial family collection of statues as well as a group of Indian monks incorrectly labelled as 'Persians'. Inscriptions in the third, **Shaedeng Village** group, indicate that the grottoes were first constructed in AD851. On the way to the Stone Bell Monastery grottoes, you will pass **Baoxiang Temple**. The temple is perched on the edge of a large cliff. A long flight of stone steps leads from here to the **Golden Temple**, the 'Residence of Sea and Clouds', at the summit of Shibao Mountain for a magnificent view of the region.

Chicken Foot Mountain (Jizushan) 鸡足山

Northeast of Dali. 70km from Xiaguan to Binchuan. 08.00 bus from the long-distance bus station. Then 24km to Shazhi at the base of Jizushan.

The 3,220m-high peak of Jizushan, Chicken Foot Mountain in Chinese, has been a major pilgrimage site for Buddhists and Taoists since the 7th century. The sacred mountain once boasted over 350 temples, sanctuaries and hermitages and a resident population of over 3,000 monks. The complex suffered badly at the hands of the Red Guards who seized on Jizushan as an example of superstition, backwardness and even, apparently, as a centre of medieval alchemy. All Jizushan's major sights and temples were either completely destroyed or badly damaged. Major renovation work is underway but it is unlikely that Jizushan will ever play host as it once did to pilgrims from all over Asia including such far-flung places as Sri Lanka and India.

There are two stories concerning how Chicken Foot Mountain acquired its name: one claims that the mountain is named after its chicken-foot shape with three hills in front and one behind; the other story is a legend of how the golden chicken, a disciple of Sakyamuni, flew through this area and, seeing the stately mountain, decided to subdue the black dragon that lived there and build a temple dedicated to Buddhism.

The mountain still attracts pilgrims from all over China and Tibet. The hike to the summit on foot is the most interesting way up, but if you are in a hurry, or not physically up to the exertion, two alternatives are to take the cablecar or ascend by pony. **Zhusheng Temple**, about an hour's climb, is Jizushan's most important temple and honours a monk called Jiaye who first established Buddhism on the mountain. Inscriptions on a large screen on the east side of the temple read 'The Grand Road to Realization' and the sobering question, directed at those who have travelled far to reach Jizushan, 'How Many Times Can You Return?'

Zhongshan Si, **Mid-Mountain Temple**, is a good place for a tea break and chat with the community of monks who live here. **Huashoumen Gate**, just before the summit, deserves a closer look as it somehow managed to avoid the excesses of the Cultural Revolution. The summit of the mountain is called Heavenly Pillar Peak. The 11th-century Jinding, or **Golden Summit Temple**, is at the end of the climb, its 13-storey pagoda taking the summit of the mountain to 3,240m.

The summit of the mountain can be chilly so it's wise to take a sweater along even in the summer, particularly if you intend to overnight on Jizushan. There are some basic guesthouses at Binchuan, a short minibus ride from the foot of the mountain, and in **Jinding Temple** at the summit. If you decide as some travellers do to stay at Jinding Temple and watch the sunrise, you may need to bring an extra blanket or sleeping bag.

Lijiang 丽江

6

'The beauty of this paradisical valley was never static or stale…The Snow Mountain was not a dead and stereotyped agglomeration of crags, ice and snow; it was a living goddess with her own way of life and moods.'

Forgotten Kingdom, Peter Goullart.

What draws travellers to Lijiang is not only its stunning backdrop, the Jade Dragon Snow Mountains, or the cobblestone lanes, canals of melted snow, and quaint, tumbledown Tibetan architecture of its old city, Dayan, but the fact that the city straddles an important cultural crossroads, the point of intersection for a number of ethnic nationalities that include the mainstream Han Chinese, the Bai peoples and settlers from nearby Tibet, Pumi, Lisu and Yi. Lijiang, however, is best known as the home of the Naxi people (also spelt Nahki and Nahi) and their ancient culture.

The genealogy of the Naxi is intriguingly arcane. Inexplicably linked with the gods of the Indian pantheon, the Naxi claim their ancestors sprang from eggs that fertilized after a torrid sexual collision between mountains, lakes, pine trees, stones, and between human females and Nagarajas. The Naxi are one of the few non-Chinese people to have their own form of writing, a rebus-pictographic script known as *dongba wen* – colourful, animation-like scrolls that represent natural phenomena, deities and infernal creatures. The *dongba* scripts contain unmistakable references to Mount Kailas and Lake Manasarowar, revealing descriptions of pitching tents in alpine meadows and the business of tending to yaks. If that were not enough, their own physiognomy bears a striking resemblance to that of their Tibetan neighbours whom the Naxi call their elder brothers.

HISTORY AND ORIENTATION

During the Qin and Han period, when nearby Baisha was the capital of the Naxi Kingdom, the area of present-day Lijiang was covered in wild forest. Exchanging their tents and nomadic way of life for houses in the flatlands of the Lijiang Valley, the Naxi settled down to cultivating fields of rice and buckwheat and establishing small clusters of villages. During the Tang and

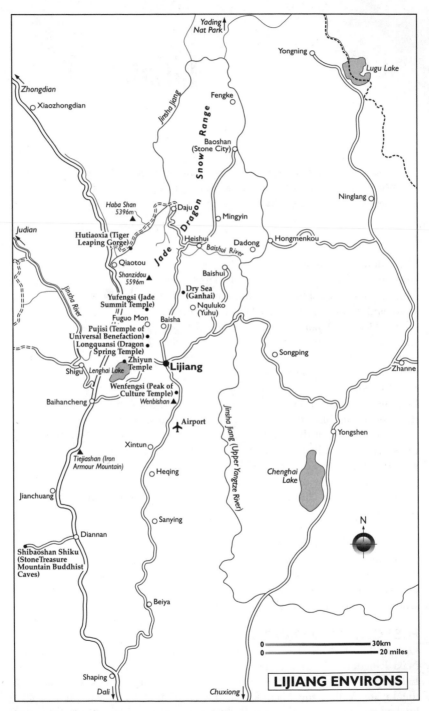

Yading
Nat Park

Yongning

Lugu Lake

Zhongdian

Xiaozhongdian

Fengke

Baoshan
(Stone City)

Ninglang

Haba Shan
5396m

Daju

Mingyin

Judian

Hutiaoxia (Tiger
Leaping Gorge)

Heishui

Dadong

Hongmenkou

Baishui River

Qiaotou

Shanzidou
5596m

Baishui

Yufengsi (Jade
Summit Temple)

Dry Sea
(Ganhai)

Jinsha River

Fuguo Mon

Baisha

Nquluko
(Yuhu)

Pujisi (Temple of
Universal Benefaction)

Longquansi (Dragon
Spring Temple)

Songping

Zhiyun
Temple

Lijiang

Shigu

Lenghai Lake

Zhanne

Wenfengsi (Peak of
Culture Temple)

Baihancheng

Wenbishan

Airport

Yongshen

Xintun

Chenghai
Lake

Tiejiashan (Iron
Armour Mountain)

Heqing

Jianchuang

Jinsha Jiang (Upper Yangtze River)

Sanying

Diannan

Shibaoshan Shiku
(StoneTreasure
Mountain Buddhist
Caves)

Beiya

N

0 _____ 30km
0 _____ 20 miles

Shaping

Dali

Chuxiong

LIJIANG ENVIRONS

Jade Dragon Snow Range

Jinsha Jiang

Song dynasties the largest of these villages, located where Sifang market is, set up a day market which opened at dawn and shut down at sunset.

As the market grew and the village prospered, Lijiang expanded in scale, becoming an important centre for the collection and distribution of commodities for trading at the great northern crossroads. It became a key staging post on the ancient Tea-Horse Road, a route for transporting tea and horses from India, through Tibet and across southwest China. The Naxi acted as middlemen for this lucrative east–west caravan route. A sound foundation for the economic progress of the old town was laid when Lijiang was linked to the all-important Silk Road. Lijiang County is still known as the Land of Horses.

Lijiang is really two parallel towns: the new, and the old, the two trying carefully not to encroach on each other. In some ways it is a good arrangement. The modernisers are allocated a designated area to despoil and vulgarise, the old town goes its own way; strict lines and parameters are set. The division between these two counter-worlds is, in fact, a very clear one: the ridge of Lion Hill with its large radio antenna. Roughly speaking the development west of the ridge belongs to the new town, the eastern section to the old.

The **new town**, with its uninspiring, Han-Soviet-style utility buildings and a more recent air of commerce, dates from the 1950s with an overlay of more contemporary white-tiled hotels with the ubiquitous blue, vinyl windows and flashy touches of chromium. The bus garages, larger shops and the post office are here. Three kilometre long Xinde Lu is the main north–south street, running towards Black Dragon Pool. Mao Square, with a couple of lacklustre cafés and some accommodation, is located here.

To local eyes, the old town, a mass of grey tiled roofs surrounded by green trees, resembles a giant ink stone. Hence its local name, Dayan, means ink stone. Dayan is preserved as a world heritage site, a remarkable place that consists of over 6,000 Naxi families, roughly 25,000 people. This is where most visitors spend their time, wandering through the labyrinth of narrow, cobblestone lanes and streams that make up one of the most fascinating and vibrant ancient cities in China.

The catastrophic earthquake of 1996 did considerable damage to Lijiang, levelling a lot of the new town. The old town fared better as the traditional wooden Naxi buildings stood up to the stresses of the tremors a lot better than the modern concrete buildings on the other side of town.

Nonetheless a lot of damage was done to the old town and some parts at the northern end of Dayan have been completely redeveloped. Visitors who knew the town before 1996 will be appalled at the changes which have made the area around East Main Street unrecognisable.

The ancient, sleepy thoroughfares have been replaced by dozens of brash souvenir shops, cafés and tour groups en masse. The redevelopment of the old town coincided with an unprecedented rise in the number of domestic tourists, with a new airport making Lijiang more acccessible to mass tourism. This placed a whole set of new demands upon the town and a rash of new shops, hotels and cafés sprung up to cater to this trade. You can, however, still find traces of an older Lijiang once you wander away from Sifang Square and the main thoroughfares. Early mornings are a good time to explore around the maze of back streets and alleys; before the day's commerce begins there are still moments of pure magic to be had in this ancient mountain town. Even with its brash new commercialism Lijiang is still a vibrant and enjoyable place to visit. It seems the Naxi culture is resilient and adaptable and has found a new pride in recent years by showcasing its unique Naxi heritage to visitors.

GETTING THERE AND AWAY

Lijiang is approximately 196km north of Dali and the road between the two places has spectacular mountain scenery and is one of the best journeys you can take in Yunnan. The new highway between Xiaguan and Lijiang is surprisingly good and has cut the journey time considerably; Lijiang to Xiaguan now takes only three hours on one of the fast new express buses that depart fairly frequently from the main bus station in either town. The fare is Y60. Ordinary buses take five hours and the fare is around Y35. Coming from Xiaguan the road ascends up through numerous mountain switchbacks before finally reaching Lijiang at an altitude of 2,400m. En route not only the scenery changes but also the peoples and culture, as you pass from typical Bai country of rolling hills to the more rugged upland areas of the Naxi people. Along the way you will see many beautiful scenes of rural Yunnan, with traditional villages clustered in the shadows of green terraced hills and mountains, river valleys and bamboo groves. There are several small towns along the way that you could stop off at if you wanted to explore further around this area. It could be a problem finding accommodation that will accept foreigners, though, in which case your only option would be to re-board another of the frequent buses along this route for Xiaguan and Lijiang.

If you are coming from Lijiang to Dali, be warned that most express buses will not stop at Dali but carry on to Xiaguan, some 15 minutes further on. In Lijiang the main bus station is at the southern end of town. Some buses heading in a northerly direction to places like Tiger Leaping Gorge, depart from the smaller north bus station. There are several buses every morning leaving from Kunming, with varying prices. The ordinary buses take a good ten hours. There are night sleeper buses as well, but try to avoid the cheap, Eastern European-made buses which have a bad record of breaking down en route. Buses depart from Lijiang for other several destinations including Shigu, Zhongdian, Jinjiang and Qiatou.

If you are arriving by air, Yunnan Airways has daily 45-minute morning flights to Lijiang from Kunming. The fare is Y420 one way and can be booked through CITS or other ticket agencies. The flights currently depart at 09.30 from Kunming and 08.40 from Lijiang. If done in combination with other destinations like Dali, taking a flight one way and then the bus back is a good plan for people with limited time. Lijiang also has a daily flight service operated by Yunnan Airlines to Jinhong in Xishuangbanna province. Timings for the 50-minute flight vary each day and should be checked locally. The fare is approximately Y730. Taking this flight can save a lot of time and backtracking if you intend to visit Xishuangbanna.

Arriving at Lijiang by air brings you into a modern new terminal located about 15km outside the city. There is an airport bus outside which departs 30 minutes after the plane arrives and takes you into the centre of town for Y10. The bus usually terminates on Shangri-la Avenue, close to the Guangfeng Hotel which is 10 minutes' walk from the start of the old town. Alternatively there are usually plenty of taxis available which will take you into town for about Y90.

GETTING AROUND

Maps are not really necessary for exploring the old town. Although there are few landmarks or large sights you will soon acquire a feel for the layout of the town although it is still possible to get pleasantly lost. Lijiang is almost entirely a pedestrian zone. Bicycles are an option, though, for getting around the new town and into some of the Naxi villages and valleys in the county. Lijiang has a good local bus service with routes to several of the places mentioned in this chapter.

PRACTICAL INFORMATION
Post and telecommunications

The main post office is along Xinde Lu, on the right hand side of the road as it climbs away from the entrance to the old town. International calls can be placed from here. Opening times 08.30–18.00.

The area code for Lijiang is 0888.

Internet

Websites: www.lijiang.com. The city is on the GeoCities website as well: www.geocities.com/lijiang

Money matters

There are two branches of the Bank of China in Lijiang, the larger one on Xinde Lu, the smaller office next to the Lijiang Hotel. The Lijiang Hotel also exchanges money. The Bank of China near the main bus station has a cash machine that accepts most credit cards.

Tourism

The main office of CITS is located along Xinde Lu. There is a potentially more useful new branch of the CITS Family and Independent Traveller (FITS) department opposite the Yunshan Hotel. Staff are very helpful.

PSB

A small office run by friendly staff usually willing to give visa extensions without a fuss. On the right side of the Lijiang Hotel grounds as you pass through the gate. Office hours are 08.00–12.00 only.

Books and maps

The Xinhua Bookshop (tel: 512 5999) on Xinde Lu has started to stock a small but decent selection of travel and photo books on Yunnan as well as translated

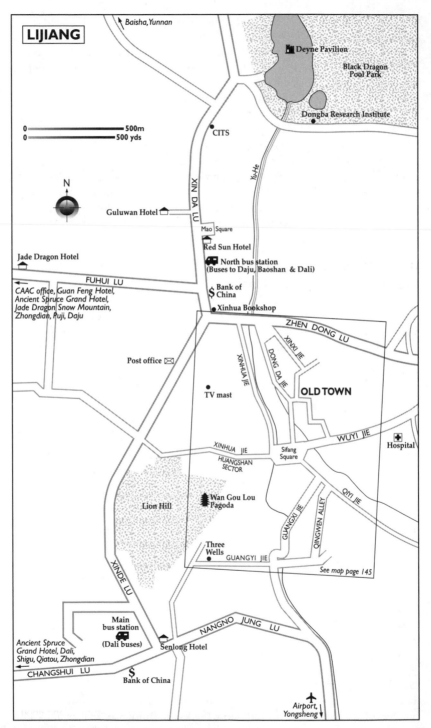

folktales and a fairly decent map of the old town, labelled in English and Chinese for Y5. Some of the bigger hotels and a few cafés also sell books. You can pick up maps at the same places and also in the main day market in the old town.

Weather conditions

The Lijiang area enjoys an annual average temperature of 12.5°C. The rainy season is a long one, lasting on and off from the end of May until the beginning of October, though there are sunny days between. Annual rainfall averages about 1,000mm. The sun can be strong because of the altitude.

Nature notes

Topographically, Lijiang lies close to the southeastern section of the Qinghai-Tibet Plateau, astride the transversely faulted Hengduan Mountains which stretch into the Central Yunnan Plateau. The disadvantage of living above these shifting geological plates was felt in February 1996 when a major earthquake, registering over seven on the Richter scale, hit an area 60km north of Lijiang, killing over 300 people, injuring a further 16,000, and triggering a massive relief operation. Although some buildings collapsed in the old town, many survived, enough, in fact, to convince the United Nations to place Lijiang county on its list of World Heritage Sites.

There are almost 3,000 species of seed plants and some 400 types of timber plants in the Lijiang area. Various micro-climates are found at different altitudes on and around the Jade Dragon Snow Mountain range where azaleas, primroses, rhododendrons, orchid, primula and alpine forests are common. Sadly, much of the timber, a valuable cash crop, is vanishing. Flowering quince, lacquer trees, mulberry and bamboo are also common. There are over 600 species of medicinal plants in the area as well. The Chinese, in fact, call this area the Home of Medicinal Plants. The valleys and rice terraces around Lijiang abut orchards of peach, citrus, persimmons and walnuts, and fields of sunflowers.

Plentiful water and deep forests support an undetermined but surely dwindling number of cranes, pheasants, quail, chamois, musk deer, and even, it is claimed, a few clouded leopards and Dian golden monkeys.

WHERE TO STAY

Most of Lijiang's accommodation is in the new town, although recently a number of fine traditional-style inns and guesthouses have opened in converted courtyard houses in the old town. Options are growing each year as more visitors discover Lijiang. The large, new, mostly Chinese tour group-patronised hotels on the edge of town are best avoided in favour of smaller hotels within a 10-minute walk of the old town.

Ancient Spruce Grand Hotel Shangri-la Av, a block south of the Guangfeng Hotel; tel: 516 6966; fax: 516 858. One of the best choices amongst the dozens of new hotels which have sprung up along Shangri-la Av. The hotel has pleasant grounds and good views towards the Jade Dragon mountain. The Ancient Spruce advertises itself as a four-star hotel but feels more like a three-star. If you want modern amenities then this is a good choice if the hotels nearer the old town are unavailable but it is still a good 20-minute walk to the old town from here. Rooms with TV, phone and en-suite bathroom cost from Y480.

Ancient Town Inn Jishan Lane, Xinyi Jie; tel: 518 9000; fax: 512 6618. The most upmarket of the traditional old town inns. Beautiful courtyards, wooden buildings with lacquered pillars and excellent service, the Ancient Town Inn (formerly the Old Town Inn) isn't cheap, although the standard singles are good value for Y200. Doubles Y320, triples Y380, four-beds Y420. There is also a rather luxurious, traditionally designed suite for Y480.

Deer Source Inn 67 Xinhua St; tel: 518 5178. Small family-run establishment whose main draw is the balcony rooms on the top floor that command great views over the old town and Jade Dragon Snow Mountains. Basic doubles with shared bathroom cost Y40, single rooms Y20.

Dongba House Minshi Alley; tel: 517 5431; fax: 517 5431; email: dongba@hotmail.com. Run by the same people who have the MCA Guesthouse and Internet Café in Dali. A Naxi-style guesthouse with attached courtyard, restaurant, bar and internet café. Rooms with shared hot showers from between Y20 and Y50 depending on size. The café has a good travel service office (www.yunnantravel.com) and can arrange personalised tours almost anywhere in the northwest.

First Bend Inn 43 Minshi Alley; tel: 518 1688; fax: 518 1688. One of the most popular old-style inns in Lijiang with independent travellers. The inn has a wonderful central courtyard where guests can sit, order tea or Naxi wine, read and meet other travellers. The main drawback is the noisy Chinese tour groups who regularly come to the restaurant at the back of the inn, shattering the peace of the courtyard and poking their heads in all the ground-floor rooms. Try to get a second-floor room if you want to avoid these inquisitive visitors. The rooms are somewhat damp smelling but clean and reasonably good value. Helpful and friendly staff. Singles with large bed Y80, doubles Y80, triples Y90, four-bed set-up Y100. Clean communal showers with hot water day and night.

Grand Lijiang Hotel Near entrance to old town and night market; tel: 512 8888; fax: 512 7878. The Grand ranks as the best choice amongst Lijiang's modern hotels, with a convenient location at the main entrance to the old town and next to the Yu He River. Rooms are well equipped, the service is excellent and its pleasant riverside café offers a great place to relax away from the crowds. The restaurant offers a buffet of Thai and Naxi food each evening for Y35. Rooms start from Y497.

Guangfeng Hotel Corner of Minzhu Rd and Shangri-la Rd; tel: 518 8888; fax: 518 1999. Lijiang's only real four-star hotel is a joint venture that has plenty of facilities and good service but lacks in atmosphere. Rooms with TV, phones and ensuite bathroom start from Y828 per night.

Guluwan Hotel Xin Daije; tel: 512 1446. On the opposite side of the road just past Mao Square. A good mid-range option. Doubles with bathrooms for Y250, triples at Y300. There are cheaper rooms at an annex behind the main hotel building; doubles with hot showers for Y150. The hotel has a small travel agency.

Hua Ma Guo Inn Next to the old stone bridge between Minshi Alley and Sifang

Above The magnificent San-Tasi (The Three Pagodas),
on the road northwest of Old Dali
Below Dali's newly renovated South Gate

Above A Yunnanese elder practising his calligraphy in the quiet courtyard of his home

Right Bamboo bird cages and calligraphy outside a shophouse in Kunming

Below Yunnanese monk, a follower of Tibetan Red Hat Lamaism

Below right Traditional Chinese oiled umbrellas in Kunming

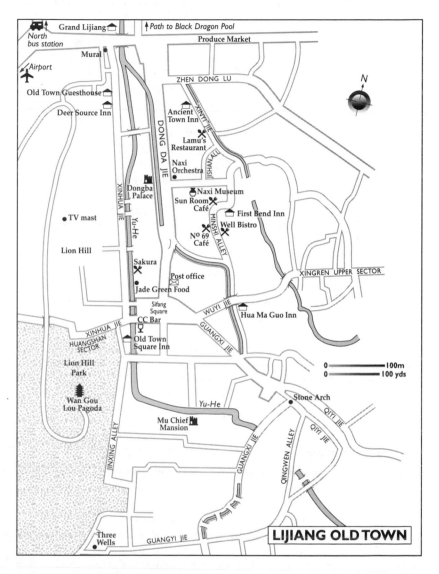

Square in the old town. This small guesthouse is a gem, with a few clean well-furnished rooms that each have a balcony and tables overlooking the river and bridge. It is an excellent spot to relax and enjoy the view over one of the main scenic spots of the old town; fall asleep to the sound of running water. Large, clean doubles with shared bathroom start from Y100.

Jade Dragon Hotel Fuhui Lu; tel: 512 2458. It doesn't look very impressive from the outside but the rooms, which are spacious and tastefully decorated, are excellent value. Doubles with TV, phone and en suite bathrooms Y200. There is a family suite for Y260. Helpful staff and good location, about five minutes from the old town.

Naxi Village House Tel: 127 8092958. Definitely not for the tourist but a unique experience. Mr He Jing Ling, an English-speaking local, can offer a room in his traditional Naxi house 4km from Lijiang. This is rather like a homestay set-up, eating and staying with the family, a good inside experience. The rooms are simple but clean and neat. The toilet is outside though. Rooms are only Y20–30. You can contact Mr Ling through Lamu's Restaurant. He will come and fetch you.

Old Town Guesthouse 61 Xinhua St at the northern end of the old town; tel: 518 8611. Another favourite with budget travellers, the guesthouse offers basic rooms built around a central courtyard with friendly staff and a common area. Double rooms with shared bathroom start from Y50 and dorm beds from Y15.

Old Town Square Inn Off Sifang Square; tel: 512 7487; email: sifang@netease.com. Probably the best value among the budget accommodation on offer, the Square Inn is built around a traditional Naxi-style courtyard and centrally located in an alley off Sifang Square. It is a popular choice for backpackers and a good place to socialise. It is probably best avoided if you are after somewhere quiet to stay, though. Internet services are offered at Y15 an hour. Doubles cost Y60 for a reasonable room with shared bathroom.

Red Sun Hotel Mao Square, off Xinde Lu; tel: 512 1018. An old favourite with backpackers, the Red Sun has large, wonderfully clean, dormitory rooms looking out over the Jade Dragon range. About five minutes' walk to the old town. Dorms are priced according to the number of beds, ranging from eight-bed dorms for Y25, to Y40 for doubles.

Senlong Hotel Opposite the main bus station on Minzhu Rd; tel: 512 0666; fax: 518 1968. This pleasant three-star hotel has one modern block and one with traditional Naxi architecture. Facilities are quite good and include a sauna and bowling alley. Rooms in both blocks are standard and it's really the Naxi decorations that you are paying extra for. Rooms with bathroom in the main building start from Y299 and Y550 for a room in the Naxi-style block.

WHERE TO EAT

Naxi cuisine relies heavily on wheat, corn and beans with a supplement of rice. Pork is the preferred meat. The moon-shaped *baba*, slightly sweet, deep-fried wheat flatbreads, are sold plain or stuffed with meats and vegetables. *Nuomi baba* is a smaller, sweeter version stuffed with glutinous rice. Naxi sandwiches, consisting of local goat's cheese, fried egg and tomato stuffed between two layers of *baba*, are tasty and good value. Naxi bean jelly is a local speciality, served cold in summer, warmed up in winter. Chick-pea jelly is also eaten. A more elaborate meal would be the Naxi Eight Bowl feast, a reference to the number of courses served.

Peter Goullart, a Frenchman who worked for the Nationalist Government in the 1940s, helping to set up many successful artisan communes in the Lijiang area, wrote about the city's many wineshops, all of which were run at the time by women. These disappeared after the Liberation but, according to Goullart, 'Everyone, men, women and children, drank wine, white or sweet *yinjiu*. No self-respecting child above two years would go to sleep without a cup of *yinjiu*.' You can still drink *yinjiu* at almost any café in Lijiang. This dark, smoky-tasting wine, similar in taste and body to port or a heavy sherry, is excellent.

THE WATER CITY

The cultural geography of Lijiang would be very different without the presence of water. Nurtured by streams issuing from the Jade Dragon River, the Naxi people of Lijiang owe a lot to the gurgling brooks and waterways that run past their homes, sub-dividing and merging into streams and canals as they exit the town to irrigate the region's lush farmland. Flowing from Black Dragon Pool, it splits into three branches before forming the dozens of channels the town is noted for.

In the old days Lijian's market place, Sifang Square, a slightly inclining expanse of stone paving, received a water dousing at the end of each market day. A sluice gate was erected across the river that flows past the higher end of the square. Closed after the market finished, water would then inundate the square, washing it clean of the day's accumulated fruit and vegetable debris.

You'll see many artesian wells as you walk around. Grateful locals even lead the water into their homes. If you glance into a Naxi kitchen you may see steps leading below the floor to a very conveniently diverted streamlet. One interesting feature of Old Lijiang are its *baima longtan*, or 'triple wells'. Tucked away in public courtyards, grouped in threes, locals make liberal use of their clear flowing water. One important rule governs the use of each unit. Different functions are assigned to each well according to the direction the water flows in. Buckets and pails of potable water are taken from the well which is furthest upstream; the middle one is used to wash vegetables, and the one farthest downstream for washing clothes and eating utensils. There is a good example of a stone *baima longtan* not far from the Black Dragon Pool. The head spring here is circular, the next square, the last rectangular.

The Naxi people believe that water is a god, and that the Naxi deity Shu resides in it. Shu is a powerful god, dominating heaven and earth as well as the wealth and fate of humans from his watery domain. The association between water and prosperity can be seen each third lunar month when water rites take place at the Anajizheng Spring on the west side of Lion Hill. In a ritual known as *maitoushui* ('buying the first bowl of water'), locals rise early to burn joss sticks, donate money, scoop out a bowl of sparkling water and pray to the god Shu to bless their families.

There are a few dull-looking canteens around Mao Square serving a mishmash of Chinese and local dishes, but the best eateries are in the old town. Both sides of Xingren Shangduan, the lane that runs off Sifang Square and passes over the Old Stone Bridge, are lined with excellent hotpot restaurants in old buildings. Simple, delicious noodles, rice and meat dishes charcoal-heated in ceramic dishes. You sit at pint-sized stalls at low tables. Very atmospheric and traditional. Unfortunately, more jade and souvenir shops are appearing along the street now. The night market which is set up in the evening at the entrance to the old town has plenty of stalls selling charcoal-grilled sticks of meat, corn-on-the-cob, *baba* and various rice and noodle mixtures.

69 Café Minshi Alley. You can recognise this restaurant from the artesian well outside. A tiny, intimate spot with only five tables. Beautifully designed and atmospheric with candles on the tables during the evening. Plenty of books, magazines, card and board games for rainy days. English, Naxi and Tibetan breakfasts, veggy soups, burgers, and creative interpretations of curry and tofu dishes. Walnut and apple crumbles, tarts and pies go well with a fine selection of teas that include liquorice, crysthanthemum, eucalyptus, ginger and Tibetan butter tea.

CC Bar Sifang Square. A tiny, hole-in-the-wall café and bar between the Old Market Inn and the river, this must be one of the most intimate and friendly places in Lijiang. Run by a couple with a good taste in local art and contemporary music and jazz, it is a great place to relax, watch the market square and enjoy a snack.

The Jade Garden Restaurant Lijiang Grand Hotel. Offers a good-value buffet of Thai, Naxi and Cantonese food for Y35, in pleasant garden surroundings by the Yu-He river at the side of the hotel.

Jade Green Food Just off Sifang Square, along Yu-he River. Simple Naxi and Tibetan dishes in a pleasant location with views of the willow-lined river outside. Has travel information.

NAXI WOMEN

Visitors to the old quarter of Lijiang often remark on the predominance of women over men. 'To marry a Nahi woman', a botanist engaged in field work in Yunnan during the 1950s remarked, 'was to acquire a life insurance, and the ability to be idle for the rest of one's days.' At some point in the history of the Naxi people, traditional Confucian-based values and roles appear to have been reversed. Applying themselves to the complexities of commerce, women became shopkeepers, traders, land and exchange brokers, merchants and money lenders. At the same time they encouraged their menfolk to idle their time away. 'Silently and persistently, like the roots of growing trees, Naxi women', as Peter Goullart observed in his 1957 classic, *Forgotten Kingdom*, 'slowly evolved themselves into a powerful race until they utterly enslaved their men.'

Exuding physical strength and obvious business acumen, Naxi women today still seem a self-assured and assertive breed, very much at the helm of a family's prosperity and, especially in Lijiang, a highly visible presence in the workplace. Followers of a polytheistic blend of Taoism, Tibetan Lamanism and older shamanist beliefs in the spirits of pine trees, wind and clouds, Naxi society continues to adhere to a matriarchal model, albeit a modified one.

Under the *azhu* (personal friend) system still practised in the remoter villages, young men and women could have relations outside marriage while both partners continued to live in their separate family houses. If a child was born to the couple it automatically belonged to the woman, although the

Lamu's Restaurant Xinyi Jie. Near the Ancient City Inn. Acclaimed by its patrons as the best food in the old town, Lamu's offers a good selection of Tibetan, Naxi and Western foods. Don't be put off by the names of some of the Tibetan dishes: 'Ants climbing trees', for example, turns out to be a wholesome potato-beef-noodle concoction. Other Tibetan dishes include a sweet, cheesy version of *tsampa*, the standard wheat flour-based staple; *tendrik* is a meat and tomato bowl. There are also yak spring rolls and various soups and Tibetan butter tea. The café has a sunny, log-wood interior. This is a good place for alternative travel information. See the hand-drawn maps on the walls, travel postings and messages. Lamu, the owner, formerly ran the Tibetan café in Zhongdian and is well acquainted with the tastes and needs of foreign travellers. A relaxed atmosphere makes this one of the best places to while a few hours, also one of the best spots to gather updated travel information from other travellers.

Old Market Inn Sifang Square. A shadow of its former self, this is no longer the cosy, ethnic joint it once was. Linoleum, glass windows and a TV set have replaced the old wooden tables, dusty sofas and open front. The waitresses are now decked out in cutesy versions of tribal costumes and the place is aggressively advertised with stick-on messages. It still commands one of the best views of the old market square and the Naxi dishes are passable.

Sakura Café 123 Xinhua St. With its quaint riverside tables the Sakura is an excellent place to sit out, particularly in the evenings. It offers a great variety of different food,

man was expected to provide financial support for as long as the affair continued. Strong matriarchal influences can still be found in the Naxi language. Nouns become more important, for example, when the Naxi word for female is added, while nouns that have the word for male added, decrease in significance. The word 'stone', with the addition 'women', turns out to mean boulder (a large rock), while the word 'stone' plus 'man' equals pebble (a small stone).

In many ways Naxi society remains strongly matriarchal. Women still control the family economy, and inheritance continues to pass to the youngest daughter in the family rather than to the eldest son. Traditionally, women worked in the fields and traded, while the men stayed at home and looked after the children. Men were known as gifted gardeners and musicians, and continue to practice these skills now. These days, women can be seen engaging in a number of different activities in the older quarter of Lijiang: running its busy street markets, restaurants and small businesses.

Apart from the persistent wearing of Mao caps among the older women, Naxi females are easily identified from their costumes which consist of a blue bodice, quilted cape and white apron. On closer scrutiny the cape, held in place with crossbands, reveals an upper indigo segment representing the sky at night, and a lower sheepskin or silk band standing for daylight. A row of seven disks, symbolising the stars, bisect the two halves. The effect, whether intended or not, unequivocally places women at the centre of the Naxi universe.

including Japanese and Korean dishes. The lasagne and other Italian dishes here are also good. Upstairs is a video room and internet service for Y12 per hour.

Sunroom Café Minshi Alley. A newish, family-owned place run by a very hip manageress with a good sense of humour and good taste in music. Light and cheerful surroundings are decorated with *dongba* art, wall hangings and tie-dye tablecloths. A very civilised hangout with a few books and magazines to browse through. Patronised by foreigners and Chinese. They have a tempting range of homemade breads, and interesting vegetarian versions of *baba* and Naxi sandwiches. Recommended are the wheat noodles, steamed Naxi cheese, and spicy tofu treats.

Well Bistro Minshi Alley. An elegant café-restaurant with good reading materials and a friendly, English-speaking staff. Excellent vegetarian pizzas, pasta dishes, buckwheat crêpes and other options like ratatouille. Delicious sweets include apple strudel and oatmeal biscuits. Their *yinjiu* (Naxi wine) is excellent.

ENTERTAINMENT

Apart from the prospect of a drunken evening of karaoke in the new town or at one of the more sleazy hostess bars or discos that have opened to cater for the growing number of Han Chinese living and working there, Lijiang's nightlife is fairly tame. One of the most rewarding ways of spending an evening is to attend a performance of Lijiang's superb **Naxi Orchestra**. Nightly concerts are held in a lovely old hall on the main street in the old town. They start at 20.00. You can also buy a CD or cassette tape of their music in the small art shop next to the hall. Another option is the more eclectic, tourist-oriented performances of Naxi and *dongba* music and dance at the **Dongba Palace** opposite.

FESTIVALS

The Fertility Festival is held in the third lunar month, usually on the 13th day. The Torch Festival is a big summer event, held in July and celebrated throughout the Lijiang area as well as among the Bai in Dali. Late August sees the All Souls Festival when different coloured paper lanterns and boats with lit candles are made and then launched into the streams of the old town during the evening. It is a magical event. A colourful horse fair takes place every April and September.

WHAT TO SEE
Jade Dragon Snow Mountain

Located 35km north of Lijiang, Yulong Xue Shan, the ice-bound Jade Dragon Snow Mountain dominates the Lijiang Plain. To the Chinese, the 13 peaks of the massif resemble jade pillars holding up the sky. The highest of these pillars, the spitting image of a crystalised dragon (but only if you are Chinese) is the 5,596m Shanzidou. Permanent snowfields and glaciers encrust the five main summits, alpine meadows and pastures the slopes, tea fields and a natural pharmacopoeia of medicinal herbs its milder, lower reaches which make fine hiking courses.

Less enthralling than climbing, but offering an equally good if not better view, is the chairlift which takes visitors halfway up the mountain. From here you can reach the snowline by continuing on foot or explore the meadows by pony.

Before reaching the mountain you will have to pay an entrance fee of Y40, which is collected at a toll booth on the road from Lijiang. After this there are two options: a cable car to the top of the Mountain itself or a smaller chairlift up to some Yak meadows on the flanks of the mountain. The first place you will see is the base and car park for the cable car, known as the Snow Flowers Mountain village, where coaches take passengers to the actual cable station about 10 minutes' drive away. Billed as the highest cable car in the world, it takes passengers up to 4,200m; such a rapid altitude gain could cause potential health problems for some people. Tickets to the top cost Y110 and the cable car base also rents out warm clothing and oxygen bags. The top station is already in a dilapidated state, despite having been open for only two years; the wooden walkway at the top had collapsed at the time of writing, leaving little room for exploration. The views over the Lijiang Plain can be outstanding on a clear day but this is probably an outing best left to the Chinese tour groups as the cable car is many ways a classic example of poor development.

The chairlift, which is located further on from the Snow Flowers Mountain Village, costs Y50 and takes you halfway up the mountain to some heavily touristed yak meadows where ponies can be hired for a trot around. This is really more of a photogenic opportunity than anything else, though the views from the chairlift and meadows are good. There are possibilities for walking on the lower flanks of the mountain but very often the vegetation is extremely dense, making walking difficult. It would be best to enquire about bringing a guide with you for extended walks.

Getting to the mountain can be a problem as there is no direct public transport. Hitchhiking is an option but an uncertain one. Private buses go to Daju, the nearest point. Local travel agencies offer pricey tours to the mountain but there are the inevitable diversions to caves and souvenir emporiums. The best method is to get together a small group of fellow travellers or Chinese who want to cut through the commercialism and rent a van. This shouldn't cost more than Y150 for the whole day round trip.

Lion Hill and Wan Gou Lou Pagoda
Wan Gou Lou Pagoda Y15.
One of the finest views of the old town is from Lion Hill. The hill is unmistakable because of its radio mast. Further along the ridge you will come to a lovely park whose grounds are home to the Wan Gou Lou pagoda, one of the landmarks of Lijiang. The 33m-high, five-storey pagoda claims to be the tallest wooden building in China. The design is certainly unique, with 16 main pillars, and a number of features that combine local lore, including *dongba* star and moon carvings. The 13 eaves bend upwards and represent the 13 peaks of the Jade Dragon Snow Mountains. The pagoda is a good place to watch the mists clearing over the town in the early morning. Paths wind down from the pagoda to Sifang Square and breakfast.

DONGBA SCRIPTS AND PAINTINGS

Dongba culture finds expression in forms as varied as dance, ghosts and the making of clay figurines of deities. The culture's curious script, and lively painting on wooden slabs, markers and paper (scripts consisting of over 50 Naxi pictographs), are its most visible expression, copies of which travellers are likely to have thrust in front of them by shopkeepers and old grannies working for craft galleries.

In the clan religion of the Naxi, the *dongba* scriptures were used by their shamans in rituals connected to the worship of nature, ancestors, totems and a host of gods and quasi-deities. The transmitters of *dongba* culture, also called *dongba* (the name means 'scripture reader' or 'necromancer' in the Naxi language), are dwindling in numbers.

Worldwide, over 20,000 volumes of *dongba* script exist in museums, universities and private collections. Some of the pictures are easy enough to interpret. The characters for tiger, crane, deer and horse, for example, are complete pictures. Characters were originally carved in stone, then drawn on ox and sheep hide, wood, and finally, paper. The most representative legacy of Naxi pictorial art is found on paperboard, and in bamboo, scroll, timber and slat painting. Wood slat paintings, called *kebiao* in Naxi, are another unique art form. Usually made of pine, the slats, depicting celestial beings and ghosts, are used in sacrificial rituals.

One of the most impressive works in the *dongba* repertoire is the Divine Road Painting, a vivid work designed like a road map, to guide the soul of the deceased to heaven, negotiating a number of tricky stages on the way. It looks a bit like a Monopoly board with some bankrupt souls being temporarily cast into hell, others proceeding to spiritual prosperity and a good reincarnation. These unique hand scrolls measure about 30cm in width and an astonishing 15m or more in length. Scholars claim that the Naxi have the oldest dance score in the world, an intriguing cartoon strip showing the choreographed steps of wolves, peacocks, white elephants and a green dragon, dating back to the 15th century.

The Dongba Research Institute in Lijiang, a small museum located on a hill in Black Dragon Pool Park, was set up to study and preserve the culture of the *dongba*. A few remaining masters are attached to the institute, while researchers are engaged in the awesome task of translating and deciphering small booklets called *dongbajing* which cover subjects from religion, magic and mythology, to accounting and exorcism. A thousand or so booklets were written and the institute contains some 5,000 copies. The institute hopes to produce a comprehensive encyclopedia of Naxi culture in the near future.

At the time of writing a new pathway was under construction which will lead directly from the back of the Mu Chief's mansion to the Wan Gou Lou Pagoda.

Museum of Naxi Culture
11 Jishan Alley.
Check to see if this small museum dedicated to Naxi culture is still open to the public as it is located in the home of Mr Xuan Ke, the leader of the Naxi Orchestra. Mr Ke is a busy man these days as the orchestra is attracting more attention. He may not be around to discuss the finer points of Naxi music and culture as he was in the past.

Mr Ke's family were close friends of the fiery botanist Dr Rock who spent 29 years in and around Lijiang before the revolution. Some of his personally made furniture is on display, along with a collection of rare travel books on Lijiang and other Naxi items, including some musical instruments.

Black Dragon Pool
End of Xinde Lu. Open: 07.00–20.00. Y8.
On the northern, slightly older edge of the new town, Black Dragon Pool (Heilongtan Gongyuan) is approached via a road lined with aromatic, herbal hotpot restaurants, and an old wooden community temple. The park's most publicised feature is the photo-perfect view it offers of Black Dragon Pool, the Moon-Embracing Pavilion, the marble arch of Belt Bridge, and the stunning, snow-capped backdrop of the Jade Dragon Snow Mountains. On a fine day, the combination is dazzling.

There is a very pleasant walk to the Black Dragon Pool from the old town. A pathway which starts at the side of the Lijiang Grand Hotel runs by the side of the river all the way to its source at the Black Dragon Pool. Winding its way through some interesting older neighbourhoods, the path is often frequented by groups of Naxi women and is a pleasant 10-minute stroll from the old town.

As you enter the park you'll see a small, nicely renovated library on your right. The painted eaves, with their complicated cross-joints are impressive. The building was brought from Fuguosi in the early 1980s and reconstructed by a highly skilled, local Naxi artisan. The next building up is the *Dongba Research Institute*. The scroll painting and other artefacts here are well worth the Y4 entrance fee. The number of *dongba* shamans is dwindling but you might be lucky enough to see one of them working on a script or scroll inside the institute. You might also catch a rehearsal of the Naxi Orchestra while you are here. They practise in a nearby wooden hall three times a week.

Another building of interest is the 17th-century **Dragon God Temple** (Longshenci), which has been converted into an art gallery. The attached garden is pleasant with cherry, forsythia and dwarf trees. One of the most outstanding buildings in the park is **Five Phoenix Hall** (Wufenglou). The hall was brought from Fuguosi, 30km west of the town which was formerly

THE NAXI ORCHESTRA

The last few years have seen an incredible resurgence in traditional music, a legacy preserved by the Naxi since Kublai Khan's invasion of Lijiang in the 13th century. The general is said to have bequeathed several musicians from his own orchestra in gratitude to a Naxi chieftain who helped his army cross the Yangzi. Four or five orchestras have regrouped in the Lijiang area, including an ensemble of village elders who perform *Baisha Xiyue*, ritual music composed to pacify the souls of those who perished in war. By far the most renowned group of musicians are the Naxi Orchestra.

The orchestra play music dating back to the Song and Tang dynasties. Known as *liyue*, the music was originally used by scholars performing Taoist rituals connected to the Dong Jin grotto scriptures. Long forgotten in the rest of China, except among a small cultural elite during the Ming and Qing periods, the music remained popular in this remote outpost of the Himalayan foothills.

The titles in the orchestra's repertoire, like 'Waves Washing the Sand', 'Ten Consecrations', and 'The Old Man at Qing River', are well tuned to the surroundings. The group also perform Han and minority music, a haunting flute solo, a Tibetan song, and a Naxi rice-transplanting song. Concerts are worth attending just to see the instruments the orchestra uses. Old instruments like this are rare today as most were destroyed during the

the largest and most important Tibetan monastery in the Lijiang district. The eaves of the building are supposed to resemble an outstretched phoenix and date, like the hall, from 1601. There is a small museum on the first floor with a musty collection of amulets, Tibetan prayer wheels, *dongba* swords and other ritual items.

The park's hyacinth-choked pool is known as Yuyuan, meaning Jade Spring, an allusion to its cool, pale green water. The poet Guo Moruo dedicated two gushing couplets to it, one of which reads, 'Thirteen peaks are reflected in the Dragon Pond with plunging dragons up in heaven and flying dragons down on earth. Jade waters flow, with jet as the body, and turquoise the soul.' Although the current building is a 1962 reconstruction, the centrepiece of the park, floating majestically at the centre of the pool, is the **Moon-Embracing Pavilion** (Deyuelou). The original building burnt down in a dramatic double love suicide in 1950. A high official and his lover repaired there for cakes and wine and then, once the moon had risen, set fire to the pavilion.

Dongba Palace

Along Dong Dajie.

A minor site but worth a quick look, the Dongba Palace has a small shop selling copies of *dongba* scripts, paintings and other rather commercialised paraphernalia, a restaurant and some travel service facilities. On a more

Cultural Revolution, a period during which the Naxi Orchestra was banned from playing. Many of the instruments – a fish-shaped drum, ancient lute, three-stringed instruments, cymbals, an exquisite, lacquered copper gong-frame – were buried to save them from the zeal of the Red Guards.

The orchestra's director and chief exponent of Naxi music and culture, is the youthful Mr Xuan Ke. As a renowned Naxi scholar, Xuan He paid a high price, spending 20 years in labour camps, before the Cultural Revolution was discredited. Now in his 60s he has the energy of a man with a mission. Having rebuilt the Naxi Orchestra, Xuan Ke founded the Dayan Naxi Ancient Music Association which, besides researching and promoting their own activities, trains young students. Due to a dwindling number of older musicians only 23 pieces out of an original repertoire that exceeded 60, are performed.

The orchestra gave eight sell-out recitals in Britain in 1995 and participated in the 7th Hong Kong Art Festival. Xuan Ke quips that the most difficult thing about performing abroad was not transporting their antique, weather-sensitive instruments, but their antique, weather-sensitive musicians. The orchestra claims, in fact, to have 'three old rarities': namely, ancient musical compositions, authentic instruments, and ancient musicians. The average age of members is 80, a fact that may account for the solemn, dream-like atmosphere created during their concerts.

positive note it has a fascinating permanent exhibition on Dr Joseph Rock in the form of original monochrome photos. There is a restaurant here and nightly performances of *dongba* dance and music from 20.15. The commentary is all in Chinese and the peformances recreate traditional *dongba* shaman's dances and Naxi folk songs. Quite interesting but a second choice for an evening's entertainment after the Naxi Orchestra.

Mu Chief's mansion

Located in the southwest corner of the old town, directly below the Wan Gou Lou Pagoda, this elaborate reconstruction of a Naxi chief's home has been completed recently after three years of building financed by the World Bank. The project originated from damage done to this part of the old town by the 1996 earthquake. The hereditary title of Mu has passed down through 22 generations from the Yuan dynasty, when the Mongol invaders appointed the Naxi tribal chieftain (*tusi*) as their administrator. The Naxi enjoyed important development during the Ming dynasty and the *tusis* were trusted and relied upon by the Ming rulers. Lijiang became very prosperous and the *tusis* reflected this wealth and importance with a large-scale architectural complex of palaces. The mansion is a reconstruction of what would have originally stood here in Ming times, as the original palace was long since destroyed during wars in the Qing dynasty and the remaining gateway finished off by the Red Guards. The famous Ming dynasty traveller and geographer Xu Xiake

A VISIT TO THE CLINIC

You don't have to be sick to visit the Clinic of Chinese Herbs in Jade Dragon Mountains of Lijiang, run by Mr He Shixiu, better known as Dr Ho. Dr Ho's celebrity began on 16th March, 1986, the day British writer Bruce Chatwin's article, 'In Lijiang: Rock's Kingdom', appeared in the New York Times Magazine. Chatwin was a guest (seated 'beside the east window') at a feast held to honour the doctor's firstborn grandson. Chatwin's finely tuned writing and affectionate description sets the scene: The doctor appears 'in a white clinician's mobcap and silver-grey cotton greatcoat', surveying the company 'with the amused, slightly otherworldly air of a Daoist gentleman-scholar, and flicks his wispy beard from side to side'. Those who make the effort to visit the doctor at his clinic, and plenty do – some Chinese are even starting to turn up to see what all the fuss is about – will find it hard to resist a smile at the precision of Chatwin's eye. Two decades later the doctor remains much the same as in his Times debut, only the greatcoat gone, replaced with a long, well-worn Chinese surgical frock coat.

A steady stream of visitors and attention has made the doctor a prosperous member of the Baisha community, but prosperity and comfort in a less doctrinaire China have come late. His house, like many others, was

wrote of its 'beauty like a palace and similarity to the monarch's' in his account of *Travels through Yunnan*, arousing suspicions that the Mu *tusi* had modelled their palace on the emperor's in Beijing. Indeed, the modern reconstruction of the palaces closely imitate in style the Forbidden City buildings of Beijing.

The mansion comprises several buildings, the most interesting of which is the Wan Juan building which houses a collection of Naxi cultural heritage items, including ancient paintings, sutras and important works of literature. The inscription over the entrance archway says 'Let's read', reflecting the Naxi people's passion for knowledge.

SIDE TRIPS FROM LIJIANG CITY
Forest temples and monasteries

Many of the monasteries and lamasaries that dot the forests and hills around Lijiang, including the five main sites mentioned here, owe their existence to Mu Tian Wang, an early 17th-century ruler of the Naxi and a benevolent sponsor of religious works. The current leader of the Mu clan is still regarded as the titular headman of Lijiang even now. The monks who lived at these temples were followers of the Karmapa school of Tibetan Buddhism, the Red, or Scarlet Hat sect.

Jade Summit Temple (Yufengsi), a lamasery about 11km northwest of Lijiang, was established in 1756. Laid out on terraces, each has something different to offer. The top tier, for example, has an attractive geometrically designed, pebble courtyard. The temple's main attraction, which brings droves of visitors here between February and March, is a 500-year old camellia tree.

ransacked during the Cultural Revolution. The doctor was forbidden from practicing. The house is a typical Naxi affair with mud-brick walls covered with ox-blood wood panels, and a tiled roof with tufts of grass providing an unintentional layer of thatch. If you ask, you will be shown the garden, a small walled plot planted with neat rows of vegetables and some of the medicinal herbs that make up the secret ingredients of his cure-all tea, one most visitors end up sampling. It is an unexceptional brew but its powdery, menthol flavour strongly laced with aniseed or liquorice, served from a dented pot, is refreshing and its amusing trying to guess the ingredients. Whether it cures or alleviates the long list of illnesses and diseases, some fatal, that the doctor claims, is another question.

The doctor will show you his extensive collection of scrapbooks packed with articles and other clippings. It seems that every journalist – including this one – who has passed through Baisha, turns out an article or two on the doctor. The doctor's bedside manner and hospitality is, to some extent, part of a well practised patter intended to extract a generous donation from you for his time and tea. Average donations seem to be around the Y20 mark, a small price to pay for time spent in the company of a Daoist gentleman-scholar.

The so-called Camellia Tree of 20,000 Blossoms may fall quite a bit short of that figure but its amazing display of red flowers, certainly in their thousands, is a sight to behold.

The **Temple of Universal Benefaction** (Pujisi), lies about 5km northwest of Lijiang, a pleasant hike past a couple of ponds just outside the town and then up a steep goat trail. Two giant crab-apple trees stand in the courtyard before the main, copper-tiled Buddha Hall. Like all of these temples, the Red Guards did their best to destroy anything that smattered of art or religion, but there are still a few Buddha images, Tibetan scroll-banners, and murals on display. If you continue the climb up to the summit of the hill there are rewarding views of the plain and fields below.

The most important buildings at the **Kingdom of Blessing Temple** (Fuguosi), once the most prestigious temple complex in Lijiang, have been removed for safety and better exposure to visitors, to the Black Dragon Pool area. Hufa Hall, however, has some frescos worth looking at. A visit here could be combined with a side trip to nearby Baisha. **Zhiyun Temple**, 18km southwest of town, is another site that, unless you are already in the area or have a special passion for desecrated temples, can safely be bypassed. The temple was built in 1727 and is now being used as a school for the kids who live in Lashiba.

More rewarding is an excursion to the **Peak of Culture Temple** (Wenfengsi), 8km southwest of Lijiang. This Tibetan monastery dates from 1733. The centre for some unusual esoteric and occult practices, the monastery once housed dozens of lamas. Despite the vandalism of the 1960s,

DR ROCK: BOTANIST-EXPLORER

Asia has never been short on eccentric expatriates, but Joseph Rock (1884–1962), the Austro-American botanist and anthropologist, must surely rank as one of the strangest Europeans to have left his mark on China. A self-trained botanist and gifted linguist, Rock made Lijiang his home for some 27 years during which time he became the world's foremost authority, firstly on the flora of southwest China and, as his interests changed, on the culture and language of the Naxi. Once he had found conditions conducive to his interests and colossal talents, he worked ferociously for almost three decades, exhausting those who worked for him and, occasionally, exasperating the few Westerners he came into contact with.

Autocratic, temperamental, given to terrible fits of anger when the mood struck him, Rock was, nevertheless, popular with the Naxi. This was partly because he was not peddling Christianity like other Westerners the Naxi had brushed up against. Rock had a lifelong abhorrence of missionaries which he was not afraid of venting in their company. He also provided the Naxi with much needed medicines and limited treatment free of charge at a time when there was no clinic in Lijiang. By modern standards he can appear self-righteous and egocentric. Rock held a low opinion of the Han Chinese and described the Naxi, among whom he lived and professed to admire, in the patronising, romantic terms of the day as 'noble savages', and 'pure children of nature'.

Rock's expeditions into the field to collect plant specimens were legendary. He introduced countless new types to the West. During his

this atmospheric temple has been sensitively rebuilt and there are a couple of elderly monks in attendance. The setting, among shaded woods and orchards, is suitably holy. The roof murals, paintings, carvings and Tibetan mandalas, although damaged, are still remarkable. A holy cave and spring on the hill behind the temple has a black rock on which a devotee of Sakayamuni is believed to have placed a key for Tibetan pilgrims on their way to Mount Jizu to use to symbolically open the path. A stiff, three-hour hike to the top of Wenbishan, the hill behind the temple, offers great views of the surrounding countryside.

Getting there

Jade Summit temple can be reached on foot from Baisha, which is on the No 6 bus route. The other places involve either a very stiff hike, taxi, or arranging private transport.

Dragon Spring Temple

Northwest of Lijiang, near the village of Wenmingcun.

Little-visited Dragon Spring Temple (Longquansi), set among pine covered hills is a rather neglected but atmospheric temple that combines various energetic career as a botanist, before he returned to a study of linguistics and the compiling of a Naxi dictionary, Rock sent over 80,000 specimens of plants from China. Two were even named after him.

It was not Rock's work as a botanist and scholar, or the many well-received books and essays that he published that made him famous, but his work as a reporter for *National Geographic* in the 1920s and 30s. In features like the April 1925 'The Land of the Yellow Lama', many Westerners got their first view of southwest China. Rock illustrated his own articles for National Geographic, and photos of the reporter on location show the man at a thick-set desk with negatives pegged on a drying line in the portable tent he had his bearers take everywhere, a structure that served as living quarters and darkroom. Another photo shows Rock standing outside his tent dressed in the silk and brocade of a Mandarin. He is flanked on both sides by some of the dozens of Tibetan bodyguards he took with him on expeditions, not only to protect his caravan against bandits, but also to impress potentially troublesome local chieftains and warlords.

Rock's poor view of the Han Chinese made him believe that they were exercising a destructive and divisive influence on the more traditional minorities of China. In his last role as an authority on Naxi ethnology, he predicted the subjugation and eventual extinction of the Naxi culture, something that almost happened during the Cultural Revolution. Rock's monumental, two-volume *The Ancient Nahki Kingdom of Southwest China*, remains required reading for anyone with a serious interest in the people and culture of the region.

elements of Buddhism, animism and Taoism in its highly accomplished and well-preserved window, door and rail carvings. The god who presides over the main altar is in the *dongba* style, adding a touch of local culture to the melange. The murals are almost illegible, another legacy of hysterical Red Guards. The courtyard is a suitably contemplative place to sit and admire the resident citrus and peach trees, orchids and primula.

Baisha 白沙

10km north of Lijiang.
But for its famous frescos and the well publicised Dr Ho (see box *A visit to the clinic*, page 160–1), few people would know the name Baisha. Astonishingly, the village was once the capital of the Naxi Kingdom before Kublai Khan invaded the region and incorporated it into the new Yuan Empire in the 13th century.

The village can hardly have changed since then and provides a good insight into a typical Naxi community. Baisha consists of just two roads with muddy alleys and lanes off. Baisha has many well-preserved houses, monastic buildings and an imposing, Naxi-style gate-tower. Walls are built in the traditional style: mud-bricks fastened with chaff and pebbles are placed on top of a stone base and then topped with tile.

Most visitors come to Baisha in order to see its famed **Daboaji Hall**, also known as the **Coloured Glaze Temple** (Liulidian), across from the village school. It took over 200 years to complete and decorate the temple, work beginning in 1385. The temple is a heady fusion of Tibetan Buddhist, Taoist, Naxi and *dongba* styles. The Baisha frescos are displayed in a back hall which you reach after passing through a series of halls, gates and courtyard gardens. The frescos are sombre and powerful, rendered dark and sinister by centuries of roof soot and the spiteful gashes and gouges of the Red Guards. Despite the damage, the central fresco and side panels are impressive. Represented in a riot of figures, symbols and decoration, is a rich and pluralistic Tibetan Buddhist iconography that includes Sanskrit inscriptions, trigrams, bodhisattvas, lotus flowers, the Wheel of Life, and those damned to the underworld. The hall is rather badly illuminated. A torch would be useful to examine the frescos at the back of the main screen. Naxi elders sometimes give short concerts in the temple grounds of Baisha Xiyue (Baisha Fine Music), the classical Naxi music which includes a series of ritual music dedicated to the souls of those who died in wars.

A separate building called the **Pavilion of Great Calm** (Dadingge), just beyond the main temple complex, has some vandalised but immensely well-rendered paintings of birds, flowers and jewellery. Several stalls have set up along the path that leads to the Daboaji Hall, selling postcards of the frescos, *dongba* scrolls, wood carving and other cultural knick-knacks. There are also some useful food stalls.

Not far from Baisha, on the flat plain that the bus crosses to get to the village, lie the remains of an **old airstrip**. Few people pay much attention to the plot, but in the last years of World War II this was the site of a vitally strategic operation run by the Flying Tigers, a group of ace pilots who braved the tricky Himalayan passage to transport supplies to Chinese forces fighting the Japanese in eastern China. Nobody objects if you get off the bus and have a nose around.

To travel to Baisha from Lijiang take bus No 6 from the stop near the Bank of China on Xi Dajie. The buses terminate at the head of the main street. They are supposed to return to Lijiang every 30 minutes. If you are in a hurry there are usually one or two pickup trucks that do the trip for Y4.

Yuhu Village 玉湖村

5km northeast of Baisha.

Several locals still remember Joseph Rock who had a house here in Yuhu village when it was known as Nguluko, meaning 'Snow Pine Village' in Chinese. A steady trickle of Rock admirers trek out to Yuhu in the hope of gaining entrance to the botanist's former house which is now owned by the grandson of Li Wenbiao, Rock's muleteer. The house contains many of his possessions which were passed down to the family. When Bruce Chatwin visited the house, he was shown the camp bed and washbasin Rock used on expeditions, as well as a portable, canvas bath from Abercrombie & Fitch. The man clearly lived well in the wilds. The house appears to be a fine example of

Naxi rural architecture with a three-sided courtyard, animal and wood shelters and a fine gateway, all of which belie the fact that the family are relatively poor peasant farmers. If you must see inside the house, be sure to make a small donation to the family as they have more pressing things to do than show visitors around.

The Dry Sea
22km north of Lijiang.
Ganhai (the 'Dry Sea') is a marshland of stones, sand and grass, dotted with a few solitary pine trees that was formed when a highland lake dried up. Locals remember the area still being water-logged in the 1940s.

The road to Daju rises towards the Dry Sea, passing across a plain and through a rock-strewn valley. Ganhai, at the foot of the Yulong Mountains, is one of the most accessible places to watch the sun rising behind the glacier of the Jade Dragon massif.

Black and White Water Rivers
As the road climbs into the mountains, beyond the Dry Sea through forested valleys and ridges, you presently reach the White Water River (Baishui). Naxi and Yi tribal people stop here to rest and let their horses drink from the clear waters. The river's bed is strewn with the white rocks and chips of coral that give the river its name. The hamlet of Jiazi lies downstream from here and the traditional Naxi town of Dadong. A few kilometres from Dadong is the spot where Kublai Khan's army made the perilous crossing of the Yangzi in inflatable skin boats, before going on to conquer the Kingdom of Dali.

Further along the valley is the Black River (Heishui), named after its bed of black rock. The Yi village of Heishui is a traditional place with wood-smoke fires burning throughout the day, terraced fields and small herds of goats roaming the high pastures and slopes.

The Stone City of Baoshan 宝山石城
130km northeast of Lijiang.
A single road connects Baoshan Ancient Stone City (Baoshan Shi Gu Cheng) with the outside world. About 100 Naxi families live in this extraordinary town perched high up on a mushroom-shaped ridge overlooking steep rice terraces and the Upper Yangzi River.

The town dates from the Yuan dynasty (1271–1368) and oozes with a monolithic antiquity. Many of the houses are hewn from the rock itself or from local red stone. Many of the tools and utensils, even tables, cupboards and stools, are carved from the rock. Baoshan lies at the end of a road that passes by Mingyin. You can try hitching your way to the town or hire your own transport. (For further information, see *Chapter 10*, page 202–7.)

The easiest way to reach Baoshan is with one of the tours organised by tour operators and cafes in Lijiang, either as a day trip or with an overnight stop in the village.

FURTHER AFIELD FROM LIJIANG

If you would like to venture further off the beaten track and see some of the wilder, less explored parts of northwest Yunnan, then Lijiang is a good base for organising such a trip. Mainstream tourism is still a long way off in many parts of the area, though, so you should be prepared for rough conditions and some frustrations if you want to travel in these untouched areas. There are options for travel through the area of the three great rivers which flow through northern Yunnan: the Mekong, Salween and Yangtze. These three rivers carve out parallel courses as they journey southward from their sources high on the Tibetan plateau. If you have time it is possible to follow a circuit from Lijiang that would take you northwards to Zhongdian, Benzilan and Deqin before turning southwards along the Mekong River valley (Lancang Jiang) to Weixi and the Yangtze (Jinsha Jiang) at Shigu before finally arriving back in Lijiang. You should allow about a week for this journey if using public transport.

Local buses run to and fro between Weixi, Deqin, Zhongdian, Lijiang and Shigu on a daily basis but accommodation is very limited or non-existent in some places, so camping is the best and most reliable option. The road from Zhongdian to Deqin rises about 2,000m and after Benzilan is very high with long, plunging river valleys at its edge. The road is just wide enough for two vehicles at some points, so it can be very dramatic. Every year during the rainy season one or two buses go over the side, so try to avoid it during this time. (For more details see *Chapter 9*.) Just beyond Benzilan is Dongzhulin Lamasery, which is well worth a stop if you have independent transport or are hitching. If the sky is clear on the approach to Deqin the views of Mei Li Xue Shan and the surrounding mountain ranges are spectacular.

The section between Weixi and Deqin is a very long day's journey on a rough road so it is advisable to break the trip into two parts. The road from Deqin down to Cizhong is high, rocky and prone to landslides which are most frequent in the summer months. On this section of road you will be able to see the Mekong river far beneath you as it enters Yunnan. After Cizhong, where there is a lonely Catholic church built by French missionaries at the turn of the century, the road drops down to the Mekong and follows it as far as Baijixun where it turns off for Weixi. The change in scenery is quite dramatic as you descend from barren, high mountains to fertile valleys with distinctive red soil and plentiful greenery and rainfall. This area is also famous for its abundance of orchids, some of which sell for as much as Y10,000 in the cities. As you descend from the mountains the population changes from predominantly Tibetan to Naxi and Lisu, with the Naxi largely in the valleys and the Lisu on the mountains where they are given free land from the government. Most of the villages in this area have simple accommodation ranging from very basic rooms to Chinese local standard hotels. From Weixi to Shigu the scenery becomes even more pastoral and pleasant as you enter the Yangtze valley and the first great bend of the river at Shigu. The scenery changes to rice paddies and green hills along the route until you eventually arrive back on the Lijiang plain. (For more information on these areas see *Chapters 8 and 9*.)

Yading National Park

For those adventurous travellers with a taste for high-altitude wilderness areas, a visit to the newly opened Yading National Park might be worth considering. Shadowing the northwestern Yunnan/Sichuan border, the area has been open only since late 1999, and for all practical purposes accessible only this year. Rarely visited by foreigners, it has long been a pilgrimage site for Tibetans and is notable for its three sacred peaks named by the fifth Dalai Lama. At the foot of each mountain lies a lake, surrounded by the roughly built *stupas* found scattered throughout this area. At an average altitude of 4,500m Yading offers a beauty and remoteness unique to China, paralleling that of the Himalayas further to the west.

However, access is far from easy and Yading is only reachable by experienced 4WD drivers during the spring and autumn months. The road from Riwa, although stunning, is by reputation one of the most terrifying in southwest China and is not for the faint-hearted. Trying it, either during the summer (even if you could persuade a driver to take you), or in a cheap rental, would be ill advised.

Once at Yading the most spectacular, but costly, option, is the six–seven-day trek from Yading village to Lugu lake which lies to the southeast. This is only possible as a supported trek because horses, guides, equipment and food are all necessary. For those on a budget or limited by time, it is possible to hire guides and horses from the locals in Riwa (some basic Chinese is necessary) to trek into the park up to the tiny Chonggu monastery and from there explore the surrounding mountains for two or three days. The monks there (at the last count, all two of them) will give you a bed for Y20–30, but you'll have to bring your own food. Horses cost in the region of Y50–60 a day and the guide a little less.

If you are interested in going on a supported trek in either Yading or some of the more remote areas of this region, then the best operators to use are Haiwei Trails based in Lijiang. Haiwei are run by a team of Western expatriates who are an excellent source of useful and up-to-date information about travelling conditions in the more remote regions. In Lijiang they can be contacted through the Sakura Café in the old town. Alternatively, visit their very informative website at www.yading.com or email them at haiweitrails@chinamail.com.

The Road to Lugu Lake

'To the north lies Lugu Lake and Lion Mountain, all but dwarfed by higher peaks beyond.'

Children of the Jade Dragon, Jim Goodman

Straddling the Yunnan–Sichuan border Lugu Lake (Lugu Hu) lies at an altitude of 2,685m above sea level, the highest expanse of water in Yunnan. The lake is roughly 8km across and reaches a depth of 90m, making it the second deepest lake in China. The statistics are impressive but less so than the sight of Lugu Lake itself. One of the most beautiful bodies of water in Yunnan, this remote alpine lake is flanked on two sides by steep, partly forested slopes, hills and shoreline, two well-delineated strips of blue and green.

Its shores are inhabited by Yi, Moso, Norzu, Pumi, Tibetan and other minorities. The region has not been open that long to either foreign or Chinese tourists. Until the 1950s, the area was dominated by the Norzu clan, a branch of the ethnic Yi group. The Norzu were slave owners who made regular raids into then surrounding lowlands. Captives were brought back to the Lugu Lake area to live abject lives in total submission to their masters. A fascinating account of life under the Norzu is contained in Alan Winnington's book, *Slaves of the Cool Mountains*. Lugu Lake has achieved much notoriety recently with the Han Chinese for being the home of the still matriarchal Moso tribe. Chinese travel brochures gleefully describe this supposed region of Amazons as the 'Kingdom of Women', and 'Home of the Matriarchal Tribe'.

Lugu Lake and the approach road are snowbound for at least three months of the year, another factor that has contributed to the relative isolation of the area. Spring and early autumn are probably the best times to visit as the weather is dry, the light clear, and daytime temperatures fairly warm. Things cool down in the evening so come prepared with at least a sweater.

Nature notes

Although large tracts of woodland have been deforested in the last decade or more, county officials still claim that roughly 51% of Ninglang remains covered in forest. Among the Chinese and Yunnan pines, lacquer, camphor, kapok and dragon spruce are ancient trees of almost indefinable age. Along with Xishuangbanna and Deqin, this is one of the more likely places to spot foxes, musk, vultures, hawks, pilose antelope, even the occasional leopard.

The lake area is also the temporary home of migrant birds like the white swan and bar-headed goose. Lugu Lake and the Yongning Plain are rich in flora as well, ideal places for naturalists and botanists to hike.

GETTING THERE AND AWAY

The first bus from Lijiang's north station for Ninglang, the transfer point between Lijiang and Lugu Lake, departs at 07.10. If you can catch this one it should allow you enough time to board the connecting bus for the remainder of the trip to the lake. The ride to Ninglang usually takes about nine hours, the final stretch to the lake about five hours.

Buses returning to Lijiang leave Luoshui at 07.10. Luoshi is the main village on the shores of Lugu Lake itself – all the buses go there. The return trip should be slightly shorter. If you are lucky you could be in Lijiang by 17.00. In the unlikely event that you want to stop-off in Ninglang, the first bus leaves at 09.00.

THE YI

Over three million Tibeto-Burman speaking Yi live in Yunnan Province, scattered all over the north and northeast. One of the largest and most diverse minorities in China, the Yi have at least 30 different branches. Like the Moso, they seem to have once practised a matrilineal system. The *Annals of the Yis in the Southwest*, records that in ancient times the Yi 'only knew mothers, and not fathers'.

The Yi have their own script. A number of written histories, literary works, genealogies and medicinal tracts have survived. There are also many steles and stone tablets incised with Yi writings in existence. Many Yi folktales have been translated into Chinese. There are also English versions available in the stores in Kunming. Fictional epics, like the Yi story *Ashima,* have also been translated. Oral folk tales, proverbs and fables have also been passed down through the generations.

It's difficult to categorise Yi dress as their clothing is as diverse as they are. Typical of women, though, are large silver earrings, long, colourful dresses with frilly hems, and the Yi's signature hat: broad and kite-like, with an almost Napoleonic flavour.

Many Yi were forced into slavery under the worse-than-feudal system that prevailed under the all-powerful Norzu. Many of the men who suffered serfdom joined the ranks of the Red Army when it marched through the Lugu Lake and Ninglang region.

LIJIANG TO NINGLANG 宁蒗

The landscapes on the 280km ride between Lijiang and Lugu are outstanding, comparable only, perhaps, with those on the Zhongdian to Deqin route. The road passes through the Ninglang Yi Autonomous County. If you are on one of the later buses from Lijiang or suffer from unscheduled delays, you are likely to miss the link to the lake and will have to stay overnight in Ninglang.

The Chinese government has a new road in the pipeline which, if and when completed, will dramatically reduce travel time to Lugu Lake and see a dramatic increase in the number of visitors. Hopefully, it will be some time before this dream materialises. Make the most of the current road. At present the inconveniences of the long road to Lugu act as a filter, separating as it were, the traveller from the tourist.

Where to stay
Ninglang
Lugu Hotel Just two or three minutes' walk from the bus garage in the centre of town, this is a clean and comfortable place to stay. Beds in doubles for Y15, triples Y10. There are also some double rooms with baths for Y160.
Bus Station Guesthouse Right near the bus garage, with doubles for Y15.
Government Guesthouse A bit of a walk from the bus station but this hotel is a friendly, well run place with a couple of English-speaking members of staff who can be quite helpful at times. Dorm beds are priced at Y10 and Y15, but they also have a few double rooms for Y150.

LUGU LAKE 泸沽湖 AND THE ISLANDS

One of the most interesting things to do while staying in Luoshui is to hire a boat and spend a day or half day on the lake visiting the far shores of Sichuan and several islands and islets that dot the water. The boats used for these pleasant excursions are the traditional 'pig troughs' as the Moso call them: long dug-out canoes. The pilots are generally Moso women who charge Y15–20 per person for a return trip to Liwubi Island, the largest on the lake, or Y30–40 for a longer trip around the lake. Try to negotiate for a full day's trip and take along your own picnic. Most of the canoes are lined up outside the Moso Yuan Hotel.

In the past many of these islands were used as retreats by the Yongning nobility and were the site of gardens and pleasure pavilions. Three of the islands are considered sacred by the local Moso and regularly visited to make offerings.

The **Gemu Goddess Mountain** on the Sichuan side of the lake, with its little-explored caves and springs, is well worth a look. Children on the Sichuan shoreside are remarkable linguists, often speaking three or four languages: Mandarin, Tibetan, Pumi and Moso. The shores along the Sichuan section of the lake were once the centre of the powerful Bon religion, a pre-Buddhist Tibetan theology. Strongly animist, Bon shamans used magic spells and incantations in attempts to appease, as well as harness, the forces of nature. Traces of Bon worship still remain around the lake. If you tramp the hills

THE MOSO

Yongning is the main home of the Moso, a branch of the Naxi. Known to their Naxi cousins as Luxi, the Moso originally referred to themselves as the Hlikhin. The Moso have a number of unique and interesting customs and habits. The Moso boats used by women on the lake are carved, for example, in the shape of a pig's trough. The strangely named Boneless Pig is also associated with this group. Most visitors will wonder what on earth a boneless pig might be, and what possible use it could be put to. Apparently, these huge animals are fattened up, slaughtered, then boned and salted. After this transformation they are placed in Moso homes and used for ten or twelve years as mattresses before being sliced, then eaten along with pieces of homemade cheese and whipped yak butter. The custom seems to have started very sensibly as a way of hoarding food in the event of famine.

The Moso culture and lifestyle has made the lake area an unintentional Mecca for anthropologists. Known in Yunnan as the 'matriarchal tribe', the Moso follow an ancient practice known as the *azhu* system, whereby a flexible form of cohabitation takes the place of formal marriage. Moso women generally take the initiative in forming relationships and are free to dispense with their lovers when the time comes. The word *azhu* means 'good friends', and the relationships are often quite short-lived. Any offspring of the liaison are brought up by the mother. Family names in this system pass from mother to daughter. The household money is controlled by the Moso women and almost all decisions made by them.

Sexual activity of this kind often begins during the teen years. Needless to say, the incidence of sexually transmitted diseases among the Moso is frightful. It always has been. In his 1957 memoir *Forgotten Kingdom*, Peter Goullart noted an encounter with a Tibetan trader he met who was returning from the Moso region. Goullart was asked to examine and treat the man. The Russian-born Frenchman quickly recognised the symptoms of gonorrhea and proceeded to suggest the right course of treatment to the man, who, to quote Goullart's book, responded in the following manner: 'No! No!' the man protested. 'It is only a cold.' 'How did you get it?' the writer asked. 'I caught it when riding a horse,' the man replied. 'Well,' said Goullart, 'it was the wrong kind of horse.'

around Luoshui you can still come across curious-looking towers or masts called *nya-ta*, or demon-traps. Looking like ruined utility poles, festooned with a nest of cord, wires and strong twine, they are intended to capture evil spirits. They are usually placed above fields to protect the crops. A few old wooden **Bonpo monasteries** survive. There is one in Luoshui which has some interesting murals.

The Moso in this area celebrate two main festivals every year. Their Mountain Festival takes place on the 25th of the seventh lunar month, generally in August or at the start of September. The Lake Festival is held on the 15th day of the third lunar month which usually falls in late April.

Where to stay/eat
Lugu Lake
Moso Homes One of the most interesting things you can do while in Luoshui is to board with a Moso family. Traditionally, Moso houses face the lake and you should look for one of these for a more authentic experience. Simple meals, consisting mostly of fish, a few vegetables, eggs, potatoes or wheat-based pancakes are cooked by the family. The beds are reasonably comfortable and you will be charged about Y15 for the night. Meals are extra. The only drawback is that there are no showers.

Moso Yuan Hotel Actually a guesthouse, this is the most popular choice for most travellers who don't stay in a Moso home. A good place to pick up travel information. They also have Moso song-and-dance evenings which are quite spirited affairs. The Moso seem genuinely to enjoy dancing. Some of the more enthusiastic dance routines put on at the Yunnan Nationalities Village in Kunming are by the Yi. Dorm beds here are Y25.

Peace Garden Offers similar facilities. A nice quiet place as the name implies. Beds for Y15.

THE YONGNING PLAIN
Both agricultural centre and cradle of the Moso culture, the Yongning Plain lies roughly 20km west of Lugu Lake at an altitude of 2,900m. Shizu Shan (Lion Mountain) dominates the eastern end of the plain, while the eastern horizon is filled out by the blue and purple mountains of Sichuan. The plain itself, transected by countless streams and other water channels, is extremely fertile.

Kublai Khan is supposed to have reviewed his troops from a hill above the plain when his Mongol army passed through here in 1253 before their victory against the forces of the Dali Kingdom. The great general camped at a spot called Ri Yue He, meaning 'the union of sun and moon'. The meadow where his troops massed is now a Moso field sown with rice corn and tobacco.

Yongning Monastery lies 12km west of the lake and is the plain's most visitor-worthy historical sight. Actually a lamasery of the Yellow Hat (Gelugpa) sect of Tibetan Buddhism, with over 20 lamas in attendance, the original buildings date from the 17th century. The monastery was savagely violated during the Cultural Revolution but some well-managed reconstruction and renovation was undertaken in the early 1990s. There is a small chapel on the right side of the monastery which is still intact. You will also find a hot spring within walking distance of the monastery.

There is a public bus to Yongning Monastery which charges Y5 and stops at Luoshui. Private buses are more expensive but also more frequent.

Opium poppy

Shigu, Weixi and Tiger Leaping Gorge

'One would expect from the impressive statistics that the river would be choked with vessels of all descriptions, but this is not the case.'

The Yangzi River, Judy Bonavia

One look at the foaming, brown waters of the Upper Yangzi as it tears across boulders and through narrow gorges is enough to put most people off the idea of floating a canoe down this scornful and impatient river. Tourists who have tried to kayak down this stretch have invariably met disaster, and now few try. There are various ways to cross this lively river bereft of shipping. Bridges and ferries span the river at various points, locals still occasionally use inflated goat-skin vessels to reach the opposite bank and you might also come across precarious-looking pulley-bridges, that require the person crossing the river to sit in a basket and fly across in the manner of a funicular.

Within a few hours of Lijiang, travellers can explore the amazing cartography of the Yangzi at Shigu and, further north, at Hutiaoxia, better known as Tiger Leaping Gorge. More intrepid travellers will want to press on to the little explored, but highly scenic region of Weixi, an area between the Yangzi and Lancang (Mekong) rivers which sees few visitors.

Nature notes

Late May is a fine time to visit this region when plants and flowers are in full bloom. Naxi women collect pine and artemisia from the slopes of the mountains. Larch, wild pear and gentian are also common. Hundreds of other alpine flowers and medicinal plants thrive in this area.

The Hengduan Mountains are an area of particular interest to botanists who come from all over China, as well as overseas, to study one of the world's most botanically varied regions. There are several rare species of plants hidden in the primeval ecosystem along this range, and among the evergreen, broadleaf forests there are ancient trees, some of them over 2,000 years old. Among the more endangered fauna are takin, golden monkeys and red gorals. Wild goats and small bears are more common. The fauna of the area is, sadly, withdrawing in the face of increasing human encroachment.

SHIGU 石鼓

70km west of Lijiang.

History

Something extraordinary happens to the Yangzi when it reaches the village of Shigu. Instead of flowing south like the Mekong and Salween, the Yangzi seems to have a change of heart, swerving in a 180° turn north, running for the next 20km or so parallel to itself. Changing its course it has, to a very real degree, also changed the course of Chinese history and had a defining effect on the people of China. Travel writer Simon Winchester put it unequivocally when he stated in his book, *The River at the Centre of the World*, that 'given the central role that the Yangtze has for aeons played in the creation of China, one can say without risk of too strong contradiction that it caused China to exist as well.' Locals are immensely proud of their village, claiming that if it were not for Shigu, the country would have lost this valuable water stock to Southeast Asia, as they do with the Mekong and Salween.

Shigu (Stone Drum) takes its name from a large, 75cm thick, 150cm diameter, cylindrical-shaped memorial tablet which records and pays tribute to a victory by Sino-Naxi forces over an invading Tibetan army. The slaughter of the Tibetans here on the wide, pebble-strewn banks of the Yangzi took place in the summer of 1548. The stone drum, described by Bruce Chatwin in his essay, *In Lijiang: Rock's Kingdom,* as 'a cylinder of marble in a pavilion by the willows', records it all: 200,000 men sent packing in confusion, 3,000 decapitated in a gory victory ceremony, 'Heads heaped like grave mounds, Blood like rain…The dikes choked with armour and rattan shields.'

History was made again on April 24 1936 when 18,000 Red Army soldiers, part of a much larger group fleeing from Nationalist forces, crossed the Yangzi at this point. It took four days and nights for locals to ferry the soldiers across the river. This footnote in the story of the communist's Long March is still remembered by some old-timers, and the event, marked by a tablet called the 'Chinese Workers and Peasants Red Army Second Route Army Long March Ferry Crossing memorial', which stands on a promontory above the spot where the crossing took place. As for the Stone Drum itself, Red Guards split the tablet in the 1960s. It has since been stuck together again.

Getting there and away

There is a 14.30 bus from Lijiang to Shigu which departs from the north bus station. With more visitors discovering Lijiang, it is likely there will be extra bus services laid on to Shigu and other interesting destinations in the area.

Although Shigu is only a short journey from Lijiang (an hour and a half) it is not currently possible to visit it as a day trip on public transport because the bus timings necessitate an overnight stop. However, several Lijiang-based travel agencies offer one-day trips to see the Stone Drum.

Where to stay/eat

There is only one guesthouse in Shigu. There are a couple of attractive-looking restaurants with tables set up outside under trellises.

What to see

Shigu is an extremely pleasant place to spend a day walking around the hills in the vicinity or idling along the banks of the river. The hill above the village which blocked the southern flow of the Yangzi, is called **Cloud Mountain**. Covered in camphor trees, rhododendron and camellias, it is not difficult to climb and provides a fine view of the river and the so-called First Bend of the Yangzi River. Shigu's **Tiehong Bridge**, a 17m-long span across the river is a good example of a chain construction with wooden planks. The bridge was built during the Qing dynasty and formed a lucrative tea transportation link on the Southern Silk Road. The bridge is in perfect working order and still used today.

THE YANGZI

The titanic Yangzi, or Changjiang as it is more commonly known to the Chinese, is China's premier river. Changjiang means 'Long River', a name it lives up to. Covering a distance of 6,300km it is the world's third largest river, roughly equivalent in length to the Mississippi.

China's mother river is swollen by over 700 tributaries, a fact of great concern to those who live within flooding distance of its middle reaches. At Shigu the Upper Yangzi makes a dramatic 180° turn, changing not only the direction of the river but the course of Chinese history in the process. Because of this, the river is regarded by the Chinese as a marker, broadly dividing the country into north and south. The division is considered as much a cultural as a geographical one.

The Yunnan section of the river boasts, along with the key sights of its middle reaches like the Three Gorges, some of the most stunningly beautiful stretches of the Yangzi. Here are many of the river's most awesome gorges, unnavigable rapids, and ravines. Before its swerve at Shigu, the Yunnan stretch of the Yantgzi, known here as the Jinsha Jiang (River of Golden Sand), runs more or less parallel with three other waterways that also have their source in the high plateaus and glaciers of Tibet: the Mekong, Salween and the eastern branch of the Irrawaddy.

There are many stretches of the Jinsha Jiang which can hardly have changed much since Joseph Rock explored the area as leader of the National Geographic Society's Yunnan Province Expedition in the 1920s. One of Rock's superb photos shows two semi-naked locals about to cross the river on rafts made from inflated sheepskin. Skin-coracle boats are still used today for short, normally unnavigable, passages; swaying rope-bridges are also found. Even more an act of faith for those obliged to use them are pulley-bridges. A taut rope slung between respective river banks is carefully greased with yak butter, and then the rider sent across in a sling.

The river, alternatively tea-brown or frothing white according to its depth and speed, is a companionable but awesome presence for anyone travelling through the rugged northern counties of Yunnan.

WEIXI 维西

100km northwest of Shigu.

Little explored, with only a seminal tourist infrastructure, but surely destined on account of the beauty of the area to be on the traveller's circuit before long, the county town of Weixi is at the end of a road that leads northwest from Shigu. Before reaching Weixi, you pass through the Hengduan Mountains and some worthwhile stops on the way.

Liming and Liguang are at the centre of a multi-coloured forest of flat-topped hills and steep rock faces that dot a large expanse of river valley. You would need private transport to see this geological spectacle, although it is possible that you could hitch a lift from the left turning to Liguang which appears about 40km after Shigu. The 240km^2 protected area is sure to be developed as a scenic tourist spot with easier transportation and tours provided.

Just before reaching the township of Judian, the road forks left toward the Xinzhu Botanical Garden and Weixi itself. If you continue roughly 40km north instead of bearing left, you will reach the small village of Tacheng, site of several Neolithic ruins and a backdrop of towering

THE PUMI

The Pumi, a Tibetan race with a population of about 29,000, are one of the smallest minorities in southwest China. Most Pumi live within the counties of Weixi, Lanping, Ninglang, Lijiang, and Yongsheng. Pumi legends claim their ancestors were a nomadic tribe that roamed the Qinghai-Tibetan Plateau, a perfectly feasible theory. From there they descended to warmer, more verdant valleys situated in the Hengduan Mountains.

The Pumi language belongs to the large, and far-ranging Tibet-Burmese group. Pumi women can be identified from their head scarves and plaited hair, which is mixed with silk threads and yak-tail hairs. In the Weixi area, women have a preference for blue, green and white long-sleeved jackets, embroidered belts and silver bracelets and earrings.

If by chance you end up staying in a Pumi village, you are likely to be fed on maize, wheat and highland barley-based foods, though rice is also grown. The Pumi's favourite food though is called '*pipa-meat*'. Salted pork is wrapped in pork skin which is supposed to resemble the shape of a *pipa*, a Chinese string instrument. Tea and liquor are equally popular.

The most important event for the Pumi is the New Year Festival, held on the eighth day of the 12th lunar month. Houses are decked out with green branches, symbolising the hope for an everlasting green year. Adulthood rituals are held at this time of year for 13 year-old boys. The Festival of Travelling Around the Mountain, held on the 15th day of the seventh lunar month, honours the Pumi's mountain god. Wrestling, mountain-hiking, camping, and horse-racing are all part of the festivities.

mountains. It is also possible if you have your own transport or can arrange something on the spot, to visit the **Bodhidharma Cave and Temple**, about 15km from Tacheng.

About 18km west of Judian is the outstanding **Xinzhu Botanic Garden**. Some of the 300 or so species of trees in this protected park are over a thousand years old. There are several temples, pagodas and pavilions in the Weixi area you could explore.

TIGER LEAPING GORGE

100km north of Lijiang.

Reputedly the world's deepest canyon, Hutiao Xia gets its name from a story describing how a tiger, looking for an escape route from hunters, found two sides of the gorge so narrow it leapt across in one go. Truth or legend, it is a tight squeeze in places for the Yangzi to get through. Wedged between the Jade Dragon Snow Mountain and Haba Mountain ranges, sitting at an altitude of 2,500m, the cliff above and below the gorge, which hikers have to nerve their way along, rises for 3,900m from the water to the top. Some people, dwarfed by the scale of the gorge, actually find the spectacle quite oppressive. Not everyone likes the Grand Canyon, right?

The Gorge has undergone a few changes in the last few years which have made access easier but as a consequence have brought far more visitors. The Gorge's fame has spread and it has become one of the must-see attractions of Yunnan. There is now a road through the gorge from Qiaotou 桥头 which brings busloads of visitors each day, most of whom go by tour bus to the one place where you can walk down to the gorge, about a third of the way along from the Qiaotou end. There are the inevitable accompaniments to any well-known site in China: food stands, karaoke and lots of willing folk who will carry you up and down the steps in a sedan chair for Y50 or so. There is also a road currently under construction on the southern side of the gorge, which will take most of the day-visitor traffic once it is complete. If this doesn't sound like the Tiger Leaping Gorge that you have heard about and want to experience, do not despair, as the high path (also known as the 28 bend path) is blissfully free of any such distractions and is still one of the best scenic treks you can undertake in China. The new roads will, if anything, make the high path more of a wilderness experience by thinning the crowds.

You should, however, think carefully before undertaking the high path. Although it is easier than it used to be, with arrows directing walkers along the paths and a bevy of new wayside guesthouses, the walk itself is strenuous and, if the weather changes for the worse, dangerous. There have been several fatalities amongst walkers who have slipped over the edge, been trapped under landslides or simply got lost on one of the side trails and been unable to find one of the two main paths. Travellers are also advised not to walk through the gorge alone as there have been some recent, though isolated, cases of mugging along the way. Having said all that, the trek on the high path is well worth the effort and is considered by many as a Yunnan highlight. For those people who cannot do without their creature comforts, the walk is best undertaken as a day

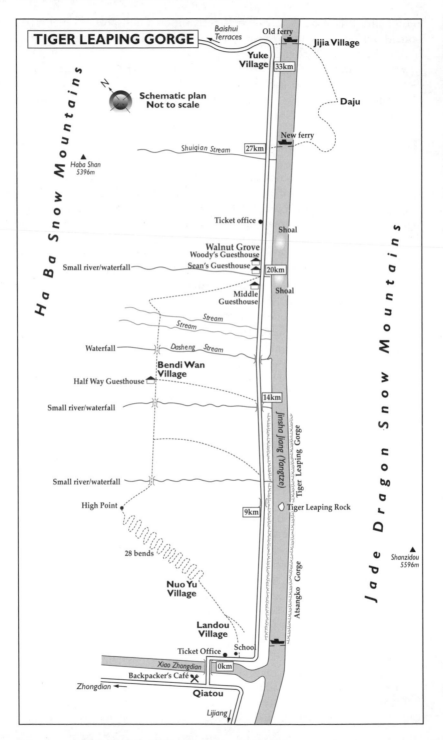

TIGER LEAPING GORGE

Schematic plan
Not to scale

Baishui Terraces

Old ferry

Jijia Village

Yuke Village

33km

Daju

New ferry

Shuiqian Stream

27km

Ha Ba Snow Mountains

Haba Shan 5396m

Ticket office

Shoal

Walnut Grove
Woody's Guesthouse

Small river/waterfall

Sean's Guesthouse

20km

Shoal

Middle Guesthouse

Stream

Stream

Waterfall

Dasheng Stream

Bendi Wan Village

Half Way Guesthouse

14km

Small river/waterfall

Jinsha Jiang (Yangtze)

Tiger Leaping Gorge

Small river/waterfall

High Point

9km

Tiger Leaping Rock

Jade Dragon Snow Mountains

Shanzidou 5596m

28 bends

Atsangko Gorge

Nuo Yu Village

Landou Village

Ticket Office

School

Xiao Zhongdian

0km

Backpacker's Café

Zhongdian

Qiatou

Lijiang

Above The feathers of this minority headdress from Xishuangbanna are coloured with vegetable dyes.

Left A member of one of Yunnan's 25 ethnic minorities

Below Detail of a headdress of Hani minority women

Above Messages beseeching good fortune are inscribed on stones.
Below Badly desecrated but still vivid, the famous Baisha frescos

trip since the guesthouses along the way, although perfectly adequate, offer only simple standards of accommodation.

Walking options

There are now several options: you could take the easier route on the road, the more challenging high path or a combination of both (by starting on the road and then cutting up to the high path by one of several trails). You could also walk the road to Walnut Grove one day and return via the high path the following day. It is also possible to do the gorge as a day trip from Lijiang, starting from the Qiaotou end. Buses leave from the main Lijiang bus station at 06.30 and arrive in Qiaotou at 10.00. If you then allow for three hours to walk up to the high point at the top of the 28 bends and three for the return journey you will be back in Qiaotou in time to catch the last bus which leaves at 18.00. The fare each way is around Y15. To sum up the differences between the road route and the high path: the road is as you would expect – a lot easier to walk and closer to the river itself – but the high path has a much wilder feel with better scenery and views.

When to go

The rainy months of July and August are best avoided, not only for the cloud and drizzle which seem to hang interminably in the gorge, but also because of the very real danger of landslides.

The winter months can be cold in the evenings and snow is not uncommon but the days can also be quite warm and sunny. April, May, September and October are the best months to visit as the weather is usually dry and bright. Whatever time of year you choose be sure to have adequate warm and waterproof clothing, as with any mountain area the weather conditions can be volatile and unpredictable.

Route details

The full trek can be done in under two days from either end, but it would be best to allow three or four days for a round-trip journey from Lijiang if using public transport. Most travellers taking the high path prefer to start at the Qiaotou end of the gorge and finish at Daju, but you could just as easily do it the other way around. (The average walking time is around seven hours.) The facilities have traditionally been better at Qiaotou but this is now changing with the addition of places such as the Snowflake Hotel at Daju. Coming from the Qiaotou end you will first cross over the bridge, turn right and then pass through a gate for the ticket office (there is a Y20 entrance fee to the gorge) and on to a school building some few hundred metres away. Behind the school building is where the arrows start which will direct you to the high path. It is worth asking directions throughout the walk to confirm that you have taken the right path, otherwise you could end up getting lost or taking a walk along the lower route. If you are taking the lower route then continue along past a concrete statue of a leaping tiger and you can expect to have a straightforward walk of about five hours until you come to Walnut Grove, where the higher trail meets the road. Mama Wu's Guesthouse is situated about an hour or so from Qiaotou but at the time of writing there is little else in the way of accommodation on the lower route until you reach Walnut Grove; this may change as this part of the gorge receives most of the visitors. If you are taking the lower route then be aware that, due to construction work and the dynamiting of cliff faces, there is a danger of landslides blocking parts of the road.

The high path continues on for a good few kilometres uphill then ascends through the tortuous 28 bends to the highest view point of the trek. Expect this to take about five hours from Qiaotou. There are excellent views back through the mouth of the gorge and of the Jade Dragon snow range. You then descend down into a pine wood and, after crossing a bridge, the path will take you to Bendi Wan, some two hours' walk from the top of the 28 bends. Once at Bendi Wan you have the option to finish your walk for the day or continue on to Walnut Grove, another two or three hours away.

Accommodation at Bendi Wan consists of the Half Way Guesthouse, a welcoming place run by the Feng family who have now expanded the number of beds available to 32; from Y15 per night. The Half Way Guesthouse is, as its name suggests, the equidistant centre from both Qiaotou and Daju. It offers not only food, lodging, hot showers and an excellent spot to enjoy the views of the gorge but also excellent guided tours into the Haba mountains and horse riding.

There is a path from Bendi Wan that connects with the road so that you could conveniently switch your route at this point or return back to Qiaotou a different way.

Continuing on from Bendi Wan it is another two to three hours descending to the road and Walnut Grove. Before arriving at Walnut Grove you should come across the Middle Tiger Leaping Gorge Guesthouse, which offers reasonable accommodation for around Y15. Once at Walnut Grove you will find the two original guesthouses of the Tiger Leaping Gorge: the Spring Guesthouse and Chateau De Woody, both of which are equally good. Sean and Woody are the two amenable owners and these two veteran operators can offer all kinds of amenities such as hot showers, good food, horse riding and interesting treks further afield from the gorge. (See below for more details.) Both places offer dorm beds and a limited number of double rooms starting from Y10. If you are coming along the path from the direction of Daju, after the Spring Guesthouse you should look for arrows pointing the way to the upper path. It is very easy at this juncture to get lost or go too high on one of the myriad small trails in this area. If after half an hour you don't see any arrows then turn back because you are probably on the wrong path. From Walnut Grove it is approximately three hours' walk along the road to the old ferry crossing, coming out of the gorge and into a wide plain dotted with hamlets and other small settlements. When the river is not running too high there is also another ferry crossing about an hour or so from Walnut Grove. This new crossing will connect you on to a path on the other side that has spectacular views but is quite a rough walk as the path winds its way up and down to Daju, about 25 minutes away. If you plan to use this ferry it is advisable to check in Walnut Grove that it is running. The walk from the old ferry crossing to Daju is easier but takes you further out and takes approximately two hours longer. The ferry crossings can vary in price but expect to pay at least Y10 per person.

Once you have crossed to the other side follow the path around until you see a track on the right. Walk until you reach the first village, following the arrows that have been provided for hikers, and then descend an embankment and cross a small stream. Carry on straight from here, ascending again and finally following the path on the left to reach the dusty stone walled houses of Daju.

Longer treks

For those who want to undertake a more challenging trek it is possible to continue trekking onwards from the Tiger Leaping Gorge to the Baishuitai Terraces and even further to the lake at Bita Hai. The trek begins at Walnut Grove and goes up into the Haba Snow Mountains stopping at Haba village on the opposite side of the gorge and further up from Daju. Along the way you will pass through forests and spectacular mountain scenery, taking two days to reach Haba. The Haba Snow mountain range is an extraordinarily rich botanical area and part of a reserve that is home to half of the 13,000 plant species found in Yunnan. There are reputedly more than 900 varieties of medicinal plants found here, as well as 50 kinds of azalea and 25 species of protected animal. The first day's walk from Walnut Grove takes about six to eight hours and necessitates an overnight stop in one of the guesthouses at Haba village. From Haba it is another six or seven hours' walk to Baishuitai. Once you are at Baishuitai it is possible to continue onwards to Bita Hai or catch a bus to Zhongdian, five hours away. The best way to undertake this is on one of the guided tours offered from either the Spring Guesthouse or Woody's; the charge is in the region of Y50 per person per day for a guided trek with horses taking your packs. If your interest is mainly a botanical one then Mr Feng at the Half Way Guesthouse runs tours into the mountains to search for rare and medicinal plants and comes highly recommended. If you undertake the trek to Haba by yourself then be sure to get good directions and take adequate supplies as it is be easy to get lost in these mountains.

Where to stay

Apart from the guesthouses listed above, in the gorge itself there are several choices of accommodation in Daju and Qiaotou. In both towns the accommodation is fairly basic but, at the time of writing, there are plans underway to build more upmarket accommodation in line with the development of the gorge. In Qiaotou the **Jade Dragon Hotel** and the **Gorge Village Hotel** both offer fairly basic rooms starting from Y12 for a bed. The **Backpacker's Café** near the bridge is the best place to pick up information on the gorge while enjoying a meal or drink. They also have an information phoneline for the conditions in the gorge, call (0887) 880 6300.

In Daju the best bet for accommodation is the **Snowflake Hotel**, just downhill from the hospital, which is a main landmark in the town. The Snowflake Hotel is run by a friendly Naxi family and has received many good reports from travellers. Beds start from Y15.

Other guesthouses include the **Tiger Leaping Gorge Hotel** and the **Weinin Hotel**.

Getting there and away

Buses for Qiaotou depart from Lijiang's main station starting at 06.30 and are fairly frequent; the fare is Y13 and takes roughly three and a half hours. Returning from Qiaotou the last bus leaves at 18.00. For those going onward to Zhongdian from Qiaotou, the last bus leaves at 18.00 and the fare is Y15.

From Lijiang to Daju the first bus leaves from the north bus station at 07.30 and the last at 13.30. Returning from Daju to Lijiang there is a bus at 08.00 and one at 13.30, the fare is Y25 and it is a five-hour journey. There is also a man in Daju who offers transport to the Yulong Snow Mountain Natural Reserve and from there onwards to Lijiang by jeep. The journey to Lijiang by jeep takes four hours and costs around Y30 per person for a party of four. This is an excellent scenic alternative to the bone-jarring bus ride. This man can be contacted through the Snowflake Hotel; his house is the first place you come to after crossing the river, if you are coming via the new ferry crossing.

Zhongdian and Deqin

'The Land bathing in god's favour,
As a carpet covering in lotus.
The village in god's beneficence.'

From a Tibetan folk song.

After passing Qiaotou and the gateway to Tiger Leaping Gorge, the road from Lijiang begins its slow ascent, following the course of the Xao Zhongdian He River. Climbing through forests and woodland hamlets which are still a part of the Yangzi River Valley, the bus suddenly pitches over the top of a ridge and, in an instant, you are rumbling across the Tibetan highlands, bearing down on Zhongdian, a town situated at an altitude of 3,160m, high enough to be quite chilly at night even in the spring and summer months.

The name Zhongdian refers both to the 300,000-strong county and to the town which is its capital. There is something distinctly sacred about this land of prayer flags, holy mountains, lamaseries and rock-piles inscribed in Tibetan characters with Buddhist sutras. Zhongdian, in fact, is a Chinese name; the predominantly Tibetan population of this region call it Gyelthang. Contiguous with Tibet in the northwest, Muli and Ganzi in the north, the Salween River Lisu Autonomous Prefecture to the west and Lijiang to the south, the county plays host to an interesting fusion of Tibetans, Hui, Bai, Naxi and Han peoples.

The town itself is nothing special, although it has an interesting old section. Zhongdian is going through a construction boom at the moment; local businessmen are opening new shopping centres, hotels and travel agencies. More Han Chinese are moving in, attracted by the region's natural resources which include deposits of gold, silver, zinc, iron, copper and lead.

Zhongdian and Deqin are considered the gateway to Tibet and Sichuan. Travellers should double-check on the prevailing rules about Tibet. At the time of writing, the PSB were adamant that, unless you were part of an authorised tour, this route into Tibet was strictly prohibited. It would be inadvisable to try and slip in unnoticed: as a foreigner in this sensitive border region you are highly conspicuous.

ZHONGDIAN 中甸
Getting there and away
Zhongdian is 198km northwest of Lijiang. These days the journey by bus can be done in slightly under five hours. Buses leave Lijiang's northern bus station at 06.30 and 08.00 and then at 13.30. You can also leave from the main bus station at 07.50 and 13.30. Buses pass by Qiaotou, the southern gateway to Tiger Leaping Gorge. Buses returning to Lijiang depart at 07.00 and 12.00. There are also sleeper buses for the long-haul to Kunming. There is a Zhongdian to Dali bus at 08.50 which takes an interesting back route. It takes about eight hours. There are lots of police barriers on this route checking mostly for drug smuggling. Worth the minor delays for the scenery and remote villages you pass through. A second bus station to the north of Changzheng Lu also has buses that make the Lijiang run.

There is now a brand new airport at Zhongdian which is located 3km outside the town. Flights to and from Kunming depart on Tuesday, Thursday, Saturday and Sunday. The fare is Y560 and the flight takes 50 minutes. A taxi from the airport into town should cost you around Y15.

Getting around
The town is extremely easy to negotiate as it is built on a simple grid system. The main north–south street is the 2km-long Changzheng Lu. This is where the bus station and most of the town's shops and hotels are located. The road leading northeast of Changzheng Lu leads to Songzhanling Monastery, Zhongdian's main sight. Changzheng Lu is transected by a number of short streets worth exploring for local restaurants. East–west running Tuanje Jie at the southern end of the street leads to a number of smaller temples and skirts the edge of the old town.

With the exception of the Songzhanling monastery, Zhongdian is easily explored on foot. Bicycles can be hired from the Tibet Hotel. Two- and four-seat motorised cyclos putter around town. It would be pleasant hiring one to go out to Songzhanling monastery.

Practical information
Post and telecommunications
The small post office is just along from the bus station. There are no facilities at present for making international calls, but improvements are likely.

The area code for Zhongdian is 0887.

Money matters
The Bank of China offices are in the People's Bank of China along Changzheng Lu. The exchange counter is on the right. The Tibet Hotel can change dollars.

Tourism
The CITS office is just south of the bus station. There are several small travel agencies dotted around town worth sounding out for trips further afield. The

Tibet Hotel has a small but well set up travel office which can arrange group or individually tailored trips and excursions at reasonable rates.

Books and maps

Decent printed materials are few and far between but hotels occasionally have hand-drawn maps that turn out to be surprisingly useful. The **Snowfield Bookstore** at the far southern end of Changzheng Lu, has the best selection of local maps (places of interest in Chinese, text in English), and plenty of books on the local 'Shangri-la' theme.

Shopping

Changzheng Lu is fast becoming a shopping and souvenir strip, although it is uncertain who actually supports such a large commodities market. Among the showcases of Japanese cameras and Scotch whisky, you will find some well-made Tibetan objects like *tankas*, silver jewellery, musk, copper kitchenware, carpets and nice examples of embroidery. You may not be interested in the furry, Davy Crockett-style hats or polished yak horns. Expensive *songrong* mushrooms are said to have curative qualities. The Zhongdian Wooden Bowl Factory, just outside town on the left of the road that runs to Benzilan, is an interesting place to visit. They make small Tibetan tea bowls from azalea wood, as well as larger, lidded containers for keeping seeds, sweets and rice.

Nature notes

Zhongdian and Deqin are located at the core of the Hengduan Mountain Range, an area which acts as a girdle of rock for no less than three great rivers and their valleys: the Upper Yangzi, the Mekong and Salween. Supporting a vertical pattern of snow-capped mountains, glaciers, snowfields, grassslands, rivers and lakes, the area provides a great environment for the growth of primeval and virgin forest. The area was popular with Western naturalists, botanists and those interested in medicinal herbs and plants in the 19th and early half of the 20th centuries. You can expect to see a good range of flora, especially on the Deqin Plateau. Red-spotted stonecrop, green and purple wormwoods, pyxie, gentian, azalea, orchid, green artemisia and other alpine plants are common. The **Mount Baimang Nature Reserve** due east of Deqin, was established in 1985 and provides a wonderful opportunity to see the flora and fauna of this region at close quarters. It is the largest reserve of its kind in Yunnan. There is also an interesting botanical garden section.

Although many of the forests are increasingly depleted, there are many tracts of woodland remaining which are the habitat of rare creatures like the black-necked crane, snow cock, snub-nosed monkey, the lesser panda, leopards, muskdeer and pangolins. This is also the home of the endangered Dian golden monkey and several domestic animals such as yak, donkeys, sheep and Tibetan horses. The region's herbs, medicinal plants and roots are highly prized. China's interest in forestry for commercial timber will surely send the region's wildlife into retreat, reducing a wilderness rich in flora and fauna to one or two showcase nature reserves.

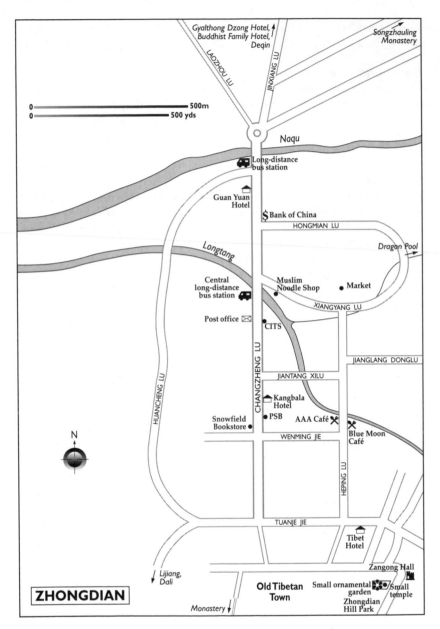

ZHONGDIAN

Where to stay

Buddhist Family Hotel Nai Zi River Bank, Jingxiang Rd; tel: 822 7505. This guesthouse is built in authentic Tibetan style and run by a friendly Tibetan family offering dorm beds and the unique experience to eat your meals with the family, one of whom is reputedly a living Buddha! The rooms and toilets are kept very clean and beds cost Y30 a night.

Guan Yuan Hotel Changzheng Lu. Next to long-distance bus station. Popular with small groups and backpackers. Friendly staff and clean rooms. Convenient for the bus station. Doubles with bathroom Y200, 'ordinary' doubles Y60, triples Y90, four-bed rooms Y120.

Gyalthang Dzong Hotel Jingxiang Rd, between the traffic circle and the monastery about 20 minutes' walk from the town centre; tel: 822 3646/822 7610; fax: 822 3620. The most interesting option for accommodation in Zhongdian and one that gets rave reviews from travellers who have stayed there, the Gyalthong Dzong is run by a Tibetan family not only as a hotel but as a Tibetan cultural centre as well. They hold regular lectures here and tours based on traditional Tibetan medicine, flora, music and dance. The building itself is built in Tibetan style and double rooms with bath cost Y331.

Kangbala Hotel Changzheng Lu. Between Wenming Jie and Jiantang Xi Lu; tel: 822 4488. A decent option in the unlikely event that you cannot get something at the above two places. Clean rooms, friendly enough staff. Doubles with bathroom Y210, triples Y180. Dorm beds go for Y30.

Tibet Hotel Tuanje Jie; tel: 222 206. The essential backpackers' and independent travellers' hangout, this accommodation, also known as the Longlife Tibetan Hotel, provides a complete life support system for the traveller. Very clean communal hot showers are available for guests in the cheaper wing, attached bathrooms for the more upmarket rooms. The hotel also has a money exchange service, international calls, laundry service, bicycle hire, a travel agency and a decent restaurant. TV and electric blankets in all rooms, even the cheap ones. Spacious doubles with nice wooden floors Y240, suites at Y300. Basic but clean, neat rooms for Y50.

Where to eat

Tibet Hotel Mediocre food but a good range and the last travellers' style cuisine that you will enjoy for a while, especially if you are headed in the direction of Deqin. Unexciting Chinese fare enlivened with some good chicken and nut, sweet and sour and fried pork with cucumber specials. The hotel's special breakfasts are worth trying: steamed bread, Tibetan tea, boiled eggs and oatmeal porridge.

AAA Café Heping Lu. Popular with travellers. In a kitschy row of log cabins. Run by friendly staff wearing ethnic bonnets and smocks. Good selection of Chinese, local and Western-style dishes. The spicy tofu dishes from Sichuan are good. The kitchen grills are outside where you can sit and watch the local dumper trucks and tractors going by from the verandah. The service can be a bit slow as they only seem to have one cook at any give time.

Blue Moon Café Heping Lu. Good all-round choice of Western and Chinese. Some Tibetan snacks and dishes as well. Would be better without the blue vinyl windows and loud pop music. The owner speaks English and can give advice. There are some simple yak meat restaurants almost next door to the Blue Moon.

Muslim Noodle Shop Xiangyang Lu. Doesn't seem to have a name but look out for the Arabic writing and crescent moon, this second from last restaurant on the left before hitting Changzheng Lu is a rough and ready place patronised by only locals at the moment. Serves a fiery beef and vegetable noodle in a delicious sauce. Ask for *niuron mian* (beef noodles in soup) and they'll give you their version of it. The noodles themselves are homemade.

Market Xiangyang Lu. The fruit and vegetable market opposite the northern end of Heping Lu has a number of good clay-pot, mostly noodle, options. Some rice and dried ham pots. You will find a number of rough and ready tables set out at the back of the market, between the fruit and vegetables section and comestibles.

What to see
Old Zhongdian
There are few real sights in the old Tibetan neighbourhood of Zhongdian, located to the south of the main drag of Changzheng Lu, but the area is well worth exploring for its insight into how the city must have felt half a century ago. The first thing you notice is how quiet and rural the district is compared to the brash, newly constructed parts of town. Unmade lanes lead past Tibetan-style block houses and back gardens full of fruit trees and poultry. In the harvest season, hay dries on huge wooden ricks set up on plots right in the middle of the old quarter. A commanding view of the old and new city can be had by climbing up a flight of steps to **Zhongdian Hill Park** where there is a small temple on the top. Just across the road from the hill is the recently restored **Zangong Hall**, a fine old building which serves as a memorial to the Red Army's Long March. Southwest of the old town, walking up a slope, is a well-preserved temple complex looked after by a handful of monks who are happy to receive visitors.

Songzhanling Monastery
5km north of town. Bus No 3 from any stop heading north along Changzheng Lu. Y10.
Apart from Zhongdian's position as a jumping-off point for trips into the deep northwest and the borderlands of Tibet, most visitors stop off in Zhongdian to spend a day exploring the Songzhanglinsi, a monastery founded in the 17th century by the fifth Dalai Lama, partially destroyed during the ravages of the 1950s and 60s, and now back on its feet after some skillful restoration work.

As the bus ascends the crest of a hill the complex, a Yellow Hat Tibetan sect monastery, comes into full view: a broad collection of buildings in the midst of rolling hills and farmland, behind rows of giant hay ricks that look like palisades. If the complex looks familiar it is because it was designed as a smaller version of the Potala Palace in Lhasa. Songzhangling is a working monastery. At present there are 780 registered monks (although not all of them are resident), making it the largest Lamaist monastery in Yunnan.

The main temple, at the top of a long flight of stone steps, is a typical Tibetan, four-storey block-house structure with a gold-plated roof. The grand Sutra-Pitaka Palace on the ground floor can accommodate up to 2,000 monks chanting the scriptures. There is a bronze statue of the fifth Dalai Lama over the altar in the main hall. If you mount the wooden stairs to the right and left of the main hall in this barn-like building, the second floor has a permanent exhibition of well-preserved *tanka* (wall hangings depicting the Tibetan view of the cosmos) and ritual costumes. Ascend to an earth roof for fine views of the surrounding countryside. During festivals or when special rituals are held you can sometimes see the Jiangmu Dance, an ancient performance

THE TIBETANS

Yunnan's 110,000 or so Tibetans are mostly concentrated in Deqin Tibetan Autonomous Prefecture, along the southeastern boundaries of the Qinghai-Tibetan Plateau, with smaller communities inhabiting the districts of Ninglang, Gongshan, Yongsheng and Lijiang.

The Tibetans in Yunnan cultivate wheat, corn and rice. Animal husbandry is one of the main occupations in these areas. Yak, Tibetan sheep, goats, and pien cattle are native to the region. The long-haired yak is an important source of meat and milk. Also a useful means of transport, it is known in Tibet and Yunnan as the 'Boat of the Plateau'.

Although dried mutton and beef are common, *tsampa* is the most typical Tibetan food staple. Highland barley is left overnight in water and then, after being scooped out, it is placed in a pot to dry. The barley is then roasted with Chinese prickly ash, stirred with butter tea, and then made into loaves of yellow bread.

Butter tea, made in a wooden tub, is the daily Tibetan drink. Made from a tea-brick which is boiled with yak butter, salt, sesame seeds and a touch of fresh milk, butter tea and *tsampa* are also offered to visitors. In some rural areas, women use butter as an ointment to protect their skins. Most families in the regions of Deqin and Zhongdian ferment their own barley wine.

Barley and other, sweeter wines are drunk while couples court each other. Snippets of song, their lyrics a running commentary on each persons' feelings, hopes and expectations, are exchanged at this time. Marriage is a serious business, the prospect of children and the uniting of the couple's respective families generally taking priority over love. In one song, for example, a woman, level-headed despite the barley wine, will sing the following, sobering refrain:

> 'Do not be carried out by a beautiful feather of
> The snow-capped chicken,
> Test the power of its crows and wings.
> Do not focus on a strong appearance,
> Test his morals and behaviour.'

accompanied by Tibetan music, requiring monks to wear masks representing demons, spirits and mythical animals. The biggest occasion in the life of the monastery is the assembly for worshipping and commemorating Sakyamuni which falls from the 5th to the 15th of the first lunar month each year. At other times it is quite likely you will be able to catch monks in small ensembles of Tibetan musicians practicing somewhere in the building.

Festivals

Zhongdian's **Horse Racing Festival** or 'Heavenly Steed Festival' as it is also known, falls on the 5th day of the fifth lunar month (usually June) and is a spectacular affair that draws a mainly Tibetan crowd from all over the surrounding regions and lasts for several days. Horse traders, magnificently attired in furs and silk robes, arrive from distant mountain villages looking as though they have ridden straight out of the pages of history. The festival is held on an extensive meadow outside Zhongdian at an elevation of 3,288m and whole families come to camp out around the horse-racing ground. Large picnics are laid out and there is a lively sense of celebration as competing riders test their equestrian skills and try to win honour for their home villages. The **Horse Racing Festival** is without doubt one of the most colourful of Yunnan's many festivals and a must for anyone with a serious interest in Tibetan culture and customs.

The other festival in the town is the annual September **Minority Arts Festival** which was launched in the late 1990s as a means to drum up more interest in the region. The festival features the work of artists who are mostly from Zhongdian, Deqin, Sichuan and Gansu. Like the Horse Festival this event draws crowds of people and it can be very difficult to find accommodation. If either one of these festivals is your main reason for visiting this area you would be best to book your accommodation in advance with a tour operator to avoid disappointment.

Side trips from Zhongdian
Baishuitai 白水台
108km southeast of Zhongdian.
In the right weather conditions, the limestone, stepped terraces at the Naxi village of Baidi make a good one-day trip from Zhongdian. Similar in some respects to the white, calcium carbonate terraces at Pammukale in Central Anatolia in Turkey, the surrounding green landscaped hills and valleys make this a unique and dramatic location.

Each terrace has its own pool of shallow water, fed from a spring in a field above Baishuitai (White Water Terrace). The terraces are thought to have begun forming as long as 2–300,000 years ago and Baishuitai was an attraction for travellers as long ago as the Tang and Song dynasties. The White Water Terrace is revered as the birthplace of the Naxi *dongba* culture and practitioners of *dongba* make pilgrimages here. The story goes that the beautiful scenery here attracted Dingbashiluo, the founder of *dongba*, on his way back from Tibet, where he had studied Buddhism, and he decided to settle here to popularise his beliefs. Near the source of the pools is where Dingbashiluo is said to have sat and meditated and there are some inscriptions and a poem written by a Mu chieftain of the Ming dynasty, describing the spectacle of the terraces and paying homage to Dingbashiluo. The spring is sacred and the local Naxi place painted, with holy wooden markers around it. In March, when the waters are at their highest, thousands of pilgrims pour into the area to honour the spring and terraces, joined by groups of picnicking tourists. The waters are believed to be curative and women who cannot conceive come here to drink from the spring.

The terraces can be slippery after rainfall. Late afternoon when sunlight falls on the terraces is the most beautiful time to see them. The Tibet Hotel and other travel agents around town can arrange transport to Baishuitai. There is also supposed to be a bus that leaves Zhongdian every morning at 07.00 from the bus station, but some travellers have reported unreliable times and frequency. It would certainly be worth checking as the fare is said to be only Y15.

Dongba Gu Dong Cave
In the valley opposite Baishui.
While you are in the Baishui area it is worth a quick look at Dong Gu Dong Cave, actually two caves, associated with the home of the half-mythical hermit and spiritual leader Shenrap. Tibetans claim that he was the founder of the Bon religion, the belief which pre-dated the arrival of Buddhism in the region. The Naxi also revere him as the second founder of the *dongba* religion.

The cave is supposed to be the site where Shenrap developed his spiritual powers. The interior of the cave is almost empty except for some dongba writings on the wall which look as if they are quite recent. Locals call these adjacent grottoes the Cave of the Ancient Sorcerer and they certainly have an aura. It takes just under two hours to walk to the caves from Baishui. You may need to ask one of the local woodcutters for directions. They are sure to guess why you are there.

Bita Hai and Napa Hai
25km east of Zhongdian.
The centrepiece of these nature reserves is the two lakes which Chinese tourists come to admire for their flowers which burst into bloom in the early summer. *Bita Hai*, which means quiet lake in Tibetan, lies at an elevation of 3,539m and at some 3km length is the smaller of the two lakes. The road to Bit Hai stops a few kilometres short of the lake in order to preserve its peace and visitors are required to walk in or ride on horses. Rowing boats can be hired to take you out to the island which is covered by spruce and azalea woods. The nature reserve contains a number of rare and protected species including black-necked cranes, red-tailed pheasants, rhesus monkeys, lynxes and supposedly even clouded leopards. The second lake, Napa Hai, is located 8km northwest of Zhongdian and attracts less visitors. Napa Hai is a seasonal lake that expands during the rainy season and mostly contracts into marshland during the dryer months.

The surrounding grasslands are also home to a large variety of water birds and grazing Yaks.

Napa Hai is best explored on horseback, which can be arranged through local tour operators who will have a mount waiting for you when you arrive. Expect to pay around Y50 for the trip including the horses. There is a bus every morning at 09.00 from the bus station but it may be easier to join a small tour group.

Xiagei hot springs
14km southeast of Zhongdian.
You will probably have to arrange transport to the subterranean hot spring at Xiagei in order to find it, which could otherwise be quite tricky. A few

kilometres before the springs on the same route brings you to the a natural limestone bridge over the Suoduogang River. The **Tiansheng Bridge** as it is called is another popular half-day trip from Zhongdian. The **Dabao Temple**, an important and early Buddhist centre in this region, is a short distance from the bridge.

Benzilan 奔子栏

Benzilan's position roughly halfway between Zhongdian and Deqin has turned it into a well-serviced waystation for buses and trucks on this route. A pleasant town to walk around, Benzilan sits at an altitude of 1,968m on a strip of road that runs between steep cliffs and the waters of the Upper Yangzi. Sichuan Province lies on the far bank and can be reached by ferry. There is a small Tibetan temple called **Gochen Gompa**, with attractive murals below the southern end of the main street. Another temple and stupa are located at the northern head of the town. Like Zhongdian, Benzilan has a well known tea bowl factory.

The restaurants along the main street are excellent and offer a surprisingly wide range of dishes, all prepared and served at lightning speed. One of the best is a long, one-storey restaurant at the end of town as you are exiting in the Deqin direction. The ceiling is covered in trellises of plastic grapes, and some of the booths have good views over the river. Lots of yak meat dishes and hashes, mandatory noodles, and spicy Sichuanese treats. Benzilan would be a good place to break the journey to Deqin and have more time to explore the superb Dongzhulin Temple and Monastery.

Dongzhulin Temple

22km north of Benzilan in Shusong village.

One of the most important temples in northwest Yunnan and the second largest of the Yellow Hat sect complexes, Dongzhulin has the appearance of great antiquity. The present buildings, however, are reconstructions of the original temple constructed in 1667 and then dynamited by the People's Liberation Army in the 1950s.

In its heyday the temple housed over 700 monks and several 'living Buddhas'. The original monastery stood on a remote mountain 10km from here. The present location though, below the main road in a gully with a backdrop of dry mountains, is still stunning. There are 300 monks in residence at the monastery. There is one incarnate lama, or *tulka*, also residing at the monastery who, despite his revered status, is quite approachable. When rituals are held and music performed, the temple's main courtyard seems like the stage for an exotic costume drama. It may be possible to stay overnight in the monastery. Try to enquire.

DEQIN 德钦

Deqin is the end of the line as far as travel goes in northwestern Yunnan. Abutting both Sichuan and Tibet, its massive mountain ranges, valleys and gorges are awesome and, at the time of writing, yet to be fully exploited as a

YUNNAN'S LOST HORIZON?

If he were alive today, British writer James Hilton might be surprised at the uses his 1933 novel, *The Lost Horizon*, is being put to by the tourist department in Deqin county. A few years ago it was announced that the fabled Shangri-la, the mountain utopia that forms the setting for Hilton's bestseller, was none other than Deqin county. Apparently substantiated by research and the statements of several Western 'specialists' invited to the region to verify the claim, the authorities are waiting expectantly for the tourist dollars to start rolling in.

With all the publicity the Chinese government is providing for its 'Shangri-la Found' campaign, and the expected completion of a new airport near Deqin, high up on the Tibetan Plateau, they may even succeed. The promoters' case is founded on a number of rather unconvincing coincidences and similarities, including the apex shape of Mount Kagebo which is supposed to resemble a key landmark in the novel. Now that the tourist people have decided that this is the real Shangri-la, there's no turning back. At least three photo books (in English, Chinese and Japanese) with the name Shangri-la have already appeared. The name Shangri-la is a Tibetan one, meaning 'the sun and the moon in the heart', and refers to a place of idyllic beauty.

Joseph Rock's accounts of the region which began to appear in the West in various journals in the 1920s, including National Geographic, are credited as one source of inspiration for Hilton's book. Accounts of the secretive Himalayan kingdoms of Bhutan and Mustang are others. All the tourist hype aside, in the right weather conditions Deqin's magnificent scenery lends a certain romantic credence to the Shangri-la theory. Lost or found, Deqin may be about to take its place beside other fabled worlds like Xanadu, Atlantis and Camelot. Cynics will likely compare it to another famous utopia novel, Samuel Butler's *Erehwon*. Spelt backwards as intended, the title reads NOWHERE.

destination, though a hugely optimistic tourist infrastructure is already well beyond the drawing board stage.

The region is dominated by the titanic (when it comes to Deqin, travel writers easily slip into superlatives!) Kawa Karpo Range with its tallest peak, Mount Kagebo (Meili Xue Shan to the Chinese) at 6,740m. In clear weather the Meili Snow Mountain Range, as it is also known, is one of Nature's most formidable displays.

Deqin county is gloriously under-populated for China, with less than 60,000 people in the entire county. Tibetans are in the majority but there are a number of Naxi and Lisu as well. A small community of Tibetan, rather than Hui Chinese, Muslims live in Deqin. They are the descendants of families who were involved in the caravan trade that once brought tea, medicines, gold, cloth and other valuable items across the mountains from Tibet and India.

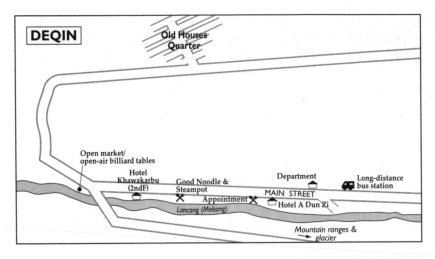

Deqin itself feels like a chaotic frontier town, which is exactly what it is, a riotous melange of old Tibetan buildings, concrete stores and flashy hotels, roaming monks in ruby robes and bright orange woolly hats, and mud streets currently being hastily surfaced. By the time you read this, Deqin should be in better shape. The mood in the old part of town to the north, a collection of Tibetan style blockhouses and unmade lanes with yaks wandering about, is more restrained. The town centre, if such a thing can be said to exist in Deqin, appears to be the corner where the road loops around in the direction of the bus garage, where the market gate is. There are a few small restaurants, curio and souvenir shops here. It also seems to be a meeting place for people at a loose end.

Zhongdian to Deqin Road

A trip to Deqin should not be taken lightly. The road there, which can take anything from ten hours to infinity, is one of the most stunning in the whole of China. Rising to over 4,000m at certain points, it winds along spectacularly steep gorges, valleys, rice and wheat terraces, ravines and limestone rock faces. The road, which is unmade most of the way, is frequently snowed out for indefinite periods from mid-October to the end of May. During the long rainy season the road can be equally treacherous as buses will take the risk and run at these times.

The road, which is only just wide enough to allow two vehicles to pass each other, can be very slippery at this time. The rear wheels of the bus I took on my last trip to Deqin got wedged over a ravine after slipping off the road, and there was a long wait until help arrived in the form of ropes and pulleys. This happened both going and coming. Even more dangerous is the prospect of land and mud slides, a fairly frequent occurrence. When it rains there is always slippage. Some of the rock faces the bus glances are extremely friable. Add to that the erratic antics of some of the drivers, punctures and mechanical problems and you have one very risky road.

Having said all that, this is one journey that travellers should not miss if they have the time. Allow an extra day or two for unforeseeable problems. A bus leaves Zhongdian at 07.00. It can get cold at any time on this route, so come prepared. There are sleeper buses that do the long run from Deqin to Kunming, though this is not recommended. Private jeeps can be hired from the Tibet Hotel in Zhongdian for the journey. If you can get together a group of three or four travellers it's good value. They charge roughly Y400 a day.

Where to stay

At the time of writing accommodation in the Deqin area is very limited, but then so are the number of visitors. This is likely to change as great plans, including a massive airport project, are in the pipeline. There are one or two alpine-style guesthouses in the forest near the glacier which might be worth checking out.

Adunzi Hotel Nanping Lu; tel: 841 3378; fax: 841 3388. A surprisingly swish hotel for these remote parts, the Adunzi is a good place to recuperate after the long bus ride or hold out and console yourself in the event that you are trapped in the town as a result of one of Deqin's fairly frequent snowfalls or landslides. Well furnished and equipped rooms with hot water. Y218 doubles, Y388 singles. These are the rates posted on the board, but seem to be negotiable. Travellers have often ended up with doubles for as little as Y100. The staff have only a smattering of English but are very keen to help.

Hotel Khawakarbu Nanping Lu. Cheap and conveniently located, this has backpacker potential, though all of the guests appeared to be Chinese when I stayed there. The rooms are spartan but clean and tidy. Guests pay Y10 for the bed. If it is a double room and you want it to yourself, you'll have to pay Y20. Very basic toilets, but better than the standard of public loos in China. No showers.

Department Hotel Nanping Lu. Dingy rooms at low rates. Y50 doubles, Y60 triples. Some depressing dorm beds on offer. A last ditch choice if there is nothing else available.

Where to eat

The local barley wine is more like a liqueur. Served in a small glass this transparent concoction is very potent, more like a slightly sweet Japanese sake or a potato-based firewater.

Steampot Restaurant Nanping Lu. Between the Hotel Khawakarbu and the Hotel Adunzi there is a good hotpot restaurant without a name, that also serves excellent beef and pork noodle dishes all cooked over a charcoal brazier.

Hotel Adunzi Restaurant Nanping Lu. A good selection of mainstream Chinese cuisine. Reasonably priced but expensive for Deqin. Has a bar and coffee service.

Appointment Restaurant Nanping Lu. A spotlessly clean Chinese place. Good all round selection but few local foods. A little more expensive than average for these parts.

What to see
Mount Kagebo and Minyang Glacier

The highlight of any trip to Deqin is a hike or pony trek up to the foot of Mount Kagebo, also known as Mount Meilixue, China's most sacred peak.

Tibetans come to the glacier at the foot of the mountain to pray and make offerings. Guides are recommended for this route. The CITS office in Zhongdian can help.

Yunnan's highest mountain

Kagebo is regarded as the first of eight magic mountains in the Tibetan region of Yunnan. According to local legend the mountain was originally a demon with nine heads and 18 arms. Under the influence of Tantric instructions it became a Buddhist general, guardian of the 13 peaks that make up the Meili Snow Mountain range, all of which are over 6,000m in height and are known as the 13 *taizi* (prince) peaks. Pilgrims travel from Tibet, Gansu, Sichuan and elsewhere to worship at the base of the mountain from late autumn to early winter. Like circumambulations of great pagodas, it is considered a great achievement to walk full circle around Kagebo.

Perhaps there are some mountains which are just not meant to be climbed. Astonishingly, the summit of Kagebo has yet to be conquered. At 6,740m, it is Yunnan's highest mountain. Highly unpredictable climbing conditions, thick fog and clouds, frequent snow-slides and storms, not to mention precipitous cliffs, have so far thwarted all attempts. The failure to scale the pyramid-shaped mountain is not for want of trying. A British team undertook the first unsuccessful expedition in 1902. Four groups of mountaineers from China, the United States and Japan followed. In January 1991, a team of Chinese and Japanese climbers died after making an apparently well organised and planned ascent.

Kagebo peak remains one of the world's last great mountaineering challenges.

Markets

Although the markets here are rather tame compared to other cities in Yunnan, there is an interesting open-air market just behind the main intersection, reached through a Disneyesque, Ming-style arch. It is essentially a fruit, vegetable, meat and comestibles market but you'll find a good deal more if you look closely. Notice the hessian sacks full of huge blocks of yak butter, the large Ali Baba jars stuffed with pickles, marinated vegetables, and pungent red pepper sauces. There are about a dozen billiard tables lined up smack bang in the middle of the market, a popular game with local truck drivers and monks.

De Profundis in Cizhong

Nineteenth-century French missionaries, seeking converts in the fastnesses along the upper reaches of the Mekong Valley had more success 'harvesting souls' among the Tibetans of northwest Yunnan than in Tibet itself.

An anomaly today, the **Cizhong Catholic Church**, 80km south of Deqin, in a secluded village of the same name has, like a carefully concealed religious relic, managed to survive some of China's most tumultuous times. Although the church, originally built in 1867, was destroyed by fire in 1905, funds from the local government helped to reconstruct the building in a more or less exact version based on the design of French cathedrals. Interestingly, all the interior decorations are pure Tibetan.

The church is still used by mainly Tibetan parishioners on Sunday mornings, the sounds of 'Cantique au Saint Coeur' a curious refrain issuing from the lips of the farmers and yak herders of Cizhong village.

Travel to Tibet and Sichuan

At the time of writing, independent travel onwards from Yunnan to Tibet was still officially prohibited and things look set to continue that way. Travel into Tibet is permitted only as part of an organised group with the requisite Tibet travel permit. If you are interested in travel to these eastern regions of Tibet then you should contact one of the tour operators (listed in *Chapter 2*) who specialise in overland trips through eastern Tibet and onwards to Lhasa. This is not a cheap option but is the only way to travel overland into Tibet from Yunnan. Occasionally very intrepid travellers do manage to hitchhike into Tibet from Yunnan, but they tend to be very much the exception rather than the rule. Expect frequent checkpoints, and little accommodation and food along one of the toughest road journeys in the world; it could take up to three weeks to reach Lhasa. Travel on the Sichuan–Tibet highway is a risky business and should not be undertaken lightly on account of the Chinese authorities, the severity of the terrain, the scarcity of lodgings, food, transport and the high frequency of landslides and road accidents. If you are determined to reach Tibet a better option would be to reach Chengdu in Sichuan province from where you can usually buy an air ticket (approximately Y2600) from local tour agents, who will list you as part of a group for the flight to Tibet. Once you are in Lhasa you are then free to go your own way. Chengdu can be reached by an overnight train from the railhead at Panzhihua (a journey of some several hours from Lijiang) or a flight from Kunming.

The road to Xiancheng and Litang in Sichuan was open at the time of writing, but is frequently prone to closure and has been off limits to foreigners in the past. If you cannot make it to Tibet but want to get a good taste of Tibetan culture and similar scenery then this route is a good alternative but a lot of the factors mentioned about the Tibet highway apply to this route as well. Buses to Xiancheng in Sichuan province leave from Zhongdian at 07.30 each day and the journey takes around 11–13 hours on some very rugged mountain roads. The service can be quite erratic though and if you find that a bus is not running then you could try asking for a lift at the local truck stop. Post office trucks are another good bet for hitching rides. Once you reach Xiangcheng, there is some basic accommodation at the bus station hotel.

Buses leave Xiancheng for Litang on the Sichuan–Tibet highway every second day and from Litang a journey of two to three days via Kangding will bring you to Chengdu. The scenery along this route is spectacular but you should be prepared for some very basic conditions. Check in the cafés in Zhongdian and Lijiang for the latest information on this route.

Rhodendron Yunnanense

Baoshan and Tengchong

'The valley of the Salween is nothing short of magnificent...'

Yunnan, Patrick R Booz

Although it was only given the status of a city in 1983, Baoshan is the biggest city in western Yunnan after Xiaguan. Despite being an important industrial and transportation hub, it feels more like a booming, very lively provincial town. Despite its modern pretensions, there are still fine examples of old wooden architecture in Baoshan, some winding, stone-paved back streets, pleasant walks around the outskirts of town, and the sensation of being on the road to a milder, more exotic climate to the west.

Commerce has always been the life blood of Baoshan, a fact that is still evident in its bustling commodities markets along Qingzhen Jie and its surprisingly well-stocked shops, supermarkets and department stores with their offerings of imported goods and luxuries, Yongchang silk and other Baoshan items such as pressed, salted duck, crystal sugar and the famous, locally produced and much exported Coffee Arabica, and its equally revered Reclining Buddha Baoshan Tea. Baoshan's street markets are also an excellent showcase for the region's natural products. The area's slightly acidic but mature soil is perfect for growing lychee, longans, water chestnuts, pepper, walnuts, mulberries, oil crops, tea, coffee, tobacco and a host of medicinal plants.

Located at the southern end of the Hengduan Mountains, east of the great Salween River valley and close to the massive Gaoligongshan range, the region is home to diverse ethnic minorities including the Bai, Yi, Lisu, Dai, Hmong, Yao, Deang and Wa.

Nature notes

The Baoshan–Tengchong area is a treasure trove for naturalists, botanists and visitors with an interest in the flora and fauna that distinguishes this part of Yunnan. As always, in the case of China, it is difficult to assess just how much of the flora and fauna of this region still survives, or how much faces imminent extinction, or the propensity of the authorities to exaggerate the well-being of the environment.

In the botanical garden formed by this region, ornamental plants such as azalea, orchids and camellias grow in wild profusion. The 33m Huangxinnan (yellow-core nanmu) is the largest and oldest lily-magnolia of its kind in the world.

The Gaoligongshan Mountains, close to northern Tengchong, are rich in timber diversity. A list of precious trees in this region would have to include the hawthorn, *Taiwania Flousiana*, lacquer trees, Chinese fir, Bhutan cypress and giant rhododendron trees. In 1982, forest workers in Tengchong discovered a patch of wild rhododendron bushes on the mountain, several of which measured over 25m in height and almost 4m at the root. Spinulose tree ferns and various kinds of medicinal herbs are common.

Although it is difficult to verify exact numbers, rare and curious animals are more common here than almost anywhere else in China. Species include macaques, golden monkeys, gibbons, lesser panda, pangolins, water deer, leopards, tigers and takins. Birds and fowl like the Chinese nightingale, sunbird, green peacocks and silver pheasants make the denser parts of the forest their home. The area is also a meeting ground for birds migrating southwards and those flying north.

BAOSHAN 保山
History
Yongchang, the ancient name for Baoshan, straddles the halfway mark on the old Yongchang Route, a staging post at the southwestern end of the Southern Silk Road – the all-important Indian-Sichuan trade route. The route was extended as far as Yongping, 105km west of Xiaguan, under the Emperor Wudi, and further developed by Emperor Mingdi in AD69. In that year the region became known as the Yongchang Administrative District.

By the time the 3rd-century Sichuanese minister, Zhuge Liang, visited Baoshan the city's wealth and prestige was well established. Indian merchants lived here during the Tang dynasty, trading in precious gems, gold, peacock feathers, elephants and rhinoceros. It was and remains, to some extent, a textile centre, a valued producer of silk, kapok and sisal. Kublai Khan won another terrifying victory in this part of Yunnan in 1277, defeating the Burmese king Narathihapade, his archers turning the advancing Burmese elephants full circle so that they stampeded their own troops. Marco Polo, always careful to appear after, rather than before, one of the great Khan's victories, turned up in the town a few years later, leaving a memorable description of 'Vochan' as he called Baoshan.

In the 1940s the town was heavily garrisoned with Chinese troops trying to keep the Japanese from invading across the Yunnan-Burmese border. Baoshan still has a military bearing today and supports a large contingent of army recruits who can be seen exercising and jogging in formation around town.

Getting there and away
These days connections to Baoshan, which is 592km from Kunming and 120km from Xiaguan, are excellent. Baoshan airport is about 10km from town.

Flights between Baoshan and Kunming run three times a week: on Tuesday, Thursday and Saturday. The fare is Y370 one way. These may very well increase as other routes are added. At the moment few foreigners use this route as most people seem to be drifting in overland from places like Dali. The CAAC office (tel: 216 1747) is well hidden on the first floor of the yellow-coloured building where Minhang Lu and Longquan Lu cross.

Baoshan really comes into its own with buses. Its gigantic, spanking new long-distance bus station offers routes all over Yunnan. Its western routes cover Tengchong, Ruili and several places between. The first Tengchong bus leaves at 06.50 and takes about six hours, a little less if the current upgrading of the road continues; the fare to Tengchong is Y22. Buses to Ruili begin at 06.50 and pass through Mangshi and Wading, taking about eight hours all told. Xiaguan buses start to depart at 06.50 for the six-hour ride; the fare is Y27. Sleeper buses bound for Kunming leave in the afternoon generally. The first departs at 15.00. It's an 18–20-hour run. If you are a glutton for punishment, you can also pick up a sleeper bus for Jinghong for the minimum two-day ordeal. Should you opt for the longer routes, it is advisable to take along some snacks, reading material, toilet paper and, if you are a non-smoker or have any thought for your lungs, a cotton surgical mask of the type worn by Bangkok traffic duty cops.

There is a second city bus station nearby which serves more or less the same destinations as the above. The departure times, though, are slightly different.

Getting around

Baoshan's town plan is a simple one, following the square, north-south, east-west grid lines of the old Ming dynasty walls that once stood here. Maps of the city are available from the small shops in the new Baoshan long-distance bus station.

Despite its size and strategic location, Baoshan's tourist infrastructure is fairly basic compared to somewhere like Dali. The Bank of China office is on Baoxiu Donglu and opens Mon–Fri, 09.00–11.30, 14.00–17.00. The post office is a block south on Xia Gang Jie.

Baoshan is still small enough to get around on foot. There are pedicabs if need be. There are also a few motorcycles with Wallace and Gromit-style sidecars puttering around.

Post and telecommunications

The area code for Baoshan is 0875.

Where to stay

Baoshan has a good choice of cheap guesthouses and hotels. Most are within walking distance of the bus station, reflecting Baoshan's role as an important transportation hub.

Baoshan Guesthouse Shang Gang Jie; tel: 212 2804. Usually quiet and friendly, the Baoshan has simple doubles for Y50, but the showers are communal. For private bath you'll need to get into one of the Y130 doubles.

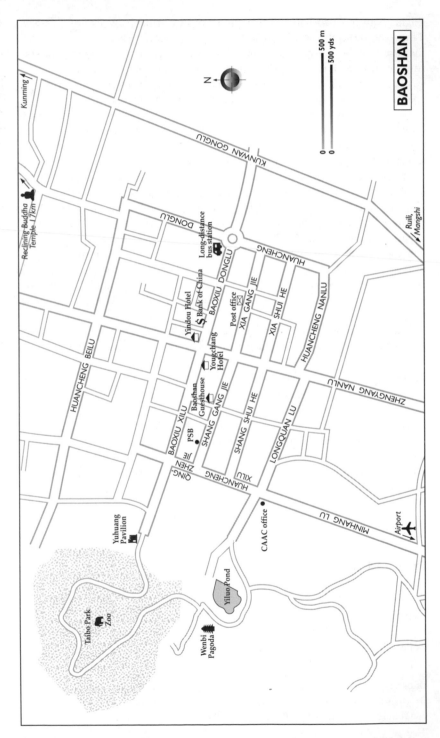

BAOSHAN

Yindou Hotel Baoxiu Donglu; tel: 212 0948. Owned by the Bank of China, this is Baoshan's fanciest hotel and a very good deal it is too. You can stay in a clean double here for Y150, with 24-hour hot water, air-conditioning and satellite TV all thrown in. More expensive rooms are also available.

Yongchang Hotel Baoxiu Xilu; tel: 212 2802. The friendly staff here offer clean singles (a rarity to even find a single in Yunnan) for Y50–130, doubles for a little less. Triples go for Y100. All have attached bathrooms that work.

Where to eat

Food is varied and plentiful in Baoshan where the national pastime of eating is well to the fore. You will find plenty of old wooden restaurants along Shang Gang Jie and Baoxiu Lu serving casseroles, hotpots and sizzling, stir-fry dishes, some of them nice and spicy. The bus station area is a good option for quick, cheap dishes: dumplings, pancakes, soups and bowls of noodles. Golden Dragon noodles, a local make, are particularly good. Crisp and salty pressed duck is a local favourite.

Hotel food is alright as a last resort but not recommended in a town whose kitchens are begging to be explored. Hotels offer mostly fairly stodgy food with a glazed, been-in-the-tureen-too-long look.

There are several Muslim restaurants around town. A concentration of them, recognisable from their green crescent signs, can be found along Qingzhen Jie. Near to the Baoshan Guesthouse there is an Across-the-Bridge-Noodles restaurant that doesn't appear to have a name. Unless you have pigged out enough on this very Yunnanese preparation while in Kunming, their version is recommended.

What to see
Taibao Park

One and a half kilometres west of the city centre, this 100ha park, with chestnuts, birches, cypresses, pines and other trees gracing the hill the park stands on, makes a pleasant stroll and provides some good views of the city and the Baoshan Plain.

Wuhou Si, a large hall commemorating the Three Kingdoms character, Zhuge Liang, stands at the top, an enormous statue of the leader at the front. There are other pagodas in the park worth a look. Paths to the south of the park lead to a rather lacklustre zoo.

Yuhuang Pavilion

This attractive 16th-century, Ming-Taoist temple, with its octagonal dome, flanks the northern entrance to Taibo Park. It is no longer used for worship. There is a museum inside displaying maps and photos connected to the war with Japan. The building has been dubbed the 'Cultural Relics Bureau'.

The architecture is quite elegant, and the inner ceiling of Yuhuang (Jade Emperor) Pavilion, quite exquisite. There is a small chapel next to the main temple with several alabaster Buddhas.

Graveyard of the National heroes

This military cemetery is dedicated to the 8,000 Nationalist Chinese troops buried here who died in the fierce battle to recover Tengchong against Japanese troops attempting to push forward to Burma. It is China's largest cemetery for troops killed in the anti-Japanese war and was completed in 1945 with funds from Chinese merchants living in India. There is a memorial hall attached to the graveyard which contains a large number of graphic pictures showing the battle for Tengchong and a number of couplets written by military officers to honour the dead, including one by the Generalissimo himself, Chiang-Kai Shek. Similarly the tower at the top of the graveyard displays another dedication called 'The National Heroes' by Chiang-Kai Shek. (Presumably the lingering hatred of the Japanese in the following decades must have been much stronger than any dislike of the Nationalist leader and this is what must have saved the memorial's inscriptions from the attentions of local Red Guards.) The cemetery is located at the foot of Laifeng Hill, 3km south of town.

Wenbi Pagoda and Yiluo Pond

Wenbi Pagoda stands on the southern flank of Taibao Mountain. The 13-storey pagoda, which is surrounded by graves, has an air of antiquity. A short stroll southeast of the pagoda brings you to the walled **Yiluo Pond** which affords a fine view of Wenbi Pagoda. The Teacher Training College and its one or two foreign teachers are nearby. They will be glad to see an English speaker if you are interested in a chat.

Side trips from Baoshan

Reclining Buddha Temple

17km north of Baoshan.

It can be hit and miss getting here, but the temple and its reclining Buddha, an hour's walk from the town of Shuizhai, are worth the effort as this is one of the main historical attractions in the area.

The Ming dynasty temple is located in the Yunyan Mountains. Behind the temple is a cave housing the impressive 9.5-ton marble statue, depicting the Buddha on the point of entering Nirvana. It is over 6m long.

There doesn't seem to be any public transport to the site. Inevitably there will be tour groups going there from Baoshan, but until that happens you may have to either take a taxi (this cost me Y100 for the return trip), or hop on one of the motorcycle-and-sidecar contraptions mentioned earlier. Providing that the road is relatively traffic-free and your driver doesn't take it into his head to overtake every truck he meets on a bend, this could be a very pleasant way of travelling. Sidecars generally ask for Y50 for the return trip but can take two passengers.

Rainbow Bridge

58km southwest of Yongping.

Jihong Qiao, or Rainbow Bridge, one of the only chain bridges in China to have been in more or less continual use for over 500 years, was built in 1475.

When it was constructed it consisted of 17 main chains, each one made from 176 separate rings. The current replacements amount to 15 chains.

Spanning the Mekong River, pavilions nearby have inscriptions recording the former importance of the bridge (now used mostly by locals and the occasional tour group) on the southern trade routes. Marco Polo and the Emperor Kangxi were among its illustrious visitors.

TENGCHONG 腾冲

The road west from Baoshan to Tengchong, though bumpy in places, pitching you around hairpin bends and over pot-holes as well as newly surfaced stretches of asphalt, is unlikely to bore you. Police roadblocks soon give way to fields of abundant crops, river valleys, the luxuriant forest and jungle growth of the Gaoligongshan Nature Reserve and, finally, on to the geological faultlines that will, hopefully, stay gelled together for the duration of your stay.

Earthquake-prone Tengchong was formerly positioned on the Southern Silk Route, and much foreign trade passed through the small town during the Qing dynasty. Its fortunes continued to rise, the British even regarding it important enough to establish a consul there in 1899. In the 1930s, however, the road swung farther south, bypassing the town, at which point it seems to have reverted to the backwater it used to be.

Trapped somewhere between the past and the future Tengchong is likely to see a good deal of activity in the near future as its hot springs and volcanic landscapes are turned into holiday resorts, something which is already happening to some degree. Though there are parts of Tengchong that retain a certain lost world charm with their winding, cobblestone streets, wooden houses and private courtyards, the town is tottering on the brink of change, and demolition work, sadly, has already begun in some districts.

Getting there and away

The bus station is located on Huancheng Donglu in the eastern section of town. Buses to Ruili, stopping off at Yingjiang and Zhongfeng on the way, easily take ten hours. You can always stop off at Yingjiang or catch a bus to Mangshi and overnight there if you wish. The first bus for Baoshan departs at 07.30. There are others throughout the morning. Xiaguan-bound buses start at 07.00. Sleepers for the long-haul to Kunming start leaving at 09.30 for the 24-hour minimum run.

Practical information

One of the best sources of information, though the staff have only scant English, is the travel service counter at the Tengchong Guesthouse, a sort of unofficial CITS. They have a good map of the area which should prove handy. The Bank of China is on Yingjian Xilu, the small post office along Fengshan Lu.

Where to stay/eat

Tonglida Hotel Huancheng Donglu; tel: 518 7787. Good value with extremely clean doubles for Y80, and shared rooms starting at Y30. 24-hour hot water is shared.

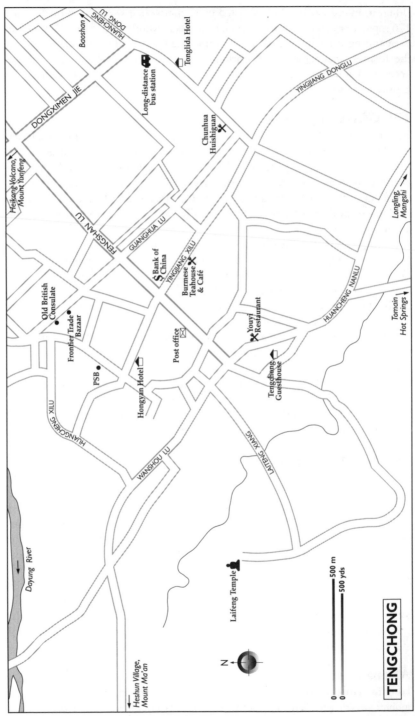

TENGCHONG

N

500 m
500 yds

Dayung River

Heshun Village,
Mount Ma'an

Laifeng Temple

Wanshou Lu

Huangcheng Xilu

PSB

Frontier Trade
Bazaar

Old British
Consulate

Fengshan Lu

Heikang Volcano,
Mount Yunfeng

Dongximen Jie

Huancheng
Dong Lu

Baoshan

Long-distance
bus station

Tongliida Hotel

Chunhua
Huishiguan

Yingjiang Donglu

Guanghua Lu

Bank of
China

Yingjiang Xilu

Burmese
Teahouse
& Café

Post office

Hongyan Hotel

Youyi
Restaurant

Tengchong
Guesthouse

Huancheng Nanlu

Longling,
Mangshi

Tomain
Hot Springs

Laifeng Xiang

Hongyan Hotel Yingjiang Xilu. A nice courtyard setting for this guesthouse. For reasons unknown, the place has periodically been off-limits to foreigners, but it is worth enquiring as the setting is very attractive, and the prices right.

Tengchong Guesthouse One block behind the Youyi Restaurant. A peaceful place away from the main roads, the Tengchong has spacious singles and doubles with attached bathrooms for Y60, and a good selection of dorm beds in the Y15–25 range. There are also a couple of higher grade doubles with TVs and bathrooms for Y80. The guesthouse also runs a travel agency and may be able to help you access some of the remoter locations mentioned here. They have a decent restaurant as well.

Youyi Restaurant. On Guanghua Lu. Pricey food and local dumplings are the speciality here. There is a second Youyi Restaurant just up from the Tengchong Guesthouse.

Bus station area One or two hotpot restaurants, several barbecue stalls and several noodle places.

Chunhua Huishiguan Guanghua Lu. A Muslim restaurant that has good, spicy noodles and some lamb dishes.

Burmese Teahouse and Café Tengyun Hotel entrance. Given the quality of coffee in the Baoshan/Tengchong region, the glucose-spiked, instant brew here is pretty awful, but the café itself is a relaxing place patronised by a friendly bunch of Burmese merchants posing as high quality gem dealers. They do have a few inferior rubies and crudely cut diamonds on hand if you are interested. The pancakes, samosas and beer make up for the coffee.

What to see

Tengchong might seem a backwater but is home, in fact, to quite an international community of ethnic Chinese, who have returned from overseas, and Burmese traders who have long-standing connections with the place. The town sits at an altitude of 1,650m which can be very pleasant during the daytime. Nights frequently require a light sweater.

Serendipity is your best course here, meandering around the backstreets of the old quarter in the western section of town, the markets, shops and cafés of the newer sections. The former **British Consulate** is in the northwest section of town, near the compound of the Municipal Foodstuffs company. It is a large building with upturned eaves which has been turned into a storehouse for grain and liquor. The building was constructed in 1916 and used by the British well into the 1940s.

The town's best market is the **Frontier Trade Bazaar**, a suggestive name for what is mostly a commodities market, but it's a lively place with some cross-border items like gems and Burmese jade on display.

Side trips from Tengchong
Laifeng Temple and Fengshan Forest Reserve

A 15- or 20-minute walk southwest of town brings you to the Laifeng Shan park, a woodland full of meandering paths, and an attractive waterfall called **Dieshui He**, a popular weekend picnic spot for families. Laifeng Temple, a Qing dynasty monastery, has some well-renovated halls and a museum with exhibits on the history of Tengchong.

The temple and its surrounding pine forests are a good place to embark on a hike through Fengshan Forest Reserve.

Heshun Village

Four or five kilometres west of town will bring you to the imposing memorial gateways of Heshun Xiang, a wonderfully photogenic Qing-style village.

EARTHQUAKES, VOLCANOES AND HOT SPRINGS

Yunnan's complex geology can be traced back 40–50 million years to the slow collision that took place between the Asian and Indian subcontinents. The most dramatic example of the crustal compression and shortening caused by this mammoth ramming process are the Himalayas which spill into northwestern Yunnan. As rivers eroded downwards, mountain and cliff faces rose, giving birth to spectacular gorges. An outstanding example can be seen at Huliaoxia, the Tiger Leaping Gorge, where the Jinsha Jiang (Upper Yangzi River) flows at high speed between walls of Devonian marble beneath a 4,000m snow peak.

If you have been wondering why there are so many caves, sinkholes and caverns in Yunnan, continental uplift and the disappearance of a vast sea that once covered this area exposed limestone to the air, causing hollowing and erosion.

Limestone surfaces, exposed for millions of years to wind and rain, have formed some extraordinary karst landscapes in Yunnan, the most famous being the so-called Stone Forest southeast of Kunming where needles and folds of Permian limestone stand in haunting clusters (see Chapter 3, pages 105–9).

Faultlines, where the Red River now runs in western Yunnan and other places, caused grabens, deep indentures in the earth, many of which have filled with water to form splendid lakes like Erhai and Dian. The downside of all this fault movement has been countless, high-magnitude earthquakes. The area of Tengchong in western Yunnan alone has experienced over 70 major earthquakes since records were first kept in the 16th century. An earthquake measuring over seven on the Richter scale struck the Lijiang region in February, 1996, leaving over 300 dead and many thousands injured. A second earthquake, registering 5.3 this time, shook the city in October 1997. Causing less damage and no fatalities, it nevertheless served as another reminder of how vulnerable the region is.

Faultlines have allowed heat to reach the Earth's surface in the form of hot springs. The Yunnanese have used this hydrothermal activity to good effect, turning many of their hot springs into resorts. The boiling hells around Tengchong, a volcanic region where there are some 80 hot springs, geysers and sulphur pools, are poetically referred to by the Chinese as 'Hot seas' and 'Hot fields'.

There are said to be over one thousand small houses concentrated within Heshun's encircling brick walls.

For many visitors Heshun, with its ornamental gardens, concealed courtyards and its centrepiece **Yuanlong Tan**, a splendid pond enhanced with pavilions and an old water mill, represents all that is best in Chinese rural architecture. Interestingly enough, many of the residents of Heshun are former overseas Chinese who remitted funds to the village for its maintenance, and who have now returned to a comfortable retirement there. The **Heshun Library**, established in 1924 and containing over 70,000 books, is one of the fruits of their endeavours. The finely crafted library, which is open to the public from 08.00 every morning, was made from the highest quality wood available at the time.

Mount Yunfeng
47km north of Tengchong.
The Taoist mountain of Yunfeng is an interesting place to explore without maps. Dotted with the ruins of late Ming and early Qing dynasty temples and pavilions, you could easily spend a whole day here poking around the mountain. The finest building here is unquestionably **Yunfeng Temple** which sits at the summit.

At the moment there is no direct public transport to the mountain. The cheapest method is either to try hitching all the way, or catch an early morning bus out to Ruidian, and then thumb a lift the remaining distance from the turning just past Gudong. There isn't a great deal of traffic on this road though. The more costly alternative is to hire a van for the round trip. If you can get a small group of people sufficiently interested it might be economical. On the last check drivers in Tengchong were asking Y450 for the round trip, more than it costs to fly from Kunming to Baoshan!

Touring the geothermals
If you like volcanoes, hot springs and geysers you will be in your element in Tengchong. All the volcanoes in the district have features that set them apart from each other. The same can be said of the over 80 hot springs and geysers in the area.

Dayingshan Volcano to the north, near Zhonghe village, is one of the biggest, its base measuring roughly 12km across. Its crater rim is 300m across and its cone drops to an internal depth of some 100m. Thirty kilometres north of Tengchong, **Huo Shan Kou**, near the town of Mazhan, is another awesome volcano set among a cluster of lesser cones. More inspiring stuff awaits at **Dakong Volcano**, west of Tengchong, and the tallest of the cluster at 250m. If you peep over the crater you can see heaps of pumice-stone at the bottom. **Heikong Volcano** is a mere 80m high but makes up for it with an astonishing depth of 100m. 'Heikong' means black and empty, an apt description of the hollow void within this volcano. The nearest crater to town is **Mount Ma'an**, 5km northwest of Tengchong, just off the road to Yingjiang.

Powerful hydro-thermal currents and shifts have created a wonderful diversity of geysers and hot springs in the area, some quite unique. The so-called **Bird-Snatching Pool** east of town, for example, is a geyser which draws birds down from the sky to their deaths. The geyser apparently contains high levels of carbon dioxide and hydrogen sulphide, a toxic mixture that knocks the birds out as they fly overhead.

The prosaically named '**Sea of Heat**', is a basin of geysers and hot springs located roughly 12km southwest of Tengchong. They are divided into four equally lyrically titled areas: Sulphur Pond to the north, Pine Valley in the south, the Faithful and Pious Temple springs to the east, and Banana Garden over on the west side of the sea. The hot springs contain various pools that are accessible to bathers and some indoor baths. There are also two local guesthouses that offer fairly basic but adequate rooms from Y30, so you can make an overnight stay of your visit. These baths emit a strong sulphur smell. It won't do you any harm; quite the contrary in fact. Inhaling the putrid egg-smell is said to be good for you.

There are two hotels at the entrance to the spring, perfectly nice places with indoor and outdoor pools. Expect to pay Y40–60 for a double. An overnight stay here after taking several of the baths is exceedingly relaxing. Minibuses to the hot springs depart from a turn-off point on Huangcheng Nanlu, in the southern part of Tengchong. Buses start running to the hot springs at 08.00 and entrance to the springs themselves costs Y5.

Getting to these sights can be tricky unless there is a tour being offered by the Tengchong Guesthouse. It is quite likely that there will be as the geo-thermals are Tengchong's main drawcard. Mazhan is relatively easy to get to as the Gudong-bound bus passes through the village. From the drop-off point it is an easy enough walk to the volcano or a motor-tricycle ride.

Ruili and the Borderlands

'The long white ribbon came up out of Burma twisting and turning, like a string of pearls flung carelessly over her coat by a lady back from the opera. It ended in Kunming.'

The Burma Road, Miles Kington

Westwards, towards the great watershed gorges of the Mekong and Salween (Lancang and Nu Jiang) rivers, roads wind through emerald rice fields, broad, fertile valleys and stunning monsoonal forests and jungles before arriving at small cities and townships, many of which are still well off-the-beaten-track. Whole districts near the border were under the suzerainty of Burmese-style *saubwas* (the hereditary land owning class) until as recently as the 1950s.

As an area of immense ethnic interest, the Dehong region is home to many of Yunnan's minorities. The most conspicuous groups are the Dai, Lisu, Jingpo and Burmese. Relatively few travellers pass this way, heading instead for the more publicised Xishuangbanna and its well-organised itineraries and attractions. The Han Chinese have a smaller presence in this area as well. Most are there for the trade and the very real possibility of quick money that the area offers, preferring, like most foreign visitors, Xishuangbanna as a safe bet for their holidays.

Dehong Prefecture is deeply incised with historic trade routes. At the old garrison town of Zhuge Liang, still in the domain of Baoshan, the Southern Silk Road split into two branches: one passing through Tengchong and then eventually to Mytkyina in Burma, the other through Mangshi and across the border to Lashio. These days the action has moved to Ruili, a wild frontier town on the Yunnan-Burma border. Travellers exult in the freedoms and apparent lawlessness of the region, but Ruili and the borderlands are also places where you should remain wary.

The roads around Dehong and the borderlands are severely affected by the region's sub-tropical monsoon climate which includes a long and humid wet season from the end of May into October. It rains practically every day during these months and roads are often flooded or eroded in places, making passage difficult and hazardous.

Nature notes

Flowers bloom all the year round in this sub-tropical monsoon climate, the heat and rain the only real indicators of seasonal change. Dehong's rainforests support a number of trees normally associated with Southeast Asian countries such as giant banyans, rubber trees, blue incense cedar and teak. There are over 40 varieties of bamboo in the region alone. Mango, papaya, and large, shady fig trees are common sights in villages.

Its humid jungles and tightly pinched mountains are home to a veritable menagerie of wildlife: leopards, tigers, pythons, boa constrictors, grey langurs, gibbons, jungle fowl, red deer and wild oxen. The markets in Ruili and smaller towns along the border, with their trade in ground rhinoceros and antler horns, slices of dried elephant trunk, python skins, bear gall bladders, tortoise shell and musks extracted from the livers of several endangered species, are an indication of how vulnerable the area's wildlife is.

Tengchong to Ruili

There are two simple routes to Ruili: the southern road from Baoshan, and the less used westerly one from Tengchong which, if you are going direct and are lucky, should take only five or six hours. It is an enthralling journey as associations with a more classic Chinese landscape crumble into the luxuriant growth of Southeast Asia, and the buses are subjected to a higher incidence of contraband checks as you near the sphere of influence cast by the notorious Golden Triangle.

Baoshan to Ruili

The more common road to Ruili, the one from Baoshan, quickly swerves southwest, soon cutting across the stunning Salween Valley through fields ripe with sugarcane, coffee, papaya, mango, buckwheat and corn. The bus makes brief calls at Mangshi, Dehong's administrative capital, and Wanding right on the border with Burma, giving passengers a chance to consider a stopover in these laid-back towns where the pace of life is more akin to Southeast Asia than modern China or even Yunnan.

YINGJIANG 盈江

Some travellers like to break the journey to Ruili by overnighting in the friendly, relaxed, halfway-house town of Yingjiang, where they can acclimatise themselves to the sub-tropical rise in temperatures and the Burmese influences that start to become more evident as you proceed west.

There are few sights to recommend in Yingjiang, but the **Laomian Pagoda**, 2km from town on the way to Ruili, is an interesting old Burmese-style stupa. **Jucheng**, a 15–20-minute motor-cyclo ride in the other direction is an old, Chinese town, preserved by neglect, that is worth a look.

Getting there and away

Direct buses to Ruili leave Yingjiang from 07.00 until mid-afternoon each day and cost Y16 for the five-hour journey. Buses for Mangshi also depart from here going via Ruili. Buses to Tengchong follow a similar time schedule and cost Y20 for the four-hour journey. If you intend to proceed to Baoshan and connect with a bus for Kunming then you are best going back via Tengchong.

Where to stay/eat

Bright Pearl Hotel Not recommended for a room as it is almost as expensive as the Great Wall, but its restaurant is very good and the service friendly.

Great Wall Hotel. This pretentiously named hotel is the most expensive in town and definitely a last ditch choice, although it is relatively quiet (when there isn't a karaoke-mad trade delegation in town), and very clean, with satellite TVs in all the rooms. The trouble is the prices, which start at Y80 for the bare essentials and go up to an unbelievable Y550.

State Guesthouse One of the cheapest places in town. Convenient too as it's near the long-distance bus station. Beds in the five-bed dorms are only Y5 each, singles and doubles a remarkably low Y12 and Y18.

Yingqing Hotel Good value with singles and doubles in the Y20–25 range. The same with en suite bathrooms and TV for as little as Y40.

MANGSHI 芒市

200km west of Baoshan, Mangshi, also known as Luxi, is the capital of the Dehong Dai Jingpo Autonomous Prefecture. It is also Dehong's important air link with Kunming. The town is surrounded by minority villages, especially Jingpo and Dai settlements. There are several interesting Burmese-style temples and pagodas in the area, many of them built on raised wooden piles in the Dai manner. The town has a small Bank of China branch and Post Office, but you may wish to wait until you reach Ruili.

Getting there and away

Mangshi airport is about 7km south of town. There are daily flights between Mangshi and Kunming. The fare is Y530 one way and the flying time is 50 minutes. Buses depart from outside the airport to town after the flight comes in and cost Y2. Alternatively there are taxis waiting outside as well. There is a CAAC office along the main street of Mangshi where buses depart for the return journey to the airport. If you wish to move straight on to Ruili there are also buses that depart from the airport for Y30, taking just over two hours.

The first bus for Ruili departs at 07.00 and takes about two hours. There are several minibuses to Wanding from the main street. There are more buses for Tengchong than Baoshan. The sleeper bus for Xiaguan leaves at 08.00, and the 24-hour run to Kunming sleeper at 18.30. There are two bus depots offering more or less the same itineraries: the long-distance bus station to the east of town, and the south bus station, actually located at the west end of town.

Post and telecommunications

The area code for Mangshi is 0692.

Where to stay/eat

Dehong State Mangshi Guesthouse South of the main road. A popular place with the few foreign travellers who pass through. Doubles and triples have TVs, fans and bathrooms; pretty good for Y50 and Y40 respectively. There are also a few more 'luxurious' doubles in the Y125–190 range. The location is very quiet, the staff helpful.

Nanjiang Hotel Main road. A reasonable place to stay. Clean with generally helpful staff. Doubles and triples are no bargains at Y90–100 but OK. Dorm beds better value at Y15.

There are several open-fronted restaurants of no special distinction around town. Just walk and, if you like the look of the place, the owner will take you to the kitchen where you can point at whatever interests you. The so-called '**Food Market**' near the Bank of China has a good choice of stalls preparing stir-fried dishes, kebabs and noodles. Just north of here on the rural edge of town are a number of very pleasant Dai restaurants located in raised-wooden buildings. They have good views of the surrounding fields and countryside.

Local sights

In terms of named sights, there isn't a great deal to see in Mangshi, but walking around can be rewarding. There is an interesting Bodhi Monastery, also called the **Temple of Precious Stones**, in the middle of town; an interesting mix of Han and mostly Dai styles. The altar, lintels, and incense-burners are all Dai. The **Foguangsi Monastery** is a wooden structure dating from the Qing dynasty with recently restored and painted pillars, and carved dragons. The grandly named **Mangshi Nationalities Palace** near the southern bus station may be worth a quick look for its, at present, rather meagre exhibits on local minorities.

Fapa Hot Springs lies about 7km south of Mangshi, a good half-day excursion either by private van or bicycle. Further afield, the **Grotto of the Three Immortals** is a long, 40km trek southwest of Manshi to see cave formations that are supposed to resemble various famous Buddha halls, arhats, pagodas and a nine-dragon bridge. It is situated on a precipitous overhang of a cliff. The location is stunning but you have to have a lot of imagination for this one.

WANDING 畹町

Well known throughout China for its pineapples, fermented bean curd, soybean sweets, high quality tobacco and rice, as well as its ethnic silversmithing, Wanding is also China's official gateway into Burma. The **Wanding Bridge** is splendidly decked out with miniature customs houses, blazing national insignias and flags. Wanding's rather wholesome image, at least compared to Ruili, just a few kilometers away, is explained by its official role.

Just how porous the Yunnan–Burmese border actually is can be seen a mere one-minute stroll downstream where you can see locals paddling across the narrow Wanding stream that separates the two countries. It is easy enough for foreigners to sneak across but, as it is officially illegal, you are likely to stand out and as there is, in fact, very little to see on the immediate Burmese side that you can't see in Dehong, this would be an unwise course. Even if you can't officially go there, you can contemplate the place at close hand from Wanding.

Wanding has always been a place of economic and strategic importance as it was once part of the South West Silk Road to Burma and India and later became the terminus on the Yunnan–Burma road in 1938 when the route was opened. During the anti-Japanese war Wanding was the only international passageway open to China, as the seaports were all blocked, and vital military supplies were channelled through here to the interior of the country.

Getting there and away

Wanding doesn't have a proper bus garage as yet. Buses usually stop at the intersection between Minzhu Jie and Guofang Jie. Minibuses leave for Ruili throughout the day (Y15) and also for Mangshi (Y30).

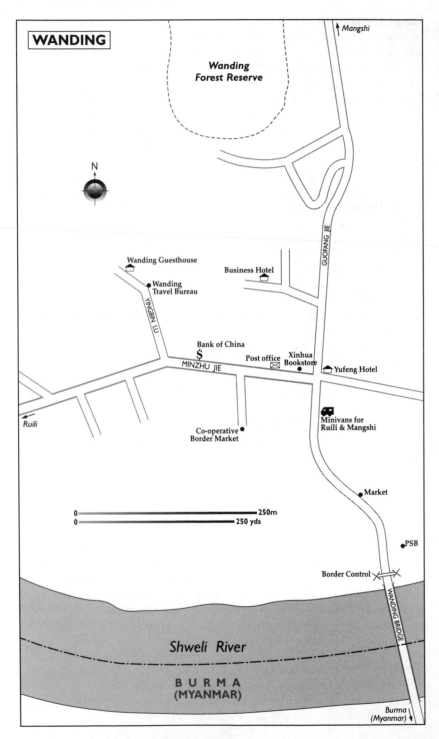

Practical information

For such a small place, Wanding, no doubt because of its critical border position, is well serviced with one of everything. The friendly, helpful staff at the PSB operate from an office just in front of the bridge, on the left side of the road. The Bank of China is on the main Ruili road, opening Mon-Fri, 08.30–11.30, 14.00–17.00. You can make international calls from the Post Office on the same street between 08.00–20.00. There is even a Xinhua Bookstore in town. The Wanding Travel Bureau, next door to the Wanding Guesthouse, is a useful place to find information and to arrange excursions.

Where to stay/eat

Business Hotel Located in a quiet back street off the road to Mangshi, this quiet hotel has good value doubles for Y50.
Wanding Guesthouse Tel: 0692 5151327. A popular place with backpackers who enjoy trying to haggle the dorm bed prices down from Y25. Doubles here have

THE JINGPO

The 118,000 strong Jingpo mostly live in the mountainous areas of Dehong and Nujiang Prefectures, but there are also smaller communities found in Tengchong, Lancang and Gengma counties.

Known in Burma as the Kachin, Jingpo men can be recognised by their round-collared, buttoned garments and head-wrappers which are decorated with small coloured balls and flower lace designs.

Jingpo women's formal attire, resembling medieval chain-mail or armour, is stitched with dozens of silver bobbles. Women wear lacquered rattan rings around their waists, wrists and ankles. The Jingpo hold that the more of these red and black rings that are worn, the more beautiful they are.

Tall, coloured pagodas are a feature of Jingpo villages, cheerful and dazzling structures that are an expression of the Jingpo's *joi de vivre*. The group have a well deserved reputation as hedonists. Drinking is a way of life for the Jingpo who carry wine-holders called *pituns* wherever they go, dispensing cupfuls to friends they meet in the fields or mountains. For detoxification, the Jingpo chew reed zhizome (a slightly narcotic root), and tobacco. They also chew betel, a nut which stains and numbs the mouth and teeth, and has a mildly narcotic effect.

The wine-loving Jingpo also enjoy singing and dancing, something they do at weddings, when a new pagoda is dedicated, a house built, friends visited, or even at burial sites. Their most spectacular event is the Munao Zongge Festival. Mass dancing festivals like this often involve more than 1,000 participants, dancing, singing and chanting to the accompaniment of gongs, cymbals, wooden drums, bamboo flutes and elephant-leg drums. Munao Zongge translates, in fact, as 'mass dancing'.

satellite TV and bathrooms. They are very comfortable and good value if you can afford the Y90. Slightly more expensive triples are available. One of the best options in town. The guesthouse is located on a hill above town.

Yufeng Hotel A large, ghostly sort of place, but it's cheap. Dorm beds are only Y15; spartan doubles go for Y70.

You can eat quite well at the **Wanding Guesthouse** even if you are not staying there. There are some good morning food stalls outside the guesthouse as well. Otherwise, there are a cluster of quite clean little family run restaurants in the Yufeng Hotel area.

What to see
Wanding's markets are not a patch on those at Ruili but worth a look while you are there. The largest is the **Co-operative Border Market**, housed in a modern building boasting several storeys. More interesting is the **Wanding Forest Reserve**, uphill from Guofang Jie. Although the zoo here isn't much, the pine forests are pleasant and, best of all, there are superb views of Burma on the other side of the river: rolling green hills, and the famous Burma Road snaking its way off in the direction of distant Lashio.

There are several **Jingpo villages** in the vicinity of Wanding. The Jingpo, a rather private people, tend to live in the remoter reaches of the Dehong mountains, so this is a good opportunity to see them close-up. On the last day of the lunar New Year, usually in February, the Jingpo stage their Munao Festival in Longlong about 15km west of Wanding. Hundreds of Jingpo gather for the event which features a communal dance inherited by their ancestors, according to Jingpo legend, from the offspring of the sun god. The Wanding Travel Bureau will be able to help you if you want to make an announced visit to one of these villages. Their tours are as authentic as you can get in the circumstances and sometimes include a very pleasant river cruise.

RUILI 瑞丽
Short on sights but long on atmosphere, Ruili's reputation as a frontier market, a place of low morals and shady deals has, ironically, helped to promote it as a travel destination. The reasons for Ruili's image as a 'Wild East' boom town are apparent from the moment you arrive. Theravada Buddhist temples and pagodas, Indian merchants, arms dealers, drug men, corrupt officials, plain clothes police of dubious loyalties, an incredible number of prostitutes, and some of the best border markets in Asia: for better or worse, Ruili has it all.

The town and its counterpart, Mu Se, over on the other side of the border, are the main corridor for Burmese heroin on its passage through China to Hong Kong, Thailand, Laos and other smuggling routes.

Burmese dialects, minority languages and alien tongues, including English, are common and friendly conversations are easily struck up. By day Ruili is a shoddily built, hustling, mercantile town; by late evening, after its batteries of neon are switched on, and its discos, massage parlours, and electronic game arcades have got going, Ruili is transformed into a nocturnal wonderland.

Masochistic levels of self-abuse, whether through intravenous drug use, prostitution, alcohol or late night, high-decibel sessions of karaoke, wait to ensnare those who linger too long in Ruili. Enjoy. Leave before it becomes a habit.

Getting there and away

There is no airport in Ruili itself. Flights arrive at Mangshi, a two-hour bus ride away. Yunnan Airways (tel: 414 8275) office is right in the centre of town on Nanmao Jie. It is wise to reconfirm your outgoing flight from here.

Ruili has buses to all sorts of places in the region and beyond. Vans and minibuses, leaving from across the road from the long-distance bus station, serve local destinations like Jiegao, Nongdao and Zhongfeng. Buses for Mangshi are frequent, the first departing at 08.00. minibuses leave for Wanding every hour. Yingjiang buses leave a little later, the first at 09.30. The first Tengchong and Baoshan bound buses leave at 07.00 and 07.20 respectively.

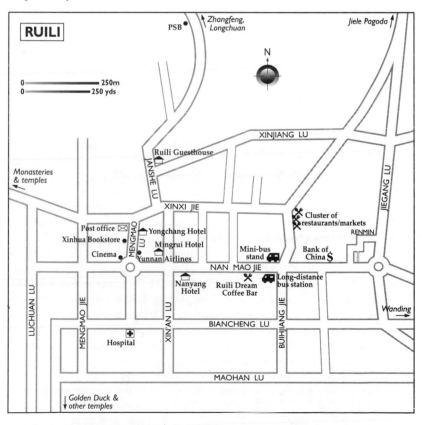

The nearest of the long-distance sleeper routes is Xiaguan. Buses depart at 19.00 and are supposed to take 16 hours. Reckon on at least 25 hours for the Kunming route. The first of many Kunming-bound sleepers leaves at 06.20. Place your travel plans on hold if you intend taking the Jinghong-bound sleeper, arrival date unknown. In normal circumstances, you might expect to arrive sometime on the third day.

Getting around
Ruili is still small and easily negotiated on foot. There is a taxi stand near the long-distance bus station but you are unlikely to require their services. Bicycle-rickshaws are handy vehicles for local trips to outlying temples and pagodas, if there are any left by the time you read this. The best way to get around is by bicycle. The Mingrui Hotel has bike hire, but demands a hefty deposit up front. The Ruili Dream Coffee Bar is a much better bet. Expect to pay Y12–15 a day for a good bike, and Y100 deposit.

Border crossings
Jiegao and its bridge, just a few kilometres from Ruili south of the Golden Duck Temple, is one of the official border crossing points that you are unlikely to be able to access for some time. Foreigners are categorically not allowed to enter Burma, or Myanmar as it calls itself these days. Resistance to foreigners crossing the border comes from the xenophobic Burmese side, not the Chinese who are perfectly amenable about the whole thing. If and when

THE BURMESE CONNECTION
The current boom in 'informal trade' between China and Burma can partly be seen as the logical reactivation of time-honoured Asian forms of border commerce. Border trade with China and other neighbouring countries was formally legalised in September 1988, only a month after the Burmese military's infamous massacre of thousands of demonstrators. China now has virtually free access to the north of Burma, with a steady flow of traders and trucks loaded down with Chinese goods and the latest arms, thundering down the old Burma Road.

Priority in national road and bridge building in Burma has been given, in fact, to routes that facilitate the delivery not only of goods but of arms from China. The first bridge to be heavily appropriated by those who manage the weapons trade spans the Shweli River, linking Ruili with roads that carry armaments into Burma. Nicknamed the 'Gun Bridge' by locals, deliveries so far have included amphibious tanks, armoured personnel carriers, rocket launchers, anti-aircraft guns, thousands of tons of recoilless rifles, mortars, light weapons and ammunition.

The border is a place where all kinds of deals are made. The Burmese say that there are three lines of business along the border and further foreigners are allowed over, it is likely to be in the form of expensive, closely scrutinised tours, probably one day trips.

Where to stay/eat

Ruili Guesthouse Tel: 414 1463. A quiet place with a palm garden away from most of the frenzied nightlife. The dorms are nothing special but alright for Y25 a bed. Bathrooms and toilets are shared. There are some overpriced doubles for Y170.

Mingrui Hotel Western end of Nanmao Jie. One of the best deals in Ruili. Clean doubles and singles at Y30 and Y60 respectively, with bathrooms. Some cheaper triples also. Good staff. Try to get a room away from the basement disco or second-floor karaoke hall.

Yongchang Hotel Mengmao Lu. Popular with Burmese merchants, a clean and relaxed place with single and double rooms with baths for Y90 and Y170. Also some triples and quads.

Nanyang Hotel Nanmao Jie. A Chinese style hotel with reasonably priced doubles and plenty of hot water for Y80. Simply furnished but quite comfortable.

Ruili Dream Coffee Bar Nanmao Jie. A favourite with foreign travellers, the Dream is run by a fluent English-speaking Chinese. An excellent source of local information, the café also has a good English language menu which includes a number of authentic Burmese dishes. Fresh juices and draught beer also available.

Hotpot stalls Most of these are located either near the long-distance bus station, which also has several noodle stands, or outside the Ruili Guesthouse.

Burmese food Can be found in small restaurants along and off Jiegang Lu and along Renmin Jie.

into the country: the so-called 'green line, red line and white line', signifying jade, rubies and heroin. Although narcotics are one of 23 listed items which are officially banned from cross border trade, contraband of this kind is often ignored by the military personnel who supervise checkpoints.

The north's trade in rubies, though less contentious than heroin, is, nevertheless, extremely profitable. Burmese rubies are considered the finest in the world. Those known in the profession as 'pigeon-blood rubies', a variety unique to Burma, command the highest prices.

The Chinese have also made inroads into the trade in jadeite which, like precious gems, has always been government managed. The Chinese have always had a special appreciation for Burmese jadeite and have imported vast quantities of it for centuries. China's finest jade figures in fact, such as those on display in Beijing's Forbidden City Museum and the National Museum collection in Taipei, or those reserved for the top end of their export market, are carved from Burmese jadeite. Jade has been described by the Chinese, who have carved the stone into ornamental and ritual objects for almost 7,000 years, as a 'symbol of protection, health, and strength, something fortunate to own and felicitous to give'.

Juice bars Also serving coffee, tea and ice-cream, these are found all over Ruili now, but especially along Nanmao Jie. The 1997, near the Mingrui Hotel, is a good place for freshly squeezed juices. Lime is particularly refreshing.

What to see
Markets
Ruili's superb day and night markets are a source of endless fascination. Among the predominantly Burmese merchants you will also find the odd English speaking Bengali, Pakistani or Indian offering their wares. Alongside the familiar tubes of Colgate toothpaste and fake Nikes are products of more local provenance: betel-nuts, Mekong whisky and Mandalay rum, succulent fruits, jaggery (unrefined sugar), incense and caged birds. Members of minority tribes come each morning to the fresh produce market held near the post office. Other highlights include a daily gem and jade market in a narrow alley off Xinxi Jie. Among the attractive but inferior moonstones, amethysts, and slivers of over-priced jade, are genuine high quality stones for the professional's eyes only.

Temples and pagodas
Whichever way you walk or cycle you will come across many temples, pagodas and monasteries. Although many of them are well preserved, the effect is often ruined by the addition of asbestos roofs. The **Golden Duck Temple**, 5km southwest of town, is one of the best known locally because of a founding legend which tells how an auspicious pair of golden ducks alighted here, harbingers of prosperity to an area that was formerly a malarial swamp.

Jiele Jin Ta, the '**Golden Pagoda**', a similar distance east of Ruili, is an interesting cluster of 17 gold-painted stupas that date back to the 18th century. West of town, **Hansha Temple** is a wooden building with a few resident monks adding a touch of authenticity. Further down the same road, **Leizhuangxiang**, a Tang dynasty stupa, is the oldest religious building of its kind in the Ruili area. The views from the stupa at the top of the hill are worth the climb. In more or less the same direction, past the village of Jiexing, the wooden **Denghannong Temple** is in the Dehong Dai style.

Twenty-five kilometres or so southwest of Ruili, the village of Nongdao, with its single hotel, is a pleasant place to spend a day. The locals are extremely friendly and the village is surrounded by other Dai settlements. There are several minibuses to Nongdao every day.

The Golden Quadrangle
The Golden Triangle, the opium growing and trading conjunction between northern Thailand, Burma and Laos also overlaps into southwest Yunnan where major smuggling routes and a flourishing heroin market exists. The area, in fact, might better be termed the Golden Quadrangle.

Much of Burma's opium is transferred along the Burma Road into Yunnan Province in southwest China, but this has become more difficult since the Chinese government launched a rather more serious effort than their neighbours to regulate the traffic on their side of the border, after alarming drug addiction statistics emerged.

The government's abhorrence of heroin is linked to the addiction of millions of Chinese as a result of the activities of British traders in the 1770s. The British tolerated, indeed benefited, from the cultivation of the drug, trading openly in the narcotic as they had with China through their entrepot at Hong Kong. They seem to have regarded it merely as a commodity like any other, on a par with their Eastern trade in tea and rhubarb. Although the opium trade was eventually condemned in the British parliament in 1906, this lucrative cash crop was to play a key role in the ideological struggles that occupied large parts of Southeast Asia, particularly Indochina, from the 1950s until the 1970s. French colonial and then American agents of the CIA both supported the growth of a huge opium trade managed by the Kuomingtang (Chinese Nationalist troops) whose resistance bases were deep in the region. Funds from opium were used to pay the thousands of American-backed mercenaries who fought against the communists in the Vietnam War, and US helicopters were even known to transport the drug.

Opium has a long history of use among hill tribes as a herbal and medicinal drug for the cure or alleviation of diarrhoea and severe coughing, and as a pain-killer. Poppy seeds, pressed oil and raw opium sap are used by some of the borderland tribes as an ingredient in their daily meals.

In many ways opium (*Papaver somniferum*) is the ideal cash crop. Light, portable and non-perishable, the high elevations at which it is grown exclude competition from lowlanders and the need to deliver the crop as dealers come to the village to negotiate a price for the harvest and then arrange for its transportation.

Poppy seeds are sown during September and October. The cultivation period generally lasts from April to August. Harvesting usually begins in the middle of December, continuing for two months or longer. High alkaline soil, preferably in sheltered mountain hollows or close to ridge lines, are perfect conditions for growing opium, although this tough plant can also thrive in nutrient-deficient fields. Discriminating users insist that they can detect a 'sweeter' flavour issuing from opium grown in limestone soil.

The Hani, Lolo, Wa and Lisu are among some of the main users of opium in Yunnan, although it has even infiltrated some of the Muslim villages along the western border counties. Little publicity is given to the fact that Yunnan's opium trade is run by Chinese gangs, reportedly with the aid of some corrupt local policemen.

226

Magnolia liliiflora

Jinghong 景 洪

Epithets like 'sleepy', 'exotic' and 'laid back', routinely used to describe Jinghong, the capital of Xishuangbanna Dai Autonomus Prefecture, the city in the jungle are, sadly, a thing of the past, albeit very recent past. Only three or four years ago the city smelt of flowers. Now it smells of concrete dust. And money.

Locals date the real construction drive that turned this provincial capital – a mixture of old wooden Dai houses and concrete, utility buildings so heat-weathered they almost fit in with the surrounding greenery – from one month in late 1998 when, almost overnight, the town underwent the first stages of a transformation they were not consulted about beforehand. As roads were torn apart, resurfaced and widened, megalithic new hotels erected, department stores planted at road junctions, more peripheral forest cleared away, the city was left choking on a fog of concrete dust. With the construction boom has come the inevitable resorting of the population as more Han Chinese have poured in to work in the booming economic sector. The spectre of local Dai people renting out their homes to newly arrived Han Chinese and moving in with their in-laws is a common story.

The sound of the jackhammer may have replaced the tinkle of temple bells and Dai drums as the *leitmotif* of Jinghong but, mercifully, some of the dust has settled now; locals no longer need to tie handkerchiefs over their noses or wrap their babies in dust-proof gauze nets when they step on to the street. Many of the palm trees that line Jinghong's broad avenues and provide much needed shade, have been left intact and, despite a noticeable build up in traffic, Jinghong is once again a pleasant place to walk around. It is still a city in a jungle, though a sprawling, increasingly ferro-concrete one.

Jinghong has become a major tourist destination for Chinese holidaymakers. More like an upland southeast Asian city than a Chinese one, tourists from the increasingly affluent east coast in particular, have discovered that they can spend their holidays in an exotic, tropical location without applying for an overseas visa. Jinghong is home to some of the best festivals in the whole province. With their southeast Asian origins and flavour, they attract tens of thousands of both Chinese and foreign tourists, creating temporary accommodation problems and overbooked flights.

Despite all the changes spearheaded by the construction boom and tourist infestation, Jinghong remains the ideal base for explorations further afield in Xishuangbanna, and now that a certain degree of calm has been restored, the city is again a convivial place to while away a few days while you ponder the next stage of your itinerary; its ethnic, culinary, and botanical microcosms of the greater Xishuangbanna region provide a useful digest of what the county has to offer. Jinghong is still referred to as the 'City of Dawn', a reference to a legend in which a local Dai hero battled for seven days in the depths of the Mekong River with a demon-king. Emerging triumphantly on the last day with a magical pearl removed from the demon's throat, the Dai youth hung the prize on a high branch of a tree, its light bathing the city and land in radiance.

HISTORY

Xishuangbanna was incorporated into the Nanzhao kingdom in the 8th century. At the time, the flatlands where present-day Jinghong stands were a loose conglomeration of tribal villages. The 'City of Dawn' was first recorded in Chinese annals when a local Dali warlord called Bazhen fought with the Hani and Bulang tribes, finally driving them off the fertile plain that surrounds the city and founding an independent kingdom in the region in 1180.

Xishuangbannna was a remote, nominal part of the Dali Kingdom until the 13th century when it became a vassal of China, a distant, rarely visited outpost. Jinghong at this time was better known for its endemic levels of malaria and occasional outbreaks of bubonic plague, than for its warm, tropical allure. Ming dynasty rulers tried with only partial success to impose a degree of authority over the area, especially the porous border regions. As the Manchus increasingly lost their grip on the country in the 19th century, European powers began to focus their ambitions on the region. The French briefly encroached on Simao, directly north of the capital, while the British actually sent a battalion of 500 soldiers to occupy Jinghong. Both eventually agreed to keep Xishuangbanna as a buffer zone between British Burma and French Indochina.

Since the Mongol invasion in the 13th century, the region had been placed under the control of Dai chieftains, hereditary heirs called the Pianling. These feudal overlords exercised enormous power over their own fiefdoms, suppressing non-Dai minorities. Taxing the common people almost to the point of extinction, they forced them – according to Qouting Heng Lan in his *Travels through Xishuangbann* – to 'till the land in tribute, buy the water they drank, the land their hut stood on, and the earth they were buried in when they died.' This tyranny continued throughout the first half of the 20th century under the rule of Ke Shexu, a Han warlord. The People's Liberation Army entered Jinghong in 1950 to a mixed reception. With time and a comprehensive programme of health care and education, the suspicion that the Chinese forces might simply be the new oppressors faded, though misgivings were rekindled during the Cultural Revolution.

GETTING THERE AND AWAY

Jinghong airport lies roughly 10km southwest of the city. The bus terminates opposite the CAAC booking office on Jingde Xi Lu (tel: 212 4774). The fare into town is Y3. The flight from Kunming to Jinghong takes about 50 minutes. The fare is Y520 one way and there are several daily flights. With the area's growing popularity there is now also a service from Jinghong to Xiaguan which currently operates every Monday, Tuesday and Thursday. The 50-minute flight costs Y680. There is also a daily flight to Lijiang which operates every morning except Saturday when it is an evening flight. The fare is Y730 and this 50-minute flight is invaluable if time is limited, as it can save several days of bus journeys. It is usually easy to book tickets except during the days leading up to the Water-Splashing Festival, although there are almost 20 flights a day at this time.

Jinghong has two bus stations. As a rule the long-distance station on Jinghong Bei Lu deals with traffic to Kunming and eastern Xishuangbanna; the No 2 Bus Station on Minzu Lu with local and more westerly destinations. Both stations have long-distance sleepers that leave throughout the day. The journey is supposed to take 24 hours but rarely makes it on time. Count on anything from 27 to 30 hours. Shop around and check out the buses in advance as there are considerable differences in price and comfort, from the basic, standard buses that leave from the No 2 station from 06.00 charging Y100, to the more upmarket private buses that do the same journey for Y180. The long-distance bus station on Jinghong Bei Lu has buses to Ruili, Baoshan and Xiaguan. In a non-stop scenario, sleepers to Xiaguan take 32 hours, but there may be unscheduled stopovers about half way in Zhenyuan if the drivers are not prepared to press on. The awesome 40-hour plus trip to Ruili is only for the very hardy. Some passengers are said to lose all sense of time on this long-haul trip which can easily degenerate into 60 or 70 hours if there are serious problems like flooding or landslides along the way.

Frequent buses and minibuses depart from Bus Station No 2 to destinations around Xishuangbanna. It is usually possible to just turn up and wait for the next departure. The earliest buses leave at 07.00 and continue until 17.00.

GETTING AROUND

Jinghong is located on the southwest band of the Lancang River which flows in a southerly direction towards Laos and Thailand where it is renamed the Mekong. The main north–south arteries are Jinghong Bei Lu which becomes Minhang Lu, and Galan Lu. The principal east-west streets are Jinghong Dong Lu and its extension Jinghong Xi Lu, and the shorter Jingde Dong Lu.

Although there are some curves and diagonals the city centre is largely based on a grid system making it easy to negotiate. Roads in the suburbs or in villages that were incorporated into the city only recently, are more winding.

There is no inner city bus service. Although Jinghong is growing into a sizable urban centre these days, it is still possible to walk almost anywhere within the city. Taxis are not usually necessary. Bicycles are an excellent way to get around and to explore villages along the Mekong River. The Banna Hotel used to have a wide selection of well-maintained bikes. Check to see if they have started renting again. If not, the Forest Café has a good choice of bikes. The Mei Mei Café should also have bike rentals. There are scores of bicycle and motor-rickshaws in and around Jinghong, although there was a rumour that cyclos would soon be banned from the increasingly car-oriented city centre. This may or may not take effect.

PRACTICAL INFORMATION
Post and communications
The post office on the corner of Jinghong Dong Lu and Minhang Lu opens from 08.00–20.30. There are cabins for placing international calls. You can send faxes also and even send email messages from the post office. The Escape Café along Manting Lu is an internet café.

The area code for Jinghong is 0691.

Money matters
The Bank of China's main office on Jinghong Nan Lu opens from 08.00–11.30, and then from 15.00–18.00. The China Aricultural Bank on Jinghong Dong Lu also has an exchange counter and can deal with travellers' cheques as well.

PSB
The PSB office is along Jinghong Dong Lu, a little way up from Peacock Lake on the other side of the road. Travellers have had few problems obtaining visas from the friendly staff here. Office hours are 08.30–11.30, and 14.30–17.00.

Tourism
The increasingly busy staff at Jinghong's two main offices of CITS are a cheerful and friendly bunch of people prepared to spend time with visitors (tel: 213 3271 or 213 0460). The main branch is on Manting Lu, the smaller one opposite the entrance to the Banna Hotel on Ganlan Lu. If you want to save the trouble of organising your own transport, food and itineraries, they may suggest several interesting day trip options around and beyond Jinghong.

Using a local guide is often a good way both to save time and learn about an area. The travellers' cafés are the best way to make contact. Check their guest books to see the comments written by other travellers. Sarah at the Forest Café can take travellers to local villages and on day or overnight treks at very reasonable rates. Zhou Yu, a fairly fluent English speaker, is a more expensive option but a highly informed guide on local cultures and the lifestyles of ethnic minorities in Jinghong, Xishuangbanna and along the western border with Burma. Zhou Yu's rates, at Y250 a day for one person, Y200 for a group of two or more (transport, food and accommodation is extra for both you and guide), are probably beyond the means of most travellers, but for those who can afford it, his services are highly recommended. You can contact him through the Mei Mei Cafe. James Dao, the Dai owner of the Wanli Restaurant is also available for day trips at Y200 a go. He speaks excellent English and Thai and is learning Japanese.

Xishuangbanna weather conditions

Xishuangbanna's tropical climate means there are only two seasons: wet and dry. The wet season, which runs from June to the end of August and into early September, is not a particularly good time to visit the area as there are downpours virtually every day. As the rains clear, surprisingly dense fog descends on Xishaungbanna from mid-September until February. This is usually no problem as the fog arrives during the evening and is usually gone by mid-morning. An ideal time to visit the area would be between November and early March when the skies are generally clear, temperatures bearable. The mercury starts to rise in April and it is quite common to experience temperatures of 25–35°C at this time.

Nature notes

Although Jinghong is surrounded by forest, jungle and fertile farmland, the city is impinging more and more on this natural garden. A good example is Management Bureau X, supposedly a UNESCO-designated biosphere reserve, forest and ecology protection project located at the upper end of Ganlan Lu on the very edge of town. When I visited, a freshly deforested area stood accusingly at the back of the complex, bulldozers levelling the ground for what looked like a new road or apartment block.

Jinghong's botanical gardens, parks and fruit markets still offer an interesting glimpse into the surrounding area, and it doesn't take much to hop on a bus or cycle off to the countryside to find jungle, Rousseauesque glades, tea and coffee plantations, or farms growing pineapples, bananas and custard apples.

Entertainment and leisure

The upper section of Manting Lu, a rather tacky but lively and atmospheric tourist strip, is where you will find a concentration of restaurants and cafés that look like prairie cabins and Austrian taverns. Dai women drape themselves from the second-floor balconies of restaurants or bang drums and gongs at entrances in the hope of luring tourists in for performances of Dai music and dance, worth seeing once if you can't hit upon a village festival. There are lots of nice, authentic touches and saving graces along this road: charcoal chicken grills on the pavement, taxi-cyclos floating along the dusty street, candle-lit open cafés and monks drifting around nearby Wat Changliarn.

THE DAI

The first recorded contact between the Dai and Han Chinese occurred in 109BC when the Emperor Wu Di set up the Yizou Prefecture in southwestern Yi, the name for the minority regions of Yunnan, Sichuan and Guizhou provinces. History, as recorded in Dai scripts, dates their culture to over a thousand years. The Dai belong to the Tai ethnic family who, like their counterparts in Thailand, Burma, northwest Vietnam, Laos and Assam, were driven south by invading Mongol armies in the 13th century.

The 1,025,000 strong Dai mostly inhabit the plains, river and lake shores of Xishuangbanna and Dehong Prefecture, but there are also Dai settlements in Lincang, Honghe, Yuxi, Simao and elsewhere. The name Dai roughly translates as 'freedom and peace-loving people'. Far from the main centres of Chinese authority, the Dai have exercised considerable freedom over the centuries and even today, like many other minorities in this region of Yunnan, practise a blithe disregard for the concept of borders and passports.

Their costumes, textiles, musical instruments and the design of their villages and homes bear a remarkable resemblance to those found among certain ethnic groups in Burma, Laos and Thailand. Their bamboo houses are usually built on stilts, the upper storey serving as the living space, the lower a storehouse, place for weaving or shelter for livestock. Ideally, the house is enclosed behind a bamboo fence and surrounded by fruit trees. Rice is the staple Dai food. Its cuisine, consisting of such specialities as sticky rice in sweet bamboo, deep-fried moss and yellow ant-eggs in sour meat, seems immensely exotic to the Chinese tourists who visit Dai areas.

Like their ethnic cousins in Thailand and Laos, the Dai are Theravada

Apart from the ubiquitous karaoke bars and hotel lounges with expensive bars, there are a few discos around town, though few seem to have live music yet. The **DDDisco** along Jingde Xi Lu is said to be one of the best. Don't expect an evening of hip hop, hard house, acid jazz or trance though. The **People's Cultural Hall** between Minhang Lu and Jinghong Nan Lu have occasional performances by troupes of musicians and dancers. There is a large open space in front of the hall used for playing billiards and pool, and rollerskating.

Masseurs in white clinician's aprons set up along central Ganlan Lu in the evening, administering to regular customers and travellers back from treks. Jinghong's parks have a spontaneous nocturnal life involving mostly impromptu dance and music displays. There is a public **swimming pool** opposite the CAAC office and vegetable market. It costs Y3. The Dai Hotel Garden offers a more upmarket set-up with a good pool, weights, a fitness room and squash and tennis courts, all for Y20.

Buddhists. A Dai landscape is easily spotted not only because of its stilted houses and fruit orchards, but its many temples and pagodas.

Women's costumes, more reminiscent of Southeast Asia than China, are highly distinctive. Sarongs, a colourful bodice and a jacket with buttons on the right are worn. Hair is often tied in a bun at the back of the head and ornamented with combs or fresh flowers or, when working, tied in a flannel-wrap head dress. Slim, silver waist-bands are worn as fashion accessories but also to indicate marital status. Other customs that have Southeast Asian parallels are the fondness for betel-nut chewing which leaves the mouth with dramatic orange and red stains, and the habit among young people of having their teeth capped in gold, a sign of beauty.

The Dai's sophisticated culture includes highly developed musical genres. The best known are narrative operas called *zhang khap*, solo performances in which singers are accompanied by the Dai flute. Weddings, courtship and the ordination of monks are the main occasions on which these miniature operas are held.

Tattooing among men is a tradition among the Dai and is still practised in the more remote areas. When boys reach the age of 12 a tattoo artist is brought to the village to begin the long ordeal of injecting colours under the skin, usually geometric patterns, the forms of flowers and animals, and designs using the Dai script.

There are a number of books – legends, poetry, fables and children's stories – published in the Dai script. The Dai have their own calendar which dates from AD638. Several books exist for calculating lunar and solar eclipses. Many books are still published in the Dai language. In Xishuangbanna and Dehong radio news is broadcast in both Chinese and Dai, and there are newspapers published in the Dai script.

Festivals

Jinghong and Xishuangbanna in general play host to some of the liveliest, best supported festivals in Yunnan. The **Tanpa Festival**, during which boys are initiated as temporary novice monks, and the **Tan Jing Festival** in which sacred Buddhist texts are honoured, take place between February and March during the second lunar month.

Poshui Jie, April's **Water-Splashing Festival** is the best known and most beloved of Jinghong's three or four main cultural knees-ups. It would be wise to book a hotel well in advance as accommodation is at a premium during the few days of the festival. The alternative is to find accommodation in a private house in one of the surrounding villages and then come in by bus or bicycle.

The **Closed-Door** and **Open-Door Festivals** are closely linked to the seasons and the agricultural calendar. The first, more austere event sees young men ordained as monks for periods of anything between a few days and months, the latter is a celebration of the harvest.

October or early November's **Tan Ta Festival** is a colourful event involving pilgrimages to local temples, rituals and the building of bamboo towers from which hot-air balloons and rockets are launched. Lucky charms are often placed inside the rockets, and those who find them among the surrounding fields, are guaranteed to be lucky in whatever enterprise they desire.

WHERE TO STAY

With the exception of the days during which the annual Water Splashing Festival takes place, there are plenty of places to stay in Jinghong. Few, however, are exceptional. Chinese-style accommodations like the Traffic Hotel (Minzu Lu), Banna Dasha (Jinghong Nan Lu), and Banna Hotel can be noisy as they cater for big tour groups. Room rates are quite competitive and reasonably good value.

Banna Hotel Ganlan Lu; tel: 212 3679; fax: 212 3368. A long-term favourite with travellers. Blocks of rooms at the Banna, also called the Banna Guest House, are set around pleasant, well kept gardens with lawns and tall palms. The hotel has a travel agency as well. Helpful and friendly English-speaking staff. Rooms are grouped according to price. Standard rooms in the newer Peacock Building are Y240, and in the old Riverside Building Y190. The so-called Bamboo Building has economy three bed rooms for Y90. These are approximate figures as prices change quite quickly here as the buildings are improved or fall into various states of disrepair.

Dai Building Inn Manting Lu. Also known as the Dai Building Hotel. Popular with backpackers and couples, accommodation here is in Dai style bamboo bungalows built on raised stilts. The courtyard where the bungalows are can seem a little claustrophobic, the rooms a bit dark, but the atmosphere here is good. A small restaurant-bar and hot showers powered by solar panels. The owner, an English speaking Dai named John, is a mine of information on the locality. Y25 per bed. Four people can occupy one room. Also doubles for single travellers.

Dai Garden Hotel 8 Nonglin Nan Lu; tel: 212 3888; fax: 212 6060. This is Jinhong's top-of-the-range five-star hotel, with a range of facilities including a swimming pool, business centre, two restaurants which serve Cantonese and local Dai dishes and a third with a Western-style menu. Pleasant grounds and good service make this the best choice if you want some creature comforts while you explore the nearby jungles and villages. Twin rooms with en-suite, TV and phone cost $80 and suites range from $150 upwards.

Jiaotang Fandian Minzu Lu. Right next to the long distance bus station. By garage hotel standards this one is not bad, though the rooms are dusty and drab. Standard doubles with bathroom and fan Y120. Deluxe doubles with fan and attached bathroom go for Y200, which seems a little steep.

Jinghong Hotel Jinghong Dong Lu; tel: 212 3727; fax: 212 3727. A centrally located government-run hotel with a good choice of clean, well-maintained rooms. Standard doubles at Y168 and Y188. Economy twin dorms go for Y88.

Mengyuan Hotel Jinghong Nan Lu; tel: 212 3028. Foreigners are beginning to stay in this smallish hotel, also known as the Ming Hotel, because of its cheap rates, clean rooms and helpful staff. Singles Y40, doubles Y 230, triple at Y20 per bed.

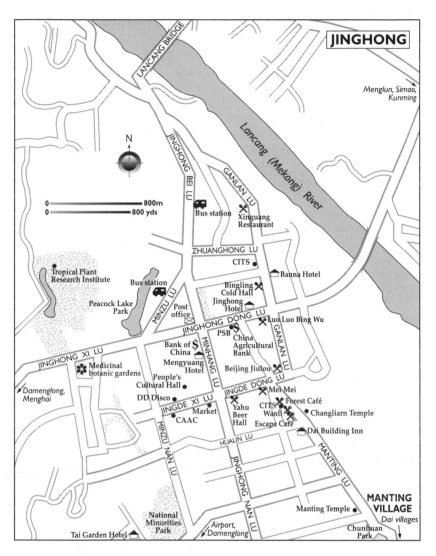

JINGHONG

Menglun, Simao, Kunming

Lancang (Mekong) River

LANCANG BRIDGE

JINGHONG BEI LU

N

0 ——————— 800m
0 ——————— 800 yds

GANLAN LU

Bus station

Xinguang Restaurant

ZHUANGHONG LU

CITS

Banna Hotel

Tropical Plant Research Institute

Bus station

Bingling Cold Hall

Peacock Lake Park

MINZU LU

Post office

Jinghong Hotel

JINGHONG DONG LU

Luo Luo Bing Wu

GANLAN LU

PSB

China Agricultural Bank

Bank of China

MINHANG LU

Mengyuang Hotel

Beijing Jiulou

JINGHONG XI LU

Medicinal botanic gardens

People's Cultural Hall

Damenglong, Menghai

DD Disco

INGDE DONG LU

Mei Mei

Forest Café

INGDE XI LU

Market

CAAC

Yahu Beer Hall

CITS Wanli

Escape Café

Changliarn Temple

Dai Building Inn

MINZU NAN LU

HUALIN LU

JINGHONG NAN LU

MANTING LU

National Minorities Park

Airport, Damenglong

Manting Temple

MANTING VILLAGE
Dai villages

Tai Garden Hotel

Chunhuan Park

WHERE TO EAT

Like every medium-to-large-sized Chinese town, there are no end of eating options in Jinghong. Having made all the effort to get down to Xishuangbanna it makes sense to try out as much of the local cuisine as possible. Most of the Dai restaurants are found along Manting Lu, although some of them include rather perfunctory song and dance performances put on by minority groups. Rice is a Dai staple which is served plain or in more interesting versions such as coconut and pineapple rice, glutinous black rice, wrapped in banana leaves or placed into lengths of bamboo and then steamed or grilled. Rice-based pancakes, sweetened and stuffed with nuts make a good breakfast along with coffee. Fish or beef cooked in lemon grass, dried banana wafers, fried river moss, and sour and spicy bamboo soups are other local specialties. If you are up to the challenge, there are also more exotic foods to sample like steamed frog in piquant sauce and fried wasp larva. Monkey liver, for obvious reasons, is not recommended.

A cluster of good food stalls at the bus station sell bowls of wheat and rice noodles for Y4. You can also buy provisions like biscuits, sponge cakes, buns and fruit for the journey. The café at Peacock Lake is a pleasant place to have a mid-morning cup of Yunnan coffee. If you want to pig out, the breakfast buffet at the Tai Garden Hotel is good value at Y25. Burmese pancakes are sometimes sold in the mornings near the souvenir market north of the bus garage. There are several decent bakeries along the south end of Jinghong Lu – either side of Jingde Lu and Hualin Lu intersections.

Wanli Manting Lu. Along with the standard travellers' fare are some authentic Dai dishes. Vegetarians will love the peanut sauce, eggplant, cucumber, fried banana and plain rice combinations. Roasted fish dishes prepared in lemon grass, fried river moss are mouth-watering. Fresh fruit juices and Burmese black tea are good accompaniments. Eat at one of the tables on the upstairs balcony which has a good view of this lively street. The restaurant, which also has cheap accommodation, is run by James Dao (real name Dao Yuam Chun), a Dai minority person who can also organise tours to local places of interest. He also runs the James Coffee Shop next door.

Forest Café Manting Lu. One of the best cafés to hangout, browse through the town's best selection of books, and enjoy homemade food. Bread is baked on the premises and tastes like it. English, American and Scottish breakfasts, an excellent goat's cheese salad, and what one expat of several years' standing in Yunnan has billed 'the best hamburger in the entire province'. The owner Sarah, a friendly women from Hunan, can also take you on insider tours of local hill tribe villages.

Mei Mei Manting Lu. One of Jinghong's two or three backpacker cafés. Good all-round menu with Western breakfasts of muesli, yoghurt, toast, eggs and ham, Yunnan coffee. Some books for sale and reference. Staff tend to be glued to the telly most of the time. See the guest books which carry some useful, sometimes disgruntled or slanderous, comments and recollections on local sights, restaurants, hotels and other travel tips.

Xinguang Restaurant Ganlan Lu. A basic, no-nonsense, working class canteen restaurant that serves real Dai food. There's no English menu or anything like that, so you'll have to point at dishes on other people's tables. They'll get the message. Lunch times are crowded and boisterous.

Bingling Cold Hall Ganlan Lu. Opposite the Banna Hotel, an unassuming-looking place that has cheap dishes, drinks and snacks. A lot of Burmese people from the nearby souvenir market in Zhuanghong Lu come here.

Beijing Jiulou Jingde Dong Lu. A good-quality Chinese restaurant for those missing spare ribs, roast duck, Great Wall wine and rice crackers.

Yahu Beer Hall Jingde Dong Lu. A brewery and bar that serves great pitchers of draught beer for Y30–40. You can also eat here.

Luo Luo Bing Wu East end of Jinghong Dong Lu. A clean and cheerful noodle and tea shop with a good view of the street.

WHAT TO SEE
Tropical Plant Research Institute
Off Jinghong Xi Lu. Daily 08.00–17.00. Y10.
In the western part of the city centre the grounds of this well laid out plant and crop research garden are one of the delights of Jinghong and a nice initiation into the flora of the region in general. There are over 1,000 species of plant at the institute and an almost equal number of researchers and gardeners. Much of the research is in the field of economic plants. Among other ventures, the institute runs a large rubber plantation. You can watch the trees being tapped from the end of March until well into December. In the middle of the plantation you can find a concrete memorial to the ever-popular premier Zhou Enlai, who met his Burmese counterpart U Nu, on this very spot on April 14 1961 to discuss the sensitive Sino–Burmese border situation.

About half the trees and plants are labelled in English, others with their Latin or Chinese names. The gardens, lawns and nurseries here contain closely planted shrubs, flowering bushes, bougainvillea, paper flowers, and bonsai. Fruit and rainforest trees are well represented and include plumeria, cassia, calabash, cinnamon trees and the small leaf fig. There are also Liberian coffee bushes, and a Mango Germplasm centre whatever that is.

Continue through the gardens and you will come to a large building called the **Traditional Medicine Clinic**. The staff here are friendly and welcome foreign visitors. A small shop near the entrance to the research institute sells an interesting collection of herbs, traditional Chinese medicines like 'dragon's blood', ground coffee and other horticultural products. Across the road on Jinghong Xi Lu, you can also visit the **Medicinal Botanical Gardens**, a pleasant enough garden, but it pales against the institute.

Peacock Lake Park
Jinghong Xi Lu.
The park beside Peacock Lake, an artificial pond halfway along Jinghong Xi Lu, is a pleasant place to have a morning coffee at one of the open air tables near a pergola. Locals come here to go through their morning life-enhancing exercises and practise tai chi. There is a small zoo tucked away in the corner and some miniature children's attractions.

The English Corner is held here on Sunday evenings, a good chance to meet locals. On other evenings during the week you may find musicians and singers here, running through excerpts of Chinese opera or local Dai songs. Foot masseurs and weighing machines add to the recreational and health character of the park.

Changliarn Temple
Manting Lu.
The first main temple you come to along Manting Lu, Wat Changliarn has a temple school. Dai boys used to come to this ancient temple for a three-year

period of Buddhist training and instruction. It is a pleasant wooden building with an interesting interior. Unlike other parts of China, Korea and Japan where people have traditionally followed the Mahayana (Greater Vehicle) school of Buddhism, Dai patronised temples are associated with the Theravada (Lesser Wheel) school of thinking which originated in Sri Lanka and is common to countries like Cambodia, Thailand, Laos and Burma.

Manting Temple
Manting Lu.
You will recognise this important temple from its wall and the balustrade which leads up a few steps to the main compound as both are topped with the

THE WATER-SPLASHING FESTIVAL

Poshui Jie, the Water-Splashing Festival, is the Dai people's most important festival. Like Thailand's Songkran, the festival, a week of unbridled hedonism, which seems like an unrestrained carnival, originated as a solemn Brahmanist rite.

Dai folklore has its own way of explaining the origin of the festival. According to their account, the Dai Kingdom was once oppressed by a tyrant with magical powers. Among his hundreds of consorts, there was a woman who took pity on the Dai. She discovered that her master's vulnerable point was his neck which could be easily broken. When the king slept she plucked a single hair from his head, placed it around his neck and strangled him. To the woman's horror, the head dropped off and a torrent of blood, spume and fire spurted forth, endangering the whole kingdom. Steeling herself, the woman grabbed the head while her Dai friends poured water over it, quelling the fires and washing away the blood. With the spell broken harmony was restored to the land of the Dai and each year, in thanks for their delivery from the demon-king, and to wash away their own sins, they have held the Water-Splashing Festival.

In traditional Dai culture, water symbolises emotion and wisdom. It follows that drenching people – strangers are also fair game – is not a taunt but a token of goodwill. Besides the water dousing, other activities which have been worked into the festival include peacock and elephant-foot dancing, dragon-boat racing, the slaughtering of buffaloes, singing contests and, echoing a similar event held in northeast Thailand and Laos, the building and launching of giant, bamboo sky-rockets. The festival used to run for weeks until it exhausted itself and everyone involved. The government has now limited it to April 13–18, with the main events taking place over three consecutive days. The festival attracts droves of tourists, but also provides an opportunity for one of Yunnan's biggest ethnic gatherings, an intriguing cross-section of Yunnan minorities dressed in all their finery.

form of a *naga*, a mythical water-serpent common to the cultures of Laos, Thailand, Burma and elsewhere.

Wat Manting is Jinghong's principal Buddhist place of worship, a large but simple design in wood, raised on piles to avoid termites. The temple, which is said to have been founded over 11,000 years ago, is being gradually restored with the help of donations from Thailand. Always remove your shoes when you enter a temple in Xishuangbanna.

Chunhuan Park

Manting Lu. Daily 08.00–17.00. Y12.

Chunhuan Park, the former location for the Dai chieftain's royal slaves, is on the tourist circuit but doesn't in all honesty have a great deal to offer, although it is a pleasantly green, usually quiet spot. The tropical flowers and trees here are worth a look. Some of the tour groups who show up here can sometimes get a bit excitable as they stage a daily water-splashing event for those who can't make the real one in the spring.

You can wander to the back of the park where there are real peacocks wandering around (the bird is a symbol of well-being and grace to the Dai people, one you will see represented on temple carvings, paintings, menus and other places); then cross over a bridge that spans a tributary of the Mekong, where there are several mock temples and pagodas on a small island. Zong Temple is a prestigious Buddhist school, **Baijiao Ting** a replica of the well-known Octagonal Pavilion near Jingzhen.

Chunhuang means 'Garden of the Soul' in the Dai language. It's certainly a calm place when there are no groups around. A stroll further on through the small rainforest area will take you to an auspicious bodhi tree, supposedly planted by a Thai princess, and the inevitable Zhou Enlai statue.

If you take the path that runs past the entrance to the park you will reach the village of **Manloh Hon**. The village is interesting because its water source is a large bamboo waterwheel. You can get a ferry here across the Lancang where there are several villages tucked away among the banana groves and rice-paddies.

National Minorities Park

Minzu Nan Lu.

This 20.5ha park was opened in 1987 as a showcase for the minority cultures of Xishuangbanna. It is nowhere near as big as its equivalent venture in Kunming but the idea is more or less the same.

If you turn up on Wednesday and Saturday evenings between seven and eleven o'clock you can attend 'parties' in which professional singers and dancers perform shortened versions of the Dai Peacock Dance, the Hani Bamboo Tube Dance, the Great Drum Dance of the Jinuo and so on. The performances are fake to the hilt but the audiences are usually immensely appreciative and a good mood prevails. In the daytime you can see various tribal peoples drifting around the park looking picturesque. There is a small museum here as well, with ostriches, coypus, giant lizards and a couple of elephants. There are also some amusement stalls for kids and a couple of shooting galleries. They seem to have removed the offending live chicken and crossbow shooting gallery.

Better is the setting itself, the walks under the foliage, the collection of tropical plants and medicinal herbs, and some half-decent Yao and Jinuo exhibitions. There are several outdoor cafés concentrated in one area of the park selling fresh tropical fruit juices, charcoal barbecued sticks of meat, and cold summer noodles. It is a green, relaxing setting in which to enjoy a snack or light lunch.

Markets

Jinghong is full of interesting street markets, many of them no more than just a few, hastily thrown-together stalls selling durians, gnarled roots and ear-wax cleaners. A large, generalised, semi-covered day market at the top end of Minzu Lu is worth a look. A covered market at the southern end of Minzu Nan Lu is good for fabrics and local Dai costumes, dresses and blouses. A small market appears every morning outside the gates of the Changliarn Temple, and disappears as quickly. Just around the corner several stalls appear outside the primary school just before the children are let out, offering very cheap hot bowls of noodle and snacks.

A completely tourist-oriented market can be found along Zhuanghong Lu, a pedestrian-land just up from the Banna Hotel, on the left off Ganlan Lu. Its main product is jade. It is known locally, in fact, as the Jade Street. There are several salesmen here from India as well as Burma where deposits of the world's finest jade are found. There are several other trinkets including impossibly heavy and overpriced wooden elephants, peacocks and sets of camels. I suppose that if you really wanted one, you could haggle the prices down. There is a good night market with lots of food stalls outside the People's Cultural Hall along Jingde Xi Lu.

Exploring Xishuangbanna

'Ever since this region of Xishuangbanna fell to the Mongols in the thirteenth century, the Chinese have rumoured it an earthly paradise: "the Land of Peacocks".'

Behind the Wall, Colin Thubron

Xishuangbanna is where the influences of a more monolithic China subdivide and dissolve into the rich ethnic morass of Southeast Asia's borderlands and culture. Known as the Xishuangbanna Dai Autonomous Prefecture, the region consists of the three counties of Jinghong, Menghai and Mengla. The name Xishuangbanna (locals just call it 'Banna'), is the Sinicised rendering of the Dai wording Sip Song Ba Na, meaning 'Twelve Rice-Growing Regions', an administrative convenience for measuring land distribution.

This hugely fertile region, lying just beneath the Tropic of Cancer, was once plagued by malaria and cholera. Until the early 1950s, when these risks were finally eradicated, the region was known by the unfortunate epithet 'Land of Lethal Vapours'. Among the minority nationalities that live in Xishuangbanna, the Dai people are the largest. Fine agronomists and architects of Xishuangbanna's landscape, they have been engaged in agriculture for over 2,000 years, firstly clearing the jungle with elephants, and then planting rice.

Nature notes

A natural laboratory for botanical research, Xishuangbanna is one of the few areas remaining in China with primeval rainforests. Over 30% of Xishaungbanna is forest cover, much of it virgin forest. Species of tropical trees number over 5,000. This figure includes species of fast-growing trees. Over 500 types of medicinal and food plants and trees like pepper, benzoin, cassia and sandalwood have been recorded, plus a high yield of oil-bearing plants.

Tropical and sub-tropical crops grow well in the fertile soil, farmers enjoying two or three harvests a year. Home to the famous Pu'er tea, the region also produces quinine, rubber, camphor, coffee, cocoa, and a wide range of fruits like pineapple, mangoes, bananas, plantain, cashew and coconut.

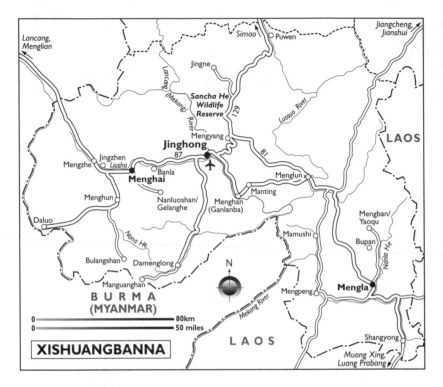

THE MEKONG RIVER

Watching the sun set along the banks of the Lancang (Mekong) River in Jinghong, in temperatures that can rise to 35°C or more, it is difficult to imagine the river's snow-fed source up in the Himalayas on the Tibetan Plateau. There it is known as Dza Chu, or 'Water on the Rocks'.

The Chinese have another name for these waters. As they tumble through the awesome gorges of northwestern Yunnan, the currents become Lan-Tsan Kiang, the 'Turbulent River', a sobriquet that hints at the Mekong's dual character. Depositing on the one hand, rich alluvial topsoil over rice fields, it is also known at certain points along its course down through southeast Asia, to cause disastrous floods, loss of life and crops.

The third longest river in China and the world's 12th largest, the Yunnan stretch of the Mekong is navigable for 320km. You would expect the broad, sinuous course of the Mekong to be a major highway for passengers and trade, but in fact the river is underworked, though it is deep and navigable enough to accommodate a flotilla of different vessels from cruise ships and ferries to light tankers.

Its warm, humid forests and nature reserves are home to wild oxen and elephant, gibbons, green peacocks, leopards, mongoose, takin, golden-haired monkeys, hornbills, boa constrictors and many rare fowl. Almost one-third of China's birdlife can be found here. Many animal and bird species are being hunted down to the point of near extinction, not only to fill the cooking pot but also to feed China's ravenous hunger for ingredients for its more unusual and rarefied medicines and cures. Tiger bones and bear gall bladders are a case in point.

The government has designated slightly over a quarter of a million hectares of forest as parkland reserve. It can only be hoped that this is not interpreted as providing a licence to plunder the remaining non-protected areas.

BANLA 班拉
37km west of Jinghong.
If you don't have time to trek into the wilderness and find an untouched Hani village, the one at Banla is a decent option. Its proximity to Jinghong and location a short distance from the main road has meant a certain amount of encroachment. They have built a Hani meeting hall, for example, so that they can put on performances for visiting Japanese tour groups.

Despite such pandering to the tourist market and the odd TV aerial sprouting from thatched roofs, the village follows fairly traditional seasonal patterns. You won't find that many people around during the morning and early afternoon, for example, as almost everyone is working in the fields. The houses at Banla are all built in the traditional style: large, single structures raised on stilts. Cooking is done at an inside, sunken hearth.

To reach the village, join any bus on the Menghai to Jinghong route and ask to be let off at Banla. Once off the bus descend to the Flowing Sands River near the road. Cross the bridge and you will be in Banla territory. After viewing the village, continue along the unmade road that rises above Banla's spirit gate (a typical Hani touch), and walk for about 2km until you come to a small Lisu settlement. It is a pleasant walk between slopes neatly planted with tea bushes, and the views of the river valley below are excellent.

MENGHAI 勐海
53km west of Jinghong.
Menghai's varied geographical surroundings, its hills, mountains, and river basins, are considerably more attractive than the dusty, unprepossessing town itself. Menghai, however, is the centre for the cultivation of Pu'er tea and one of the most important tea growing areas in China, and possibly its first.

Rare tree and tea varieties are grown, and research undertaken at the **Mangao Nature Reserve** and the **Yunnan Tea Research Institute**. At 1,400m Menghai is perfect for this type of tea. Pu'er is a world famous brew, exported not only to Hong Kong and Japan but also Europe where it has its followers. Compressed into bricks it is also sent over the border into Tibet, and as such was once used as a trading unit. In its slimmer's version called

THE HANI

The majority of the 1.273 million Hani live in regions of Honghe, Xishuangbanna and Simao Prefectures, specifically in the valleys that lie between the Ailao and Mengle Mountains and the great Yuanjiang and Lancang rivers. Linguistically they belong to the Yi branch of the Tibetan-Burmese language group. In neighbouring Thailand they are known as the Akha in Laos they are called the Kaw.

Polytheism and ancestor worship add interest to their micro-culture. Rituals are held to worship and appease family patron gods, the deities of earth and heaven, and the sacred Dragon Tree. It's all fairly esoteric to the outsider, but the flavour of their beliefs, and some of the substance, can be sensed during their festivals and ceremonies. The Hani, in common with many tribes who live close to the animistic world that thrives in remote places, spend an enormous amount of time trying to avert misfortune. At times when someone dies, a fire breaks out, a wild animal roams the village, or a dog manages to climb onto the roof of the house – a particularly bad omen this last one – the Hani will make offerings to mollify or redirect the cause of evil. In accordance with their own lunar calendar, the Hani celebrate New Year in October.

Rice is the staple diet of the Hani people, great quantities of sticky rice cakes being consumed over the New Year. If you stay in a Hani village you will likely be fed on a mixture of fresh vegetables and wholesome soups, as well as Hani predilections like sour and spicy bamboo shoots, salted beans and vinegar meat. Another food staple of the Hani is corn. They also cultivate a certain amount of opium.

The Hani are a highly visible tribe. Their traditional clothes and jewellery – hand-embroidered tunics, silverware breast-plates, and elaborate headdresses, bedizened with pom-poms, dyed feathers, beads and old silver coins from China and French Indochina – are instantly recognisable, as is the design of their homes and their amazing water-terraced rice fields. The terraces in Yuanjiang County in Honghe Prefecture are particularly impressive and little visited. Hani homes, two or three storeys built of bamboo and hardwoods, are constructed on the slopes of hills, villages sometimes comprising as many as 300–400 individual families. A modest people, they are rarely seen outside their villages except when they appear at weekday markets to trade.

The Hani's age-old custom of hospitality, of offering wine and tea to passersby and strangers, is something that should not be abused or taken advantage of by travellers.

tuocha, it is exported to France. It used to be possible to join tours of the **Menghai Tea Factory**. Check through your hotel in Jinghong or locally to see if these are still taking place. An alternative would be to join a tour of the

Nestlé Company's coffee plant. You can see the gates to the plantation, which is located along the Liusha He (Flowing Sands River) valley, from the bus on the way to Banla.

The **Sunday market** at Menghai is a colourful event attracting, as all the best ones seem to, a lively cross-section of minority peoples. There are about a dozen different ethnic groups in the Menghai area, including the Lahu, Dai, Hani and Bulang. A rich cluster of over 30 hot springs can be found at nearby Mengman, on the Nanbenghe River.

The two cheapest places to stay in town are the **Banna Hotel** and the **Liangyuan Hotel**, both on Xiangshan Xinjie. Both offer reasonable dorm beds with shared bathrooms. Better rooms in the Y170–190 range can be

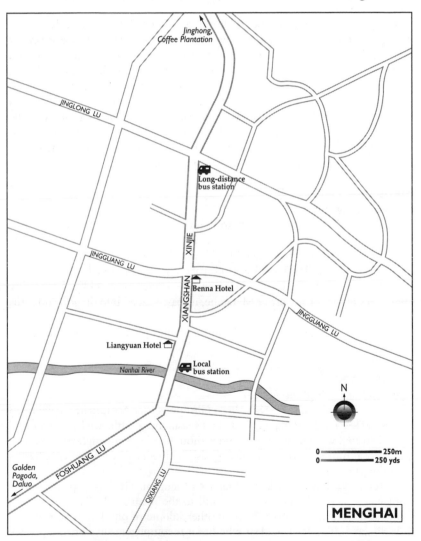

found at the **Commercial City Hotel** near the main long-distance bus station. Getting to Menghai from Jinghong's No 2 Bus Station is easy enough, with vehicles leaving every 30 minutes from 07.30 onwards. The journey takes about 90 minutes.

Jingzhen's Octagonal Pagoda
14km northwest of Menghai.
Bajiaoting, the Octagonal Pagoda or Pavilion, is Jingzhen's main tourist draw. Standing on a man-made hill visible from the main road, the temple was built and completed in 1701 with the dual purpose of honouring the Buddha and acting as a talisman against misanthropic wasps, apparently a major problem in the area at the time.

Badly damaged during the Cultural Revolution the pagoda has been through a number of renovations over the years. Its colourful base is one of the features of this unique building which is now a designated protected monument. The blue, green and yellow base rises to mid-level covered with gold flowers, stupa, legendary beasts and tree motifs. The pagoda's main feature is its steep, ten-tiered, eight-piece roof and cupola crowned with a complicated spire. The renovations may have detracted quite a bit from the original but it is still worth seeing. There are some other buildings on the hill including a monastery and library. The library has some naive scenes from the Jakata tales, stories from the Buddha's former lives.

Mengzhe 勐遮
8km west of Jingzhen.
If you happen to be in Jingzhen try to visit the small town of Mengzhe, an area rich in pagodas. The best known one is **Manlei Pagoda**. The central of its two painted stupas reaches a height of 20m. The second stupa in Mengzhe is called the 700 **Buddha Temple**. Both pagodas were built in 1746.

Wat Manduan, an even older temple dating from 1132, lies a few kilometres to the southwest of Mengzhe, its base shaped into dragon and lotus forms.

Mengzhe and Jingzhen are both on the main bus route from Menghai to Menglian.

Nanluoshan 南罗山
43km southwest of Jinghong. Y2.
Getting to Nanluoshan (the 'Southern Glutinous Rice Mountain'), celebrated for its 800-year old King of Tea Trees, can be a little tricky. Dedicated naturalists will want to see this wonder though – the 5.5m-high tree, planted by the local Aini minority – if only to test the theory that tea growing has its origin in Yunnan.

To reach Nanluoshan, take the bus from Menghai. The bus stops at a bridge from where it is a 5–6km trek up a hill to the main road. The tree is well signposted from here and is about another kilometre on. The tree itself is a little disappointing. It's not clear whether it is completely alive or not, or why so many visitors have defaced it with names, messages and attempts at graffiti. There are reputed to be better tea trees elsewhere.

A larger and older wild tea tree can be found in a valley at **Hesongzhai Village** in the district of Baba. Reputedly 1,700 years old, the tree rises to over 14m and is in better shape than the one at Nanluoshan.

Gelanghe 格朗和
30km southeast of Menghai.
If Banla failed to satisfy your curiosity about the Hani people, a trip to the little visited town of Gelanghe might. The main minority here are the Ake, a less known sub-branch of the Hani who can, nonetheless, be found near both Simao and as far away as Menglian. The Ake wear their hair long. Married women tuck their hair under caps which they decorate with silver coins and beads; single women adorn their headdresses more ornately.

If you follow the track that leads up above the town into the hills and past a lake, you will come to several wooden Ake villages. The people here are not used to visitors so tread gently.

MENGLIAN 孟连
Just over the border from Xishuangbanna, Menglian is a town set among attractive green hills with potential for exploring, although it may seem at first sight to be just another hideous Chinese construction site. Overland travellers coming from the Dehong region will find this a convenient place to stay overnight before continuing by bus for the seven- or eight-hour run to Jinghong.

Chinese painters are said to be drawn to this area because of its supposed similarity to the karst hills of Guilin. I didn't see any. But it is certainly an interesting area for those interested in Yunnan's minorities. There are some 15 or more represented here, including the Lahu, Hani, Dai, and the normally elusive Wa.

If you are approaching from the Jinghong direction, the bus passes over some extremely dusty roads, though some are made of compacted stones. It is a superb route visually though, with rice-terraces, water courses, and sugarcane fields growing on steep slopes overhanging boulder-strewn streams and gorges.

Getting there and around
The No 2 bus station in Jinghong has departures for Menglian at 08.30 and 11.30. Return buses from the long-distance station in Menglian start to leave at 07.30. The journey takes around seven or eight hours and costs Y35. A few buses each morning also connect Menglian with Simao; the six-hour journey costs Y35. This could be another alternative to flying back from Jinhong as Simao has its own airport with connections to Kunming. There are also bus connections from Menglian to Baoshan via Lancang.

You can easily walk up and down the two main streets that constitute most of Menglian. There are also motor-cyclos around town which are a fun and comfortable means of travel. If you follow the local Nanlei River some 6km outside town it is supposed to be possible to rent boats. Enquire at your hotel, they might be able to help. Communication, though, can be a problem. Menglian doesn't have many foreign visitors, so very few people speak English. There is no tourist infrastructure to talk of here, so it might be worth checking with the CITS office in Jinghong if you are interested in exploring some of the tribal areas. Alternatively, some of the guides mentioned in the Jinghong chapter know this area and may be of help. (See Chapter 12, *Where to stay* and *Where to eat*, pages 234–6.)

Where to stay/eat

Nanxiang Hotel Tel: 872 3777. If you don't mind the sound of jackhammers and oxyacetylene flashes at the window at night, the rooms here are very spacious and reasonably clean. No hot water though. Doubles for Y80 with large beds, TV and basic bathroom with non-flush toilet.

Menglian Hotel Near the canal at the entrance to the old town. Friendly and good value. Has singles and doubles with bathrooms and hot water for Y70. Also some dorm beds for Y20. The best choice in town.

Shunjun Restaurant At the intersection up from the bus station. A friendly, family run place where they will take you into the kitchen and show you what is available. There are two or three similar places in the same row.

Bus station area Several noodle stands, and one or two small Dai and Muslim restaurants in this vicinity. Near to the large produce market with its tasty breakfast and early lunch, open canteen-style eateries.

What to see

Menglian has a couple of quite lively **markets**. The largest is one block in front of the Nanxiang Hotel. If you are staying on one of the front rooms you can see the tiled roofs of the market's sheltered stalls. It's largely a produce market but a fascinating place visited each morning by several different ethnic groups from the surrounding villages. There is a row of cheap breakfast kitchens along the left side of the market. There is a smaller market frequented by locals and tribal peoples near the canal, just off the street at the west end of Menglian Dajie.

The **Old Town** is just up the hill from here, running more or less parallel with the canal. There are some fine old wood and clay houses still standing here. Though small, it feels light years away from the town's main drag with its half-baked concrete-and-glass modernity. The old town seems orderly and clean by comparison. Although there are some new, intrusive houses here, most are traditional with nice courtyards and balconies. There is an impressive Burmese style temple at the top of the hill, with wooden, ox-blood coloured walls, sweeping roofs and some resident monks. There is a second temple in the centre of this quarter whose stencilled walls between the upper roofs are reminiscent of Lao and Thai designs.

The highlight of this area is the Mengliang **Dai People's House Museum**, a splendidly preserved clan house for Dai leaders and their families. The original construction dates from the 13th century. The courtyard with its miniature

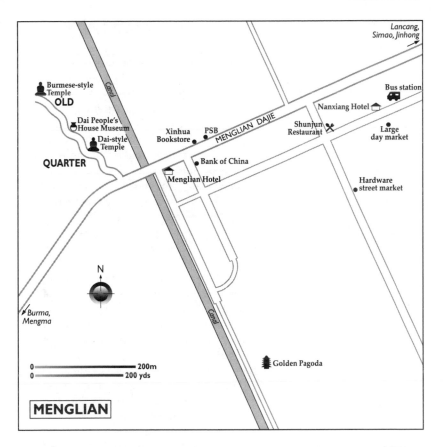

MENGLIAN

rainbow bridge and watered garden, lacquered walls, decorative tiles and shaded walkways is a delight. The interior has been made into a museum. The rooms are nothing short of superb, with highly polished floors, latticed windows and odd bits of antique furniture lying around. The upper floors house an interesting collection of silk costumes with dragon and peacock embroidery, manuscripts, ceremonial umbrellas and other artefacts of the Dai culture. There are very few visitors to the museum. You'll probably have the place to yourself and the services of a very pleasant woman who has a smattering of English. She will collect the Y5 entrance fee from you and then give you a tour of the grounds and rooms.

Follow the canal south of the old town and after a couple of minutes you will come to the **Golden Pagoda** on your left. There is a Y2 entrance fee to see the Dai and Burmese scripts within and the mandatory Buddha statue.

MENGHUN 勐混
27km southwest of Menghai.
The main reason for a visit to Menghun is to take part in its extraordinary **Sunday market**. If any of the guides in Jinghong offer to get you there and back in a one-day excursion, make sure you leave early: the market, which gets

THE WA

Mention the name Wa and many people think of head-hunting and drugs. The Burmese Wa certainly were head-hunters until only two or three decades ago and are still deeply implicated in running sectors of the lucrative Golden Triangle drug trade. Narcotics are inseparable from the life and economy of many of the tribes inhabiting Yunnan's southwestern border with Burma, but the 347,000 Wa who live in Lincang, Simao, and the Cangyuan and Ximeng regions of the Awa Mountains generally follow more innocuous pursuits.

This Mon-Khymer, animist worshipping, cross-border ethnic group are essentially an agrarian people. The Wa exult in festivals, especially those connected with the important totem of the drum. During the Lamu Drum Festival, which is observed just before the harvest in the 12th lunar month, cows are sacrificed, incantations chanted by shamanistic priests and prayers for a bumper crop offered. At one time the Wa kept their drums in special bamboo drum rooms, replacing them with newly made ones if disaster befell the tribe in the form of disease, a bad omen or crop failure.

Contrary to their fierce reputation, the Wa are a hospitable people. Guests are honoured and made welcome with *shuijiu*, a strong alcoholic drink served in a bamboo bowl. You will be expected to swallow the first offering in one go. Women make *shuijiu* by steaming wheat corn, millet and buckwheat with yeast. The mixture is then sealed and fermented in a container that contains banana leaves. The resulting firewater, a milky coloured liquid, is called 'water wine'.

Wa women are gifted weavers, but are best known for the visual impact they make from wearing heavily ornamented silver and antimony bracelets, hoops, bangles and belts over their bare arms, embroidered sarongs and tunics, hair tied in a black turban or plaited into a chaplet and decorated with woollen flowers. If you see the Wa you are unlikely to forget them.

going just after dawn, starts to fizzle out around noon. It is best to stay overnight beforehand, though the options are not that inviting.

It's all worth a little discomfort, though, to see the rich mix of locals and minority people. The Hani in all their tribal finery stand out, but there are the turbanned Bulang, Dai and several other groups swirling around in various costumed and bejewelled states. The market itself is a good place to buy ethnic textiles, clothes, shoulder bags, silver belts and handmade paper.

The town itself is not spectacular but there are some interesting pagodas scattered around the nearby hills and countryside. An octagonal monastery, modelled after the one at Jingzhen, stands in a bamboo grove on one of the hills near the town and there is a small group of pagodas dating from the 18th century in the village of **Nanban** on the outskirts of town.

Getting there

From the No 2 Bus Station in Jinghong you will have to take a bus bound for Daluo and then get off at Menghun. Buses start at 07.30. There is a special market bus which departs at 07.20. The James Café along Manting Lu in Jinghong has a minivan that goes there. Enquire at the café for departure time and cost. (See Chapter 12, *Tourism*, pages 230–1.)

Where to stay

If the accommodation in Menghun is not that enthralling it is at least absurdly cheap. The best place is probably the **White Tower Hotel**, a quiet place with a pond in its grounds. Beds in double rooms cost Y10. The second best choice might be the **Yunchuan Hotel** near the bus stop, which also runs a decent restaurant. The rooms here are even cheaper.

DALUO 打洛

2km from Burmese border in Menghai County. Buses from Menghai.
Although there are few real sights in Daluo, its proximity to Burma and the daily **cross-border market** which attracts an interesting mixture of different hill tribes, justify a trip if you happen to be in the area. The road to Daluo passes through dense green countryside and the villages of minorities like the Bulang and Hani.

Daluo is a popular excursion for Chinese tourists because of a famous, giant fig tree. Its elevated roots descend to the ground, forming, in the popular Chinese imagination, a '*Tree That Looks Like a Forest*', as they have dubbed it. A more bizarre feature of Daluo is its popular half-day tours (Chinese only) over the border into Burma, supposedly to purchase jade, but in fact to see specially staged transvestite shows.

DAMENGLONG 大勐龙

70km southwest of Jinghong. 8km from Burmese border.
A lively area of pagodas and religious sanctuaries, it is just possible if you leave early enough, to make it here and back to Jinghong in one day. The first noteworthy sight on the road off the main road to Damenglong is the **Manguanglong Monastery**, a functioning Buddhist centre with some 40 or so young monks in residence. You pass through an entranceway flanked by dragons before entering the main Buddha hall. The monks and their teachers are a friendly lot and, despite more overseas visitors turning up, still seem pleasantly surprised at the sight of foreigners. **Manfeilong Reservoir**, a popular picnicking and boating spot, is just up the road from here.

The road meanders from here through rubber plantations, rice-paddies and patches of jungle to Xiaogai, the commercial and agricultural hub of the Dongfeng State Farm, located about 15km northeast of Damenglong. A large **Sunday market** is held here every week which has a rural feel and attracts several minority groups, including the Lahu and Bulang, from the border area.

The village of Manfeilong itself comes into view just before you reach Damenglong. An imposing, but mostly concrete, Burmese-style pagoda stands at the top of a hill just beyond the village. The history of **Manfeilong Bei Ta**, the White Bamboo Shoot Pagoda, goes back to its founding in 1204, but innumerable restorations have transformed it beyond recognition. Its configuration seen from a distance is said to resemble a cluster of emerging bamboo shoots, hence the name. There is something in this. All in all it is still quite an impressive sight, with its massive concentric base, central spire and surrounding stupas. A giant pair of 'Buddha feet', models of the footprints you find all over the Buddhist world, are kept in a small room crammed with offerings of flowers, money and coloured cloth under the stupas. The Buddha is supposed to have visited Xishuangbanna and left this monumental calling card. The pagoda is decorated in bright paint and covered in small digits of evil-spirit-repelling glass, creating a crazy paving, mosaic effect. The outside of the prayer hall is covered in a riot of brightly painted figures: unicorns, elephants and dragons. Despite the tacky embellishments, the pagoda is well contoured and graceful. During the lively **Tan Ta Festival** at the end of October or early November, the pagoda plays host to hundreds of visitors. The inferior **Black Pagoda** lies a little south of Damenglong, worth the small effort of getting there for its setting and commanding views of the valley.

Damenglong is a good base for **hiking** around the surrounding area and borderlands. As some of the countryside is quite dense and there are few English, or even Chinese-speaking locals around once you leave the main town, this would be a good chance to use one of the guides mentioned in the Jinghong chapter (see *Tourism*, Chapter 12, pages 230–1). One interesting three-to-four-day hike involves 45km of local trails along the Nan He river and tributaries to the town of Bulangshan. You would need a minimum amount of camping equipment and food for this adventure through tracts of land without roads, although there is a very basic guesthouse once you reach Bulangshan.

Getting there
Regular buses depart for Damenglong from the No 2 Bus Station in Jinghong. The first bus is at 07.00 with departures every 30 minutes thereafter until 17.00. The destination is written on the front of the bus and on some maps as 'Menglong'.

Where to stay
One of the only places to stay at the moment (this is likely to change with a new Burma–China–Thailand highway up and running) is the unexciting **Damenglong Guesthouse** near the main local government building. The Y15 a night dorm beds are passable. You can also hire bicycles for Y20 a day here. The **Bus Station Guesthouse** just as you enter town is another option. There are some quite good Dai-style restaurants on the approach to the Black Pagoda.

THE JINUO

The Jinuo people were only recognised as a separate minority in 1979. Traditionally exceptionally hostile towards outsiders, particularly Chinese officials, their scattered highland homelands were identified under the collective name Youle, meaning 'Hidden from the Han'. In 1942 they showed their hostility towards outside interference by poisoning a Dai tax inspector, an act that led to them being almost wiped out by the Han tyrant Ke Shexun and the Dai aristocrats in his service.

The Jinuo number about 18,000 today. Formerly slash-and-burn, swidden farmers, these days the Jinuo cultivate tea which they sell as a cash crop. Since throwing in their lot with the Chinese government and getting themselves declared an official nationality minority, they have been the recipients of state aid programmes.

The origins of the Jinuo are obscured in the half-light of myths. Some credence is given to their own claim that they descend from the survivors of an expedition to Yunnan that took place in the third century under the leadership of one Zhuge Liang. The Jinuo are easily identified from the white, Flemish-like, peaked bonnets or cowls worn by their women and the pierced ears of both sexes. Teeth are blackened like Edo-period Japanese geisha, with the help of sap removed from lacquer trees. Until recently the Jinuo practised tattooing. Traces of tattoos can still be seen on the older Jinuo.

The majority of Jinuo live in the settlement of Jinuoluoke, about 20km southeast of Mengyang. This is where they celebrate the most important annual event among the Jinuo, January or early February's New Year Drum and Dance Festival.

Some travellers find the Jinuo standoffish, even hostile. Judge for yourself.

NORTH OF JINGHONG
Mengyang 勐养
34km northeast of Jinghong.
Mengyang is home to the Huayao, or Flower-Belt Dai, one of the three Dai sub-groups. The Huayao, who wear highly decorative costumes and turbans hanging with silver chains, are not Buddhists like the mainstream Dai.

The market town is on the tour group route because of its famous **Elephant Tree**, another anomaly of nature much beloved of the Chinese. The tree is, in fact, a banyan whose lavish roots appears to resemble an elephant.

The Sancha He Wildlife Reserve
48km north of Jinghong. Y10.
About 18km beyond the Huayao village of Mannanan, are the dense rainforests of the Sancha River basin. One of the main attractions at the

reserve is a family of elephants which can be glimpsed in the early hours of the morning from observation platforms. The further you walk into the reserve the more isolated it feels and the less likely you are to encounter other visitors. Some people feel more comfortable taking one of the park's rangers along with them, even though they don't speak any English. With a total area over 1.5 million hectares, it is not difficult to get lost. Stay close to the Sancha River and you cannot go wrong. If you don't penetrate the forest cover enough you may not glimpse the rarer species reputed to make the reserve their habitat, but you are guaranteed to see exotic birds, butterflies and snakes at least.

Virtually any form of traffic heading north from Mengyang along the Kunming road can drop you off at the entrance to the reserve.

Simao 思茅

165km northeast of Jinghong.

Simao, just over the county border, used to be the gateway to Xishuangbanna. You can still fly here and then overland to Jinghong but far fewer people take this option these days. If you are coming from Kunming on the marathon 740km bus ride, though, you will pass through Simao, capital of Simao District. Buses follow a paved mountain road through a lush green landscape which is a good introduction to Xishuangbanna.

Simao was part of two ancient trade routes that ran through the town. The ancient Tea–Horse Road and the Southern Silk Road both traversed here. Simao is close to one of the main production areas of Pu'er tea and is a major distribution centre. In the past, numerous caravans loaded with tea would set off from here on the long journey up through Yunnan and on to Sichuan and Tibet.

Although the town gets rather unenthusiastic write-ups from foreigners, there is a moderately interesting old town with wooden houses and meandering cobblestone alleys and the odd teahouse. The **Plu River Reservoir Park** a few kilometres south of town has good swimming facilities in clean water, the usual paddle-boat rides and assortment of picnic areas. **Manzhongtian Hot Spring** to the east of Simao is not far either.

If you are flying in or out of Simao you can find the CAAC office (tel: 223 234) off the main street near Hongqi Square. Flights go from Simao to Kunming on Monday, Tuesday, Wednesday and Saturday. The flight takes 40 minutes and the one-way fare is Y390. There are buses from here to Jinghong, Baoshan and Xiaguan.

The area code for Simao is 0879

MENGHAN 勐罕 AND THE OLIVE PLAIN

45km southeast of Jinghong

The market town of Menghan lies at the heart of the immensely fertile flatlands of the Olive Plain (Ganlanba), one of the Dai people's most important agricultural regions and one of the highlights of Xishuangbanna. Dai villages and hamlets are dotted all over the plain. Dai houses are easily identified from stilts supporting broad wooden homes topped with massive thatched roofs. The sensation of being in tropical Southeast Asia, only a bus journey away after all, is reinforced by groves of coconut, plantain and mango, emerald rice fields, and Thai and Burmese-style pagodas. Despite some recent developments in tourism which include a newly widened road, parking lots for tour buses and a flurry of new mercantile activity along Menghan's main road, the Olive Plain is a wonderfully quiet, refreshing area to arrive in after a few days in an increasingly commerce-driven Jinghong. At night, when the last tourist bus has left town, Menghan reverts to its old, unfazed self. Travellers often end up extending their stay on the plain.

As you approach the Olive Plain on the bus from Jinghong, there are some fine views en route of the **Lancang (Mekong) River**. On the far side of the river there are thatched hamlets seemingly untouched by time. During the dry season some of the river banks are requisitioned by locals as temporary kitchen gardens, growing watermelons, squashes and tomatoes. Steep fields beside the road are closely planted with pineapples. As you turn into the town you will see a **white pagoda** at the top of a hill. The views of the plain from here are superb.

Itineraries for this area are not really necessary. The best course is to rent a bicycle and simply wander from village to village, exploring the area by following the shaded pathways and narrow roads that criss-cross the plain. You are certain to stumble upon something interesting. Good mountain bikes can be hired from several bike rental shops that have recently set up shop along the main road. Look out for a bicycle rental sign pointing down an alley to the left off the main road as you head towards the Sarlat Restaurant (which also has bicycles). Being largely flat this is ideal bike country. You would be advised to wear a hat if you are cycling out onto the plain, as it can get hot out there.

The most interesting areas of Menghan are in the old southeast and southwest sections of town. **Wat Ban Suan Men** dates from the 13th century and is one of the finest Dai temples in Xishuangbanna. The temple lies southwest of town along a path that follows the river. The **Weijiang Baita Pagoda** in the village of Manting was considered the most historically important religious building in the area until Red Guards completely dynamited the structure in the 1960s. The current reconstruction, completed in 1985, cannot compare with the original but is worth a look none the less.

The southeastern section of tree-lined Manting Lu is a pleasant place to cycle along, with its old Dai houses and kitchen gardens. The **Mengbala Banna Xiwang Park** on the right has a Burmese-style pagoda with some curious statuary. They have just finished building a massive processional gate along the road and a new paved area on the approach to **Menghan Chunman Temple**, an ominous sign. This beautiful, Burmese-style temple has an impressive golden pagoda in its grounds, a covered gallery of *Jakata* wall paintings and well-crafted carvings and stencil work.

Getting there and away

It used to be possible to cruise up and down the Mekong through the Olive Plain to Menghan, but in the new, high-speed China, the service has been

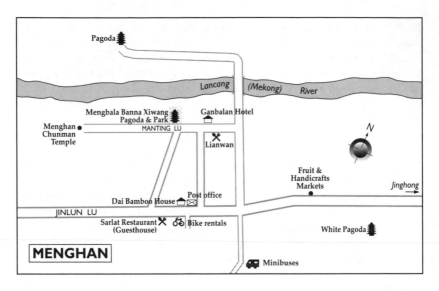

suspended in favour of minibuses. Menghan is easy enough to get to. Buses leave from the No 2 Bus Station in Jinghong from 07.00 and leave every 45 minutes. The journey only takes 45 minutes. It is possible to cycle from Jinghong to Menghan in under three hours. The road is increasingly busy though, so if you decide to cycle watch out for reckless truck and bus drivers.

Where to stay and eat
Most people will want to stay at least a night or two in Menghan in order to explore the plain. The **Dai Bamboo House**, a Dai-style family house, is on the right side of Jinlun Dong Lu as you head away from the Jinghong direction. Lionised in the past by independent travellers, the guesthouse gets mixed reviews these days. 'Bed bugs, noisy at night, hot food served cold, rats and lecherous relatives of the family who run the place', are some of the remarks recorded in the notebooks left for other travellers in cafés in Menghan and Jinghong. Others swear by the place. Doubles here are Y35, dorm beds Y15. The family-run kitchen used to have a very sound reputation.

If in doubt about the Dai Bamboo House, make for the **Sarlat Restaurant**, a traditional Dai building that doubles as guesthouse and café. The friendly and very considerate family who run the place offer Dai-style rooms with comfortable mats on the floor and mosquito tents above. The pevelboard walls do not reach the ceiling but this is good ventilation as the rooms are ranged just inside the open terrace area at the front of the restaurant. Rooms are Y15. The showers are exceptionally clean and there is plenty of hot water. You can rent good bicycles here for Y5 a day. The Sarlat is past the Dai Bamboo House, on the left. Look out for the carved *nagas* that grace the balustrades that flank the staircase up to the building.

The **Ganlanba Hotel** (tel: 241 1233) south on Manting Lu has dorm beds for Y35 which are reasonably clean. Good communal showers with 24-hour hot water.

There are several places to eat in Menghan. One of the oldest is the **Lianwan Restaurant** along Manting Lu, which specialises in excellent Dai food and is a good place to pick up travel information. The Dai food at the Sarlat Restaurant is first class.

MENGLUN'S 勐仑 TROPICAL BOTANICAL GARDEN

103km southeast of Jinghong. Y20.

Menglun, a small ribbon of streets overlooking the Luosuo River, would probably be ignored by most travellers if it were not for the fact that a narrow peninsula of the river is set aside for the Tropical Botanical Garden, one of Xishuangbanna's premier sights.

The gardens were founded in 1959 by Cai Xi Tau, a brilliant chemist and botanist, who, with a talented, hand-picked team of fellow scientists, cleared the jungle and set up research facilities on the spot. Today the gardens boast almost 3,000 different species of plants, and there are almost 500 workers conducting research into the cultivation of medicinal and economic plants, and biochemistry.

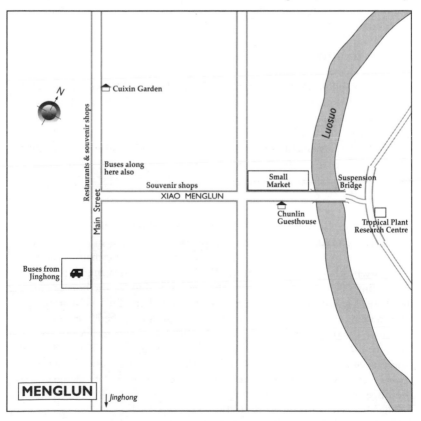

For the casual visitor the gardens are quite overwhelming. Groves of giant palms, bamboo and camphor, masses of vines, shrubs, rainforest species and giant lily pads smother the visitor and fill the air with a heady fragrance. It is best to take the gardens slowly. You could, in fact, easily spend a whole day here. The gardens receive a lot of visitors so don't expect to be alone all day, but you can usually find quiet patches away from the tour guides in their Dai national costumes and their charges.

The gardens are easy enough to find. Just look for the largest concentration of souvenir stalls, cafés and restaurants, then follow the street downhill through a small open-air market until you see a pedestrian suspension bridge. This is the entrance to the garden. The ticket office is on the right.

Getting there
Buses leave Jinghong's No 2 Bus Station every 45 minutes from 06.45 onwards. The journey takes about two hours, stopping off at Menghan on the way. There is no official bus stop or station. Vehicles usually pull up alongside the rows of restaurants and souvenir stores along the main road on the eastern side of town.

Other gardens, reserves and tourist attractions are apparently planned for the Menglun area.

Where to stay
There are several accommodation options if you decide to stay overnight, both in the town and inside the botanical garden itself. The **Cuixin Garden Hotel** (tel: 871 5711) on the road to Jinghong is considered to be the best place in town with rooms with attached bathrooms for Y180. The **Chunlin Guesthouse** (tel: 871 7172) near the entrance to the gardens is the best cheap option. Clean, reasonably spacious doubles here with a shared bathroom are Y40. Dorm beds are only Y12.

MENGLA 勐腊
200km southeast of Jinghong.
Though set in the middle of wild Aini, Dai and Yao country, the county seat of Mengla is a rather drab, Sinicised town with few sights of note. Travellers do not come to Mengla for the sights though. This is the main stopping off point after the long journey from Jinghong for an overnight stay before proceeding 60km southeast of here the next morning for the border crossing into Laos. Mengla once had the famous Qingtong Jiangdin Ta (**Bronze Spire Pagoda**), an important cultural monument, but during the 30 or so years that the town was off-limits to foreigners, the building seems to have disappeared without a trace and locals seem reluctant to own up to its former existence. There is one rather plain temple up on the hill to the west of town which appears to have a few resident monks, the remnants of Mengla's great Buddhist past.

The area code for Mengla is 0691.

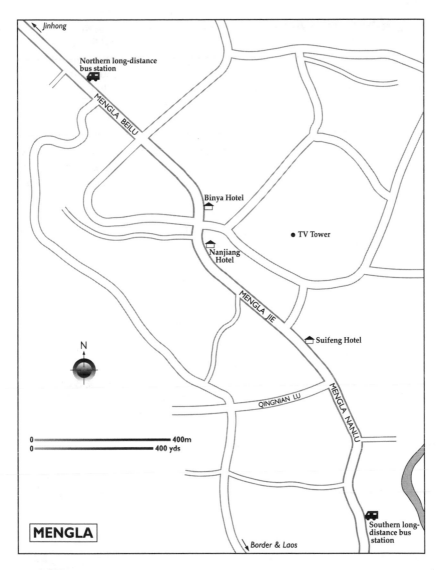

MENGLA

Where to stay and eat

Mengla has a few decent places to stay and eat, though nothing fancy. The **Nanjiang Hotel** has quite good doubles with attached bathrooms for Y70. The friendly **Suifeng Hotel** offers a similar deal but is a little cleaner than the Nanjiang. The rather uncomfortable (but conveniently located for the northern bus station) **Binya Hotel** is a last choice, but not bad with dorm beds going for Y20.

There are a few basic restaurants along the main road, Mengla Jie, and some Sichuanese joints along Qingnian Lu. Uigurs run a number of kebab stalls along the main street.

THE ROAD TO LAOS

Laos has eased its visa and internal travel restrictions in the last few years. 1999 was 'Visit Laos' Year. More travellers are opting for this route into what is touted, with some justification, as southeast Asia's ultimate lotus-land. In Laos the rules seem to change at whim so it is best to check the prevailing regulations in Kunming. The Lao, for example, now issue visas on the spot in the airport at Vientiane, the capital, and at the Mekong Bridge crossing from Nong Khai in Thailand, something which they never did before. Officially you cannot get a transit or any other kind of visa at the border. A contradictory rumour states that, if you forget to obtain a visa in Kunming, you can pay slightly over the odds and get one issued on the Chinese side. Don't depend on it. The correct procedure is to apply for a visa at the Lao Consulate in Kunming and get it dated to coincide with your arrival at the border. Unless they have been extended since the research for this book, transit visas are valid for seven days only. This allows you time to hop on a bus from the southern bus station in Mengla for the two-hour ride to Mo Han. From there you cross to the Lao village of Ban Boten where you will find plenty of trucks, tractors and private vehicles waiting to take you into Laos proper.

Laos is one hour ahead of China. It is highly advisable to get to the border crossing as early as possible as the relaxed guards on the Lao side are prone to unscheduled early closing times. Drivers seem to accept Chinese money but the first thing you will have to do is get some Lao *kip*. It shouldn't cost more than about Y15 to get a lift into Luang Namtha, the nearest town with a bank. A popular route from here is to carry on and overnight at **Muong Xing** which has a tremendous **early morning market** that attracts dozens of local Yao, Akha and Thai Lu tribals, and then take the fascinating boat trip the next day to **Luang Prabang**, the former royal capital and, arguably, one of the most ravishing small cities in Indochina. From there travellers can fly or bus down to Vientiane.

South to Hekou

'I'd travelled by the narrow-gauge railway from Hanoi to Kunming five years before, four days and three nights, amidst marvellous mountain scenery...I'd looked down and seen the winding track by which I'd travelled hundreds of feet below. I'd come over a steel bridge, which crossed an almost bottomless chasm.'

China-Burma Vagabond, Harold Rattenbury

Less visited in many ways than Yunnan's remoter but better publicised destinations, the region between Kunming and the border crossing into Vietnam at Hekou, is a rewarding area to explore if you have the time or plan on adding Indochina to your itinerary.

Here you will find Yunnan's lake region immediately south of the city, old market and trade towns set along rivers, plains and fertile basins, French period railway stations, the descendants of a lost Mongolian army, the old Ming city of Jianshui with its great Confucian Temple, and an area of Bronze Age tombs. Yunnan's most densely populated areas are around these lakes where many Han Chinese have settled. South of the lakes, however, a more interesting ethnic mix emerges, the Yi dominating the Tonghai region, pockets of Hui, Miao, and Yao appearing further south, and the Hani inhabiting the banks and valleys of the Yuan Jiang, the 'Red River', as it flows across the border on its course to Hanoi.

Nature notes

As you travel south beyond the central lakes, towards the forests and reserves along the Yunnan–Vietnam border, a more luxuriant verdure asserts itself. High temperatures and abundant rainfall have created great swathes of monsoon forest, montane rainforest and mossy, evergreen broad-leaf forest. The southern mountains are divided into high and middle arborous levels, with layers of bamboo, shrub, tree ferns, herb and plant species. These include flowers such as orchids, camellia and azaleas which are common to Yunnan, as well as rarer species ideally suited to growth in areas of varying climatic conditions.

Naturalists are drawn here for the insights it provides into the origin, evolution and classification of various animal and plant life. Rare animals, such as loris, red deer, goannas, and black-crowned gibbons inhabit this southeastern region of Yunnan. This is also the home of the Malabar pied hornbill, several varieties of parrot and mynas, and green turtledoves, as well as migratory birds, including white swans and cranes.

YUNNAN'S CENTRAL LAKES

Kunming, the great Lake Dian and the other important bodies of water south of the provincial capital, constitute the central core of Yunnan. This prosperous region, home to a Bronze Age culture dating back over 3,000 years, oversaw the development of agriculture during the Yuan and Ming dynasties, turning the area into a rich granary.

Lakes form an important feature of the topography of central Yunnan. Beginning in the southern suburbs of Kunming at the shores of Lake Dian, a string of lakes appears across the high plateau, continuing as far as the city of Shiping halfway to the border with Vietnam.

East of Dian, within Yiliang County, lies **Yangzong Hai**, a beautiful body of blue water that few visitors seem to know about. Landlocked Yunnan often adds the suffix *hai*, signifying 'sea' to the name of its lakes. There are few trees around the lake but its grassy shores and absence of visitors makes for a nice picnic spot or day outing from Kunming. The northern shore of the lake is easily reached as the narrow-gauge, Hanoi-bound train stops here.

Lake Fuxian is the deepest lake in Yunnan with a water volume that far exceeds both Dian and Erhai. Fuxian Hu is the third largest lake in Yunnan, covering a total area of 212km^2, and reaching an average depth of 151.5m. Its distinctive blue-green surface is caused by deposits of phosphorous which bleed into the lake from the earth of its surrounding hills and shores. Steep mountains drop to its western edge but the rest of its shore is dotted with villages and fields bursting with crops. Fishermen generally work at night from the side of the lake, building special stone ditches called *yugou*, to trap the fish. The lake is a popular spot for outings and has several attractions, including the elephant-shaped Xiangbiling Mountain, some attractive **hot springs** near the village of Jiucun, and an original Qing dynasty arched, stone bridge near Haikou called the **Serene Lake Bridge**. The lake has one island aptly named **Solitary Hill**, which was once home to a cluster of Ming period pagodas, temples and monasteries. Monkeys from a pilot breeding centre now overrun the ruined sanctuaries.

Xingyun Lake is connected to Lake Fuxian via a short, 1km river called Haimen, which means 'sea gate'. You will find the strangely named **Fish Border Stele** at the confluence of the river. Fish apparently swim to this point from their respective lakes but never infringe beyond this demarcation line into each others' waters. Lake Xingyun is much smaller than Fuxian Hu but, at 1,722m, sits at a slightly higher altitude. Its name means 'the lake of stars and clouds', as its surface is supposed to provide perfect, still reflections of the night sky. The lake, which is slightly salty, has several resorts around its shore and some good hot springs. Four or five resorts lie within a distance of less than a kilometre of each other. The temperature of each hot spring, starting with the one in the north, is said to become progressively hotter as you proceed south down the chain. The lake, described as a 'natural fishpond', is well-stocked with carp, whitefish, bream and the so-called big-headed fish. Restaurants here serve a hotpot made from the 'big-headed fish' which is known throughout the province for its excellent taste.

Lake Qilu, also called Tonghai Lake in reference to the nearby town of the same name, is a small, windswept lake roughly the same size as Xingyun Hu. The lake was referred to in ancient times as 'the lake of water-dyed indigo', because of its deep blue hue. Monasteries and temples dot the shores of the lake. At the village of Najiaying there is an old mosque, recently much renovated and altered. Predating the Ming dynasty, it is said to be one of the oldest mosques in Yunnan. Yangguang village is the largest settlement on the lake.

The Yi word *yilou*, meaning 'city of water', seems to have provided the root for the Chinese *yilong*, signifying 'strange dragon'. Whatever the etymology, **Yilong Hu** is Yunnan's fourth largest lake. Easily accessed from the nearby town of Shiping the lake has three main islands: Water City Island, Lesser Water City Island, and Mabaolong. It is possible to visit these beauty spots by boat.

CHENGJIANG 澄 江

65km southeast of Kunming.
A little north of Lake Fuxian, the county town of Chengjiang is a market and produce centre for what the Chinese call the 'Land of Milk and Honey'. Situated on a highland plateau, this fertile, lightly populated area enjoys high yields of soy beans, sweet potatoes, lentils, wheat, corn and rice. It is also known for its salted fish from Lake Fuxian, and for its lotus root products. The area is home to large numbers of Miao, Yi and Hui.

The town has some superb, intact wooden buildings but is best known for its **Wenmiao**, a huge Confucian Temple lying towards the east of town. The temple was built in 1571 and, despite successive renovations, remains in extremely good shape. A Grand Hall of the Honoured Teacher is surrounded by seven rooms, with pillars supporting an impressive roof covered in yellow, glazed tiles. The building is large and was briefly used as both a university and county library.

There is a park at the southern foot of Feng Mountain. **Fengshan Park**, which was made in 1945 on the ruins of a long gone temple, is a pleasant place to stroll with pavilions, terraced flower beds and bamboo groves. There is a grand hall here, with glazed tiles, standing at the highest point in the park which also has a library and cultural centre.

Liangwang Shan is the area's largest mountain at 2,825m. It lies about 4km northwest of town. Several temples and other buildings from the Ming and Qing Dynasties surround a pond at the base of the mountain. Very few foreign visitors seem to know of its existence. The better known Yusun ('Jade Bamboo Shoots') Mountain lies a few kilometres to the west.

YUNNAN'S COLONIAL RAILWAY

Kunming is where the old French narrow-gauge railway begins its 468km journey to Hekou in the far southeast, before crossing the border and continuing to its Vietnam terminus at Hanoi, a complete journey of 762km. Built not so much to provide a convenient transport link for Chinese living in the remote southeast, but as a means both of extending French influence into China and extracting Yunnan's supposed mineral resources, preliminary surveys for the railway began in 1899.

Local resistance to the line and the events of the Boxer Rebellion delayed the surveys until 1901 when they were resumed on the Vietnam side of the border. The main obstacle seems to have been surmounting the steep ascent from the Red River up to the Yunnan plateau. Fiercely determined feats of engineering and physical labour eventually achieved the apparently impossible and the line was completed in 1910. But not without a heavy loss of life caused by a combination of fatigue and malaria. P H Kent, writing at the time of the line's construction, recorded that '…when the work was commenced the death rate was appalling. In one year, it is said, five thousand coolies, representing roughly 70 per cent of all those engaged on the work, lost their lives…'

The line seems to have had the intended, albeit temporary, effect on the character of Kunming. Harold Rattenbury, in his 1939 *China–Burma Vagabond*, noted that Kunming, 'from being an old world town on the borders of China', had become 'tinged, since the opening of the Indo-China railway, with French influences'.

The line was closed for 17 years after the China–Vietnam border dispute which erupted in 1979, but is now up and running. The 16-hour journey to Hekou is full of interest, and many of the French influences are still there. Paul Theroux noted them on the short stretch of the line he rode to Yiliang, where he observed that the houses he saw 'were not Chinese houses. They were stucco, with green shutters and heavy verandahs – just the sort of houses that you see in the French towns of Vietnam.'

The station at the village of Bi'se is typical of this colonial style. The curved iron eaves, speckled and peeling stucco walls, pig-iron oven in the station master's office, and a Parisian wall clock with no hands are, quite literally, timeless.

The bus to Yuxi from the main bus station in Kunming stops off at Chengjiang.

YUXI 玉溪

98km south of Kunming.

Processing the bulk of Yunnan's cigarettes, Yuxi is also known as the 'Tobacco City'. Note that on maps it often appears as Zoucheng. Easily accessed from Kunming on the expressway, the city dates back to the Kingdom of Dian. Yuxi's trade roots go back to the early Qing dynasty when it was one of the main distribution centres in Central Yunnan. Dominated by the Han Chinese, it is also home to over a dozen minorities including the Hani, Hui, Bai and Yi. Chinese people often come here to pay homage to Nie

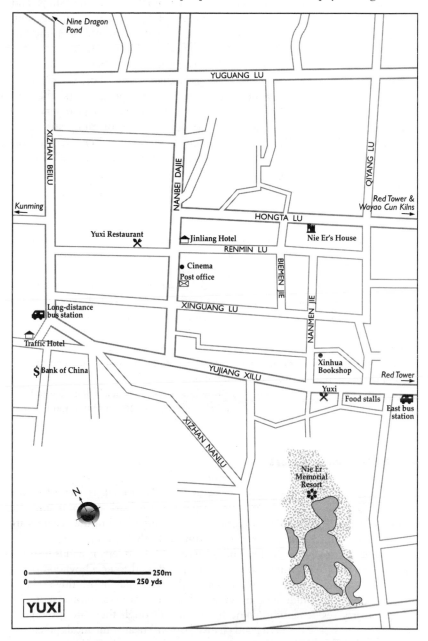

Er, the young man who composed the country's national anthem, who was also from Yuxi.

Practical information

The main city facilities, including most of its hotels, restaurant, shops and sights, are compacted into the space between Hongta Lu and Yujiang Xilu. Maps to this small city can be bought from the information desk at the bus station or from street stalls in the centre. You might be able to find some locally printed information at the Xinhua Bookstore along Nanmen Jie.

The Bank of China is located along Xizhan Beilu. Foreign currency transactions are easy enough here but they don't accept travellers' cheques. The post office is on Nanbei Dajie. The bus station has a regular service to Kunming but most people take one of the private buses or mini-vans which are far more frequent. These drive up and down Xizhan Beilu looking for passengers or wait opposite the bus station next to the Traffic Hotel. There are regular buses to Tonghai, Jiangchuan and Gejiu.

The area code for Yuxi and Tonghai is 0877.

Where to stay/eat

Jinliang Hotel Nanbei Dajie and Renmin Lu intersection. Opened in 1997, after a few years this hotel still feels newish. Good singles and doubles with bathrooms for Y70. You should take a bath on a sunny day though, as the water is solar-heated.

Traffic Hotel Right next to the long-distance bus station on Xizhan Beilu. Good value with rather spartan singles and doubles with bathrooms and hot water for only Y70. Beds in dorms are just Y12. There are some more expensive rooms available if required.

Yuxi Restaurant A popular eatery on Yujiang Xilu. A good range of Yunnanese dishes, including a fine version of the famous across-the-bridge-noodles. There is a second branch of the restaurant on Renmin Lu.

Food stalls There are countless night stalls selling barbecued sticks of chicken and lamb, clay-fired hotpots, noodles and pancakes in the Yjiang Xilu and Renmin Lu area.

What to see

Nie Er Memorial Resort

Y3 for Nie Er's House, Y1 extra for museum.

Constructed in 1985 the Nie Er Park, as it is also called, is located in the southern suburbs of the town. The purpose of the park, to commemorate China's 'People's Composer', may be of limited interest, but the grounds are very pleasant and, as you would expect, immaculately kept.

A statue in bronze of Nie Er, who drowned while in Japan, stands near the entrance to the park. Other features are its pond, said to be a boyhood haunt of the musician, a number of 'moon and crane' pavilions, flower beds, greenhouses and a children's amusement area. The park is a popular spot with Yuxi's elderly residents who come here to go through their life-prolonging morning exercises. There is a good chance you will hear some locals practicing on the *zheng*, a classic Chinese string instrument, in one of the pavilions. Nie Er's childhood home, a Qing period, two-storey, adobe and wood structure is three or four blocks north of the park on Hongta Lu. The building is the original.

The Red Tower
Southeast suburbs of Yuxi.
Formerly known as the White Tower, this limestone, Yuan dynasty pagoda was inexplicably painted red, obliging the local hacks who write the tourist blurb to change their description from 'The white tower shines brightly in the golden sunset', to 'The resplendently red tower is silhouetted in the fiery glow of the rising sun, showing a most blessing splendour'.

The pagoda really is quite impressive. Described as a typical seven-octagonal tower, it stands at 25m and is said to have been designed in the shape of a Chinese calligraphy brush. There are no direct buses to the Red Tower, although bus No 3 will drop you off fairly near. The easiest thing is to jump on a motorcycle taxi.

The Wayao Cun Kilns
South of the Red Tower.
In the far southern suburbs of Yuxi are the remains of three Yuan dynasty chinaware kilns. Excavations have unearthed some good examples and fragments of blue glaze porcelain that include plates, bowls, dishes, pots and vases. The white backgrounds are decorated with images of birds, pavilions, flowers and insects. Blue, jade-like flasks, bottles, and cremation urns unearthed in Jiangchuan, Tonghai and Lufeng have been identified as porcelain produced at the Wayao kilns. Apart from the chinaware itself the site contains worktables, moulds and stone washers, providing an insight into the way potters worked at the time.

Nine Dragon Pond
10km northwest of Yuxi.
A favourite viewing spot since the Ming dynasty, Nine Dragon Pond sits at the feet of Qilu Mountain. The Emperor Jianwen is said to have once lived here as a hermit. The park here repays an hour or two's exploration. Paths wind past temples, pavilions, fountains, cascades, an old graveyard and hundreds of ancient pine trees.

If you find the place to your liking, you can stay overnight at the nearby **Nine Dragon Pond Guesthouse**, where there are several simply furnished rooms in a traditional building with a nice courtyard.

White Dragon Pond & the East Wind Lake
7km northeast of Yuxi.
White Dragon Pond is another scenic area notable for its luxuriant evergreen trees, fountains and caves. The site is named after the White Dragon Fountain that spurts out of a nearby mountain.

Four kilometres away is the **East Wind Lake**. Built as a reservoir in 1960, the dam here is worth a quick look. Apart from that there are pavilions, tourist boats and the easy climb up to the summit of **Elephant's Trunk Mountain**.

There is no public transport to these two resort spots. You can take a normal taxi or one of the cheaper motorcycle taxis.

JIANGCHUAN 江川

38km southwest of Yuxi.

Jiangchuan means 'rivers and plains', an apt description for the rich agricultural basin the city sits in. Compounded of hills, rivers and mountains, its landform reminds Chinese people of the shape of a begonia leaf. Humans have lived in the area for millennia, a fact attested to by its archeological sites, many dating from the ancient Dian period. A vibrant Neolithic and Bronze Age culture thrived in the area and 25 tombs from the Warring States Period (475–221BC) have also been discovered.

As a city, perpetually dusty Jianchuan leaves a lot to be desired, but it has one or two redeeming features. The city's increasingly threatened old quarter has a superb set of Qing dynasty gate towers. Its proximity to the tourist lakes of Xingyun and Fuxian add appeal. The main attraction in the town itself is the **Bronze Age Museum** on Xingyun Lu. The museum highlights some of the 1,000 Bronze Age relics that were unearthed at the nearby Lijiashan site. Astonishingly, most were in perfect condition. One of the most precious objects is a bronze table with the design of a tiger cub coming across two buffalo. Yunnan's earliest coins and a collection of cowrie shells are also on display.

Connections here are limited and your best bet is to jump on to one of the frequent mini-buses that depart for Tonghai and Yuxi, from where you can catch a bus to Kunming and other destinations. If you would like to stay in Jiangchuan, the best options seem to be the **Jiangchuan Hotel** along Ninghai Lu, and the **Fuxing Hotel** with good doubles and singles for Y70.

TONGHAI 通海

10km south of Jiangchuan.

Tonghai once marked the boundaries of the empire, the limit of the Yuan dynasty's power in the region. Tonghai is a pleasant place to walk around, its old-fashioned streets and back alleys preserving a number of fine old buildings. The most conspicuous minorities represented in the region are the Muslim Hui and Mongols. There are also a number of Yi, Dai and Hani. The town has a long history of making silver ornamentation, its silversmiths having a captive market among the hill tribes and other minorities. You can still see examples of their work, now also popular with Chinese and overseas visitors.

There are a number of interesting little temples and mosques in the area. At the village of Xiaoxin the **Three Sage Temple** has some curious wood carvings of mythical creatures on its doors. At nearby Gucheng, there is an interesting little mosque whose decorative features betray both Chinese and Persian influences. **Yuanming Temple**, a superb Yuan dynasty complex in Hexi Zhen, has an extraordinary marble altar with carved reliefs. Accomplished

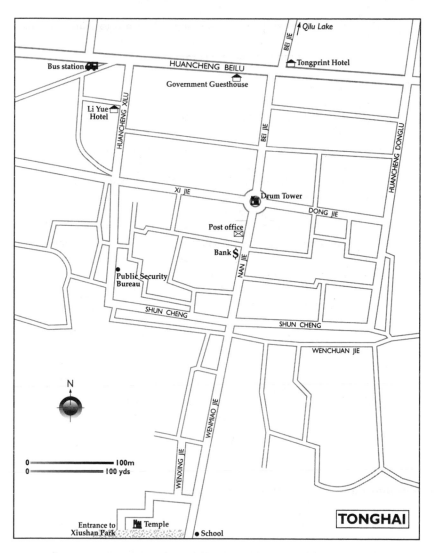

wood carving and two fine stone lions guarding the complex's Pavilion of the Jade Emperor add to the magnificence of Yuanming. The temple was completed in 1368. Nearby Lake Qilu adds to the interest of the region.

The **Old Town Gate** (Tang dynasty) is more a landmark than a sight. When I saw it last it was being restored and beautified, with several souvenir shops nearby.

Getting there and away

Tonghai is a 90-minute bus ride from Jiangchuan. Strangely, most buses depart from the Huancheng Beilu-Hubin Lu intersection around the corner from the depot. Buses leave every half hour to various destinations including

Kunming, Jiangchuan, Yuxi, Jianshui and Gejiu. The bus to Kunming takes approximately three hours and costs Y20. Delays are inevitable though, as the drivers usually wait until their buses are completely full.

Where to stay/eat

Government Guesthouse Huancheng Beilu. A good deal if you can get into this popular guesthouse. Dorm rooms at Y20 are spacious and clean, doubles in a newer section of the building with bathrooms and plenty of hot water, go for Y100.

Li Yue Hotel 56 Huangchang Xilu; tel: 301 1651; fax: 301 6101. This two-star hotel is the usual concoction of marble and mirror-faced lobby, fronting some very ordinary rooms behind it. The courtyard in the middle of the hotel is a pleasant addition though and overall it's not a bad place to stay. Standard rooms with en-suite are Y100 and smaller rooms are available for Y50.

Tongprint Hotel Huangcheng Beilu; tel: 302 1666; fax: 301 6474. A new modern high-rise hotel that seems destined to remain empty throughout its days. Purpose-built for Chinese tour groups with a huge gleaming lobby and atrium, it boasts facilities such as a swimming pool and bowling alley that seem strangely out of place here. It is undoubtedly the most comfortable hotel available in Tonghai. Rooms are clean and furnished to the usual standard Chinese hotel blueprint. A twin room with en suite costs Y300, but is negotiable.

Xiushan Hotel Xi Jie and Bei Jie intersection, near the town gate; tel: 301 1598. Definitely a second choice with rather small rooms and unreliable water supply. Dorm beds range from Y28–35. Doubles are Y50 but rather claustrophobic.

There isn't a lot of choice of eating places in Tonghai. The **Nanjie Restaurant** is essentially a noodles place with a pick-and-choose kitchen situation. A string of tiny **Muslim restaurants** along Huancheng Xilu and Xi Jie specialise in spicy stews – beef and lamb with lots of vegetables.

What to see
Xiushan Park
On the hills in the southern part of Tonghai. Y15.
A visit to Xiushan park alone justifies a stop-over in Tonghai as this delightful park contains a whole complex of temples and stele spread over thickly forested hills overlooking the town. Xiushan Mountain, which is only 200m high, was an important centre of Buddhism during the Tang and Ming dynasties. Even today the mountain still conveys a sense of timelessness and ancient China as you see old people gather amongst its shaded temples and pavilions to play music, play mah-jong and worship. The ancient complex of temples and gardens on Xiushan Mountain was first begun in 116BC during the Han dynasty and was later extended in the Dali Kingdom period by the ruler of Tonghai. Again during the Song, Yuan, Ming and Qing dynasties the temples were repaired and extended. The mountain has always been regarded as holy by both Taoists and Buddhists. Covered with lush forest, bamboo groves, and ancient cypress trees, paths wind through the leafy canopy taking in five temples, 20 pavilions and

arbours, and large stone tablets incised with wise sayings, couplets and aphorisms. The courtyards of the temples here are full of potted plants, flowers and dwarf trees. The magnolia, sweet osmanthus, plum and peach trees are outstandingly well matched to the sites.

The park is surprisingly easy to negotiate as there are several signposts written in English which include interesting snippets of information about the hill, its buildings and the legends and folklore that surround it. The views from the top of the town and Lake Qilu are matchless.

Xinmeng 新门

15km west of Tonghai.

Yuan troops who were stationed in Tonghai were there at the edge of the empire to protect its borderlands and the all-important southern trade routes. When the Yuan dynasty fell to the Ming in 1381, the Mongolian garrison stationed in Tonghai found themselves cut off, unable to return to their homeland. The remnants of this Mongolian division, about 6,000 people, continue to live at a cluster of three villages called Xinmeng. The name, aptly enough, means New Mongolia. The men in the village used to wear long gowns, the women short tunics, with their marital status determined by their headdress. Finding themselves in a different climate, the adaptable Mongols have modified their dress to shorter robes, colourfully designed.

Over the centuries these martial horsemen from the steppes turned towards the more peaceful pursuit of fishing. Because of the lowering of the water level in the lake and a depletion in fish, they have turned their skills towards metal-working and the building trade. Stalls set up around the bus station in Tonghai are a good place to see their kitchen knives and other examples of their work.

All buses and minibuses from Tonghai's regional stop at Huancheng Beilu and Hubin Lu go to Xinmeng.

JIANSHUI 建水

Jianshui is poised to become an important tourist centre. An ancient town with a full complement of sights, Jianshui's transformation is just around the corner. Its traditional architecture alone, a fascinating fusion of higher plains and local, southern styles dispersed throughout the city, justifies a visit. Apart from its historical attractions, like the Confucious temple and Zhu family gardens, the appeal of Jianshui also lies in its friendly people and the relative absence of foreign visitors, making it a delightful town to relax in for a few days.

One of the most fascinating features of the town is the disproportionately high number of venerable old ladies with bound feet. A stroll down the main street, Jianzhong Lu, will usually reveal at least a few of these ancient gentlewomen sitting chatting amongst friends or hobbling painfully on their tiny, crippled feet. As the regional centre of learning, Jianshui would have had a number of wealthy families who were the usual practitioners of this cruel but once widespread custom.

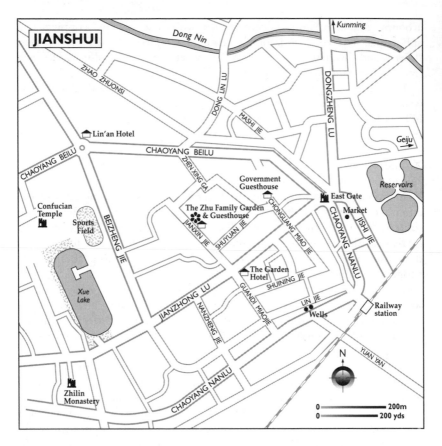

Formerly known as Lin'an, the city fell under the suzerainty of the Ningzhou, and later Nanzhou, kingdoms before entering its heyday under the Yuan Dyansty. The town entered into history again when it became the brief focus of a rebellion that formed part of the 1911 Revolution. Troops of the Southern Garrison Army were stationed here for a time.

Although the city is not large and can easily be seen on foot, a map is indispensable when trying to find particular buildings or out of the way sanctuaries. The bigger hotels have maps for sale. The county itself is rich in minority cultures, and forays into the surrounding countryside are always rewarding. In the immediate vicinity are Dai, Hui and Yi communities, while further afield along the Red River are sizeable numbers of Miao and Hani.

The area code for Jianshui is 0873.

Getting there and away

The bus station is positioned on Chaoyang Beilu, to the left of the east gate if coming from the town centre. Jianshui's bus depot has a number of frequent and good connections throughout the region. Buses to Kaiyuan run every half hour and the two-hour journey costs Y11. Similarly there are two buses an hour to Geiju and onwards from there to Hekou from Jianshui. There is also an 07.30 bus direct to Hekou that costs Y27. Several buses a day go to Tonghai and take two and a half hours; the fare is Y10. Buses to Kunming start from 08.00 until 14.30 for the six-hour journey (Y33) and there are also sleeper buses which depart in the evenings from 19.30 onwards, though the benefits of a sleeper bus are questionable as you tend to get very little sleep and miss some interesting scenery along the way.

Jianshui is also served by the narrow-gauge railway which runs from Shiping to Geiju, where onward connections can be made for Kaiyuan, Kunming and Hekou. The train station is located on Chaoyang Nanlu, close to the market. There are two trains a day in either direction. A 17.35 train leaves from the station each day for Kunming arriving at 06.35 the following day; the fare is Y26 for hard seat and Y60 for hard sleeper. Trains to Kaiyuan take around five hours and the fare is Y9. Generally speaking, though, the train is not that comfortable, takes a lot longer than a bus and should be avoided unless you are a railway enthusiast.

Where to stay/eat
Garden Hotel Jianzhong Lu. A reasonable place to stay with a fairly good restaurant attached. The rooms aren't inspiring but are clean and cost Y60–90. Dormitory beds are Y12–20.

Government Guesthouse Off Jianzhong Lu; tel: 765 6322. This guesthouse looks quite run down and has an air of communist austerity about it; probably best avoided in favour of one of the other options. Singles and doubles cost Y100 and dorm beds Y45.

Lin'an Hotel The eastern end of Chaoyang Beilu, near the Confucian temple; tel: 765 1888; fax: 765 4888. The modern Lin'an Hotel is the second best choice for accommodation after the Zhu Gardens Guesthouse. Rooms are reasonable but the décor is a little shabby. A twin room with en-suite costs Y130.

Zhu Family Gardens Guesthouse 133 Jianxin Jie; tel: 766 7988; fax: 766 7989. The Zhu Family Gardens is a real gem and one of the most unique and atmospheric places you can find to stay in Yunnan. This restored Qing Dynasty home with its beautiful courtyards and ornately carved and painted screens has recently opened a wing for foreign guests and the rooms are furnished as traditionally as the rest of the building. The courtyards are an excellent place to relax and make a wonderful escape from the bustle of the streets outside, particularly in the evening when they are lit by lanterns. There is a bar near the reception desk and an excellent restaurant overlooking the main garden. Twin rooms cost Y220 and suites Y680.

There are several tiny restaurants around the East Gate area selling roasted tofu, goat's cheese, skewers of charcoal grilled meat, and Across-the-Bridge-Noodles. Dongzheng Lu is also a good bet for street food. Several tasty Muslim and Sichuanese restaurants and bakeries are strung out between the East Gate and the bus station. Standard Chinese dishes at the **Garden Hotel** are good. Jianshui is Yunnan's main producer of the province's well-known ceramic steampots, so you will find several restaurants and stalls within the aforementioned areas offering delicious casseroles and stews. The restaurant that overlooks the rear of the Zhu Family Gardens serves a wide variety of Chinese food styles served in pleasant surroundings, with outside tables and a view of the gardens and town. A good meal for two costs around Y40.

What to see
The East Gate
Also known as the Chaoyang Gateway Arch or 'miniature Tiananmen', the reason for the East Gate's name becomes immediately apparent with first sight of the great vermilion arch that once formed the eastern entrance to the city. The East Gate was built in 1389, 28 years before the structures of Tiananmen, and was once one of four similar gate towers that were destroyed by wars in the Qing dynasty. The remaining East Gate has come to be seen as the town's great enduring symbol and meeting place. The huge three-storey structure has a height of 24m and is adorned with several calligraphy boards, aeolian bells on its cornices and a huge copper bell which was used to signify the opening of the gate in the mornings. The East Gate is an excellent place to sit and look down upon the teeming bustle of the town and in summer the building is alive with thousands of swallows, who nest under its eaves. The first floor of the building is used as a reading room and the area in front of the gate is a public meeting place, where men gather at weekends with their songbirds and waterpipes. Occasionally the gate is used for less sanguine purposes as convicted criminals are brought here and paraded before the public for their crimes; if you happen to chance upon one of these authoritarian displays then you would be well advised to steer clear of it and avoid the temptation of using your camera.

The Confucian temple
Y2.
Jianshui's main sight is undoubtedly the massive Confucian Temple of Literature, which was first started in 1285 and is the second largest Confucian temple in the country, second only in size to the mother temple at Qufu. The temple is associated with scholarship and proved highly successful as a training centre for students about to try for China's old imperial examination system. The complex, which is best approached from the southern entrance on Jianzhong Lu, stretches over several acres and includes a lake, 'the sea of knowledge', at its centre. Even now Jianshui remains a centre of learning; there are schools and colleges located next door and you can see many students walking around the perimeter of the lake hard at work reciting their lessons as they walk. The buildings of the complex include a main temple, Dacheng Hall, two side halls, three pavilions, five clan halls and eight memorial archways which are passed through on the way to the main hall. Dacheng Hall is a fine building with 22 impressive 5m-high pillars supporting it, some of which have ornately carved golden dragons wreathing around them.

Inside are eight golden boards with eulogies conferred on the temple by various Qing Dynasty emperors. The complex is full of fine archways, carvings, woodwork and dedicatory stones but it is the sense of the continued importance as a place of learning that really brings it alive for the visitor.

Zhilin Monastery
Like the Confucian Temple, an air of antiquity hangs about this huge monastery, reputedly the largest wooden structure of its kind in Yunnan. The building, located a short distance southwest of the temple, dates from the late Yuan dynasty and is a designated national treasure. That doesn't seem to have stopped several ugly modern buildings from being put up around the monastery. The building is not always open so it is a question of pot luck whether you will be able to see inside or not.

The Zhu Family Garden
Jianxin Jie. Y3.
Ten or twelve minutes' walk east of the Confucian Temple takes you to this traditional Qing dynasty ancestral home. The house was built during the late Qing dynasty by a prosperous gentleman, Zhu Weiqing, and his brothers, in the style of a typical southern Chinese-style private garden. Such large and grandiose private dwellings are rarely found nowadays in China, the last of them having usually succumbed to the destructions of the Cultural Revolution. The spacious complex contains 17 courtyards and a number of ancestral halls, gardens, pools and pavilions as well as the family's living quarters. Recent renovations have restored the house to its former glory and the wonderfully carved and gilded screen doors and ornamentations are a visual delight. There is also a small museum which has a collection of photographs illustrating local architecture and sights. The café at the reception inside is a fine spot to while away the afternoon in peaceful surroundings.

Water wells
Look out for a number of ancient water wells dotted around the town, which draw their sources from underground springs. The wells are still in use today and many people can be seen drawing their daily water from these sources. Probably the best examples are the group located on Lin Jie, a back street further along from the railway station.

The Seventeen-Arch Bridge
5km west of the town boundaries.
Also known as Twin Dragon Bridge, this structure is regarded as a masterpiece amongst ancient bridges for both its aesthetic and structural qualities. The bridge was built during the Qing dynasty in the late 1700s and originally had only three arches on its north end. Later, as the Tachong river changed its course, 14 new bridge arches were subsequently added, hence its name. The 148m-long bridge is replete with three pavilions, the centre one being 20m high with beautiful upturned eaves. The easiest way to reach the bridge is by hiring a taxi; expect to pay around Y25–30 for the round trip.

Swallows Cavern
40km east of Jianshui.
Ornithology and caves come together in an extraordinary conjunction of sight and sound, at the Swallows Cave, one of Jianshui County's main attractions. During the spring and summer months thousands of swallows will fly here from Malaysia to nest and raise their young, attracted by the steep cliffs of the cave and abundance of insects from nearby grasslands. Literally hundreds of thousands of swallows gather here, filling the caves with a cacophonous noise. Swallows build their nests with grass and saliva, which is deemed to be especially nutritious and the source of bird's nest soup. Every year from August 8–18 a bird's nest festival is held in which local men climb up the cliffs to fetch the nests. The spectacle usually attracts a large audience. Every day there are also rock-climbing exhibitions arranged for visitors. The caves themselves are on a large scale with a 50m-high entrance and large numbers of stalactites, though they have definitely become a show piece attraction with all the artificial trappings of a tourist site.

The cave is divided into two sections: the upper part is a dry area with trails through the cave that lead on to verandas and the lower section is a waterway made from the Lu river. The waterway runs for about 8km through the cave and it is possible to board a boat to explore along 3km of this.

Buses to Geiju, Kaiyuan and Menzi stop off at the cave which is just past Miandian village. Alternatively tour buses leave Jianshui every day for the trip, which takes under an hour and can be arranged through one of the hotels.

GEJIU 个 旧
318km southeast of Kunming.
Gejiu's other name, 'Tin City', is wildly misleading, at least for the overseas traveller. True, its economy is based on the extraction of tin, with commercial mining first beginning during the Qing dynasty, but this belies the reality of an extremely pleasant city, one of the most picturesque in southeast Yunnan.

Tucked into the Red River Valley, with a backdrop of cliffs, plenty of greenery and the Jin **Golden Lake** at its centre, the city has a relaxed, resort feel to it. Several minorities brighten up the place. The main groups are Yi, Miao, Zhuang, Hani and Yao. If you are interested in Gejiu's tin connections, there are plenty of tin products for sale in the city. The best place to pick up tin ornaments, tea sets and sundry other ingeniously worked items is at the market bazaar in the converted old railway station near the southern end of the lake.

Getting there and away
Gejiu has an excellent new bus station at the northern end of Jinhu Xilu, with an amazing schedule of destinations on offer. There are, in fact, two bus stations: the regional one is at the intersection of Xinyuan and Renmin Lu. You will find as many as 17 buses a day to Kunming from here, plus

medium-distance regional destinations like Yuxi, Jianshui and Jiangchuan. Routes further afield go to Qujing and the Stone Forest at Shilin. There are even sleepers from here to Jinghong and Ruili, an inconceivably long journey.

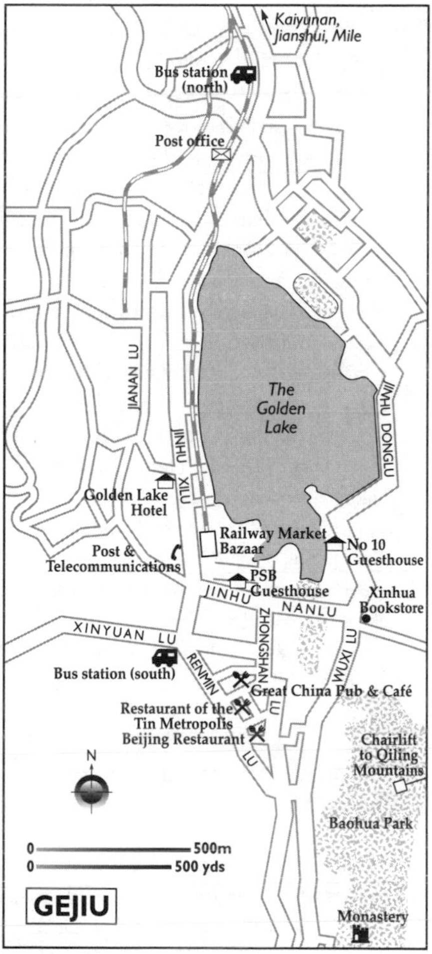

Where to stay/eat

Beijing Restaurant One street south of the Tin Metropolis. Similar food to the above.

Golden Lake Hotel Jinhu Xilu. Located on the southern shore of the lake, a new-looking building with great views of the lake and city. Very comfortable and clean with lots of hot water, but then the doubles and triples on offer do cost a bit – between Y190 and Y210.

Great China Pub and Café Along short Cailu Jie. Classic Chinese dishes, as well as some odd stabs at cuisines as diverse as Japanese and French. Incorporates a very good draught beer bar.

No 10 Guest Hotel Jinhu Donglu; tel: 2122514; fax: 2122830. Very good value with clean, comfortable singles and doubles at Y100 upwards. Also has fine views of the lake.

Map labels: Kaiyuan, Jianshui, Mile; Bus station (north); Post office; JIANAN LU; The Golden Lake; JINHU DONGLU; JINHU XILU; Golden Lake Hotel; Railway Market Bazaar; No 10 Guesthouse; Post & Telecommunications; PSB Guesthouse; Xinhua Bookstore; JINHU NANLU; JINHU ZHONGSHAN; XINYUAN LU; Bus station (south); RENMIN; Great China Pub & Café; Restaurant of the Tin Metropolis; Beijing Restaurant; N; Chairlift to Qiling Mountains; Baohua Park; 0 — 500m; 0 — 500 yds; **GEJIU**; Monastery

PSB Guesthouse Jinhu Xilu-Jinhu Nanlu intersection. Bright and cheerful place with cheap doubles for Y40. The baths are shared. Central location so it can be noisy.

Railway Market Between the lake and Jinhu Nanlu. Dozens of stalls run by Muslims, offering brazier snacks. Excellent for grilled goat's cheese, meat skewers and roasted tofu.

Restaurant of the Tin Metropolis One street south of the Great China. Easy to find two-storey eatery. Very popular. The food less of a mouthful than the restaurant's name. Standard Chinese food with some local dishes. Boisterous atmosphere.

What to see
The Golden Lake
The lake adds a lot to Gejiu's appeal. Surprisingly, the lake has a short history, dating from 1954 when a disastrous sinkhole caused by too many ill-conceived

THE YAO

Many of the 178,000 Yao who inhabit Yunnan live in the Hekou Yao Autonomous County. There are also pockets of Yao living in Jinping County in Honghe Prefecture. They can be found in six different provinces of China. Many Yao, thought by some historians to be among the first inhabitants of southern China, were driven out of Yunnan province in the 12th and 13th centuries, dispersing into Laos, Vietnam, Thailand and Burma where large numbers can be found today. The Yao are a racially homogenous group. There are no sub-groups or hierarchically differently placed clans within the Yao ranks. It follows that there are few striking differences in dress and general appearance between members of one village and another.

The Yao in Yunnan celebrate their important Danu Festival on the 24th day of the fifth lunar month. Drum contests are held in every Yao village, followed by fireworks. Essentially a festive occasion, great quantities of food and melon wine are consumed. The Panwang Festival is another big event for the Yao. The event takes place on the 16th day of the tenth lunar month. The festival, which lasts for three weeks, includes long-drum and courtship dances.

Some Yao still practise slash-and-burn agriculture. Also known as shifting, or swidden cultivation, it is a common form of agriculture among the nomadic hill tribes of Southeast Asia. After trees and underbrush are cut down, they are left to dry and then the hillsides are burnt off in preparation for planting, a process that destroys insect pests and disease. The burning usually takes place during the dry months. The resulting layer of ash then serves as a fertilizer for the crops. Swiddening may be the world's oldest existing agricultural method. Swidden agriculture works well enough when there are huge tracts of available land within walking distance of a village, which can be divided into plots and left fallow for a decade or more before reforesting or planting. This rarely happens though. One of the problems with swiddening is that, because the fields are located on hillsides which are rain-fed, their nutrients are rapidly leached from the soil. If the fallow period is too short, as it almost always is, the yield from these nutrient-depleted upland and midland fields quickly decreases. Conversely, the amount of intensive cultivation and weeding will increase. This is the Catch 22 that the Yao and their fellow swidden cultivators immediately over the border in Laos and Vietnam face.

excavations, appeared at the centre of the city, taking half of Gejiu with it. The ensuing chasm was turned to advantage.

The lake has an attractive promenade with a nice floating teahouse. Visitors usually end up hiring a boat and taking a spin on the lake.

Baohua Park

1km southeast of central Gejiu.

The main attraction at the centre of this large park is **Baohua Monastery**. Many people come here just to view this sight. Construction began on the monastery in 1670 after a Taoist monk named Li Renjie had raised enough funds by begging for alms. More buildings were added during the next century.

Many of the original structures have fallen into ruin but there is still plenty to see, including the Liang Hall, Baiyuan Tower and Lingguan Pavilion. The buildings are set amidst pleasant gardens. If you would like to continue to higher ground, there is a chairlift leaving from the north entrance to the park which will carry you up to Qiling Mountain for some fine views of the area and lunch or dinner at the restaurant there if you feel like it.

Jiasha Hot Springs

60km southwest of Gejiu.

This former workers' sanitorium is situated on the banks of the Longcha River. A good place to recuperate, the waters, which contain properties like radon carbonate and hydrogen sulphide, are said to be good for curing, or at least alleviating, neuralgia, rheumatism and various skin diseases. Sloping hills and plenty of trees and flowers add to the restful mood.

The springs are not particularly easy to get to though. The best route is probably to get on a bus heading for Kaiyuan or Jiasha from the regional depot, and then try to find local transport for the remaining ten or 12 kilometers to the springs.

HEKOU 河口

You will probably not want to stay in Hekou unless you have a special reason to. The town marks the end of the Yunnan stretch of the old French narrow-gauge railway as it creeps over to Lao Cai, its rail counterpart on the Vietnam side, and then onwards along the valleys of the Red River to Hanoi. The end also of our journey.

Tree peony

Appendix 1

LANGUAGE

Helping foreigners to pronounce Chinese words is a system called Pinyin. Although this Romanised rendering of Chinese does not cover the complete range of sounds and tones, it is a fairly good approximation. Mandarin is a tonal language. There are four tones as follows: flat and constant, rising, falling and rising combined, and falling.

Consonants

Most consonants are pronounced in a similar way to English, with the following exceptions.

c	similar to 'ts' in 'sets'		x	like 'sh' in 'shout'
g	like a hard 'goat'		z	as in 'ds' in 'beds'
q	as in 'ch' for 'China'		zh	like the 'j in 'judge'

Vowels and combinations

Vowels are more difficult to pin down. The following is only a rough guide.

a	as in 'man'		iu	as in 'yokel'
ai	as in 'Shanghai'		o	as in 'lore'
ei	as in 'ache'		ou	as in 'show'
i	as in 'tea'		u	as in 'too'
ia	as in 'yak'		ui	as in 'way'
ian	as in 'yen'		uo	as in 'war'
ie	as in 'yeah'		u	as in 'few'

Useful words and phrases

The Chinese characters are given for words/phrases that you may need to recognise.

airport	*jichang*	飞机场
Bank of China	*zhongguo yinhang*	中国银行
bus station	*gongong qiche zhan*	公共汽车站
CAAC	*zhongguo minhang*	中国民航
CITS	*zhongguo guoji luxingshe*	中国国际旅行社
chemist's	*yaodian*	药房
dentist	*yake yisheng*	牙科医生
doctor	*yisheng*	医生

hospital	*yiyuan*	医院
hotel	*binguan*	宾馆
museum	*bowuguan*	博物馆
noodles	*miantiao*	面条
post & telecommunications	*youdianju-*	邮电局
PSB	*gong anju*	公安局
restaurant	*fandian*	饭店
rice/fried rice	*mifan/chaofan*	米饭/炒饭
ticket office	*shoupiaochu*	售票处
toilet (men's)	*nan cesuo*	(男)厕所
toilet (women's)	*nucesuo*	(女)厕所
train station	*huochezhan*	火车站

Thank you	*Xiexie*
Please	*Qing*
Do you have…?	*Nimen you…ma?*
I don't understand	*Wo bu dong*
Do you speak English?	*Ni shuo yingyu ma?*
How are you?	*Ni hao ma?*
My name is…	*Wo jiao*
Pleased to meet you	*Ni hao, hen gaoxing renshi ni*
Good morning/afternoon/evening	*Ni hao*
How much is it?	*Duoshao qian?*
Do you have any vacancies?	*Hai you kong fangjian ma?*
I'd like a single/double room	*Wo xiangyao yige danren/shuangren fangjian*
I'd like a bed in a dormitory	*Wo xiangyao yige tong pu*
I am a vegetarian	*Wo shi chisu de*

Nationality

American	*meiguoren*		Canadian	*jianadaren*
Australian	*aodaliyaren*		Chinese	*zhongguoren*
British	*yingguoren*		New Zealander	*xinxilanren*

Numbers

0	*ling*	零	8	*ba*	八
1	*yi*	一	9	*jiu*	九
2	*er/liang*	二/两	10	*shi*	十
3	*san*	三	11	*shiyi*	十一
4	*si*	四	12	*shier*	十二
5	*wu*	五	13	*shisan*	十三
6	*liu*	六	14	*shisi*	十四
7	*qi*	七	15	*shiwu*	十五
16	*shiliu*	十六	50	*wushi*	五十
17	*shiqi*	十七	60	*liushi*	六十
18	*shiba*	十八	70	*qishi*	七十

LANGUAGE 283

19	shijiu	十九	80	bashi	八十
20	ershi	二十	90	jiushi	九十
30	sanshi	三十	100	yibai	一百
40	sishi	四十	1000	yiqian	一千

Days
Sunday	xingqitian	Thursday	xingqisi
Monday	xingqiyi	Friday	xingqiwu
Tuesday	xingqier	Saturday	xingqiliu
Wednesday	xingqisan		

Months
January	yiyue	July	qiyue
February	eryue	August	bayue
March	sanyue	September	jiuyue
April	siyue	October	shiyue
May	wuyue	November	shiyiyue
June	liuyue	December	shieryue

Time
| What's the time? | jidian le? | yesterday | zuotian |
| today | jintian | tomorrow | mingtian |

Food and drink
Can I see the menu, please?	Wo neng kan yixia caidan ma?
I am a vegetarian	Wo shi chisu de
Vegetables only, please	Wo zhi ao shucai
I'd like…	Wo xiagyao
Can we pay, please?	Fukuan

Muslin restaurant	qingzhen fandian
restaurant	canguan
teahouse	chaguan
vegetarian restaurant	sucaiguan
Western restaurant	xicanting

beef	niurou	牛肉
beer	pijiu	啤酒
chicken	ji	鸡
coffee	kafei	咖啡
lamb	yangrou	羊肉
meat	rou	肉
mineral water	kuangquan shui	矿泉水
noodles	miantiao	面条
Peking duck	Beijing kaoya	北京烤鸭
pork	zhurou	猪肉

rice/fried rice	*mifan/chaofan*	米饭/炒饭
rice porridge (congee)	*xifan*	稀饭
soup	*tang*	汤
spring rolls	*chunjuan*	春卷
steamed rolls	*huajuan*	花卷
tea	*cha*	茶
wine	*putaojiu*	葡萄酒

Place names

Baisha 白沙
Baishuitai 白水台
Banla 斑拉
Baoshan 保山
Stone city of Baoshan 宝山石城
Benzilan 奔子栏
Chengjiang 澄江
Chuxiong 楚雄
Dali 大理
Deqin 德钦
Daluo 打洛
Damenglong 打洛
Gejiu 个旧
Gelanghe 格朗和
Hekou 河口
Jiangchuan 江川
Jianshui 建水
Jinghong 景洪
Jizushan 鸡足山
Kunming 鸡足山
Lake Lugu 泸沽湖
Lijiang 丽江
Lunan 路南
Luxi 泸西
Mangshi 芒市
Menghai 勐海
Menghan 勐罕
Menghun 勐混

Mengla 勐腊
Menglian 孟连
Menglun 勐仑
Mengyang 勐养
Mengzhe 勐遮
Nanluoshan 南罗山
Ninglang 宁蒗
Quiatou 桥头
Qujing 曲靖
Ruili 瑞丽
Shaping 沙坪
Shigu 石鼓
Shiling 石林
Simao 思茅
Tengchong 腾冲
Tonghai 通海
Wanding 畹町
Wase 挖色
Weixi 维西
Xiaguan 下关
Xinmeng 新门
Xizhou 喜洲
Yingjiang 盈江
Yuhu 玉湖村
Yuxi 玉溪
Zhongdian 中甸
Zhoucheng 周城

Appendix 2

RECOMMENDED READING
Yunnan

Backus, Charles, *The Nan-chao Kingdom and T'ang China's Southwestern Frontier*, Cambridge, 1981.

Bonavia, Judy, *The Yangzi River*, Odyssey Guides, 1999.

Carne, Louis de, *Travels on the Mekong: Cambodia, Laos and Yunnan*, White Lotus, Bangkok, 1995.

Chatwin, Bruce, *What Am I Doing Here?* Picador, 1990.

Davies, H R, *Yunnan: the Land Between India and the Yangtze*, Cambridge University Press, 1909.

Gao Fayuan, *Women's Culture Series: Nationalities in Yunnan* (26 volumes), Yunnan Education Publishing House, Kunming, 1995.

Garnier, F, *Further Travels in Laos and in Yunnan* (1866–68), White Lotus, Bangkok, 1996.

Gill, William, *The River of Golden Sand*, Murray, London, 1880.

Goullart, Peter, *Forgotten Kingdom*, John Murray, London, 1957.

He Liyi, *Mr China's Son, A Villager's Life*, Westview Press, San Francisco, 1993.

He Liyi, *The Spring of Butterflies*, Lothrop, Lee & Shepard Books, New York. 1986.

He Zhonghua, *Where the Goddesses Live: the Naxi*, Yunnan Education Publishing House, Kunming, 1995.

Hoskin, John and Walton, Geoffrey, *Folk Tales and Legends of the Dai People*, DD, Bangkok, 1992.

Ma Yin, *China's Minority Nationalities*, Foreign Languages Press, Beijing, 1994.

Metford, B, *Where China Meets Burma*, London, 1935.

Miller, Lucien, *South of the Clouds: Tales From Yunnan*, University of Washington Press, Seattle & London, 1994.

Rock, Joseph, *The Life and Culture of Na-khi Tribe of the China–Tibet Borderland*, Franz Steiner, Wiesbaden, 1963.

Shen Che, *Life Among the Minority Nationalities of Northwest Yunnan*, Foreign Languages Press, Beijing, 1989.

The Ancient Na-khi Kingdom of Southwest China, Harvard University Press Cambridge, 1947.

The Na-khi Naga Cult and Related Ceremonies, Seria Orientalia Roma, Rome, 1952.

Tong Zhilu & Jin Zhuotang, *Lijiang*, New World Press, Beijing, 1988.

Winnigton, Alan, *The Slaves of the Cool Mountains*, Seven Seas, Berlin, 1959.

Zheng, Lan, *Travels Through Xishiangbanna*, Foreign Languages Press, Beijing, 1981.

Zhong Xiu, *Yunnan Travelogue: 100 Days in Southwest China*, New World Press, Beiing 1985.

Zhu Yintang, *The Naxi Creation Myth*, Lijiang 1991.

China

Dodwell, Christina, *A Traveller in China*, Sceptre, 1987.

Thubron, Colin, *Behind the Wall: A Journey Through China*, Penguin Books, 1988.

Winchester, Simon, *The River at the Centre of the World*, Penguin, London, 1997.

Photobooks on Yunnan

Various writers/photographers, *Mysterious Northwest Yunnan*, Yunnan Science & Technology Publishing House, 1998.

Yunnan, A Complete Guide Series of Travel & Tourism in China, China Travel & Tourism Press, 1998.

Goodman, Jim, *Children of the Jade Dragon*, Teak House, Bangkok, 1997.

Wu Jialin, *Mountain Folks in Yunnan*, Yunnan Arts Press, 1993.

Betel nuts and palm

MEASUREMENTS AND CONVERSIONS

To convert	Multiply by
Inches to centimetres	2.54
Centimetres to inches	0.3937
Feet to metres	0.3048
Metres to feet	3.281
Yards to metres	0.9144
Metres to yards	1.094
Miles to kilometres	1.609
Kilometres to miles	0.6214
Acres to hectares	0.4047
Hectares to acres	2.471
Imperial gallons to litres	4.546
Litres to imperial gallons	0.22
US gallons to litres	3.785
Litres to US gallons	0.264
Ounces to grams	28.35
Grams to ounces	0.03527
Pounds to grams	453.6
Grams to pounds	0.002205
Pounds to kilograms	0.4536
Kilograms to pounds	2.205
British tons to kilograms	1016.0
Kilograms to British tons	0.0009812
US tons to kilograms	907.0
Kilograms to US tons	0.000907

5 imperial gallons are equal to 6 US gallons
A British ton is 2,240 lbs. A US ton is 2,000 lbs.

Temperature conversion table
The bold figures in the central columns can be read as either centigrade or fahrenheit.

°C		°F	°C		°F
−18	0	32	10	50	122
−15	5	41	13	55	131
−12	10	50	16	60	140
−9	15	59	18	65	149
−7	20	68	21	70	158
−4	25	77	24	75	167
−1	30	86	27	80	176
2	35	95	32	90	194
4	40	104	38	100	212
7	45	113	40	104	219

NOTES

Index

*Page references in bold indicate major entries;
those in italics indicate maps.*